POWER, INTERDEPENDENCE, AND
NONSTATE ACTORS IN WORLD POLITICS

POWER, INTERDEPENDENCE, AND NONSTATE ACTORS IN WORLD POLITICS

Edited by
Helen V. Milner
Andrew Moravcsik

PRINCETON UNIVERSITY PRESS

PRINCETON AND OXFORD

Published by Princeton University Press, 41 William Street, Princeton, New Jersey 08540
In the United Kingdom: Princeton University Press, 6 Oxford Street, Woodstock,
Oxfordshire OX20 1TW

Library of Congress Cataloging-in-Publication Data

Power, interdependence, and nonstate actors in world politics / edited by Helen V. Milner,
Andrew Moravcsik.
    p. cm
    Includes bibliographical references and index.
    ISBN 978-0-691-14027-8 (alk. paper) — ISBN 978-0-691-14028-5 (alk. paper) 1. Non-
governmental organizations. 2. International agencies. 3. International relations. I.
Milner, Helen V., 1958– II. Moravcsik, Andrew.
    JZ4841.P68 2009
    341.2—dc22

                            2008042222

British Library Cataloging-in-Publication Data is available

This book has been composed in Sabon

Printed on acid-free paper. ∞

press.princeton.edu

Printed in the United States of America

10 9 8 7 6 5 4 3 2 1

To Robert O. Keohane,
teacher, colleague, mentor, and friend

Contents

Figures and Tables

Contributors

Vinod K. Aggarwal, *University of California at Berkeley*
Jonathan D. Aronson, *University of Southern California*
Elizabeth R. DeSombre, *Wellesley College*
V. Page Fortna, *Columbia University*
Michael J. Gilligan, *New York University*
Lisa L. Martin, *Harvard University*
Timothy J. McKeown, *University of North Carolina at Chapel Hill*
Helen V. Milner, *Princeton University*
Ronald B. Mitchell, *University of Oregon*
Andrew Moravcsik, *Princeton University*
Layna Mosley, *University of North Carolina at Chapel Hill*
Beth A. Simmons, *Harvard University*
Randall W. Stone, *University of Rochester*
J. Ann Tickner, *University of Southern California*

Preface

International relations would be a very different discipline today were it not for the contributions of Robert O. Keohane. The citation trail alone, which passes through countless and books and articles, tracks his influence. Equally important is Bob's personal imprint: his strong mentoring of graduate students at Stanford, Brandeis, Harvard, Duke, and now Princeton, many of whom have become successful academics.

On February 18–19, 2005, a group of those students came together at Princeton University to celebrate Bob's career. The large size and broad diversity of the group testify both to his tremendous energy and influence and to his determination to broaden access to the senior ranks of the profession. Not all of his former students could make it to Princeton, and not all could be represented in this volume, but we know that all share our deep appreciation and respect for Bob and his research.

The Princeton meeting explored the evolution of Keohane's research agenda in recent years. The authors in this volume, who presented papers at the meeting, and others whose work is not represented, had a chance to thank him for the support and intellectual guidance he has given us over these many years. As academics, our appreciation is most durably expressed by using his ideas to stimulate wide-ranging research and by emulating his passion for teaching. But the existence of this volume provides a specific, concrete tribute in appreciation for his lasting impact on our careers.

A great scholar sets an intellectual agenda that grows and develops in anticipated and unanticipated directions, motivating other scholars to do their best work both in furthering the animating ideas and in pushing against them. The institutionalist research program that Bob helped create has had an enormous influence in international relations. The chapters here testify to that impact. Bob has fostered an inquisitive yet rigorous research style among his students. His openness to new ideas, combined with his interest in research design, has produced novel research across a diverse set of important topics. He has trained students who agree and disagree with him. Thus the work in this volume illustrates both the strengths and weaknesses of the research program he helped found.

A great mentor guides and pushes his students at the start of their careers and then supports them wherever their paths may lead. Bob has done both. We intend this volume to celebrate his long and distinguished career and hope that it helps advance in some small way the many ideas and themes he continues to pursue.

The Authors
July 2008

Introduction

CHAPTER 1

Power, Interdependence, and Nonstate Actors in World Politics
RESEARCH FRONTIERS

Helen V. Milner

IN THE MID-1970S a new paradigm emerged in international relations. While many of the ideas in this new paradigm had been discussed previously, Keohane and Nye put these pieces together in a new and fruitful way to erect a competitor to realism and its later formulation, neorealism.[1] First elaborated in *Power and Interdependence*, this paradigm is now usually referred to as *neoliberal institutionalism*. In the thirty years since *Power and Interdependence*, this new paradigm has developed substantially and has become the main alternative to realism for understanding international relations. Keohane's seminal work, *After Hegemony*, which is a centerstone of the neoliberal paradigm, provided the most compelling theoretical justification for the existence and role of international institutions in world politics.[2] Since then the progress of the neoliberal paradigm can be plainly seen in a number of key works, such as *Legalization and World Politics*, *The Rational Design of International Institutions*, and *Delegation and Agency in International Organizations*.[3] Each of these projects, and many others, takes the key ideas of the neoliberal institutionalist paradigm and pushes them forward into new areas of research. They attest to the continuing theoretical power of the paradigm.

Furthermore, the paradigm has proven highly robust empirically. Globalization, for instance, has made the world ever more tightly connected, as *Power and Interdependence* foresaw years ago. Among other trends in world politics, including the increasing prominence of nonstate actors such as multinational corporations, nongovernmental organizations (NGOs), and international institutions, globalization has made the prevailing competing paradigm, neorealism, a less powerful explanation of international relations, and has raised the importance of the neoliberal paradigm. The key ideas articulated by Keohane and Nye in the 1970s are increasingly

---

[1] Keohane and Nye 1977.
[2] Keohane 1984.
[3] Goldstein et al. 2000; Koremenos, Lipson, and Snidal 2001; Hawkins et al. 2006.

winning the theoretical and empirical battles in international relations to understand a globalized world.

The four key elements of the neoliberal institutionalist paradigm are emphases on nonstate actors, including international institutions, on forms of power besides military force and threats, on the role of interdependence in addition to anarchy in the international system, and on the importance of cooperation as well as conflict in international politics. These elements contrast starkly with the tenets of realism and neorealism. Keohane originally developed many of these themes in his works,[4] but other scholars have taken many of his ideas and advanced them substantially.[5] This volume is intended to extend our theoretical and empirical understanding of the neoliberal institutionalist paradigm.

This volume assesses the progress that has been made in developing the paradigm and discusses areas where it has encountered new problems. Some of the chapters apply ideas from the paradigm to understand issues that have become increasingly visible, such as women's rights, religion, intellectual property rights, and peacekeeping. Others address anomalies and puzzles that the paradigm has encountered, and suggests ways that it can deal with them. The volume shows the broad range of topics addressed by, and the increasing theoretical depth of, the paradigm. Neoliberal institutionalism is alive and well as a theoretical construct in international relations today.

Neoliberal institutionalism shares a number of features with the paradigm that it contests, neorealism. The approaches in this volume also tend to share these features. Importantly, both neorealism and neoliberal institutionalism argue for a systemic-level theory of international politics. Systemic theorists believe that the international system exercises an important influence upon states; this environment constrains and shapes them powerfully. Because of this, systemic theorists argue that these external forces must be taken into account first in any theoretical explanation of international relations. To fail to do so would lead to the confusing proliferation of domestic variables to explain a systemic outcome. Neorealists see anarchy and the balance of capabilities as the central systemic factors influencing states. Neoliberal institutionalists accept the importance of these factors, but they also think that the effects of anarchy are mitigated by both mutual interdependence and the institutionalized nature of modern world politics, especially with respect to certain issues and among certain countries. While agreeing that systemic theory is preferred,

---

[4] Keohane 1989.

[5] For overviews, see Simmons and Martin 2002; Jacobsen 2000; Keohane and Martin 2003; and for examples, see Goldstein et al. 2000; and Koremenos, Lipson, and Snidal 2001.

neoliberal institutionalism does not focus solely on anarchy and the balance of power as the sole elements of the system.

Realists and neoliberal institutionalists also share the view that states are critical actors in world politics, and that they are by and large rational. Neoliberal institutionalism, however, again goes beyond neorealism in admitting that other important actors exist in world politics, such as international institutions and NGOs. Finally, the majority of neorealists and neoliberal institutionalists share a commitment to the same general epistemological orientation. They tend to be rationalists and positivists who are interested in empirical tests of the causal propositions their theories advance. Indeed, the increasing empirical sophistication of research in the neoliberal institutionalist paradigm is an important feature of the field and of this volume. The authors generally adopt these three assumptions, although some of them argue for more attention to domestic politics (see, e.g., DeSombre and McKeown) and one for a move beyond positivism (i.e., Tickner).

The Neoliberal Institutionalist Paradigm: Its Four Elements and Their Elaboration over Time

In what follows I discuss each of the four elements of the neoliberal institutionalist paradigm and their evolution over the last thirty years in the international relations literature. The four elements that differentiate this from other paradigms are an emphasis on nonstate actors including international institutions, on forms of power besides military force and threats, on the role of interdependence in addition to anarchy in the international system, and on the importance of cooperation as well as conflict in international politics. I argue that progress has been made in the paradigm and that the chapters here represent the research frontier now.

Nonstate Actors in World Politics

Starting from a systemic level theory of international politics, neoliberal institutionalism acknowledges the importance of states and their decentralized environment. But this paradigm also insists on the relevance of nonstate actors; and it acknowledges a wide variety of such actors, from multinational corporations to NGOs to international institutions. A central focus, however, is international institutions and regimes. Further, as opposed to the earlier focus on international organizations, neoliberal institutionalism takes a broader view of these actors and includes "sets of governing arrangements" that involve "implicit or explicit principles, norms, rules and decision making procedures around which actors' expectations converge."[6] This broader definition of institutions (i.e., regimes) was a step forward since it acknowledged that not all institutions had to have physical headquarters and staffs. International institutions are a broader category of actor than organizations, which they subsume. There exist many sets of state practices that are institutionalized in the sense that norms, rules, and principles exist that guide states' behavior in particular issue areas. For neoliberal institutionalism, world politics is institutionalized, although to differing extents in different issue areas and regions.

International institutions have proliferated recently, as Stone points out. Almost every area of global cooperation has been formalized into an international institution, if not an actual organization. The number of formal international organizations has risen from three hundred in 1977 to well over six thousand today. Many of these have expanded their membership; for example, the World Bank and International Monetary Fund are now global, including almost all countries in the world in their membership, and the World Trade Organization is not far behind. The European Union has also expanded greatly since its foundation. The purviews of these institutions have grown to reach many issue areas that were once considered purely domestic. The growing place of international institutions in world politics cannot be denied. Furthermore, the growing reach of international institutions brings into question the power of neorealist theory; such institutions should not be durable and salient features of international politics according to neorealism.

Early debates centered on whether these institutions mattered. The neorealist reaction was to claim that the distribution of capabilities determined this institutional framework and that the strongest powers were the ones that imposed their norms, practices, and rules on the rest of the world. Hegemonic stability theory was one version of this response, which located the genesis of international institutions for a given time period in the hands of the hegemonic power.[7] Much like Gilpin's work on cycles of war and change, hegemonic stability theory saw institutional change as a function of changes in underlying power relations.[8] Other scholars claimed that states would not cooperate on anything that was not already in their national interest, and hence that cooperation would be very thin.[9] Concerns about relative gains in cooperating were one explanation for the limits to cooperation.[10] Others noted that institutions may make cooperation more appealing but only in the sense that they

[6] Krasner 1983a, 186.
[7] Krasner 1976; Keohane 1980; Lake 1983.
[8] Gilpin 1981.
[9] E.g., Downs, Rocke, and Barsoom 1996.
[10] Grieco 1988.

make noncooperation much more costly for small states.[11] This debate over the power of international institutions has carried on for many years as neorealists have cast doubt on the evidence that nonstate actors matter.[12]

Neoliberal institutionalists have responded in a variety of ways. Keohane has argued that the post–World War II institutions were in part a product of American power but that since their establishment they have evolved into more autonomous entities.[13] He and others, for instance, have noted the continuing relevance of international institutions set up during the Cold War, such as NATO, the EU, and the United Nations, despite the end of the bipolar superpower rivalry nearly two decades ago.[14] This shows that changes in regimes are not simple functions of changes in underlying power relations, as realists assume. Rather, regime change may occur when changes in the structure of the issue area and the resources relevant to it take place. It is the interaction of power and complex interdependence that combine to create institutional change, as discussed by Stone and others in this volume.

Neoliberal institutionalists, however, have turned increasingly to explore the conditions under which and ways in which world politics is institutionalized. Keohane proposed an early theory about why countries would want to create and join international institutions.[15] His theory argues that a country, being rational, will only demand and join international institutions if those institutions can provide net benefits for them relative to the reversion point, which is the outcome if no agreement to join is reached. He sees these benefits as being reduced transaction costs, increased information flows, and reduced uncertainty. In providing these functions, international institutions help states negotiate mutually beneficial agreements that they otherwise would not be able to arrange. In part, this cooperation results from the strategies of reciprocity that can take hold more easily in such institutionalized environments. Game theorists have emphasized slightly different functions; they have focused on how regimes can reduce players' discount rates, increase information flows by signaling players' types, enhance the credibility of domestic commitments, and alter payoff structures through repeated interactions and reciprocity.[16] Others have emphasized that regimes can change actors' preferences and, more deeply, their identities.[17] The constructivist research program has grown out of this approach. It constitutes a large and vibrant

---

[11] Gruber 2000.

[12] Mearsheimer 1994–95.

[13] Keohane 1984.

[14] E.g., Keohane, Nye, and Hoffmann 1993; Keohane and Martin 1995.

[15] Keohane 1984.

[16] E.g., Axelrod 1984; Oye 1986; Mansfield, Milner, and Rosendorff 2002.

[17] E.g., Kratochwil and Ruggie 1986; Onuf 1989.

literature, which we do not touch on here except briefly in the contribution by Tickner.[18] The chapters here focus on the first two types of rationalist explanations of international institutions and their functions.

Recent work on a variety of international institutions has shown that they can perform these functions and enhance the attainment of mutually beneficial agreements. Martin shows that economic sanctions can work better if they can be multilateralized in a regime; in such a setting greater information flows make countries less likely to cheat on their obligations.[19] Burley and Mattli point out how unexpectedly powerful the European Court of Justice has become, and how autonomously from national courts it has developed.[20] Ikenberry concludes that if powerful states can bind their hands by joining international institutions, they can strike more mutually beneficial agreements with the other countries in the world.[21] Stone points out that the IMF can ensure greater compliance and hence better outcomes when powerful states do not intervene in its operations with economically troubled states.[22] Davis in her study of the WTO concludes that it can help countries overcome domestic opposition and conclude mutually valuable trade agreements.[23] Meunier shows how the EU can make a difference for European countries in their ability to strike trade bargains with other countries.[24] Some have argued that this institutionalization of world politics is becoming increasingly legalized, and that this legalization is having important effects on international cooperation.[25] Others have tried to explain the many different forms that international institutions take to perform some of the same functions but in different environments.[26] All of this research shows that international institutions of various sorts exist, function in ways neoliberal institutionalist theories predict, and have positive effects on interstate cooperation. They represent empirical progress in the neoliberal institutionalist paradigm.

The essays in this volume take a further step forward, as I discuss below. A key point of debate between neoliberal institutionalism and neorealism is the explanation of institutional change. For neorealists, institutions change when the underlying balance of power among states changes. This causal path shows the dependence of institutions on state power and

[18] E.g., Finnemore 1996; Legro 1997; Finnemore and Sikkink 1998; Barnett and Finnemore 2004.
[19] Martin 1992.
[20] Burley and Mattli 1993.
[21] Ikenberry 2001.
[22] Stone 2002.
[23] Davis 2003.
[24] Meunier 2005.
[25] Goldstein 2001.
[26] Koremenos, Lipson, and Snidal 2001.

ultimately their epiphenomenality. For neoliberal institutionalism, institutions change in part because of their success or failure in accomplishing the tasks they are delegated. In his chapter, for instance, Randall Stone takes up the question of what accounts for change in international institutions. He notes that most of the key extant institutions are under pressure to reform; the UN, IMF, World Bank, WTO, and NATO, among others, have been seriously criticized lately for failing to perform adequately. Why have these institutions seemingly failed to achieve their optimal outcomes? In Keohane's later work, he addressed three broad categories of explanations: power, international processes, and the structure of international institutions.[27] In his view, explanations based on the distribution of power in the international system fared poorly; indeed, in terms of its theoretical and empirical aspects the theory of hegemonic stability fared the worst.

According to Stone, two other factors are primarily responsible for the poor results of many international institutions. As Keohane has previously noted, the costs associated with bargaining over issues and institutional procedures are high and pose problems for states. The curse of bargaining is that the necessary condition for successful cooperation—low discount rates—is precisely the condition that makes bargaining most costly; this makes outcomes most inefficient when bargainers most value the future.[28] In addition, Stone notes that the internal dynamics of institutions can plague cooperation. International institutions change through a political process that privileges insiders, who can impose their preferences on countries that join subsequently because voting rules privilege the status quo. In general, those who create the institution can become significant impediments to new agreements that would deepen international cooperation. Thus international institutions are slow to expand and adapt to new areas of potential cooperation because of the costs of bargaining and the entrenched interests of founding members. Stone's pessimistic view, however, lays blame for the shortcomings of international institutions on features other than power politics.

Gilligan in his chapter addresses a fundamental issue about the demand for international institutions raised by Keohane in *After Hegemony*. He revisits the question of whether the transaction costs approach can explain the creation of international institutions. He notes that rationalist theories of cooperation prior to Keohane's theory, so-called decentralized cooperation theory, could explain why countries choose to cooperate, how they came to their cooperative agreements, and how they enforced

[27] Keohane and Nye 1977; Keohane 1984.
[28] Fearon 1998. Unless states can design escape clauses or renegotiation provisions, they are stuck with the distribution of costs and benefits that flows from the institution's initial structure (Rosendorff and Milner 2001; Koremenos 2001).

them in the anarchical international system, but they could *not* address why countries created international institutions. But the transaction costs approach to international cooperation explicitly answers this question. These institutions must be negotiated, and so one will only observe such institutions if the relative transaction costs of creating them, amortized over the expected lifetime of the regime, are also sufficiently small. He challenges recent empirical work that suggests transaction costs do not matter. Gilligan points out that we need more empirical work on the transaction costs approach, and offers several ideas about how to proceed. For instance, he suggests testing if the variables that the transaction costs approach claims should induce states to create institutions—such as asset specificity and the number and complexity of the transactions—are correlated with more institutionalization. These ideas for future research show the way theory and sophisticated empirical testing can lead to progress.

Ronald Mitchell asks fundamental questions about the impact of international institutions, returning to the question of their effects on state behavior. Neoliberal institutionalism, he notes, needs to take the realist challenge to the power and autonomy of international institutions seriously. Realists claim that differences in the international problem structure or distribution of power within an issue area that predate the institution may explain differences in institutional design and hence differences in state behavior. His chapter shows that if one can demonstrate that this problem structure does not dictate institutional design, then institutions can play some independent role. Theories suggest that this problem structure does not perfectly explain institutional design because of factors like uncertainty, bounded rationality, the time states take to negotiate agreements, and the unintended or unanticipated consequences of institutions. Mitchell clarifies why, and illuminates the conditions under which, so-called institution-independent interests, which states seek to enshrine in the provisions of international institutions, may diverge from the interests that subsequently drive those states' behavior. Thus factors that neoliberal institutionalism focuses on, such as information problems, normative pressures, and institutional inertia, may allow institutions to develop their own autonomous space for action.

As neoliberalism predicts, issue areas that feature much incomplete information are ripe for international institutions. Fortna and Martin focus on the demand for international institutions in peacekeeping operations in civil wars, and ask about the conditions under which governments and oppositions agree to involve nonstate actors such as peacekeeping forces. Peacekeeping, which they define as the deployment of international troops and monitors to war-torn areas, is an international institution intended to help recent belligerents maintain peace. They model peacekeeping as an institution that is able to provide information to both sides in a conflict through a signaling mechanism. Allowing peacekeeping provides a costly signal of each side's intent to abide by a peace agreement. While both sides in a civil war prefer to avoid the interference of outsiders, the costs of peacekeepers to an unreliable government—that is, one that will renege on its agreement to quit fighting—are higher than the costs to a reliable government. To test their ideas empirically, they identify several factors that should make peacekeeping more likely relative to continued fighting and to peace without peacekeepers. Following Keohane's work, their chapter shows that focusing on the interaction of nonstate and state actors and their strategic demands for institutions can produce powerful insights about the role of institutions. It also echoes his work by pointing to the critical importance of information provision as a function of international institutions.

International institutions are not the only nonstate actors of importance to neoliberal institutionalism. NGOs and private sector actors may also play key roles in world politics, especially in certain issue areas. Mosley's chapter brings attention to bear on the role of nongovernmental actors in global financial regulation, in particular financial institutions, corporations (national or multinational), industry and professional associations, and professional investors. Efforts to govern contemporary global finance take a variety of forms, including intergovernmental institutions (e.g., IMF and World Bank), transnational regulatory groups (e.g., International Organization of Securities Commissions), and private sector entities (e.g., credit ratings agencies and the London Club). A good deal of financial regulation now occurs outside traditional intergovernmental institutions and involves public-private interactions. Beginning from Keohane and Nye's assertion about the importance of private sector actors in world politics, Mosley explores the precise ways in which private sector participation affects outcomes in global financial governance. Mosley shows how these private actors create institutions that foster cooperation, but then asks whether this behavior is in the best interests of all parties to the international system.

Private sector actors also play sizable roles in the regulation of international property rights. Aronson's chapter treats international intellectual property rights as a strategic game between existing firms trying to defend and extend their power and profits in the face of technological change and global interdependence against the efforts of newcomers who desire access to existing technologies and ideas. In the intellectual property arena companies and countries seek advantage by undermining their foes' efforts. The state and nonstate players are interdependent, and power is asymmetrically distributed, currently in favor of the developed countries and existing producers. Aronson shows that nonstate actors from the private sector play a critical role in the evolution of governance in this issue area. The richness of neoliberal institutionalism is underlined by its capacity to incorporate nonstate actors into its theoretical framework.

Varieties of Power in World Politics

A second element of neoliberal institutionalism is attention to forms of power besides military force and threats. Neorealists have focused on military force as the key element of national power. As Waltz says, "In international politics force serves not only as the ultima ratio, but indeed as the first and constant one."[29] For realists, this hierarchy of power resources implies that there exists a single ranking of world powers for all issue areas, with the most powerful ones possessing the greatest military capabilities. Neoliberal institutionalism does not share this view of world politics. Beginning with Keohane and Nye's recognition of the independent logic that operates within different issues, much work in this paradigm has emphasized the importance of, and variation across, issue areas.[30] Power resources for exercising influence in international trade negotiations differ from those in nuclear nonproliferation, which in turn differ from those in climate change negotiations.

There is no single hierarchy of power resources, and states vary in their capacities to influence outcomes by issue area. Japan may be very powerful in the area of whaling or international trade, but much less so in oil and nuclear proliferation. The conception of what resources count as power is much broader for neoliberal institutionalism than for realism. One reason why scholars in this tradition have emphasized the analysis of particular issue areas is to be able to deal with the important differences in capabilities across issues. As Keohane notes, such "disaggregation is progressive rather than degenerative."[31] Interesting works in this issue area approach to power in world politics include economic sanctions,[32] monetary relations,[33] and international trade.[34] World politics in this view looks much more variegated than it does in the realist one, where military force is the only coin of the realm.

Many of the chapters in this volume examine particular issue areas and demonstrate that differences among the issue areas matter for institutionalization and for power relations. Simmons in her chapter, for example, focuses on the compliance of states with international institutions pro-

[29] Waltz 1979, 113.
[30] Keohane and Nye 1977; Baldwin 1979, 1989.
[31] Keohane 1986b, 189.
[32] E.g., Martin 1992; Shambaugh 1999.
[33] E.g., Kirschner 1995; Cohen 1998; Andrews 2006.
[34] E.g., Hirschman 1980; Reinhardt 2001; Zeng 2004.

moting human rights, in particular women's rights. She shows that it is not state power that leads to compliance but rather a complex mechanism that forces states to take into account their obligations under these agreements. Enforcement of most human rights agreements has to be highly decentralized, relying on nonstate actors and the information they can provide. Intergovernmental organizations designed to monitor governments' practices, transnational women's advocacy groups, and most especially domestic interests who demand that their government take their treaty commitments seriously are the primary enforcement mechanisms. Her data thus show that treaties can have meaningful effects, even in the absence of formal international mechanisms for their enforcement. Power over states is exercised by a variety of nonstate actors through power resources available to actors in complex interdependence situations.

DeSombre turns her attention to the role of international institutions and power within the environmental issue area. She claims that the idea of complex interdependence helps one understand the power dynamics that underpin cooperation in this issue area. She shows how the structure of the issue area itself affects the power resources that countries can employ and the types of agreements that they can make; it is not state power and military resources that matter. Complex interdependence suggests that even in situations where everyone gains from cooperation, some actors will have a greater ability than others to influence the shape and content of the cooperative arrangements. Most environmental issues contain some aspect of prisoner's dilemma incentives combined with a common pool resource problem, thus requiring cooperation from all relevant actors to successfully address a problem. Influential actors may not be those who possess traditional power resources like military or economic might, but instead ones who can threaten credibly to stay outside the process of cooperation and thereby reduce its value to others. In this issue structure the prisoner's dilemma is stark, because any major actor that remains outside of the cooperative system does not just decrease cooperation, but may be able to prevent it altogether.

The structure of this issue area enables one to understand the seemingly disproportionate level of influence that developing countries have had in international environmental cooperation. Because of this issue structure, developing states can offer to exchange their participation in global environmental agreements for economic and technical aid. DeSombre points out that the first serious instance of this "greenmail" was in the negotiation of the international agreements to protect the ozone layer. Because of this characteristic, environmental issues call forth different types of power resources. States with traditional power resources may find that these are not effective for enticing cooperation or removing incentives to free ride, but that other ways in which states can use their global linkages may prove more conducive to changing incentives to cooperate. The nature of the issue area and the complex interdependence it engenders mean that traditional power resources are not the key to understanding this issue area.

Aggarwal shows that traditional power resources are less important for the trade system than realism would lead one to expect. His institutional bargaining game approach begins by identifying an initial impetus for new trade accords, which generally comes about through some external shock. For instance, problems with extant international institutions or a financial crisis can create pressure for change, as many argue is happening with the proliferation of PTAs (preferential trade agreements) in the wake of the stalled WTO negotiations. Countries respond to external shocks in various ways based on three factors: the "goods" involved in the negotiations; their individual political-economic situation, which consists of their international position, domestic political structure, and beliefs; and the context of the existing institutional environment. Outcomes in trade depend, by his account, on the nature of the issue area and the preexisting institutional environment more than on the global distribution of power.

As Aronson makes clear, international intellectual property rights involve forms of power different from traditional power resources in international relations. His approach shows that the structure of the issue shapes both the relative power capabilities of the state and nonstate actors involved and the character of the international regimes developed to regulate intellectual property rights (IPR). Since the mid-1980s, as international treaties broadened and strengthened the scope of IPR protection and extended its range into new information arenas, the balance of power has shifted in favor of firms and countries with intellectual property. The strong protection of intellectual property runs counter to the interests of consumers, innovators, and developing countries. Developing countries and firms seeking to innovate have growing power resources because of the issue area's structure, however. While these groups may lack traditional power resources, they have been able to find new sources of influence to challenge the current IPR regime. For instance, piracy and parallel imports are costly to copyright holders. An even more serious problem comes when developing countries re-export cheap or pirated products to industrial countries, lowering sales from those who could otherwise afford to pay. The current IPR regime may help define property rights, lower transaction costs, and reduce uncertainty. But it is not optimal from Aronson's perspective and is in the midst of change, as developing countries and firms exert their new-found power.

Following on Keohane and Nye's *Power and Interdependence*, McKeown focuses on transnational relations and power resources in such relationships. Transnational ties, he notes, can be a source of influence for either party in a relationship. The existence of numerous low-level or mid-level contacts between governments is a necessary but not sufficient condition for transgovernmentalism, which occurs when governments confront an "agency problem" in the sense that their efforts to control the behavior of subordinates fail. Transgovernmental contacts become interesting when on at least one side control from the top is ineffective. As a corrective to earlier ideas, which implied that weaker states could best exploit transnational ties, McKeown argues that transgovernmental relations can be exploited by any government that desires to do so and has the capabilities.[35] Such tactics are not just the tool of small and weak countries. But, McKeown asks, what makes us believe that government officials are ignorant of the effects of transgovernmentalism or simply tolerate its unwanted outcomes? If government officials realize the power of transgovernmental and transnational ties, they may be able to resist such influences or use them to their advantage without seeming to do so. These ideas about transgovernmental relations as power resources deepen our understanding of its causal mechanisms. They take us a step further in understanding the nature of power in a world of complex interdependence.

Interdependence as a Defining Feature of the International System

A third characteristic of neoliberal institutionalism is its description of the international system as one embodying both anarchy and interdependence. Neoliberal institutionalists agree that the system is decentralized and often relies on self-enforcing behavior, but they do not think that anarchy dominates the system. As noted before, particular issue areas and relations among certain countries may be highly institutionalized. But even in the absence of this pattern, relations among countries tend, in the view of neoliberal institutionalists, to be highly interdependent. Extensive flows of goods, raw materials, people, and capital across borders benefit all countries involved, and often are critical to each country's economy. Severing these flows would cause economic damage, and political repercussions as well. Interdependence means mutual dependence, not necessarily symmetric, which brings benefits for all parties involved. These benefits and potential loss of them through international conflict make countries vulnerable, and thus are a potential power resource for the side that is less dependent.[36] The potentially pacifying effects of such economic interdependence have been noted for years.[37]

Complex interdependence involves more than just economic interdependence; it implies a world characterized by at least three features. First,

[35] See, for instance, Keohane 1971.
[36] Hirschman 1980.
[37] E.g., Angell 1912; Morse 1976; Keohane and Nye 1972.

transnational relations are important; these relations involve multiple channels connecting societies, from formal and informal ties among government officials to informal ties among nongovernmental elites in different countries. Second, the agenda of relationships among countries includes multiple issues without a clear hierarchy; security relations are not the be-all and end-all of the relationship. Third, military force is not the primary means of resolving disagreements among the countries on the key issues; rather, other power resources are central to solving problems. One such power resource comes from participation in international institutions themselves. As Keohane and Nye note, "in a world of multiple issues imperfectly linked, in which coalitions are formed transnationally and transgovernmentally, the potential role of international institutions in political bargaining is greatly increased[;] they help set the international agenda and act as catalysts for coalition formation and as arenas for political initiatives and linkage by weak states."[38] Recent literature on the impact of globalization has painted a similarly complex picture of the relations among domestic and international politics and the effects on state behavior.

Many of the chapters in this volume assume that the world is one of complex interdependence, and their descriptions of different issues show the importance of distinct power resources for different transnational and nonstate actors. DeSombre's chapter on environmental issues is exemplary. She shows that most international environmental issues involve complex interdependence, containing aspects of prisoner's dilemma combined with common pool resource problems. Given the structure of the issue area, cooperation from all relevant actors is required to successfully address problems, and so actors who can threaten credibly to stay outside the process are empowered. Furthermore, complex interdependence can illuminate the particular character of cooperative agreements in environmental policy. Many international environmental agreements are shaped by the issue's incentive structure. For instance, in most recent environmental treaties concerns with free riding have led to the adoption of the standard clause requiring a certain number of ratifications before the treaty enters into force, but also a mandate that those ratifiers account for a certain degree of the activity responsible for the environmental problem. Most international environmental agreements also make information gathering their first priority in the process of addressing an environmental problem, as neoliberal institutionalism would suggest. Environmental cooperation fosters the development of certain types of international regimes to regulate the global environment because of its particular issue

---

[38] Keohane and Nye 1977, 35.

area structure. Its heavy reliance on information and the resolution of uncertainty, its tendency to involve repeated interactions, and the extent to which successful cooperation requires the maximal participation mean that certain forms of institutionalized cooperation are more likely than others. Neoliberal institutionalism and complex interdependence, rather than realism, help one better understand the dynamics of international environmental issues.

For Aggarwal, trade relations are an area of complex interdependence. He explores the particular structure of international trade institutions as a function of the characteristics of the issue area. Using the transaction costs approach of Keohane, he asks what types of cooperative arrangements are institutionalized when countries seek trade liberalization. First, he systematically categorizes the different types of arrangements that are increasingly populating the global trade landscape by focusing on several dimensions of such institutions: their number of participants, product coverage, geographical scope, the extent of market opening or closing, and the degree of institutionalization. This categorization also enables us to understand the origins and evolution of different types of arrangements by better specifying the dependent variable. Aggarwal employs a bargaining game approach to examine the evolution of trade arrangements. This institutional bargaining game is used to understand emerging developments in the trading system with a specific focus on northeast Asia. Aggarwal's chapter demonstrates that, as neoliberal institutionalism predicts, trade institutions depend less on the global distribution of power than on the preexisting institutional environment and the nature of the issue area.

As Aronson makes clear, international intellectual property rights are a new area for neoliberal institutionalist analysis. Since the 1980s international intellectual property protection has become a critical issue on the international economic agenda. Today IPR rules are stronger and more global, but not harmonized. The structure of the issue area is key to the outcomes as it shapes both the relative power capabilities of the state and nonstate actors involved and the character of the international regimes developed to regulate these property rights. According to Aronson, international intellectual property issues involve a strategic game between older, established firms and their home countries, which are trying to defend and extend their power and profits in the face of technological change, and developing countries and new, innovating firms, which desire access to old technologies and ideas. States and firms are thus interdependent, and global governance in this issue area requires that developed countries and their firms cooperate with developing ones and their rising firms.

Tickner's essay on religion as a new source of power in world politics

concludes the volume. It challenges the conception of complex interdependence as depicted by Keohane and Nye. The 9/11 attacks and their
aftermath reveal a world that is more complicated than the one Keohane
and Nye described in 1977. The acts of informal violence since 9/11 require that institutionalism's association of nonstate actors with forms of
nonmilitary power be rethought. Such informal but potent violence raises
questions about international relations (IR) theory's assumption that the
state is both the primary perpetrator of large-scale international violence
and the primary protector against it. Neoliberal institutionalism and
other theories must expand their notions of nonstate actors and the
power resources open to them. Perhaps ironically, globalization has increased the scope and magnitude of informal violence because of the decline in the cost and increase in speed of communications and transportation. The power of ideas, in this case religious ideas, in a networked
global society allows nonstate actors with little military capability to mobilize supporters and execute acts of informal violence with large-scale
consequences. Tickner's challenge to neoliberal institutionalism is a powerful one; it forces IR theory to rethink who the key nonstate actors in
world politics are and what power resources they possess.

Cooperation in World Politics

The fourth area where neoliberal institutionalism has differed from neorealism is in its focus on cooperation in world politics. Realism, and especially neorealism, has generally focused on conflict among states, and
especially on the use of military force and war. In *Power and Interdependence,* Keohane and Nye first sought to redress the imbalance between
the scholarly attention paid to conflict and that paid to cooperation. Neoliberal institutionalism has since looked at the world through different
lenses and identified substantial and enduring patterns of cooperation,
much of it institutionalized since 1945. A "security community" in which
war is unthinkable and states do not use the threat of military force to resolve issues seems to exist in the North Atlantic region.[39] The expansion
of the EU to more than twenty-five countries in Europe has added greatly
to the number of countries that have relinquished a great deal of their
sovereignty and autonomy for the sake of peace and prosperity. International trade and investment relations have been deeply institutionalized in
the GATT (General Agreement on Tariffs and Trade), and now the WTO,
as well as in hundreds of bilateral agreements, called PTAs and BITs (bilateral investment treaties) (see Aggarwal's chapter). The chapters point

[39] Deutsch et al. 1957.

to other areas, such as peacekeeping (Fortna and Martin), human rights (Simmons), international financial regulations (Mosley), the environment (DeSombre), and intellectual property rights (Aronson), where complex interdependence seems to prevail and institutionalized cooperation is becoming the norm.

A distinctive point about the evolution of neoliberal institutionalism has been the move from cooperation to institutionalized cooperation—or global governance. Realists do not doubt that countries can at times cooperate; indeed, alliances and balancing are important forms of cooperation central to realist theory. But neoliberal institutionalism has gone further and tried to explain institutionalized cooperation, that is, sustained policy coordination among states often guided by norms, rules, and practices codified in treaties, agreements, or international organizations (as noted by Gilligan in this volume). In such arrangements countries often relinquish substantial degrees of sovereignty and autonomy over important policy areas. For such institutionalized cooperation to exist countries must comply with the norms and rules embodied in the institutions. And they must generally comply in good times and bad, that is, both when they benefit and when they are adversely affected. Realists would, of course, not expect this; they would predict that countries would defect whenever such policy coordination negatively affected their interests, and thus that cooperation would be fleeting.

To what extent and under what conditions countries comply with the rules, norms, and practices of the international institutions to which they belong is an area of important, ongoing research. Some scholars have argued that compliance with international institutions is very high.[40] Others have pointed out that this may not indicate high levels of cooperation since countries may only join institutions that prescribe the policies they would otherwise adopt.[41] To show the effect of international institutions, one must demonstrate that the policies adopted would have been different without the institution, and this task is difficult. Establishing this counterfactual often relies on comparisons of the country's policies with other similar countries or with the same country when it was not a member of the institution. But countries that join an institution may differ systematically from those that do not join, and these differences may also affect their likelihood of complying. Countries that join may already have policies close to those promoted by the institution, or they may have to pay the fewest costs to change their polices in the direction of those promoted by the institution. Simple comparisons to establish the counterfactual may

---

[40] Chayes and Chayes 1995.
[41] Downs, Rocke, and Barsoom 1996.

not alleviate these problems.[42] Joining an institution and complying with it are related decisions.[43]

The problem of untangling the effects of institutions may be even deeper. The particular design of the institution itself, that is, its norms, rules, and practices, may also be endogenous. The states that end up joining a regime may design it such that its procedures and rules require the least change for them or advantage them the most. Indeed, the rational design of such institutions implies this type of behavior.[44] Hence, neither membership in nor the character of the institution itself can be considered exogenous to the institution's creation or its levels of compliance. Neoliberal institutionalism has recently come face to face with these difficult issues involved in addressing the causal claims of the theory.

A number of the chapters in this volume (e.g., Simmons, Mosley, DeSombre, Aggarwal, and Aronson) focus on institutionalized cooperation and compliance. They try to deepen our understanding of the conditions under which institutionalized cooperation, or global governance, emerges and high levels of compliance arise. Simmons, for instance, focuses on the compliance of states with international institutions promoting human rights. From virtually nothing before the Universal Declaration on Human Rights (1948), governments have constructed a dense web of human rights treaties by which they have committed themselves to observe basic standards of rights protection. She asks whether these institutions make a difference: do governments that join human rights institutions protect their citizens better than those that do not? In particular, she focuses on the effect of the Convention on the Elimination of Discrimination against Women (CEDAW), begun in 1979, on various measures of the educational gender gap around the world. The CEDAW is an example of an international institution that has few enforcement mechanisms; hence there is a real question whether it should have any effect on states' behavior. Simmons's argument is that governments that join human rights institutions find it increasingly costly to ignore these institutions' basic principles, largely because of domestic audience costs. Enforcement of the agreement has to be highly decentralized, relying heavily on nonstate actors. The primary enforcement mechanisms she identifies rely not on powerful states, but rather on intergovernmental organizations designed to monitor governments' practices, international nongovernmental women's advocacy groups, and most especially domestic interests who demand that their government take their treaty commitment seriously. The information effects of these international institutions and nonstate actors on domestic politics and their ability to help form transnational coalitions

---

[42] E.g., Simmons and Hopkins 2005; von Stein 2005.

[43] Keohane and Martin 2003; von Stein 2005; see Mitchell in this volume.

[44] Koremenos, Lipson, and Snidal 2001.

provide strong evidence for the neoliberal institutionalist theory about the role of institutions in fostering cooperation.

In her chapter Mosley hypothesizes about the possible causal mechanisms by which private actors may enforce financial regulations and achieve greater cooperation. She demonstrates that three broad types of private actor involvement in governance exist, which allow such actors to play a central role in this issue area. Private financial actors can serve as autonomous authorities developing and enforcing rules; they can be joint sources of rules, developing them in concert with governmental authorities; and they can serve as enforcers of standards, applying rules developed by other authorities. Private sector involvement in global governance could lead to more successful global cooperation as a result of higher compliance rates because such actors have a variety of ways to induce compliance. They can act as enforcers of agreements, against third parties (e.g., private markets pressuring national governments to comply), or as self-regulators, implementing rules that govern their own behavior (e.g., accountants following international standards).

But Simmons asks, pushing neoliberal institutionalist ideas forward, whether private sector enforcement efforts are superior to those of governments. Data show that global standards that are entirely in the private sphere do not have higher compliance rates than those in the public sphere. Thus private sector involvement in global financial regulation may not be very effective. Private sector participation in governance also has distributional consequences, as privately developed regimes are likely to reflect and benefit financial sector interests. If their participation does not lead to higher levels of compliance, she notes, engaging private sector actors in global governance may reduce both accountability and compliance. Neoliberal institutionalism points out the growing role of private sector actors in world politics, but it has not carefully assessed the costs and benefits of such cooperation.[45] Who benefits from international cooperation and global governance is an important issue that early work on neoliberal institutionalism did not address.

Empirical Puzzles and Progress in Neoliberal Institutionalism

A final element of the neoliberal institutionalist paradigm has been its increasing methodological sophistication. One element of this development has been the use of game theory to better specify the causal arguments in the theory. As shown in the chapter here by Fortna and Martin, formal models of strategic interaction among countries can often show how

[45] Keohane and Nye 1977; Slaughter 2004.

international institutions help overcome coordination problems, provide information, and lower transaction costs.[46] Similar to the *Rational Design of International Institutions* volume and the *Delegation and Agency in International Organizations* volume, a number of the chapters here (Stone, Gilligan, Fortna and Martin, Simmons, DeSombre) turn to concepts in rational choice theory—and especially game theory—to develop the causal logic of neoliberal institutionalism. Ideas about transaction costs and uncertainty, delegation and principal-agent problems, signaling models and information provision, and prisoner's dilemma and common pool resources problems all help illuminate the causal logic of the interaction between state and nonstate actors in a world of complex interdependence.

Another important element has been the increasing sophistication of the empirical methods used to evaluate the causal claims in neoliberal institutionalist theory. Especially since King, Keohane, and Verba, research on international institutions has been increasingly aware of the extensive problems involved in assessing the causal claim that these institutions matter.[47] As noted above, this claim involves a counterfactual, which is difficult to assess. The selection of the cases that one uses to evaluate this claim are very important since selecting on the dependent variable is likely to give biased results. Downs, Rocke, and Barsoom years ago pointed out key problems with assessing international institutions, namely selection bias and endogeneity.[48] Gilligan in his chapter about whether the transaction costs approach can explain the creation of international institutions touches on critical issues related to case selection and empirical evidence necessary for evaluating this claim. These institutions must be negotiated, and so one will only observe such institutions if the relative transaction costs of creating them, amortized over the expected lifetime of the regime, are also sufficiently small. Selection bias arises since the transaction costs approach expects transaction costs to be low in cases where states are bargaining unaided by institutions, which are in his opinion precisely the types of cases covered by most empirical analysis of transaction costs in international relations. Careful design of research to address issues of selection bias, Gilligan notes, is important for making progress in the neoliberal institutionalist paradigm.

Furthermore, the exogeneity of the membership of the institution or its own internal design and procedures cannot be guaranteed; they are likely to be endogenous, given that they are created by rational actors interacting strategically. Ronald Mitchell in his chapter asks fundamental questions about states' compliance with international institutions and the methodological issues associated with testing such claims. He notes that

[46] E.g., Stone 2002; Mansfield, Milner, and Rosendorff 2002.
[47] King, Keohane, and Verba 1994.
[48] Downs, Rocke, and Barsoom 1996, 1998; Keohane and Martin 2003.

neoliberal institutionalism needs to take the realist challenge to the power of international institutions seriously, which raises two charges of endogeneity. Membership endogeneity means that countries that join are systematically different from those that do not. These differences, and not membership per se, may explain their behavior in the institution. Comparisons with countries that did not join or with the country before it joined are biased unless they take into account these differences. The second problem he labels *design endogeneity*. This problem is caused by the fact that differences in institutional design, which are often used to explain differences in state behavior, themselves result from differences in the problem structure or power distribution that predate the institution. Mitchell, like Keohane and Martin, agrees that neoliberal institutionalism must address these endogeneity issues.[49]

Fortna and Martin in their chapter on the demand for peacekeeping operations in civil wars attend to issues of both case selection and endogeneity. Although a substantial literature on peacekeeping exists, analyses of it as an institution promoting cooperation have not come to terms with several methodological handicaps. One is the problem of case selection; a majority of studies examines only cases where peacekeepers are involved, with no comparison to cases of nonpeacekeeping. Such selection on the dependent variable can pose problems for causal analysis. Endogeneity is also a problem since peacekeepers are not deployed to conflicts at random, so any analysis of their effects must begin with an analysis of which conflicts peacekeepers enter. The chapter by Fortna and Martin asks why belligerents sometimes agree to have peacekeepers and sometimes do not by focusing on peacekeeping as a mechanism that enables warring sides to signal their intentions to one another. By addressing concerns about selection bias and endogeneity, Fortna and Martin can better explain the adoption of institutional solutions to informational problems.

Simmons also has to be concerned with endogeneity. She wants to understand compliance with human rights regimes, in particular CEDAW. But compliance may depend on who joins an institution; those who join may be those who already or most easily can comply with the regime. Hence to see if the institution really affects behavior, one has to control for who joins in the first place. Simmons does this in a two-stage regression design and shows that even when controlling for who joins, ratification of the CEDAW has improved women's educational opportunities globally. Most importantly, because her empirical tests endogenize the making of the treaty commitment itself, it is difficult to claim that these improvements "would have happened anyway." Her seminal research demonstrates that the world's women have, on average, been made better off when their

---

[49] Keohane and Martin 2003.

governments make an international legal commitment to work toward their educational equality.

All of these methodological problems deepen the complexity of establishing an independent causal effect for international institutions in world politics. These problems, which are general to social science, also affect case study investigations, as McKeown notes, since governmental and nongovernmental actors have incentives to misrepresent their causal roles. He points out the serious methodological issues associated with determining the influence of transnational linkages. If the success of transnational and transgovernmental contacts is related to their appearance of being unconnected to the influencing government's central decision-makers, then those decision-makers have strong incentives to conceal any impetus that they provided to these private or unauthorized interactions. Government officials who are colluding with foreign governments are also likely to have strong incentives to conceal their behavior. The public record should therefore understate the degree to which significant transgovernmental interaction occurs, as well as the degree of high-level government knowledge and control of its occurrence. Some apparently transgovernmental or transnational interactions may really be instances where one or even both central governments play a controlling, but concealed, role. Assessing causality and showing the power of transnational relations, then, may be fraught with difficult empirical problems that McKeown brings to light. The increasing awareness of these methodological problems has helped the field advance and has contributed to the progressive nature of the neoliberal institutionalist paradigm.

Finally, Tickner's chapter challenges the rationalist, positivist approach in neoliberal institutionalism and opens up the methodological toolbox of international relations theory to explore religion's role in world politics. Tickner argues that since 9/11, international relations must develop a better understanding of worldviews, including religious ones, that could motivate nonstate actors to acts of informal violence. Extremist religious groups all over the globe decry international institutions and what they describe as the "new world order" led by a secular United States. They do not see a neoliberal institutionalist world as preferable to a realist one. She suggests that the rationalist tools of neoliberal institutionalism and realism are not capable of helping us understand such views. Incorporating religious motivations into international relations theory is difficult because these theories were constructed upon the epistemological foundations of secular rationalism and therefore are not useful for understanding worldviews of those with deep hostility toward secular thinking. She suggests that religious worldviews may be better understood using hermeneutic, reflexive, and dialogical methodologies traditionally associated with religious studies. Beliefs about gender and race are constitutive features of most religious worldviews, and hence linguistic constructivism, she opines, can be helpful in understanding worldviews based around views of race and gender. To understand these religious trends and their influence on foreign policies, Tickner claims, requires international relations scholars to pursue new methodological and theoretical avenues—beyond neoliberal institutionalism.

Another Generation of Neoliberal Institutionalism: This Volume

The chapters in this volume seek to extend our thinking about each of these four elements of the neoliberal institutionalist paradigm. The first three chapters, by Stone, Gilligan, and Mitchell, deal with some of the most important theoretical problems in the neoliberal institutionalist paradigm. They address the causes of international institutions, the sources of problems in the operation of such institutions, and the degree of compliance with them. The next set of six chapters turns from purely theoretical and methodological questions about neoliberal institutionalism to analyses of issue areas where institutionalization is occurring. The five chapters by Fortna and Martin, Simmons, Mosley, DeSombre, Aggarwal, and Aronson explore particular issues to see how international institutions have operated in each of them. They deal with questions about the creation, evolution, and influence of specific instances of institutionalized cooperation. They show the importance of focusing on issue areas to understand the key players and their power resources in a world of complex interdependence. The structure of the issue area, rather than the global balance of traditional military or economic power, shapes who the main actors are and what kinds of resources they can use to realize their goals as well as what kinds of cooperative institutions can be realized in the area. The possibilities for cooperation in each issue area vary according to this structure, much as Keohane and Nye predicted thirty years ago. The last two essays by McKeown and Tickner return to the central questions raised by neoliberal institutionalism about the role of nonstate actors in world politics and the methods for understanding their role. Both raise serious concerns about the use of standard empirical and rationalist methods in international relations.

The research inspired by neoliberal institutionalism has been broad ranging. The studies in this volume push forward on the research frontiers of this paradigm. They address the four central claims of neoliberal institutionalist theory and ask hard questions about the validity and power of those claims. Neoliberal institutionalism placed great faith in international institutions. It saw them as voluntary means for states to work together to devise cooperative solutions to important global problems.

The chapters here ask why these institutions seem to be operating so poorly and why many people today do not support them. Why are major post–World War II institutions like the UN, World Bank, IMF, and the WTO under attack today? Is the new intellectual property rights regime in the WTO (the TRIPs agreement) efficient, effective, or equitable? The studies inquire about the strength of the evidence in favor of a transaction costs approach to international institutions. They question whether the design of most institutions is indeed optimal or whether different designs could make them operate more effectively. They specify much more clearly the value of issue area approaches and the elements of the structure of issue areas that matter to the creation and design of international institutions. They inquire about the role of nonstate actors and how important and beneficial these actors are. Do they play an important role in transgovernmental relations? Do they lead to better outcomes in the global financial and IPR regimes?

The authors of these studies point out that many previous attempts to assess neoliberal institutionalism have been deeply flawed by methodological problems. Two of the most severe are selection bias in choosing cases and endogeneity in both membership and design of institutions. The impact of international institutions and nonstate actors cannot be understood unless these problems are addressed in the research design. They also force us to reflect upon whether the rationalist, secular approach embedded in neoliberal institutionalism and most other international relations theories is appropriate for understanding a new world order where religion and religious motivations are ascendant.

At the end, however, the studies in this book do seem to affirm the progressive nature of neoliberal institutionalism. Each of them shows how viewing the world through neoliberal institutionalism changes and probably improves our understanding of major elements of international politics. Relations among some countries and in some issue areas are heavily institutionalized. And more areas are becoming subject to attempts at institutionalized cooperation. Nonstate actors are important in numerous areas of world politics, and increasingly so as they deal more and more with governance in a globalized world. Traditional sources of power in world politics remain important, but in many issue areas, such as human rights, the environment, and trade and financial market regulation, other forms of influence may be more effective. Moreover, the issues faced today do not fall neatly into some hierarchy of concerns; rather, countries face many issues and place different valuations on them. Issue areas have particular structures of interaction, which shape who the important actors are and what the key power resources are in the area.

Even the rise of terrorism as a major security concern in world politics underlines some important elements of the neoliberal institutionalist paradigm. Terrorists tend to be nonstate actors, even if some are supported by governments, and part of their ability to wreak havoc comes from their nonstate status. Terrorists also exert influence through untraditional channels. They rarely have the military ability to defeat a state, but they use various technologies to undermine people's sense of security and of their government's ability to protect them. And in many ways they utilize and depend upon high levels of interdependence among countries to be effective. Many of the central tenets of neoliberal institutionalism help us to understand terrorism and the threat it poses, and they may provide us with a better understanding of it than realist assumptions. Hence even in the area of security studies, the neoliberal institutionalist paradigm may give us useful analytical tools to understand world politics.

In sum, complex interdependence is a good descriptor for the world around us in many regions and on many issues. Asymmetric interdependence is a powerful force for influencing cooperation and conflict. Neoliberal institutionalism remains a vibrant research paradigm. Indeed, in this increasingly globalized world it may be the most useful international relations paradigm we have.

Institutions and Power

CHAPTER 2

Institutions, Power, and Interdependence

Randall W. Stone

THE TWO AND A HALF DECADES since the appearance of Keohane and Nye's *Power and Interdependence* have witnessed a profound institutionalization of international relations. International institutions have proliferated, expanded, and deepened. The number of intergovernmental organizations has increased, and their memberships have expanded: The United Nations has 192 members, the International Monetary Fund and World Bank currently have 185 members, and the World Trade Organization grew from 128 members in 1994 to 153 a decade later, with 30 more countries at various stages in the application process. The European Union expanded to fifteen member countries in 1995, to twenty-five in 2004, and to twenty-seven in 2007. Substantial decision-making power has been delegated to international organizations, and a few dispose of substantial resources. The IMF held approximately $400 billion in assets, of which $190 billion was available to lend in 2007, while the World Bank had $230 billion in outstanding loans and $33 billion in capital. International institutions have extended their influence into policy areas traditionally the prerogative of states, and patterns of international cooperation have become progressively formalized in international law. By the beginning of the twenty-first century there was virtually no problem of broad international concern for which no international regime existed to express principles and norms of formalized cooperation, and this cooperation almost always involved the participation of international organizations.

On the other hand, international institutions consistently fail to solve the problems they were created to address. This is not simply to say that international institutions are suffering from unpopularity; indeed, the fact that dissatisfaction with institutions such as the IMF, the WTO, and the EU is on the rise is not necessarily a bad sign. Public institutions that evoke no dissatisfaction cannot be very significant, and if public opinion identifies problems and interest groups organize to influence these institutions, this is a sign of their growing importance. As a result of this pressure, international institutions across the board are engaged in efforts at reform, and they are evolving at an ever-increasing rate, becoming more transparent, publishing more data, and creating independent evaluation agencies. Nor can we hold institutions to blame for failing to coordinate states when their leaders have opposed preferences, as in the recent case of the U.S.-led war against Iraq: International institutions can only facilitate cooperation when there are common objectives to be achieved. However, across a wide spectrum of issues, the pattern is consistent that international institutions are failing to provide satisfactory solutions to international problems, and there appear to be important constraints that prevent them from achieving optimal solutions.

This returns us to the central question Robert Keohane and Joseph Nye posed in *Power and Interdependence*: what explains institutional change? Keohane and Nye suggested three broad categories of explanations: power, international processes, and the structure of international institutions. These three categories have structured many of the subsequent debates in the field. Progress in European integration has variously been ascribed to a coincidence of great-power interests, to economic incentives created by markets, and to initiatives promoted by the European Commission.[1] The pattern of IMF lending has been attributed by some to the interests of the biggest donors, by others to the logical imperatives of market reform and global stabilization, and by still others to the private agenda of an out-of-control agency. When international bureaucrats are weak, path-dependent arguments often arise nevertheless, in which the design of earlier institutions plays an important role in shaping subsequent decisions. For example, did the transformation of the international capital control regime from a closed to an open system come about because of the inherent vulnerabilities of the closed regime?[2] Alternatively, was it driven by the interests of powerful states, or by the market pressures created by private actors?[3] The three categories of explanation capture the broad outlines of many significant debates; but, as their authors acknowledged, they are too underspecified to serve as testable theories.

Rather than seeking general answers, this essay selects a few rational-choice hypotheses about international institutions that have become prominent since the appearance of *Power and Interdependence*. The focus is on five central incentive problems that explain many of the failures of international society to achieve common goals: public goods, delegation, institutional design, bargaining, and agenda control.

[1] Moravcsik 1998.

[2] The capital controls regime instituted at Bretton Woods enshrined the principle in the IMF Articles of Agreement that members had the right to establish capital controls at their own sole discretion, and even foresaw the possibility of bilateral or multilateral cooperation to enforce capital controls. This permissive regime was gradually undermined, until by the 1990s dismantling capital controls became obligatory for members of the OECD and strongly encouraged for members of the IMF.

[3] Helleiner 1994.

The Underprovision of Public Goods

When international institutions perform unsatisfactorily, the most prominent explanation is that international governance has some of the characteristics of a *public good*; although sometimes excludable, the benefits of international cooperation are generally non-rival, so that the countries that enjoy international cooperation never fully internalize its social benefits. Robert Keohane and others have used this logic to link the underprovision of international cooperation to the distribution of power: Only a powerful state could take on the role of an international hegemon, which is willing to provide public goods because it alone internalizes enough of the benefits of cooperation to be willing to pay the costs. Writing in 1984, Keohane believed that it was too early to test his contention that international institutions could support cooperation in the absence of a hegemon. Only if his forecast of U.S. decline over the next decade turned out to be correct would it be possible to test the theory.[4]

Whether U.S. power has in fact declined since the mid-1980s is an interesting question, and answers will depend on definitions of power and the selection of objectives.[5] In any case, U.S. decline cannot explain the underprovision of international cooperation, because the hegemonic stability argument had the logic of the distribution of power backward. Robert Pahre shows in a fairly general model that large leading states are able to shift a disproportionate share of the cost of providing public goods onto their allies, precisely because they are so large that everyone else has to adjust.[6] On the other hand, in a repeated public good model it becomes clear that the more powerful the leader, the narrower the scope of an enforceable cooperating coalition, because bigger states have bigger credibility problems.[7] In this model, the leader can only keep countries in the contributing coalition if they contribute enough to be worth punishing, and the opportunity cost of imposing the punishment increases as the leader grows relative to the followers. When we enrich the model to allow country-specific punishments, the type of cooperation chosen varies as

[4] Keohane 1984, 219.

[5] U.S. global military preeminence at the beginning of the twenty-first century is without historical parallel. U.S. influence in the former Soviet bloc and in areas that were contested spheres of influence during the Cold War has increased vastly, and there is no longer a formidable rival that can deter U.S. military adventures. Per capita income has not quite kept pace with America's closest rivals, increasing 43 percent since 1984, as compared to 45 percent in Europe and 47 percent in Japan, but U.S. per capita income remains 1.4 times that of Europe and 1.3 times that of Japan. Record fiscal and trade deficits are troubling and unsustainable, but the ability to run them for so long served as a signal of the extraordinary strength of the U.S. economy.

[6] Pahre 1998.

[7] Stone, Slantchev, and London 2008.

well: When possible, larger leading states choose to build discriminatory regimes rather than multilateral ones that provide public goods; this compensates for the disadvantages of size, which make the leader easy to exploit. When discrimination is not feasible, we find that dominant leaders build institutions, but again they do this to reduce the disadvantages of great power. Given these formal results, U.S. decline cannot explain the underprovision of international cooperation, although perhaps U.S. preeminence may do so. It is striking in this regard that the United States has taken an increasingly unilateral posture since the end of the Cold War.

Agency and Delegation

The familiar realist argument about international institutions is that states do not delegate authority to international organizations because they fear that cooperation will allow rivals to make disproportional gains in military power.[8] This logic only applies to intense, bipolar military rivalries,[9] but two more sophisticated arguments related to agency are plausible. First, states are reluctant to delegate because they anticipate that agency problems will make intergovernmental organizations difficult to control. Second, if states do nevertheless delegate functions to international institutions, they will do so in a way that allows them to retain substantial control, so international institutions will not have the autonomy to exercise much influence that is independent of the power and interests of states.

The study of agency in international institutions is thriving, particularly in studies of the European Union and the International Monetary Fund.[10] Roland Vaubel argued that international organizations should be analyzed in a public choice framework that focuses on the agency problems created by elected officials and international bureaucrats.[11] The domestic version of this account argues that elected officials delegate to international organizations in order to escape from their own accountability to voters and other principals such as nongovernmental organizations. This is a harsh verdict, but it finds echoes in the popular argument that the IMF is able to provide political cover for governments that want to reform their economies but face opposition at home.[12] According to this view, governments seek to deflect the blame for the social cost of economic reform by using as a scapegoat an international organization that

[8] Waltz 1979; Mearsheimer 1994–95.
[9] Snidal 1991.
[10] Hawkins et al. 2006.
[11] Vaubel 1986.
[12] Putnam 1988; Haggard and Kaufman 1995; Vreeland 2003.

is not accountable to voters. At the international level, the public choice critique argues that the objectives of international bureaucrats are to increase their power, perquisites, and organizational slack. For example, Rawi Abdelal argues provocatively that the EU Commission, the Secretariat of the Organization for Economic Co-operation and Development, and the IMF senior management played key roles in promoting the liberalization of capital controls in the 1980s and 1990s, in part because they were competing with each other to control the issue area.[13] This returned to the agenda subsequently, as the IMF staff unsuccessfully tried to use the development of its Medium Term Strategy as an opportunity to expand the IMF's authority to regulate capital controls.[14] In a less critical vein, but along similar lines, it has been argued that the European Commission[15] and the European Court of Justice[16] have played important roles in promoting European integration, often over the objections of some of the states involved.

These arguments suggest that international organizations seize authority and that international governance may be more robust and intrusive than is optimal from the point of view of voters or other relevant principals.[17] Alternatively, it may be the case that principals would like to delegate more functions to international institutions, but do not do so because they cannot control the institutions' policies. This could be the case for one of two reasons. First, agency problems may arise because there are multiple principals with divergent preferences. Second, agency problems may be due to the difficulty of monitoring the policies international institutions implement, but only if the preferences of international bureaucrats are unknown or it is costly when international bureaucrats shirk.

The influence of multiple principals is the most convincing account, because alternative agency arguments must assume that international bureaucrats have substantial information advantages over national authorities. This seems consistent with the widespread assumption that international institutions provide information that facilitates cooperation.[18] However, the most convincing empirical stories that have been told about this suggest

---

[13] Abdelal 2007.

[14] Work on the Medium Term Strategy began in June 2004 under managing director Rodrigo de Rato, and culminated in its publication in September 2005. The proposal to extend the Fund's jurisdiction to capital controls was first advanced by staff, subsequently embraced by management, and finally killed by the IMF executive board.

[15] Sandholtz and Zysman 1989.

[16] Garrett 1992.

[17] A parallel argument in a constructivist vein attributes mission creep and bureaucratic dysfunction to organizational cultures that arise within IOs and can become pathological (Barnett and Finnemore 2004).

[18] Keohane 1984.

that institutions reduce transaction costs by making authoritative determinations about what counts as defection from an agreement.[19] That is, institutions help to facilitate correlated strategies by resolving uncertainty about the definition of the rules. There are not many examples where institutions really have superior information. Most intergovernmental organizations, as for example the WTO, rely upon member states to put violations of rules on the agenda: they rely on "fire alarms" rather than "police patrols."[20] Even the European Union, the most impressive international institution in terms of its bureaucratic capacity, cannot rival the analytic and data collection capacities of its member states. The IMF does not have an information advantage over borrowers, which filter and often falsify the data that they feed to it, and arguably has no advantage over international financial markets, where major investors have the resources and incentives to procure information. Although it has subsequently modernized and made significant strides in creating incentives for members to provide it with quality data, during the Mexican crisis of 1994–95 the IMF relied on incomplete data reported by the Mexican Central Bank with a three- to four-month lag, when more complete data were available daily from Reuters and Bloomberg's. The IMF management has an information advantage over its executive board, but the degree of advantage varies significantly across countries. The Fund has developed procedures that allow it to withhold confidential information from the executive board, including internal memos.[21] However, informal consultations allow the U.S. Treasury much more extensive access to information, and in important cases such as Mexico, Indonesia, Korea, Russia, and Argentina, Treasury officials were directly involved in the negotiations.[22] Confidentiality in the IMF has more to do with centralizing control than with delegating.

Even when institutions have an informational edge over states, an agency problem arises only if the agents' types are unknown or the costs of shirking are substantial. If shirking is not very costly (i.e., discretion is important, but effort is not), the principal can achieve the desired policy by appointing an agent who is known to share the principal's preferences.[23] A great deal is indeed known about agents' types, to conclude from the recent public discussions over selection of EU commissioners, ECB presidents, IMF managing directors, and WTO directors. The problem of shirking, on the other hand, is not very costly in international organizations. The IMF has a staff of 2,700, so how much money can it

[19] Reinhardt 2001.
[20] McCubbins and Schwartz 1984.
[21] Martin 2006.
[22] IEO 2003, 2004.
[23] Moe 1990.

waste?[24] The EU is capable of spending more than any other international institution, and the issue of mismanagement of EU funds is significant enough to motivate conservative candidates in EU parliamentary elections, but it is not important enough to excite voters very much.

On the other hand, the existence of multiple principals with divergent preferences is sufficient to create agent discretion, even in the absence of asymmetric information.[25] Discretion, in this formal sense, means that the agent is able to choose among a range of policies to implement. In the case of the EU, the Commission exercises a substantial degree of discretion when the status quo lies outside the voting core of the states represented in the European Council, because it can make proposals within a wide range that will be approved by a qualified majority.[26] Along similar lines, Martin argues that multiple principals account for the substantial degree of autonomy that the IMF staff enjoys in crafting the conditionality attached to its loans.[27] Stone likewise finds that the Fund enjoys considerably more autonomy in program design than in lending or enforcement decisions, although this autonomy can be revoked in a crisis when the United States is deeply interested.[28]

The existence of multiple principals can explain an agency's discretion, but it is not clear that this should make the principals unwilling to delegate. For the problems created by multiple principals to explain the underprovision of international governance, governments would have to be unable to coordinate their votes. Otherwise, they could agree on a voting rule that would constrain the agent and leave them all better off than they would be without institutionalized cooperation. For example, when the European Commission appeared likely to enforce the rules of the Stability and Growth Pact to the disadvantage of Germany and France in 2003, Germany and France traded votes to prevent the rules from being enforced against either. When the agent seemed in danger of getting out of control, the principals coordinated their votes and reined it in. Similarly, discretion over the design and enforcement of IMF conditionality is often delegated to the donor country most directly interested in the borrowing country (France in Francophone Africa, Britain in former British colonies, the United States in Latin America), which prevents the IMF from

---

[24] The issue of compensation for Fund employees is controversial, but not because of cost. The United States consistently tries to limit Fund compensation because the greater attractiveness of working for the IMF than for the U.S. bureaucracy makes it difficult to retain qualified personnel at Treasury. Similarly, clientelism arises because former executive directors find it attractive to join the IMF staff. Executive directors from poor countries consistently support Fund proposals to increase staff compensation.

[25] Banks and Weingast 1992; Calvert, McCubbins, and Weingast 1989.

[26] Tsebelis 1994; Tsebelis and Garrett 2001.

[27] Martin 2006.

[28] Stone 2008.

exploiting disagreements among its principals about how rigorously to enforce its programs.[29] When there is disagreement on the executive board about lending to particular countries (as in the case of Argentina in 2001), the G-7 countries coordinate their positions ahead of time, and there is a virtually unbroken norm that dissenting executive directors abstain rather than voting against the management proposal. (Abstentions do not count against approval.) Coordination failure may be unavoidable when there are extreme divergences of preferences, severe commitment problems, or a lot of *ex ante* uncertainty. In most areas of economic cooperation, however, coordination among the principals appears to be able to mitigate agency problems enough to make the costs of delegation tolerable. Furthermore, when *ex ante* coordination is difficult, it is nevertheless possible for powerful states to limit their losses by circumventing the formal voting process: They buy votes or threaten to exercise outside options.[30] Agency does not provide a compelling explanation for the unwillingness of states to delegate to international institutions.

The principals' lack of commitment to institutional independence does pose a significant obstacle to effective international governance, however. Principals may prefer to retain discretion because they are uncertain about future states of the world, and are unable to write complete contracts that cover all possible contingencies. When devising the WTO's adjudication procedures and rules covering export subsidies, for example, the United States and the European Union could not be certain whether they would ultimately be directed against Boeing or Airbus. Until the issue became caught up in the 2004 U.S. presidential campaign, both sides preferred not to roll the dice, and this explains the long-standing informal ceasefire over enforcement of WTO rules against either aircraft producer. On the other hand, there exist areas of international cooperation in which the temptations to defect are very predictable, where commitment is optimal *ex ante* and reneging is optimal *ex post*. This situation, known in economics as a time consistency problem, arises whenever current policies affect the payoff to decisions made in the past.[31] For example, when sudden reversals of capital flows make it impossible for important sovereign borrowers to service their short-term debt, there are strong incentives for creditor countries to use the IMF to provide financing to bail out their banks—but this rewards the irresponsible borrowing and investment decisions that led to the crisis in the first place.[32] When the United States pushed the IMF to lend an unprecedented $17.8 billion

---

[29] Stone 2004.
[30] Fang 2005; Voeten 2001.
[31] Kydland and Prescott 1977.
[32] Aggarwal 1996; IEO 2003.

to Mexico in 1995, it met fierce resistance from Germany and the United Kingdom, whose leaders feared that this would exacerbate moral hazard—creating incentives for banks to make destabilizing short-term loans in the future in the expectation of future bailouts. Indeed, over the next six years the IMF struggled to cope with the systemic consequences of short-term capital flows to Russia, Brazil, Korea, Indonesia, and Argentina, which seemed motivated by the expectation that important debtors were "too big to fail," because the IMF would be compelled to provide financing, which would give creditors a breathing space to withdraw their capital. The IMF's commitment problem may explain why lending to systemically important countries invariably fails to catalyze private capital flows: asset prices do not move after an IMF loan to a truly important country because it was fully anticipated, and therefore contains no new information.

The best solution to time consistency problems is commitment. Facing such dilemmas, farsighted national leaders may attempt to tie their hands—or those of their successors—by delegating authority to an international organization. From this point of view, the existence of such dilemmas is a key functionalist explanation for international organization. However, it is a feature of the anarchical international environment that such commitment devices are generally unavailable and always imperfect. Even when they attempt to delegate important functions to international institutions, states always retain the capacity to renege, and the most independent international institutions remain vulnerable to the efforts of member states to influence their policies. To the extent that commitments are kept in international relations, it is generally because they rely on reputation building in repeated interactions. These reputational equilibria are generally only second-best solutions, however, in the sense that the optimal degree of cooperation is unattainable without resort to punishments that would turn out not to be credible.[33] In practice, the best reputational equilibria are messy and may not always look much like cooperation, because states' strategies only require them to refrain from exercising discretion when the temptation is tolerably small, and allow them to defect to myopic behavior when the temptation is compelling.

Both time inconsistency and agency are clearly important concepts for analyzing international institutions, so what is gained by emphasizing one or the other? One of the most popular targets of the agency critique is the IMF, and the enforcement of IMF conditionality offers an illustration of how the agency and commitment views lead to opposite expectations. Quantitative studies find rather weak effects of IMF conditionality

---

[33] Barro and Gordon 1983.

on countries' policies, and a host of case studies indicates that the conditions attached to IMF loans are only weakly enforced.[34] Why? An agency interpretation would argue that poor enforcement is a function of incentives for the IMF to shirk in order to "push loans." (At present the Fund is suffering from severe budget shortfalls because it does not have enough customers, and conditionality is the main deterrent to borrowing from the IMF.) The testable implication is that enforcement should be most robust in the most important cases, where financial instability poses real risks to the stability of the global economy, and where the major donors have the strongest incentives to monitor the IMF's performance; when monitoring is weak, the IMF should shirk.

A time-consistency approach makes the opposite prediction. In this view, the IMF is ineffective because it has a commitment problem: enforcement is weak because the largest shareholders prevent the Fund from rigorously enforcing its conditions. The industrialized countries benefit from IMF efforts to impose fiscal discipline and market openness on developing countries, but in particular cases they find compelling reasons to interfere. In some cases, such as Russia, Egypt, Turkey, and Pakistan, they trade their leverage with the IMF for concessions on other issues that seem more pressing at the time than economic reform. In others, such as Argentina in 2001, they waive conditionality in an effort to stave off a default that could rock the international financial system. The testable implication is that enforcement should be least effective in the most important cases, because these are the cases in which the major shareholders face the strongest temptations to interfere. The evidence to date suggests that poor enforcement is due to interference rather than shirking. The most influential post-Communist countries—those that received the most economic aid from the United States—were subject to the least rigorous enforcement and violated their conditions most often, and consequently suffered from higher inflation and more devaluation.[35] Similarly, African countries that received more U.S. aid, that were members of the CFA Franc Zone or the Commonwealth of Nations, or that voted with France in the UN General Assembly were subject to less rigorous enforcement of IMF conditionality.[36] This evidence suggests that the difficulty is not convincing the IMF to enforce its conditions, but rather convincing its principals to grant it enough autonomy to allow it to enforce conditionality when they might rather not.

[34] Steinwand and Stone 2008.

[35] Stone 2002.

[36] Stone 2004. In each of these studies, the rigor of enforcement is measured in terms of the length of program suspensions when programs go "off track."

Institutional Design

Having decided to provide international governance over a particular issue area and to delegate powers to an international organization, the society of states must resolve issues of institutional design. Should the rules of the regime be informal or legalized? Should commitments undertaken be permanent, or limited in duration? Should decision-making procedures be participatory or centralized? Each of these choices has implications for the effectiveness of international governance.

The dominant approach to studying institutional design, which Michael Gilligan reviews in this volume, has followed the logic of transaction costs economics. According to this view, institutions exist to reduce transaction costs, and the variety of institutional designs reflects the variety of political market failures that they are intended to address.[37] Thus, for example, Barbara Koremenos argues that states choose to make agreements of limited duration when they anticipate that circumstances may change, making long-term agreements untenable.[38] In much the same way, Rosendorff and Milner explain escape clauses, which allow states to temporarily set aside their legal responsibilities: they represent an efficient response to uncertainty about the short-term domestic political costs of compliance.[39] Duncan Snidal and coauthors advance a wide range of hypotheses linking transaction costs to decisions to centralize or decentralize decision making, expand or contract membership and the substantive scope of agreements, and legalize commitments or leave them informal.[40]

According to this approach, and to the transaction costs approach generally, institutions are efficient by assumption, or if second best, provide the best feasible set of incentives. For example, vertical integration of firms is an efficient response to commitment problems created by asset-specific investments[41] and executive compensation packages are designed to efficiently align executives' incentives to take risks with those of investors.[42] There are powerful insights here, and these claims may indeed be correct in particular cases; certainly impartial institutional designers would pay attention to incentives. Institutional designers are rarely impartial, however; it may also be the case that vertical integration is a way to increase market power and that executive compensation reflects collusion

---

[37] Keohane 1984.
[38] Koremenos 2005.
[39] Rosendorff and Milner 2001.
[40] Abbott and Snidal 2000; Koremenos, Lipson, and Snidal 2001.
[41] Williamson 1985.
[42] Milgrom and Roberts 1992.

between executives and board members. There is, furthermore, some danger of circularity in a functionalist approach that explains causes in terms of effects (e.g., explaining institutional features in terms of reductions in transaction costs), because some incentive problem can almost always be found to explain the existing state of affairs.[43]

For current purposes, the functionalist transaction costs approach is not very helpful for explaining failures of international governance, because it only explains efficient adaptations to incentive problems. It cannot shed light on the reasons why institutions might be designed inefficiently, or might be designed deliberately to fail. Historical accounts, on the other hand, tend to present the origins of international institutions as rather haphazard, marked by conflicts of interest, and shaped by the distribution of power that prevailed at the time.[44] To take a prominent example, the degree of legalization of the international trade regime has provoked sharp conflicts of interest since the dawn of the postwar era. The United States prevailed—over the obstreperous opposition of its allies—in imposing a template of legalized cooperation on the International Trade Organization, which was prevented from coming into force only by the reluctance of the U.S. Senate to ratify the treaty. Years later, developing countries objected to U.S. and EU-led plans to recast the informal trade regime of the General Agreement on Tariffs and Trade under the legalized aegis of the WTO, and acquiesced only after the United States and the European Union threatened to revoke the trade privileges they enjoyed under the GATT unless they complied.[45] This episode sharply underlined the importance of power in determining institutional design.

However, it would be a mistake to conclude from examples like this that institutions simply reflect the distribution of power and the interests of the powerful. Effective institutions depend on voluntary participation, so they must be at least minimally legitimate, and this need for legitimacy can itself be a constraint on effectiveness. The origins of the Global Environment Facility are a case in point. The GEF was conceived as a way to soften the economic impact of adjusting to global environmental targets by transferring resources from developed countries with high abatement costs to developing countries with lower costs.[46] In principle, there was a surplus to be gained by reducing CO_2 emissions where the reductions would be least costly, so both parties to the transaction should win. How-

---

[43] Thanks to Robert Keohane for pointing this out to me almost twenty years ago.

[44] Keohane 1984; Helleiner 1994; Milner 1997; Moravcsik 1998.

[45] Barton et al. 2006.

[46] The Global Environment Facility was established with a mandate to make grants to deal with four problems: global climate change, biodiversity loss, pollution of international waters, and ozone layer depletion. Two more areas were added subsequently: persistent organic pollutants in 2001, and land degradation in 2002.

ever, a conflict arose between developing countries, which insisted upon the principle of unconditional financing and sought to funnel GEF resources through United Nations organs where they held substantial leverage, and developed donors, which insisted on channeling their money through the World Bank under the existing framework of conditionality. In the end, a compromise was reached that left neither coalition satisfied, and the consequences were low levels of funding and an ineffective institutional structure.[47] The GEF was launched with only a symbolic level of funding—$1 billion over three years—and although this was gradually increased, it remains small: In the area of global climate change, for example, the GEF made 227 grants during its first decade, with an average size of $3.9 million.

Conflicts over institutional design are ubiquitous, because institutional details determine how the risks of international cooperation will be shared. Developing countries, with poor populations and weak states, are much more vulnerable to international market forces than are advanced industrial countries, and are therefore more risk averse; developed countries, for their part, attempt to use their market power to shift risks to developing countries.[48] The more-or-less legitimate compromises that emerge from the resulting struggles may or may not be efficient. Rather than assuming efficient design, we might do better to return to Keohane and Nye's prescription to explain institutional change in terms of power, international processes, and the opportunity structure provided by existing institutions. The next two sections suggest some hypotheses along these lines.

Bargaining

Apart from the substantive questions of how best to govern international society, there remains the procedural obstacle of how to secure the acquiescence and active participation of at least a subset of its members. If international institutions were not costly to create and modify, they could have no independent explanatory power; the supply would always equal the demand, and institutional design would simply reflect the short-run power and interests of the leading states, their leaders, and their supporting coalitions.[49] Indeed, in conventional terms such as budgets and overhead, all international institutions but the EU are extraordinarily inexpensive compared to the value of the issue areas over which they preside. The WTO, for example, had a staff of 625 and a budget of 182 million Swiss francs in 2007. Bargaining, however, is what makes institutions costly to

---

[47] Fairman 1996.
[48] Krasner 1985; Strange 1988.
[49] Krasner 1985.

create and reform, because bargaining involves strategic delay in reaching agreement, the investment of leaders' time, and the risk of their prestige.

Bargaining remains a substantial obstacle to international cooperation. Every GATT round faced delays and teetered on the edge of collapse before it was successfully concluded. Some meetings ended in dramatic failure, as in Cancún. Similarly, every major advance in European integration has been delayed, sometimes—as in the case of Economic and Monetary Union—for decades; and every significant change in the rules has come about after high-stakes brinkmanship.[50]

The peculiar curse of bargaining is that the necessary condition for successful cooperation—low discount rates—is precisely the condition that makes bargaining most costly.[51] In the familiar alternating offer game with incomplete information, for example, the length of the delay before agreement depends upon the patience of the players; more patient players hold out longer before they make concessions.[52] Similarly, when bargaining is modeled as a war of attrition, the size of the prize dwindles as the wrangling proceeds, and the bargaining drags on longer when the agents are patient.[53] The same logic has been used to explain the duration of wars.[54] The lesson is general, and does not depend on which bargaining protocol is chosen, so long as delay is possible: Outcomes are most inefficient when bargainers most value the future.

The fate of the Framework Convention on Climate Change is a sobering case in point. In 1992, mobilized by an emerging consensus in the scientific community, 194 countries signed the agreement in Rio de Janeiro.[55] Members of the OECD and twelve post-Communist countries agreed to stabilize their emissions at 1990 levels by the year 2000 and to negotiate an agreement to reduce emissions in the following decade. The details remained to be worked out in the Kyoto Protocol, however, and the proposals steadily became less ambitious in the course of the substantive negotiations.[56] Even the commitments at Kyoto remained abstract until the next stage of negotiations, completed at Marrakech in 2001, which defined the credits to reward land-use policies that remove CO_2 from the atmosphere, or "carbon sinks." The bargain struck at Marrakech dramatically relaxed the earlier targets: The average quota represented a 3.4

---

[50] Schneider and Cederman 1994.
[51] Fearon 1998.
[52] Admati and Perry 1987.
[53] Alesina and Drazen 1991.
[54] Slantchev 2003, 2004.
[55] Bodansky 2001.
[56] The European Union pushed for a target of 15 percent emissions reductions by 2010, but the Kyoto Protocol of 1997 pushed off the target until 2012 and called for only a 3.6 percent aggregate reduction below 1990 levels, setting targets that ranged from 8 percent cuts to 26 percent increases for individual countries.

percent reduction of emissions below 1990 levels at Kyoto, but a 1 percent increase after Marrakech.[57] In the end, even the nominal level of commitment implied by the Kyoto regime depended on the market power and selective incentives deployed by the European Union.[58] Developing countries refused to participate, and the United States, the most important producer of greenhouse gasses, failed to ratify the agreement. With only a few exceptions, the countries that adopted binding CO_2 quotas were members of the European Union or those seeking accession, and countries that were further from the European sphere of influence made fewer concessions.[59]

The fate of the Kyoto Protocol illustrates the difficulty of achieving multilateral cooperation through bargaining. There was no immediate cost to signing the protocol, but because countries cared about the future in which they would have to cooperate, they gradually whittled away at the cooperative agreement until it failed even to stabilize the carbon emissions that it was originally intended to reduce.

Agenda Control

International institutions evolve through a political process that privileges insiders, who are then able to impose many of their preferences on countries that join subsequently. All voting rules privilege the status quo, and many international institutions use supermajority rules that make the status quo very hard to change. In some cases this may be good for international cooperation.[60] In general, however, the privileged status of insiders is a significant impediment to deals that would deepen international cooperation.

Downs, Rocke, and Barsoom argue that the privileged position of insiders allows international institutions to choose consistently higher levels of cooperation by initially including only the most committed cooperators, and gradually broadening membership to include laggards.[61] In their model, late entrants prefer membership in an international institution such as the WTO or the EU to exclusion, even if they must accept a high level of cooperation as the price of admission, and the level of cooperation

[57] Den Elzen and de Moor 2001.

[58] McLean and Stone 2005.

[59] Russia's effective target after Marrakech was a 5 percent increase over 1990 levels, although actual CO2 production had fallen 28 percent since 1990, and still Russia refused to ratify the agreement until the European Union dropped objections to its admission to the WTO.

[60] Downs, Rocke, and Barsoom 1998.

[61] Downs, Rocke, and Barsoom 1998.

within the institution is chosen by voting. By expanding membership gradually, a group of intensive cooperators can assure a high level of co-operation, which then becomes the reversion point for future votes. A subsequent entrant is faced with a fait accompli: The status quo is more cooperative than it would prefer, and the pivotal voter, which likewise prefers more cooperation than the new entrant, will block any proposal that it does not prefer to the status quo. As new states enter, the intensity of cooperation is gradually diluted—there is a trade-off between the depth and breadth of cooperation—but cooperation remains consistently more intense than it would have been had all states entered the arrangement simultaneously.

The necessary condition for this logic to work is that previous entrants prefer higher degrees of cooperation than subsequent entrants, which is plausible if cooperation occurs on only one dimension and high cooperators are most interested in joining institutions. Indeed, this story explains aspects of integration in the European Union, as more committed cooperators gradually co-opted states that were initially reluctant. However, the European Union also serves as a counterexample. Cooperation in the EU proceeds on numerous tracks that touch virtually every area of public policy, and these have gradually proliferated, so that the original co-operators could not anticipate all of the forms cooperation eventually took. On some of these dimensions the original cooperators have more conservative preferences than many of the countries that have joined more recently. To take a prominent example, Britain refused to sign the Treaty of Rome in 1957, and acceded to the European Economic Community only in 1973, by which time the interpretation of the Common Market had become well established. Under a variety of Labor and Conservative governments, Britain consistently pushed for a more liberal trade regime in Europe; France was often able to block these proposals, relying upon its position as a veto player and the fact that the status quo was favorable to French interests. The logjam was finally broken only in 1986, when the Single European Act provided an opportunity to reopen the package deal of European integration. On other dimensions, of course, it was France rather than Britain that was in favor of deepening European cooperation in 1986, but this is the point: Voting rules may favor deeper cooperation on some dimensions and shallower cooperation on others, depending upon which countries entered first.[62]

The international trade regime likewise provides examples of the pernicious effects of gradualism. There is a persuasive argument that gradually expanding the membership of trade agreements helps to overcome

[62] Britain was reluctant to accept the institutional innovations of the SEA, and agreement was only reached after France and Germany threatened to move ahead without British participation (Moravcsik 1998).

free-rider problems by diverting trade away from nonmembers.[63] The same bargaining tactic, however, shields early members from the need to make concessions to new entrants. Early members of the General Agreement on Tariffs and Trade were developed countries, which tended to share a preference for lower tariffs for industrial manufactured goods, which they exported, and for higher tariffs for textiles and agricultural goods, which were produced more cheaply abroad. Subsequent rounds of trade negotiations have expanded the range of goods and services covered by the regime, until the Uruguay Round extended it to cover services, foreign direct investment, and intellectual property rights. As new members have joined the regime in the 1990s, they have been required to accept the status quo and harmonize their trade policies with those of the WTO in return for equal treatment with existing members; the existing members have not been required to make corresponding concessions. As a result, the international trade regime remains asymmetric, tolerating high subsidies and barriers to trade in agricultural goods. Annual U.S. cotton subsidies, for example, have exceeded total U.S. foreign aid to sub-Saharan Africa for a number of years, and indeed, exceed the GDP of any of the small West African countries that depend heavily on cotton exports.

The examples of the EU and the WTO illustrate the point that when institutions are used for cooperation on multiple issues, gradually expanding membership may create a bias against deepening cooperation. More generally, supermajority voting rules create a bias against cooperation whenever a new issue emerges: For example, new scientific knowledge identifies a previously unknown threat to the international environment, or a dramatic terrorist attack focuses attention on a previously marginal group. The status quo level of cooperation in new issues is zero. The strongest policy response that can be chosen is one that the pivotal voter prefers to the status quo, and if a supermajority is required to initiate a policy, as in the United Nations Security Council, the pivotal voter will be one that prefers a minimal policy.

Conclusions

Power and Interdependence inspired much of the subsequent work on international institutions, and if its concepts of power, interdependence, and organizational process do not specify a rigorous theory, they nevertheless provide a framework for organizing many of the insights that subsequently emerged. Interdependence provides the rationale for international organization, and trends in international finance, trade, and the environment in

[63] Oye 1992.

the last three decades have raised the costs of failing to address the problems of governance in an anarchic system of states. The rapid proliferation of institutions, broadening of memberships, and expansion of functions that we have witnessed are testimony to the increasing demand in democratic political systems for coordinated solutions to problems that states cannot solve unilaterally. Interdependence, however, fails to predict failures of international governance. To do this, we have to turn our attention to theories of power and institutions.

The standard agency perspective fails to solve our problem. First, agency conventionally predicts excessive institutionalization of international affairs rather than weak governance. Alternatively, a principal-agent view could hold that states fail to delegate precisely because they anticipate agency problems, and this explains why we do not observe them. This begs the question of why such farsighted states are not clever enough to coordinate their behavior to limit the cost of delegation, however; and in fact we observe that they often are. Second, the agency view does not correspond well to empirical observation. Whenever excessive autonomy of international institutions has been alleged, it has turned out that states had never really released their hold on the reins. The pattern of cooperation is consistent with the interpretation that influential states interfere in the operation of international institutions when their interests are affected, rather than the view that international agencies generate policies largely autonomously.

Explanations based on sheer power have fared equally poorly, and on both theoretical and empirical grounds the ill-fated theory of hegemonic stability has fared worst. The realist claim that states refuse to delegate important functions to international institutions because they are obsessed with security concerns is similarly implausible. The problem is rather that irrevocable delegation is simply not feasible. International governance, in short, remains a form of cooperation in a society of autonomous states. Institutions cannot serve as commitment devices because full delegation is never really possible; instead, only reputational equilibria are available, and long-term cooperation is only sustainable when the short-term costs for the governments involved are tolerably low.

Complex theories of interactions between power and institutions are more persuasive. Powerful states delegate authority to international institutions, but they do so in ways that allow them to retain substantial degrees of control. International cooperation is negotiated, and the bargaining depends on the resources and outside options that states bring to the table. Institutional membership and voting rules provide resources that shift the range of feasible agreements. Influential states manipulate institutional rules, hold out for privileged treatment for their own interests, and exploit their agenda control, and these strategies undermine the ability of institutions to provide effective international governance. The results are that international institutions suffer from credibility problems, that progress in forging new cooperative projects is slow, and that cooperation in many areas is blocked by the entrenched interests of founding members. State power and international institutions interact in subtle ways, and the possibilities of achieving the common interests that are emerging in an increasingly interdependent global society may depend more upon those interactions than upon the distribution of power or the formal design of international institutions.

CHAPTER 3

The Transaction Costs Approach
to International Institutions
Michael J. Gilligan

IN A WELL-KNOWN EDITED volume of *International Organization* Robert
Keohane asked:

> Why should it be worthwhile to construct regimes (themselves requir-
> ing agreement) in order to make specific agreements within the regime
> frameworks? Why is it not more efficient simply to avoid the regime stage
> and make agreements on an ad hoc basis? In short why is there any de-
> mand for international regimes apart from a demand for international
> agreements on particular questions?[1]

Keohane's answer to these thought-provoking questions, which employed
insights from the work of Coase, Williamson, and others,[2] pointed to the
importance of transaction costs as an independent variable in understanding international cooperative phenomena. Keohane's approach explicitly
focused on the institutional features of international cooperation, which
distinguish it from the more abstract game-theoretic treatments of the
subject. The standard game-theoretic account of international cooperation, which Snidal and Abbot and Snidal call *decentralized cooperation
theory*,[3] cannot answer Keohane's questions because in that theory institutions are not necessary to facilitate international cooperation.

One of the purposes of this volume is to assess "the progress that has
been made in developing the [neoliberal research] paradigm and discuss
areas where it has encountered new problems."[4] This chapter contributes
to that joint enterprise by returning to Keohane's insight about the role
transaction costs play in the creation of international institutions. I will
make the case that the international institutions literature has failed to
fulfill the great promise of the research agenda suggested by Keohane's insightful questions because systematic empirical tests of the theory have

I would like to thank Duncan Snidal for his very insightful comments on an earlier draft
of this chapter.

[1] Keohane 1982, 334.
[2] Coase 1960; Williamson 1983.
[3] Snidal 1996; Abbot and Snidal 1998.
[4] Quoted from Helen Milner's introduction to this volume.

yet to be conducted. If this gap in the transaction costs research program is to be closed, several methodological challenges must be met. I highlight two: measurement of key variables and selection problems. I then offer some suggestions about how to deal with these challenges.

In making these arguments I will draw heavily on an analogy to the contributions that transaction costs economics (TCE) has made to the standard study of economic transactions both theoretically and empirically. Transaction costs theory in economics arose out of a desire to explain the emergence of the firm and other economic institutions—something that the standard treatments of economic phenomena did not address. By analogy decentralized cooperation theory can explain why countries choose to cooperate, how they arrive at their cooperative agreements, and how they enforce them in the anarchical international system, but they do not address why countries create international institutions in the process.[5] The transaction costs approach to international institutions can help explain that puzzle. Continuing with the analogy, I argue that the empirical transaction costs literature from economics also offers insights into how to proceed with more systematic tests of transaction costs theories of international institutions.

The chapter is organized as follows. In the next section I discuss the inability of decentralized game-theoretic accounts of international cooperation to explain the presence of international institutions and the contribution of the transaction costs approach in explaining that puzzle. The succeeding section reviews existing empirical applications of the transaction costs approach and points out that, while enlightening, these studies are not really systematic tests of the theory. I address two challenges to systematic testing of transaction costs theories: measurement and selection issues, and offer some solutions to them. The final section draws conclusions.

A Comparison of the Transaction Costs Theory of International Institutions and Decentralized Cooperation Theory

My argument about the transaction costs approach to the study of international institutions hinges on an analogy to the contributions of TCE to the more traditional study of markets. Thus it may be worthwhile spending

---

[5] Space limitations prevent me from going into constructivist explanations of international cooperation; however, I would argue that the point I am making about decentralized cooperation theory is equally applicable to the normative constructivist account of international cooperation. Specifically, constructivists have failed to ask why formal institutions are necessary to create international norms. Some recent examples include Klotz 1995; Florini 1996; Finnemore 1996; Legro 1997; Finnemore and Sikkink 1998; Keck and Sikkink 1998; Price 1998; Clark 2001; and Rudolph 2001.

some time distinguishing between these two approaches to economic transactions. The unit of analysis for these economic theories is the transaction. In the traditional decentralized market approach these transactions are completed via "contingent contracts" in which the price at which suppliers are willing to provide the good or service in a given state of the world equals the price at which consumers are willing to buy it in that state of the world. If the contract will not be fulfilled until a future date, any uncertainty that may exist about future states of the world is factored into the price. Allocations resulting from these transactions are efficient, including who bears the risk arising from uncertainty about the realization of the state of the world when the contract is executed.[6]

If the price mechanism is as efficient as this traditional economic theory claims, why are not all transactions conducted by it? Many transactions are conducted not within markets via the price mechanism but within organizations (typically firms) at the direction of a manager. As Coase put it:

> Those who object to economic planning on the grounds that the problem is solved by price movements can be answered by pointing out that there is planning within our economic system . . . which is akin to what is normally called economic planning.[7]

The free market of neoclassical economics does not exist in an unadulterated form—within markets that we would typically characterize as "free" there exist pockets of central planning within firms.

Why are some transactions conducted within markets, while others are organized within firms? The traditional market-based approach, which does not admit a role for organizations, is incapable of answering this question or such questions as "How do transactions within organizations differ from behavior within markets?" "Are there ways to design organizations to make them more efficient and effective?" Coase's answer to the question "Why do firms exist?" or "Why are some transactions conducted impersonally via the price mechanism while others are conducted within organizations (firms)" was of course *transaction costs*.[8] Coase posited that there are costs to concluding transactions via the price mechanism— negotiation costs, contracting costs, costs of monitoring and enforcing the contract, and so on. Coase and his successors argued that, by concluding these transactions within firms, economic agents are able to reduce or eliminate these costs. The notion of transaction costs is, by design, as

[6] The classic work on the traditional approach to markets can be found in Arrow 1964 and Debreu 1959. A textbook treatment such as Mas-Colell, Whinston, and Green 1995 offers a thorough review of the topic.

[7] Coase 1937, 387–88.

[8] Coase 1937.

comprehensive as possible, a feature that can imbue the concept with a frustrating vagueness. North defined transaction costs as "the costs of measuring the valuable attributes of what is being exchanged and the costs of protecting rights and policing and enforcing agreements."[9] Williamson defined them as "comparative costs of planning, adapting and monitoring task completion under alternative governance structures."[10]

Coase's answer to the question of why firms exist only begs the next question: "Why then are not all transactions conducted in one big firm?" Coase's response was that inefficiencies arise when resources are allocated by managerial fiat within an organization rather than in response to relative prices.[11] In such a case resources are no longer necessarily allocated so that their marginal costs equal their marginal benefits. Coase was able to use his transaction costs approach along with simple notions of marginality to speculate about the size of firms. Firms would increase in size until the marginal cost of the inefficiencies of conducting a transaction within an organization were equal to the marginal cost of conducting that transaction with an outside agent.

To illustrate, consider an example of the "make or buy" decision that is paradigmatic to the TCE literature. Suppose a firm makes a product that requires a specialized part. The manager of the firm has one of two options in acquiring these parts. She can either (1) contract with an outside manufacturer to produce them or (2) purchase the necessary machinery and hire the necessary workers so that her own firm can make them, or, what amounts to the same thing, purchase the outside manufacturing firm, that is vertically integrate. Option 1 itself has a vast variety of forms of contracting, ranging from simple arm's-length spot market transactions to much more complicated contracts that may include renegotiation provisions, dispute resolution mechanisms, and so on. Coase is simply claiming that the manager will choose the lowest-cost option, taking into account the costs of contracting.

The literature has posited that costs of using the price mechanism should be higher, and therefore we should observe more institutionalized transactions, when two factors are present. First there must be *incomplete contracting*. Contingent contracts must be impossible, either because agents are boundedly rational and therefore cannot specify all possible contingencies *ex ante* or because it is impossible to independently verify when a specific contingency has occurred. Second, the transaction must require investment in some *specific asset*, meaning an asset that has substantially lower value outside the transaction in question than within it. Both of these factors are necessary for institutionalization. If these two

[9] North 1990, 27.
[10] Williamson 1989, 142.
[11] Milgrom and Roberts 1990 refer to them as *influence costs*.

factors are not present, either contracts will be able to be written to cover all contingencies or the threat of finding an alternative partner for the transaction will keep both sides of the transaction honest. However, if these factors are present, the owner of the specific asset may fear being held up by the other party to the transaction when some unforeseen contingency that changes the value of their exchange arises.[12]

We may fruitfully compare decentralized cooperation theory with the traditional approach to markets. The "transaction" at issue in the international political context is simply an agreement or treaty. I will be more specific later, but this definition will suffice for now. Understanding international agreements as transactions is straightforward: two (or more) countries agree to change their policies in exchange for changes in policies another country (or countries). Examples might include

1. The Kyoto Protocol in which the transaction is "Our country will reduce our CO_2 emissions by x percent if your country will reduce your CO_2 emissions by y percent."
2. The North American Free Trade Agreement in which the transaction is "Our country will eliminate barriers on trade in your goods if you do the same for ours."
3. The North Atlantic Treaty in which the transaction is "Our country pledges to come to your aid if you are attacked as long as your country pledges to come to our aid if we are attacked."

Obviously there are countless other possible examples of such arrangements. The point is that international agreements can be thought of as straightforward barter arrangements—a service for a service.

Decentralized cooperation theory relies heavily on game theory, typically characterizing an international cooperation problem as a prisoner's dilemma where Pareto-inefficient mutual noncooperation is the single-shot equilibrium.[13] Choosing to cooperate offers a Pareto improvement. Cooperative agreements are created by states via bargaining.[14] Decentralized cooperation theory posits that the enforcement/compliance problem that arises from the anarchical nature of the international system is solvable because the games are repeated—as long as actors do not discount the future too heavily, they will comply with their international agreements.[15] In this way decentralized cooperation theory has offered convincing answers to a certain set of questions (when will countries cooperate? how will they enforce their agreements?), and it continues to offer

---

[12] Williamson 1983, 1985, and 1989.

[13] There are other types of cooperation problems, coordination games, for instance. I focus on the prisoner's dilemma for illustrative purposes.

[14] Gilligan 2004; Fearon 1998.

[15] Simmons (1998) offers a helpful review of the compliance literature.

new and important insights today.[16] However, it is incapable of answering a different set of questions about the effects of institutions because institutions play no role in that theory.

In decentralized cooperation theory, international cooperation can occur in an institutionless void. Cooperative policies are decided upon by states via international bargaining and enforced via trigger strategies. The details of the institutional structure are unimportant—thus motivating Keohane's puzzle quoted at the start of the chapter. By invoking Coase, Williamson, and the others, Keohane pointed the way to an explicit focus on institutions—not just cooperation (whether countries do it or not and whether countries comply with their agreements or not) but on the institutional features that make cooperation possible by removing some of the impediments to it.

In a purely economic setting Coase's argument implies that we would expect transactions with relatively low costs to take place via arm's-length transactions. Transactions with relatively high costs should be undertaken within the confines of an organization—the firm—or should not be undertaken at all. By analogy international cooperative transactions with relatively low transaction costs should be undertaken via relatively simple negotiated agreements without any need to create an international regime. International cooperative transactions with high relative transaction costs, if they are undertaken at all, should take place within international institutions. These institutions themselves must be negotiated, of course, and so we will only observe such institutions if the relative transaction costs of creating them, amortized over the expected lifetime of the regime, are also sufficiently small. It is important to recognize that in all cases the concern is with transaction costs *relative* to the total value of the transaction. States may be willing to pay enormous transaction costs if the value of the treaty they are negotiating is even more enormous, and negligible transaction costs may be sufficient to induce states to forgo negotiations altogether if the expected value of the treaty is sufficiently small.

The virtue of the transaction costs approach is that it not only tells us that states may, under the right circumstances, cooperate, but it gives us insight into the great varieties of forms that that cooperation may take. Consider two countries each of which has a policy that produces some external cost in the other country (think of it as a level of pollution).

---

[16] Early examples of this approach include the articles in the Oye 1986 edited volume; Stein 1982; and Snidal 1985. A by-no-means-exhaustive list of a few of the more recent extensions might include Downs, Rocke, and Barsoom 1996, which discusses selection bias in the compliance record of international agreements; Fearon 1998, which elucidates the dual roles of states' discount rates in both bargaining and enforcement; and McGillivray and Smith 2000, which augments the basic repeated prisoner's dilemma with an agent-specific framework.

Roughly speaking, we might say that the two countries have four classes of options: (1) do nothing; (2) negotiate a single treaty that reduces their level of pollution by some specified amount, perhaps for some specified period of time; (3) negotiate a treaty to reduce the pollution and in addition create a more formal international institution to help settle disputes that may arise about the parties' compliance with the treaty, aid in the conduct of future negotiations, and so on; or (4) integrate, that is, create a supranational institution that sets a level of the policy for the two countries.

Item 1 is particularly important because it reminds us that if the costs of a cooperative transaction are too high relative to the value of that transaction, the two countries will simply forgo cooperation. This has important methodological implications because it indicates that we cannot really infer much about the presence of transaction costs from observing international negotiations. If transaction costs are too high, countries will not even bother to negotiate, as I will discuss in greater detail later. Both items 2 and 3 represent fairly large categories; indeed, casual empiricism would suggest that almost all of the international cooperation that we observe falls into these categories. Breaking them up in two categories is somewhat artificial. Even within these categories international cooperation can take any form along a continuum of one-time agreements, where two countries merely agree to alter a particular policy, all the way to more complicated agreements, where new organizations may be created with explicit dispute resolution procedures, renegotiation provisions, "escape clause" provisions, voting rules, and so on. Instances of item 4 are, of course, not unheard of in international politics, as the creation of the Common External Tariff and the recent events in the creation of the European Monetary Union attest. Lake makes a compelling case that empires are essentially an example of number 4 whereby a powerful state integrates (often via "hostile takeover") the security policies of weaker states into its own.[17]

Testing

In his review of the new economics of institutions and transaction costs economics literatures, Herbert Simon remarked:

> the [new economics of institutions] suggests a whole agenda of . . . empirical work that must be performed . . . Until that work has been carried out the new economics of institutions and related approaches are acts of faith, or perhaps piety.[18]

[17] Lake 1996.
[18] Simon 1991, 27.

A quarter-century after Keohane's seminal insight the same statement could be made about the transaction costs approach to international institutions. Several studies employ transaction costs arguments to understand particular cases, but there is only one study of which I am aware that explicitly attempts to test the implications of a transaction costs approach to international institutions (reviewed below),[19] and that study claims to refute the importance of transaction costs in the creation of international institutions.

Existing Studies

The transaction costs approach to international institutions has been fruitfully applied by a variety of scholars. Some very interesting insights have come in the field of international security, particularly in the way alliances are organized. Lake offers a fascinating study in which he uses the transaction costs approach to explain why some security relations are organized as alliances while other are organized as empires.[20] Weber also applies these concepts to international security relations to explain the level of what she calls "bindingness" of alliances, and she discusses NATO and plans for a European Defense Community using these concepts.[21] Abbot and Snidal focus on formal international *organizations* rather than on the broader category of institutions referred to by Keohane, and they provide a long list of possible functions for such organizations.[22] International trade policy has been a particularly common area where the approach has been applied. Dixit provides a case study of some GATT rules within the context of the transaction costs approach, as do Yarbrough and Yarbrough, who also extend their analysis to regional trade agreements.[23]

The articles in the "rational design" school of international institutions[24] employ some transaction costs ideas, and they attempt to test them via a set of case studies provided by contributors to the volume. However, the rational design research program is an entirely new theoretical venture. While it does address questions regarding international institutions, it is not a transaction costs approach to international institutions. The dependent variables that the rational design school seeks to explain, such as size of membership and degree of centralization, are different from the international cooperation equivalent of the "make or buy" decision, namely whether to conduct a cooperative venture inside an institution or

---

[19] Moravcsik 1999.
[20] Lake 1996.
[21] Weber 1997.
[22] Abbot and Snidal 1998.
[23] Dixit 1996l; Yarbrough and Yarbrough 1992.
[24] Koremenos, Lipson, and Snidal 2001 and sources therein.

outside of it. Furthermore, the independent variables used to explain those outcomes are not typical to transaction costs explanations, which focus specifically on asset specificity and incomplete contracting.

These studies, while enlightening and generally supportive of the transaction costs approach, cannot be thought of as real tests of it as much as applications of transaction costs concepts to understand particular cases of institutionalized international politics. As Masten, Meehan, and Snyder state in their discussion of the empirical TCE literature, "claims that observed institutions minimize transactions costs were easy to make and impossible to refute."[25] It is difficult to see how the research designs of these studies could have produced evidence that would have refuted the claim that the institutions under examination were chosen so as to minimize transaction costs. True testing should at the very least establish the hypothesized correlation (recognizing that this does not prove causality) between the degree of transaction costs and the degree of institutionalization of international cooperative episodes.

By this standard the only study of which I am aware that attempts to test the hypothesized correlation between the presence of transaction costs and the institutionalization of international politics is offered by Moravcsik,[26] and he argues that the evidence does not support the transaction costs approach. Employing case studies of the negotiation of five major European integration treaties, Moravcsik concludes that EC/EU staff did little to further integration and in some cases even lagged behind the efforts of state leaders in bargaining the agreements. By his account, states seemed to have little trouble making agreements on their own, and so he concludes that *ex ante* transaction costs are generally unimportant impediments to international cooperation. However, before we accept his findings as the final word, we should address some methodological challenges that affect both Moravcsik's analysis and further attempts to test the transaction costs theory of institutions. I will focus on two: (1) definition and measurement of key variables and (2) selection bias.

Definition and Measurement

One of the greatest difficulties in testing transaction costs theories in economics has been measurement of key variables, and this difficulty is no less present in testing transaction costs theories of international institutions. Before we can even begin to discuss measurement, we must be clear about what we seek to measure. Some clarification of the key concepts of *transaction* and *institution* is required. Frequently these concepts (espe-

[25] Masten, Meehan, and Snyder 1991, 3.
[26] Moravcsik 1999.

cially "institutions") have been defined as broadly as possible. The urge to create all-encompassing definitions with which all scholars can agree, regardless of theoretical orientation, is understandable, but such a definition may not useful for the purposes of testing a particular theory. A transaction and an institution are phenomena that play specific roles in the transaction costs theory. Including phenomena in one's definition that do not play these roles will only dilute the power of one's tests. My purpose in proposing definitions for these concepts is not to achieve consensus but to motivate testing of the transaction costs theory of international institutions.

In the economic context it is fairly obvious what is meant by the term *transaction*. It is the exchange of one good or service for another (typically money). In the international cooperation context the meaning is perhaps less clear. I suggest that a transaction is a specific, agreed-upon change in the policies in one country in exchange for specific agreed-upon changes in policies in another country or countries.

This definition avoids confusion generated by other definitions. Trachtman, for example, says that states are transacting *power*.[27] This terminology confounds the issue, in my opinion. States are merely agreeing to alter their policies by a specified degree perhaps for some specified period of time as long as the other state also alters its policy by some specified degree for some specific period of time. They can continue the transaction as long as they benefit from it, and they can withdraw from the transaction as soon as they see fit. No power actually exchanges hands in these transactions. States retain sovereign power after the transaction as before. International transactions, as I understand them, are nothing more arcane than a simple exchange of services.

An *institution* in the transaction costs framework is an agreement about how to *govern* transactions. Transactions are agreements to change policies, and institutions are agreements about how to govern transactions. Examples of the provisions of such "agreements that govern agreements" might include *dispute settlement procedures*, that is, agreements about what to do if two or more of the parties disagree about whether they are changing their policies in the ways they said they would. Other such provisions might address what the parties will do if unforeseen circumstances arise that alter the benefits that the parties obtain from the agreement—so-called escape clause provisions. Still other features might include decision making or bargaining procedures for the conduct of future negotiations.

Comparing two examples may clarify the difference between transaction and institution. Consider the Marrakech Agreement of 1994, which

---

[27] Trachtman 1996.

regulates global trade. Specific trade policy commitments by member states are not even listed in the treaty itself because they would comprise a document of approximately thirty thousand pages. The text of the treaty and its annexes is well over four hundred pages long. Elaborate dispute resolution mechanisms and escape clause provisions are specified, as well as membership rules and voting procedures.[28] There is a transaction—states are agreeing to set their trade barriers at specific levels in exchange for similar commitments from other members—however, there is also an institution. The way in which the transaction will be governed is spelled out in great detail.

The Convention Providing for the Protection of Migratory Birds and Game Animals concluded between the United States and Mexico in 1936 is rather different.[29] The treaty concerns the exploitation of a common pool resource. It specifies the birds that are to be protected, the length of hunting seasons for these birds, and so on. The transaction in this case is "The United States will regulate its hunting of these birds according to these rules as long as Mexico does and vice versa." The entire text of the treaty is two pages long. The signatories did not create a "North American migratory bird regime," nor did they even specify the consequences if one of the parties failed to comply with the treaty. Presumably the signatories understood that if they failed to regulate the hunting of the specified birds as mandated by the treaty in a way that harmed the other party, there would be diplomatic protests that if left unheeded would lead to noncompliance by the other party. In such a case both parties would be worse off than if they had complied with the treaty, and so governance structures were unnecessary.

By my definition the convention protecting birds and game animals and agreements like it are transactions but not institutions, while the Marrakech Agreement is an institution. Many agreements will be both; that is, they will include both quid pro quo changes in policies (a transaction) and provisions for how to govern that transaction. A measure of whether a transaction is conducted inside or outside an institution would need to be coded from the treaty text itself. Does the treaty contain governance provisions about how disputes will be handled, escape clause provisions, and renegotiation provisions? If cooperation is conducted within a framework such as this, it should be considered institutionalized cooperation.

A successful confirmatory test of the transaction costs approach to international institutions would show that cases of cooperation like the Convention Providing for the Protection of Migratory Birds and Game

---

[28] These facts are taken from http://www.wto.org/English/docs_e/legal_e/legal_e.htm (accessed July 13, 2007).

[29] There are thousands of similar examples, but this will suffice for the purposes of illustration.

Animals are characterized by relatively low levels of transaction costs, while highly institutionalized cases of cooperation like the Marrakech Agreement are characterized by relatively high levels of transaction costs. But how do we measure transaction costs? Unfortunately, transaction costs cannot be directly measured. Transaction costs economists have dealt with this problem by gathering data on the *covariates* of transaction costs. Transaction costs are said to be greater when transactions are (1) *frequent*, (2) *complex*, and (3) *require transaction-specific investment* (that is, asset specificity). Economists have used measures of these variables as proxies of transaction costs.[30]

Within the international relations context, "frequency" might be proxied by the geographic proximity of countries, suggesting that the cooperation of neighbors should be more institutionalized than that with countries that are farther away. Economic integration may play a similar role. Geographic proximity has the virtue of being exogenous, so we do not need to be concerned with reverse causality between frequency and institutionalization. The same cannot be said for economic integration; however, we do not need to be overly concerned about reverse causality (is greater frequency causing institutionalization or is institutionalization increasing the frequency of transactions?) because causality in both directions is consistent with the theory.

The term *complexity* is meant to capture the assumption that individuals are boundedly rational in transaction costs theory. If individuals could see all contingencies in advance, they could include them in the contract (treaty) and they would not need an institution. The constraints of bounded rationality are hypothesized to be more binding in complex transactions. Multilateral agreements are probably more complex than bilateral ones.[31] Complexity may be mitigated when countries have similar domestic political systems, languages, and cultural traditions.

The proxy for transaction costs that has garnered the most attention from economists is asset specificity. For example, some economists have used research and development expenditures as proxies.[32] Others have conducted surveys of engineers in a particular industry to ascertain how specialized particular parts are to the relevant industrial process. These studies have typically shown that transactions that require specific assets are more institutionalized.

The equivalent of asset specificity in the political context would have to capture the extent to which countries were "locked in" to a particular policy (and therefore more susceptible to opportunistic behavior) once they had signed on to the agreement. Scholars may be able to obtain some

[30] Shelanski and Klein 1995.

[31] These same predictions are mirrored in the "rational design" volume cited above.

[32] Armour and Teece 1980; Globerman 1980; Joskow 1985; and Pisano 1990.

leverage from differences between domestic political systems. Perhaps it is more difficult to change policies in a democracy than a nondemocracy. Federal systems and separation-of-power systems also probably make it harder for countries to change policies. Do countries characterized by these feature demand greater institutionalization of their agreements? Similarly, executive agreements are presumably easier to change than full-fledged treaties. Are executive agreements less institutionalized than treaties?

Selection Bias

A further methodological challenge facing testing of transaction costs theories of international institutions concerns selection bias. We must be careful about making inferences that transaction costs are negligible from cases where states are in the forefront of negotiating agreements. We should expect to observe governments negotiating in cases where transaction costs are low relative to the surplus to be divided by the treaty. If that were not the case, states would simply forgo negotiating altogether because the value of the transaction would not cover the transaction costs. The fact that we even observe governments negotiating on these matters suggests that they are cases where transaction costs are low relative to the surplus to be divided.

This is quite plausibly the case in the negotiations that Moravcsik examines.[33] His cases were major events in the formation of the European Community/Union. Transaction costs, even if they were high in some absolute sense, were probably quite low compared to the huge potential surplus to be divided by the treaties. The types of *major* institutional innovations that Moravcsik examines are precisely the sorts of situations where stakes are high and therefore states are probably willing to pay the transaction costs of negotiating these treaties, particularly when one considers that once the new institutions are created, the transaction costs of creating them will be amortized over a long period of time.

Indeed Keohane himself recognized this methodological problem and its implications for regime creation:

> If transactions costs are negligible it will not be necessary to create new institutions to facilitate mutually beneficial exchange; if transactions costs are extremely high it will not be feasible to build institutions. . . . Therefore according to this theory one should expect international institutions to appear whenever the costs of communication monitoring and enforcement are relatively low compared to the benefits to be derived from political exchange.[34]

[33] Moravcsik 1999.
[34] Keohane 1989, 166–67.

Furthermore, this selection bias problem is exacerbated by the fact that international institutions may be created to lessen the costs of expected *future* transactions. Some of the transaction costs that states are trying to minimize are not even observed at the time of the negotiations. They would only occur in expectation in the future if the institution were never created. Focusing on negotiations over the institution will completely miss these costs. Indeed, if the institution is created and reduces transaction costs as intended, the full extent of these future costs will never be observed—they will be counterfactuals.

Again we can see this problem manifest itself in Moravcsik's test of transaction costs in the development of the European Union. His cases are all examples of major *institutional* innovations in the process of European integration. If transaction costs are generally negligible, one must wonder why the members of the EC/EU deemed it necessary to create these institutions in the first place—to paraphrase Keohane's questions, why not simply skip the institution creation and innovation stage and make agreements on an ad hoc basis? According to the transaction costs approach, the very institutional innovations that Moravcsik describes were undertaken to reduce costs on *future* transactions conducted within the framework of those institutions. In other words, Moravcsik could be accused of changing levels of analysis. He looks for transaction costs in the *formation* of institutions, but the claim of transaction costs theory is that these institutions reduce transaction costs of other cooperative ventures in the future, such as engaging in trade negotiations with outside states and setting common agricultural and monetary policy.

In summary, when we look for a link between transaction costs and cooperation, negotiations may not be the best unit of analysis. The fact that negotiations between states are occurring at all probably means that transaction costs are relatively low compared to the value of the transaction, and furthermore one must be careful about drawing conclusions from states' negotiations to create institutions that may be designed to lower expected transaction costs in the future, which are counterfactual and unobserved. The relevant comparison in those cases is not the costs of the particular negotiation over the institution but the costs of all future negotiations that will (according to the theory) be lessened as a result of the creation of those institutions. To effectively test the predictions of the transaction costs approach in cases such as these, a better tack might be testing if there was a statistically significant increase in the number of cooperative agreements following the creation of an international institution in the relevant issue area and whether these effects were interactive with measures of the three variables mentioned above, such that increases in international cooperation were larger in percentage terms where those variables are more prevalent. Alternatively we might look across countries or types of agreements, as indicated above: Do democracies or federal systems demand greater institutionalization of their agreements? Are executive agreements less institutionalized than treaties? And so on.

Conclusion

In the standard game-theoretic treatments international agreements are arrived at via decentralized bargaining and enforced with some form of trigger strategy in a repeated game. These studies have extended our understanding of international cooperation greatly; however, they are incapable of answering why states bother to create international institutions. Why do they not just cooperate in the decentralized fashion modeled by the game-theoretic treatments? This was the question Keohane asked a quarter-century ago. His answer, which drew upon ideas from transaction costs economics, was that states create institutions when the costs of bargaining and enforcing agreements in the decentralized fashion are too high compared to the benefits of cooperation.

I have argued that the time has long since passed to subject these important conjectures to empirical testing. However, daunting obstacles must be considered before undertaking that task. One must think carefully about the key concepts of *transaction* and *institution*; measurement of transaction costs is highly problematic; and one must be cognizant of selection effects when choosing case studies, because the transaction costs approach expects them to be low in cases where states are bargaining unaided by institutions. I offered a few ideas about how to address these issues. With regard to the definitional issue I suggested maintaining a clear distinction between *transactions*, which are agreements to change states' policies, and *institutions*, which govern transactions.

Ultimately a positive correlation between institutionalization (provisions in agreements that govern transactions) and the presence of transaction costs must be exhibited if the approach is to be convincing. Measuring transaction costs directly, however, is impossible. I suggested taking a leaf from the transaction costs economists' book and rather than attempting to measure transaction costs directly use variables that should be correlated with frequency, complexity, and asset specificity and therefore transaction costs. I suggested geographic proximity and economic integration may be good proxies for frequency, and the similarity of countries' languages, cultures, and domestic political systems may be good proxies for complexity. Multilateral treaties should also be more complex than bilateral treaties. Regarding asset specificity, I suggested that if perhaps policies were harder to change in democracies, federal systems, and separation-of-power systems, countries with such institutions may demand more institutionalized agreements. Furthermore, executive agreements should be less institutionalized than treaties.

Selection effects will plague case studies of negotiations over institutions because the transaction costs that will be reduced by the resultant institutions would have come in the future, not at the time of negotiation. Thus it will be difficult to establish a correlation between the relevant transaction costs (those that would have occurred in the future had the institution not been created) and the institutionalization of the cooperative problem. Furthermore, the transaction costs of the negotiation of these new institutions must have been relatively low or states would not have bothered to negotiate in the first place. These selection effects make tests that focus on negotiations unreliable. A better test of the transaction costs approach is to compare the number of cooperative transactions pre- and postinstitution to see if their volume increased. An alternative test would be to see if the hypothesized correlation exists between covariates of frequency, complexity and asset specificity (as described above) and the presence of governance provisions (institutions) in international agreements.

The field of international relations has barely scratched the surface in testing the implications of the transaction costs approach to international cooperation or employing them proscriptively. There are literally tens of thousands of agreements, the institutional characteristics of which have gone unstudied by this approach, and which could render numerous insights as to how best to craft agreements so as to bring about more effective international cooperation. My hope in writing the chapter is to encourage international relations scholars to return to the insights of the transaction costs approach and advance the important research program that Keohane began.

CHAPTER 4

The Influence of International Institutions
INSTITUTIONAL DESIGN, COMPLIANCE, EFFECTIVENESS,
AND ENDOGENEITY
Ronald B. Mitchell

IDENTIFYING THE INFLUENCE of international institutions requires taking
into account how problem structure influences institutional design. Three
claims are central to the relationships among international institutions,
state interests, and state behaviors. First, states act to further their goals;
second, states use international institutions to advance those goals and
"design institutions accordingly"; and third, states "fight over institutional
design because it affects outcomes."[1] Yet if states behave in ways that
reflect their goals and interests but also push for designs of international
institutions that reflect those goals and interests, how can those institutions be said to "affect outcomes" in the sense of causing states to behave
differently than they would have otherwise? Making sense of these claims
simultaneously requires us to assume (and have a logic for assuming) that
the goals and interests that states codify in international institutions differ from the goals and interests that drive their behavior.

In short, to demonstrate the influence of international institutions on
state behavior convincingly requires taking the realist challenge seriously.
The ability of international institutions to promote cooperation in the
presence of preexisting conflict is central to Robert Keohane's intellectual
legacy.[2] Realists contest this claim about institutions, arguing that states'
interests drive not only their behavior, but also both the form of the institutions they create and their choices about membership in them. Therefore, those institutions cannot have any independent effect on their
behavior. Behavior is driven either directly by structure or indirectly by

Acknowledgments: This chapter has benefited from valuable comments and discussions
with R. Charli Carpenter, Page Fortna, Erin Graham, Helen Milner, and Craig Parsons. The
material presented here is based upon work supported by the National Science Foundation
under Grant No. 0318374 entitled "Analysis of the Effects of Environmental Treaties," September 2003–August 2008. Any opinions, findings, and conclusions or recommendations
expressed in this material are those of the author and do not necessarily reflect the views of
the National Science Foundation.

[1] Koremenos, Lipson, and Snidal 2001, 762.
[2] Keohane 1984.

"structure-through-institutions" with any observed institutional "effects" being spurious or epiphenomenal.[3]

The realist challenge involves two different charges of endogeneity. *Membership endogeneity* involves the claim that, for any international institution, countries that join differ systematically from those that do not. Those preexisting differences drive the decision to join and explain any subsequent differences in behavior between members and nonmembers. What appear to be institutional influences are simply the postagreement expression of preexisting differences. *Design endogeneity* involves the claim that variation in institutional design reflects systematic differences in the underlying structure of the problem being addressed. In this case, differences in problem structure dictate the variation in what provisions countries negotiate and accept in international agreements and also explain systematic differences in how states respond to those agreements. What appears as one institution wielding greater influence than another is simply the postagreement expression of differences in problem structure. Thus, an individual institution's effects cannot be identified by contrasting the behaviors of members to nonmembers because countries are not assigned randomly to treaties. Nor can the effects of multiple institutions be compared because institutional provisions are not assigned randomly to treaties.

This chapter argues that accurately evaluating institutions requires paying more attention to why states design international institutions as they do and why, once institutions are negotiated, some states join and others do not. As Keohane and Martin note, "institutional theory needs to deal forthrightly with the endogeneity problem."[4] We need to better distinguish between cases in which problem structure dictates institutional design (and therefore, the correlation of behavior with institutional rules is epiphenomenal) from those in which problem structure underdetermines institutional design (and, therefore, institutional design choices have the potential to exercise real influence over behavior). Making those distinctions convincingly requires identifying the influence of problem structure on institutional design, the behaviors that problem structure would dictate absent an institution, and the ways in which behaviors influenced by institutional rules are distinct and distinguishable from those influenced solely by the forces of problem structure.

The chapter first outlines how problem structure influences—but does not dictate—institutional design. It clarifies why (and the conditions under which) the "institution-independent" interests that states strive to codify in international institutions may diverge from the interests that subsequently

[3] Strange 1983.
[4] Keohane and Martin 2003, 73.

drive those states' behaviors. The chapter then outlines the ways in which problem structure and country characteristics also influence—but do not dictate—institutional membership. I then delineate methodological strategies for analyzing institutional effects that take design endogeneity and membership endogeneity into account. I provide a framework for analyzing institutional influence that recognizes that even institutions that reflect the interests and capabilities of the states involved nonetheless may lead those states to engage in different behaviors than they would otherwise. Using this framework, one can conduct research that would more convincingly distinguish whether actual behaviors reflect institutional influence or not.

The Endogeneity of Institutional Design to Structure and Behavior

Both realist and institutionalist assumptions pose theoretical challenges to claims of institutional influence. I focus here on the influence of those international institutions that derive from treaties, conventions, protocols, and other formal agreements "negotiated among international actors, that prescribe, proscribe, and/or authorize behavior."[5] Although international institutions can take many forms, the formal and public nature of international legal agreements facilitates analysis by removing analytic ambiguity about the commitments states have made to each other.

Realist claims of institutions as epiphenomena take two forms. The first critique is that international agreements reflect "wishful thinking" and a "false promise" on which they cannot deliver: states are no more likely to engage in the behaviors they commit to in international treaties than they would be in the absence of such commitments.[6] This critique predicts high levels of regime-inconsistent behavior whenever such behavior is inconvenient or costly. The second realist critique is that international agreements simply codify the existing constellation of power and interests among the states involved—states negotiate and accept only those rules that prescribe behaviors they would have engaged in anyway.[7] This view predicts high levels of regime-consistent behavior because such behavior is not costly. Thus, one interpretation of the high degree of Soviet and American compliance with arms control agreements during the Cold War is that those agreements simply put in writing previously planned weapons buildups rather than curtailing them. Likewise, the quotas established under the International Convention for the Regulation of Whaling throughout the 1960s and 1970s closely correspond to the catch in

[5] Koremenos, Lipson, and Snidal 2001, 762; Krasner 1983b.
[6] Mearsheimer 1994–95.
[7] See, for example, Werner and Yuen 2005.

the previous year, suggesting that catch was dictating quota more than quota was dictating catch. In the first critique, the behavioral dictates of structure and the behavioral dictates of institutional rules diverge, but behavior follows the former; in the second critique, structure dictates both institutional rules and behavior. In neither case, however, do institutions have any independent impact on behavior.

Institutionalist theory also poses obstacles to demonstrating institutional effects. Existing functionalist theories of the factors that determine why and when international institutions form and what dictates their terms imply "complete endogeneity" since they contend that "states create institutions when they expect them to be useful."[8] But if both the terms of international agreements and the behaviors those agreements regulate are influenced by problem structure, then research on institutional effects faces a troubling, omnipresent, and difficult-to-refute alternative hypothesis, namely, that any change in behavior after an international institution is created or amended is caused by a change in the underlying problem structure that leads states both to behave differently and to codify their intention to do so. Indeed, within this logic, the creation or modification of an international institution itself becomes evidence that the problem structure has changed; otherwise, why did states create or change the institution when they did? Thinking across institutions, this logic implies that variation in design simply reflects variation in underlying problem structure. The fact that one type of institution performs better than another stems not from one set of negotiators doing better at institutional design but from their facing an easier problem, that is, one more susceptible to institutional influence.

Those studying institutional influence and regime effectiveness have yet to respond adequately to these challenges.[9] To be sure, the literature on regime effects has grown considerably in the past three decades, not least through Keohane's extensive theoretical and empirical contributions.[10] This scholarship has often engaged the first realist critique, with many scholars quite carefully demonstrating that states behave consistently with institutional rules more frequently than structural factors would predict.[11] Scholars have also provided considerable evidence of Keohane's argument that the distribution of power differs across issue areas, with corresponding variation in the ability of states to influence outcomes (see Milner, introduction to this volume). Nonetheless, too little work has made

[8] Keohane and Martin 2003, 98 and 82. See also Keohane 1983, 1984.

[9] Keohane and Martin 2003, 98.

[10] See, for example, Keohane, Nye, and Hoffmann 1993; Keohane, Haas, and Levy 1993; Keohane and Levy 1996.

[11] See, for example, Brown, Weiss, and Jacobson 1998; Young 1999; Miles et al. 2002; Breitmeier, Young, and Zürn 2006.

evaluating the influence of structural and country-level factors on institutional design a central feature of efforts to evaluate how institutions influence behavior.

Scholars have begun addressing problems of membership endogeneity, that is, the difficulties arising because states that become members of an international institution differ in systematic ways *that influence their subsequent behavior* from those that do not become members. Thus, Simmons demonstrates institutional effects by contrasting behaviors of states that make international commitments and those that do not only after accounting for the factors that lead states to make those commitments.[12] Von Stein's research further highlights that institutional influence can be accurately assessed only after ensuring that members and nonmembers of international institutions do not differ in systematic but unobservable ways that lead to behavioral differences between the groups.[13]

The second realist critique, however, or the design endogeneity problem, has received far less attention to date, despite being evident since institutional theory was first developed. As Nye and Keohane note, precisely because "institutions often reflect the conditions of their origin, it is helpful to understand those origins."[14] Or consider Stein's claim that, because coordination problems pose inherently less risk of defection than do collaboration problems, the institutions states create to address the former will contain fewer, if any, monitoring and enforcement provisions than those they create to address the latter.[15] The arrangement of states' power and interests in coordination problems imply predictable postagreement behaviors *regardless of the specifics of the agreement*; and these behaviors are predictably different from those in response to collaboration problems. Precisely because states recognize these predictable differences in postagreement behaviors, they incorporate different provisions in regimes addressing coordination and collaboration problems. The coordination/collaboration distinction provides merely one example of the larger point that differences in problem structure often imply quite different postagreement behaviors and that differences in institutional design reflect states' recognition of these differences.

Why has so little analytic effort addressed the design endogeneity problem? In part it is a by-product of the numerous factors that have led most scholars to investigate institutional effects via individual agreements. A focus on individual agreements results from several forces: a desire to engage realist claims of epiphenomenality with sufficient empirical richness to draw confident causal inferences; from a belief that "it is hard to find

---

[12] Simmons 2000.
[13] von Stein 2005; Simmons and Hopkins 2005.
[14] Nye and Keohane 1993, 111.
[15] Stein 1983.

enough comparable cases, across which institutional form varies but structure does not;"[16] from the difficulty of identifying multiple institutions whose effects it makes sense to compare and for which comparable data is available; from a desire to control for variation in problem structure; and from methodological predilections. Even the best quantitative studies usually focus on a single agreement or even a single provision, comparing variation over time and across countries but not across institutions.[17] Whatever the reasons, design endogeneity is not particularly salient when evaluating a single agreement. Analyzing single cases, even cases that involve multiple observations, tends to control for problem structure, which facilitates isolation of institutional influence but precludes analysis of how variation in problem structure influences both institutions and outcomes. Fortna's work on peacekeeping missions, although not looking specifically at international agreements, engages problems that parallel design endogeneity by addressing how factors that influence the existence and type of peacekeeping missions deployed also influence the relative effectiveness of those missions.[18]

Endogeneity and the Possibility of Institutional Influence

To the extent that institutional design is completely endogenous to structure, no room exists for institutional influence.[19] We therefore need a theory of institutions that recognizes and identifies the important ways in which structural factors influence both institutional design and institution-related behaviors but allows for the possibility that those factors do not dictate either. In a tension that reflects the larger theoretical debate regarding structure and agency, structure sometimes dictates institutional design but at other times allows negotiators flexibility to make meaningful choices about some aspects of institutional design.

I define *problem structure* as that array of factors which influences state behavior in such a way that at least some states view current outcomes as suboptimal and are, therefore, motivated to develop an international institution to improve them. Considered broadly, this definition includes realist factors such as the power and interests of states relevant to a problem, institutionalist factors such as preexisting institutions and rules, and constructivist factors such as ideas, norms, discourse, and identities. Taken together, these factors generate some set of "institution-independent" interests. I do not use the term *preinstitutional* interests since I want to

[16] Keohane and Martin 2003, 83.
[17] See, for example, Simmons 2000; von Stein 2005.
[18] Fortna 2004a, 2004b; but see also Werner and Yuen 2005.
[19] Keohane and Martin 2003.

capture the notion that these factors continue to influence interests even after an institution is established. In examining endogeneity, the relevant questions are how, why, and under what conditions might interests as "institutionally codified" diverge from institution-independent interests. Clearly, institutional influence is epiphenomenal unless such a divergence exists. Yet there are several reasons to believe that such divergence can occur.

First, to accept the proposition that problem structure influences institutional design does not require that one accept that it dictates it. Both theoretical reasons (e.g., uncertainty, bounded rationality, and unintended or unanticipatable institutional consequences) and empirical evidence (e.g., the time states take to negotiate agreements and the difficulty of predicting their terms until negotiations are complete) suggest that the interests that emerge from a given problem structure constrain but do not uniquely define an agreement's features. Problem structure surely determines the "zone of possible agreement" but not what agreement—within that zone—states reach.[20] Put differently, most international institutions arise from non-zero-sum games whose solutions have multiple equilibria[21] in which the common desire to avoid suboptimal outcomes does not identify a unique point on the Pareto frontier.[22] Even some skeptics of institutional influence recognize that structure rarely uniquely dictates institutional form. Thus, the claim that international institutions that require "deep" cooperation, that is, that require significant behavioral change, will be ineffective unless they contain strong enforcement provisions implies that states can and do choose between strong and weak enforcement provisions in designing such institutions.[23] Structural factors and foresight surely incline states toward particular solutions to particular problems, but they can make both choices and mistakes in doing so. Constructivists further caution us that states' interests neither preexist nor are fully exogenous to international negotiations—states may only define (and may redefine) their interests during negotiations.[24] At the extreme, if interests were perfectly known—and if they fully dictated institutional terms—then, presumably, negotiations would be short and their outcomes readily predicted, which they are not. Indeed, precisely because interests do not dictate institutional terms, states use negotiations as a means of defining and choosing among mutually acceptable alternatives. Because structure usually, though not always, gives states and their nego-

[20] Raiffa 1982.
[21] Keohane and Martin 2003.
[22] Krasner 1991.
[23] Downs, Rocke, and Barsoom 1996.
[24] Risse 2000.

tiators some freedom in choosing design features, "gaps will appear between problem and form."[25]

Second, states are unlikely to be able to perfectly anticipate future situations and incorporate institutional design features that will foster their interests in those situations. If states can perfectly anticipate the future and can design institutions to achieve their preferred outcomes in those situations, then international institutions are epiphenomenal. But whenever the assumption of perfect anticipation seems unreasonable or when institutional design cannot be made flexible enough to address the expected range of contingencies, then institutions have the potential to exert influence, that is, to generate outcomes that would not occur otherwise. Indeed, Keohane identified this issue and its methodological implications over two decades ago in *After Hegemony*.[26] In that book and many others, Keohane's methodological insight was that institutional effects are most visible not when regimes are first established but at subsequent points at which the original power and interests that led to, and are codified in, the institution's design have shifted enough that the behaviors they would predict differ from those that the new constellation of power and interests would predict.[27]

Third, states cannot always accomplish their goals without institutions. Problem structures may predetermine particular outcomes in situations in which states cannot achieve their objectives by any means other than creating an institution. Thus, states may not be able to undertake an exchange that all sides prefer without creating a contract-like institution that helps reassure all sides that others will carry out their parts of the bargain.

Fourth, norms exist that constrain the institutional forms that states can use to codify their interests. Institutional provisions require relatively universal language, with assumptions that states have equal rights and obligations or that differentiation of rights and obligations must be based on general—not state-specific—criteria. In the absence of institutions, "the strong do what they can while the weak suffer what they must."[28] By contrast, in negotiated institutions, the strong and the weak are presumed to deserve equal treatment. Processes for modifying collective obligations, opting out of such obligations, withdrawing from agreements, settling disputes, and so on, are standardized so that all parties receive equal treatment. Joint obligations and individual commitments are assumed to remain operative until explicitly revoked.[29] Although many

[25] Keohane and Martin 2003, 106.
[26] Keohane 1984.
[27] Keohane, Nye, and Hoffmann 1993.
[28] Thucydides 1982, book 5, chap. 89.
[29] Keohane and Martin 2003, 101.

agreements violate these metanorms, most follow them, suggesting that these metanorms influence which terms are incorporated—and which eschewed—in international agreements.

Finally, institutionally codified interests tend to diverge from institution-independent interests over time because the former tend to change more slowly than the latter. Even if negotiators could perfectly codify institution-independent interests in institutional rules, inertia prevents smooth and rapid institutional responses to changes in structural variables. Only "when institutions remain stable in the face of changes in structural variables, [do] we have an opportunity to observe the independent effect of institutions."[30] This drift of institution-independent interests from institutionally codified interests also can arise in international agreements that establish institutional agents that have both autonomy from, and different interests than, the states they represent.[31]

These observations imply that those interested in institutional effects must distinguish the influence of "structure-through-institutions" from an institution's independent influence. Those who contend that institutions are epiphenomenal see design endogeneity as complete, with problem structure perfectly embedded in institutional form and no room for any independent institutional influence. The argument just delineated leaves as an empirical question whether institutions exhibit complete or less-than-complete design endogeneity, and hence whether institutions can have any independent influence. To answer that question requires far more focus on the conditions under which, and extent to which, institutional designs vary, having controlled for problem structure. For some types of problems, we should expect problem structure to dictate—or very tightly constrain—institutional form, whereas for others, we might expect considerably more variation in institutional form in response to problems with essentially similar problem structures.

Problem Structure and Endogeneity

Discussions of problem structure to date have focused on how states' incentives and interests regarding a problem influence both the institutions they establish and their behavioral responses to them.[32] This section discusses specific examples of such influence and then delineates three additional parameters of variation in problem structure that have implications for both institutional design and behavioral responses.

[30] Keohane and Martin 2003, 101.

[31] Keohane and Martin 2003.

[32] Krasner 1983b; Koremenos, Lipson, and Snidal 2001; Hasenclever, Mayer, and Rittberger 1997.

The Incentive Structure of Problems

Certainly, problem structures vary with regard to the interests relevant actors have both in seeing a problem resolved and in contributing to its resolution if agreement can be reached. Variation in these interests has implications for what institutions states negotiate, which states join those agreements, and how states that join them behave. As examples, consider the implications of the structures of upstream/downstream, coordination, and collaboration problems for institutional design, the subsequent behavior of relevant actors, and analysis of the influence of institutions. I use *relevant actors* to refer to those actors that the states concerned about a problem view as required for—or capable of contributing to—its resolution.

In upstream/downstream problems, the institution-independent interests of those causing the problem make them indifferent or even antipathetic to seeing the problem resolved. France's upstream position meant that their dumping of chloride into the Rhine was a problem for the Dutch, but not them.[33] Britain's position upwind meant that its emissions of acid precipitants were a problem for the Scandinavian countries but not for the British.[34] We might assume that the interests in such asymmetric externalities would preclude creation of cooperative institutional solutions. But, if downstream states (i.e., the "victims" concerned about the problem) would benefit enough from resolving the problem and have access to appropriate inducements, they can identify institutional terms that make upstream states prefer institutional membership to nonmembership. Institutions responding to such problems will reject sanctions in favor of carefully delineated exchanges in which concerned actors reward those causing the problem for changing their behavior.[35] Upstream states will only join agreements if they contain such rewards, a point illustrated by the refusal of China, India, and other developing countries to join the Montreal Protocol designed to protect the Earth's ozone layer until amendments established a developing-country-focused financial mechanism. It is quite clear that the "no-institution" counterfactual involves no behavior change: upstream states have no incentives to change their behaviors without remuneration, and downstream states have no incentives to offer remuneration unless there are institutional arrangements that protect them against reneging by the upstream state. The design and degree of influence of institutions addressing upstream/downstream problems are likely to vary with the attractiveness, credibility, and contingency of the rewards being offered.

[33] Bernauer 1996; Bernauer and Moser 1996.
[34] Levy 1993.
[35] Mitchell and Keilbach 2001.

In coordination problems, most relevant actors have institution-independent interests in seeing a problem resolved and, once a solution is established, have little interest in defecting from that solution.[36] In coordination problems—as illustrated theoretically by the Battle of the Sexes and empirically by ocean navigation and air traffic control—the advantages to relevant actors of *some* resolution to the problem lead them to conform to the rules of *almost any* resolution of the problem. Since relevant actors will either adopt the agreed-upon behaviors or clearly announce their intention to defect, institutional provisions may vary considerably in the detail needed to identify equilibrium behavior but will be quite similar in having few, if any, monitoring or enforcement provisions. In coordination problems, an institution's influence will be most visible when no institution-independent focal points exist: if states do not have the option to coordinate informally around some "natural" or hegemonically preferred focal point,[37] then institutions cannot simply codify behavioral preferences since those preferences are indeterminate prior to negotiations. In such cases, states want to coordinate their behavior but collective creation of an institution is necessary to identify how they should do so.

In collaboration problems, many and perhaps most relevant actors have institution-independent interests in seeing a problem resolved, but their interests in contributing to its resolution are institution-dependent since they depend on the probability of defection being detected and the costs of detected defection. Institutions designed to address such problems often entail reciprocal restraint and incorporate specific monitoring provisions linked to a system to induce credible and potent sanctioning for those who defect.[38] Yet problem structure allows institutional flexibility—Coasean remuneration or side-payments can be substituted for sanctions.[39] Indeed, as Keohane noted, states that are quite capable militarily may find it to be less costly to rely on "forms of power besides military force and threats."[40] Thus, in a 1911 agreement, the United States and Russia resolved a quintessential coordination problem involving open access to fur seal stocks by paying Canada and Japan to halt their fur seal harvests.[41] As in upstream/downstream cases, the resource transfers required careful monitoring provisions but provide empirical evidence that sanctions are not the only viable response to collaboration problems. Collaboration problems not only have alternative institutional solutions but may fail to be resolved because of the difficulty of collective action, particularly among

[36] Stein 1983.
[37] Lipson 1991.
[38] Downs, Rocke, and Barsoom 1996.
[39] Coase 1960.
[40] Milner, introduction to this volume.
[41] Slunaker 2005.

states that distrust each other. As with coordination problems, estimating the "no institution" counterfactual depends on determining whether the hegemon's incentives were such that regime formation was a foregone conclusion and, if not, how the hegemon might have wielded its power to achieve the same objectives. When no hegemonic state exists, institutions that arise in response to collaboration problems among mutually distrustful states present strong counterfactuals: we can expect the problem to remain unresolved without an institution, and so any behavioral progress can more confidently be attributed to the regime. By contrast, highly interdependent states (e.g., European Union states) are more likely to create institutions to address their coordination problems but also more likely to make progress in mitigating the problem even without such an institution.

These three descriptions—although only a sample of problem structures—illustrate the larger point that variation in incentive structures produces predictable variation in institutional design, institutional membership, postagreement behavior, and no-institution counterfactuals. Problems, however, also exhibit variation in their capacity structure, informational structure, and normative structure, as discussed below.

The Capacity Structure of Problems

The distribution of state capacities to contribute to problem resolution also varies across problems in ways that influence institutional form and effects. In some cases, positive interstate externalities may go unrealized if states lack the financial, technical, or administrative capacity to undertake behaviors that would benefit themselves and others. Consider the cases of drug interdiction, controlling AIDS and other diseases, and providing advanced military hardware to alliance partners.[42] In such cases, incentives still matter since states will not form international institutions if states that would benefit from other states addressing their own national problems do not see those potential benefits as greater than the costs they must incur to fix the other states' incapacity problems. Yet resolving such problems requires institutions that address incapacities, not incentives, through transfers of knowledge, technology, or financial resources. Donor states will seek to minimize their costs and to ensure the transfers are used as intended. If they have only weak incentives to resolve the problem, they can dictate explicit terms of exchange, transfer less fungible resources, and limit the value of the transfers to the minimum needed to make the behavior possible. If donor states have strong incentives to resolve the problem, recipient states can extract more, and more

---

[42] See, for example, Darst 2001; Connolly and List 1996.

fungible, transfers. The strength of monitoring that states incorporate depends on whether the resources being transferred are relatively fungible or nonfungible, with agreements that transfer AIDS drugs likely to have weaker monitoring provisions than those that provide surveillance planes for drug interdiction. Recipient states are likely to be eager to join institutions addressing incapacity problems, whereas prospective donor states are likely to be reluctant to do so. Problems for which incapacity is central provide clear no-institution counterfactuals that differ markedly from postagreement outcomes if the institution is influential: states that are incapable of an activity and of developing the capability indigenously but begin engaging in that activity in ways that institutional resource transfers made possible provide strong evidence of institutional influence.

The Informational Structure of Problems

Institutional form and effects are also influenced by a problem's informational structure. Behaviors that give rise to interstate problems vary considerably in how visible they are and how well they can be kept secret. Thus, arms races and tariff wars are usually considered to be prisoner's dilemma problems, but vary considerably in their institution-independent transparency: states have strong incentives and often the ability to keep military activities secret, but they cannot collect tariffs without revealing them to actors that have strong incentives to report rates that exceed institutionally sanctioned levels.

Institution-independent transparency varies within as well as across issue areas: compare tariffs and quotas to nontariff barriers; large-scale troop deployments to nuclear weapons development; or denying equal suffrage to torturing prisoners. To be influential, institutions addressing the latter of each of these pairs must craft far more careful monitoring provisions. Indeed, inherently nontransparent behaviors tend to prompt institutional innovation to enhance transparency, as evident in the surprisingly cooperative procedures for on-site inspection developed in U.S.-Soviet nuclear arms agreements and in states facilitating monitoring by nongovernmental actors in areas of human rights that governments are less capable and less inclined to monitor.[43] When states develop careful and cooperative monitoring provisions in response to inherently nontransparent activities, such as International Atomic Energy Agency inspections, the no-institution counterfactual claim that those activities otherwise would not have come to light and, therefore, would not have changed, gains plausibility. By contrast, claims of influence for institutions addressing inherently transparent activities are more challenging

[43] Keck and Sikkink 1998.

and must demonstrate that observed behavioral responses were not a response to the institution-independent existence of that information.

The Normative Structure of Problems

Finally, problems vary in normative structure. Institutional design and postagreement behaviors vary considerably depending on when in a normative life-cycle states succeed in creating an international institution.[44] At one end of the spectrum, states may negotiate international agreements only after both norms and behaviors have stabilized, as in the codification of customary international law. At the other end, nonstate activist networks may successfully press states to negotiate agreements designed to promote a normative consensus where none yet exists, as in signature of the land mines convention at a time at which most nations still viewed them as legitimate weapons.[45] In the spectrum's middle are many cases in which states that have accepted certain norms create international institutions to induce others to do so.

Normative variation also exists along a spectrum from issues in which interests are at stake and norms play little role to those in which norms are central. Thus, most arms control, trade, and natural resource negotiations involve interest-based dialogues based in a logic of consequences. By contrast, most human rights negotiations involve norm-based dialogues based in a logic of appropriateness.[46] We can expect institutions designed to reduce behaviors already viewed as morally "bad"—such as torture or genocide—to specifically define what constitutes a violation and to rely on sanctions for violations. By contrast, we can expect institutions designed to foster behaviors viewed, by some, as morally "good" but insufficiently frequent—such as equal treatment of women and minorities or ensuring citizens' economic and social well-being—to be broader or more exhaustive in their definitions of commitments. To promote internalization of norms, these latter institutions will tend to foster extended normative dialogue, persuasion, argument, and the praise of those doing well rather than instrumental mechanisms such as sanctions or side-payments, since the latter undermine efforts to induce the internalization of norms.[47]

Normative variation also has implications for estimating counterfactuals: the later in a normative life-cycle that an international institution is established, the more difficult it becomes to plausibly claim that behavioral conformance with institutional rules is due to the institution. Equally

[44] Finnemore and Sikkink 1998.
[45] Price 1998.
[46] March and Olsen 1998.
[47] Risse 2000.

important, the longer after the creation of a norm-based institution that one attempts to assess institutional influence, the more difficult it becomes to disentangle whether normative strengthening is caused by institution-independent normative maturation or by the institution's contribution to that maturation. Thus, in most human rights cases, the appropriate no-institution counterfactual is probably to assume that the norm would have gained some strength even absent any institution; evidence for institutional influence must come from a rate of norm internalization and acceptance that is higher than what would have been expected otherwise.

Other Considerations

Problems also vary with respect to whether they involve acts of omission, acts of commission, or accidents; whether states and civil society are tolerant or intolerant of violations; whether a consensus does or does not exist about the problem and its resolution; and whether resolution of the problem requires dramatic and costly behavioral changes or all-but-costless changes. Variation in these and other parameters of problem structure may well influence both institutional terms and state behaviors in ways that pose analytic risks of endogeneity and hence require attention when evaluating institutional influence.

Multifinality and Equifinality

The foregoing discussion of a subset of different problem structures illustrates that the relationship of problem structure to institutional design can involve both multifinality and equifinality. In multifinality, negotiators have sufficient freedom to incorporate different institutional features in response to a given problem structure; in equifinality, negotiators addressing problems with different structures may end up selecting similar institutional features. Both aspects of the relationship provide analytic opportunities: situations of multifinality allow evaluation of the relative effectiveness of different institutional design elements, with the investigator controlling for problem structure; situations of equifinality allow comparison of the performance of a given institutional design element in different problem contexts.

Methodological Implications

Recognizing the endogeneity of institutional design to problem structure generates several methodological insights. Those interested in identifying institutional effects must avoid assuming that problem structure and institutional design are perfectly correlated or, conversely, assuming that they are totally independent. If design endogeneity is likely but neither necessary nor perfect, then it is an empirical question whether a given institution's design is endogenous to problem structure. Those interested in institutional effects cannot take institutional design features as given but must examine the extent to which those features were independent of problem structure. Keohane's dictum to "think like a social scientist"[48] suggests researchers must carefully identify the values of various parameters of variation in problem structure independent of evidence regarding institutional change (not by taking institutional change as evidence of problem structure change) and then examine the extent to which variation in problem structure covaries with institutional design.

Making a convincing claim of institutional influence requires explicitly demonstrating that institutional design was not completely dependent on problem structure, whether by demonstrating that problem structure was indeterminate with respect to institutional design or by demonstrating the presence of institutional variation in the absence of problem structure variation. Researchers also must avoid assuming that—and instead carefully evaluate whether—an institution's members and nonmembers are otherwise alike. As noted, some scholars have begun to address membership endogeneity.[49] As with design endogeneity, the extent of membership endogeneity is an empirical question that cannot be identified by assumption. When comparing the behavior of members to nonmembers or of states before and after becoming members, scholars must try to identify what factors make states likely to join particular agreements at the time that they do independent of evidence regarding when they joined them.

Analysts should also explicitly consider what alternatives to the observed institution, if any, were possible given the problem structure. This requires assessing theoretical arguments and empirical evidence to determine how much leeway, if any, negotiators had in institutional design. How "inevitable" was it that states would create an institution and that the institution would take the form it did? Knowing whether states might have forgone the institution and what alternative institutions they might realistically have created is crucial to generating plausible counterfactuals that are the foundation for claims of institutional influence.

Addressing both design endogeneity and membership endogeneity requires methods that distinguish an institution's independent influence on behavior from both problem structure's direct influences on behavior and its indirect influences through its influence on institutional design. One approach involves comparing cases for which the analyst has verified,

[48] King, Keohane, and Verba 1994, 32.
[49] Simmons 2000; Simmons and Hopkins 2005; von Stein 2005.

rather than assumed, that problem structure was held constant. Whether looking for the effects of changes in a single institution's design over time (e.g., adoption of protocols or amendments) or the effects of institutional variation across institutions, the possibility of endogeneity demands that the analyst explicitly evaluate the values of problem structure parameters and demonstrate that they do not vary. A second approach, which addresses how well a given institutional design does in varying circumstances, involves comparing cases that exhibit a change in problem structure but institutional constancy, the methodological underpinning of Keohane's argument in *After Hegemony*.[50] Here, too, the analyst must clearly demonstrate that problem structure changed in ways that would be expected to produce an institutional change but did not.

With respect to design endogeneity, analysts should start by assuming that some part of any correlation between behavior and institutional design arises because both are driven by problem structure. With respect to membership endogeneity, analysts should start by assuming that member states are more likely to adopt institution-consistent behaviors than nonmember states even in the absence of an institution, not because of institutional influences but because states that become members are more concerned about the problem, face lower adjustment costs, or both.[51] Analysts should begin with these assumptions but then look explicitly for variation in the problem structures being addressed or in the characteristics of states that joined an institution and those that did not. Institutional influence can be shown either by identifying behaviors that differ systematically and in predicted ways between the institutional and noninstitutional setting or by finding evidence that the processes and causal mechanisms that led to certain behaviors more closely match the predictions of an institutional argument than those of a problem structure argument.

Quantitative analysis of institutional effects opens up additional possibilities, so long as the foregoing arguments about endogeneity are taken into account.[52] Standard regression techniques separate institutional influences from structural influences but do not usually separately identify structure-through-institution influences. Design and membership endogeneities require explicit modeling. A particularly appropriate approach involves two-stage modeling in which the influence of structure on institutional design is determined in one regression and the results of that regression are used as inputs to a regression that assesses the influence of institutional design and structure on behavior, having already accounted for the influence of structure on institutional design. These and related

[50] Keohane 1984.

[51] Sprinz and Vaahtoranta 1994.

[52] Miles et al. 2002; Helm and Sprinz 2000; Hovi, Sprinz, and Underdal 2003a, 2003b; Young 2003; Mitchell 2002.

strategies offer opportunities to evaluate the extent to which institutional design reflects or diverges from the dictates of problem structure; by accounting for that variation in analyzing behavioral responses, they can distinguish the influence of problem structure *through* institutions from the independent influence *of* institutions.

Conclusion

Endogeneity of institutional design raises an analytic obstacle that has received insufficient scholarly attention. The same states whose (presumably self-interested) behavior is leading to suboptimal outcomes negotiate agreements (that presumably reflect their self-interests) to regulate those behaviors. If the international institutions states devise to regulate behavior and the behaviors being regulated are simply different expressions of the same constellation of power and interests, how can those institutions be said to have an independent influence on state behavior? The proper question is, as Keohane has argued in many settings, not either/or but "Under what conditions?" Institutions do reflect the power and interests of the states that create them, but they also can wield independent influence over those states' behaviors. Our task is to determine, convincingly, the conditions under which the latter happens given the methodological obstacles posed by the former.

The processes and constraints of creating international institutions produce institutional designs that can diverge, at least at times and to some extent, from what problem structure alone would dictate. That said, some problem structures may generate perfect design endogeneity, and, in those cases, any correlation of behavior with institutional dictates is epiphenomenal. But when structure underdetermines institutional design (or even whether states will create an institution), the collective institutional choices that states make may produce outcomes quite different from those predicted by problem structure alone. Distinguishing these two types of cases requires considerably more attention than recent institutional scholarship has given to three analytic tasks: (1) identifying how problem structure influences institutional design, (2) identifying what behaviors structural forces would dictate absent an institution, and (3) identifying how the behavioral dictates of institutions diverge from those of structural forces. In short, those interested in institutional effects cannot ignore the factors that influence institutional formation. It is only by recognizing the theoretical and methodological implications of endogeneity that scholars can take advantage of the many insights that Robert Keohane has contributed to our understanding of institutional influence over the past quarter-century.

The Role of Institutions across Issue Areas

CHAPTER 5

Peacekeepers as Signals
THE DEMAND FOR INTERNATIONAL
PEACEKEEPING IN CIVIL WARS
V. Page Fortna and Lisa L. Martin

PEACEKEEPING—THE DEPLOYMENT of international troops and monitors to
war-torn areas—is an international institution intended to help recent
belligerents maintain peace. The literature on peacekeeping has exploded
in the last fifteen years,[1] but analyses of it as an institution promoting cooperation have been hampered by several methodological handicaps.
One is a matter of case selection—the majority of studies examine only
cases where peacekeepers are involved, with no comparison to cases of
nonpeacekeeping.[2] The second is an endogeneity issue—peacekeepers are
not deployed to conflicts at random, so analysis of their effects must begin
with an examination of where peacekeepers go. Recent studies of peacekeeping have begun to address the first problem,[3] but much less has been
done to remedy the second.[4] We know very little about why peacekeepers
are sent to maintain peace after some conflicts but not others. By definition, peacekeeping missions operate with the consent of the belligerents
(this analysis excludes enforcement missions, known in the UN lingo as
"Chapter VII" missions, that do not necessarily rely on the participants'
consent). In a civil war, the consent of the government is particularly important. But there has been little systematic analysis of the conditions under
which warring parties request or consent to peacekeeping by the international community. This chapter begins to answer the question of why belligerents sometimes agree to be "peacekept" and sometimes do not, by focusing on peacekeeping as a mechanism that enables warring sides to signal

We thank the participants in the Robert Keohane Festschrift Conference, Princeton University, February 2005, for comments, especially Robert Keohane, Helga Haftendorn, John
Owen, and Helen Milner.
[1] For a review, see Fortna and Howard 2008.
[2] Among many examples, see Coulon 1998; Diehl 1993; Durch 1996; Findlay 2002;
James 1990; Krasno, Hayes, and Daniel 2003; Stedman, Rothchild, and Cousens 2002; and
Zacarias 1996.
[3] For example, Doyle and Sambanis 2000, 2006.
[4] For recent work on this issue, see Gilligan and Sergenti 2007. Fortna 2008 builds on
the analysis presented in this chapter.

their intentions to one another. While the argument applies to consent-based peacekeeping in both civil and interstate conflicts, we focus here on civil wars, as the most common form of warfare in recent years.

Robert Keohane revolutionized the study of institutions in international relations by insisting that we think about the demand for international institutions.[5] We follow in his footsteps here by concentrating on the institution of peacekeeping, and modeling the demand for it. We also build on Keohane's work in general terms by thinking about how the willingness to bear the costs of acting within an institutionalized setting can serve as a signal. We conceive of the institution of peacekeeping as a costly signal of intent to abide by a peace agreement, and ask about what patterns of behavior we would expect to follow if this is an accurate conceptualization.

Considering peacekeeping as an international institution, and asking about how the demand for peacekeeping acts as a signal, connects this research closely to many of the central themes of Keohane's work. As Helen Milner spells out in the introduction to this volume, Keohane's research inspired renewed interest in nonstate actors of various types, including international institutions. Peacekeepers are intriguing nonstate actors; their presence is approved and supported by states, but their status is clearly differentiated from direct intervention by third-party states in domestic conflicts. Keohane's research also emphasizes sources of power that are not solely military. While peacekeepers are militarized actors, in fact they are often lightly armed and operate under strict constraints on their ability to use force. We argue here that the power of peacekeepers comes not from their military capacity, but from their ability to act as a signal of governments' intentions to seek a resolution to ongoing conflicts.

Milner also highlights themes of cooperation, the creation of institutions, and the importance of appropriate empirical methods in Keohane's work. In the instance we consider, the obstacles to cooperation are high. Generating cooperation between governments and rebel groups involved in bitter civil wars is very difficult. We shed light on the puzzle of how relatively weak peacekeeping forces can nevertheless be effective, and under what conditions. Thinking of peacekeeping as an institution, and studying the demand for it, provides a new perspective on the creation and use of institutions. We also attempt to use appropriate, rigorous methods to study issues with complex causal chains. We provide a formal model from which we derive explicit testable hypotheses; discuss observable proxies for the parameters of the model; and use multivariate logit analysis to test the hypotheses.

The chapter connects insights from Martin's work on treaties as signaling devices and Fortna's work on the causal mechanisms of peacekeep-

[5] Keohane 1983, 1984.

ing.[6] Martin examines the choice made by U.S. presidents between formal international treaties that require ratification by two-thirds of the Senate and executive agreements that require no such blessing. Because the former is a costly and time-consuming endeavor, formal ratification serves as a credible signal of reliability. Similarly, Fortna argues that one of the ways in which peacekeepers can have a causal effect on the duration of peace is by serving as a costly, and therefore credible, signal of benign intent. Belligerents who have no intention of abiding by a cease-fire or peace agreement will be less willing to have a contingent of international observers and troops inspecting their actions. Consenting to a peacekeeping mission is more costly for unreliable types than for reliable types. Such consent can therefore provide a credible signal. The signaling model of peacekeeping that we develop here provides a number of empirically testable insights about when agreements are feasible and when belligerents will consent to peacekeeping. We test these hypotheses on a data set of civil wars from 1989 to 1997. We find relatively strong support for the model's predictions. Factors such as the potential benefits of peace, government costs of allowing peacekeepers in, and rebel assessments of the government's reliability are related as expected to the incidence of peacekeeping.

The small existing literature on where peacekeepers get sent focuses on the supply side of the equation—where does the UN decide to send peacekeepers? Some arguments emphasize the strategic or economic interests of the permanent five members of the Security Council and argue that there is a strong regional bias to where peacekeepers get sent. Some debate whether the UN is motivated by the humanitarian impulse to stop the worst bloodshed, or perhaps the worst bloodshed televised by CNN. Others suggest it is driven by a desire to spread democracy.[7] As Gilligan and Stedman point out, much of this literature is based on impressionistic accounts or on flawed research design.[8] The methodological sins include tautology, especially with reference to Security Council interests, and selection on the dependent variable, that is, inference only from the set of peacekeeping cases, not all civil wars.[9]

Very few studies test these hypotheses systematically.[10] Gilligan and Stedman use duration analysis to show that the UN sends peacekeepers

[6] Martin 2005; Fortna 2008.

[7] On these points, see De Jonge Oudraat 1996; Neack 1995; Jakobsen 1996; and Andersson 2000.

[8] Gilligan and Stedman 2003.

[9] Beardsley 2004 addresses some of these issues in a study of intervention in interstate crises.

[10] See Gilligan and Stedman 2003, 38–42, for a review and critique of the existing literature. Fortna 2004a and Andersson 2000 examine the question of where peacekeepers go, but only in passing.

most quickly to conflicts with higher death tolls; that the international organization tends to avoid peacekeeping in countries with large armies; and that while there is a regional bias, Asia is the most neglected, not Africa. They find that levels of democracy, primary commodity exports, or whether the country is a former colony of a permanent Security Council member have no statistically significant effect on the hazard rate of peacekeeping. Mullenbach argues that peacekeeping is less likely when the interests of great or regional powers are most highly engaged, for example, when the target state is itself a great power.[11] Carter argues that the UN intervenes strategically, where the probability of success is high.[12]

The most important difference between the approach we take here and existing studies is that we develop hypotheses about the demand side of peacekeeping—about when belligerents will agree to a peacekeeping mission.[13] While a peacekeeping mission requires an active decision by the UN or a regional organization (or sometimes an ad hoc group of states) to deploy, it is exceedingly rare for the international community to refuse peacekeepers if the belligerents themselves request them. Despite U.S. admonitions during the 1990s that it learn to do so, the international community rarely "just says no." Whether or not peacekeepers are deployed in civil wars is a decision made largely by the combatants themselves. We focus on the demand side of peacekeeping for two reasons: first, this is the aspect most overlooked by the literature on where peacekeepers go, and second, for consent-based peacekeeping it is belligerents' choices that are most important. However, once they arrive, it is peacekeepers' actions as independent agents that underlie the fact that peacekeeping provides a costly signal. It is because they act independently to monitor behavior and raise the cost of aggression that consenting to them is a credible signal of benign intentions.

Below we present a model of the government's decision to continue fighting or to offer an agreement with or without peacekeeping, and the

[11] Mullenbach 2005. Others, however, argue that great power interests must be at least somewhat engaged (De Jonge Oudraat 1996; Durch 1993, 22–23).

[12] Carter 2007; Fortna 2008, chap. 2, shows just the opposite, however, that peacekeepers go to the hardest rather than the easiest cases.

[13] See also Fortna 2008. Gilligan and Stedman (2003, 40) suggest two hypotheses that they describe as demand-side but that are either indirectly or partially supply-side arguments: that stronger states are better able to resist pressure to consent to peacekeeping, and that the war aims of rebels affect both the willingness of the government to agree to peacekeepers and the willingness of the UN to send them. Mullenbach 2005 examines several state or conflict level variables, but the analysis faces several methodological problems. For a number of variables, such as the death toll, duration, and intensity (death toll per month), each of which is treated dichotomously, multicolinearily makes inclusion in a single model potentially problematic. For several other categorical variables, the baseline category to which effects should be compared is unclear (e.g., for ethnic, religious, and ideological wars).

rebels' decision to accept an agreement or reject it in favor of continued warfare.

Model and Comparative Statics

In this section we introduce a game-theoretic signaling model of the interaction between a government and rebel group involved in an ongoing militarized conflict. We believe that formalizing our ideas about the nature of strategic interaction in this manner has a number of benefits. It forces us to state our assumptions about actors, the options available to them, and their payoffs precisely. The model then identifies certain parameters that will specify the conditions under which peacekeeping can effectively serve as a signal. The interaction of the parameters leads to the specification of fairly precise hypotheses, and points us toward finding observable variables that are reasonable proxies for the major concepts of the model. As we will see, some of the parameters function in ways that are not entirely intuitive until one works through the strategic logic of the model. Thus, while the model itself is a minor modification of a standard signaling model, we find that it has high payoffs in the way that it structures the ensuing empirical analysis.

Model

To explore the demand for peacekeepers as a signal of intent to comply with a peace agreement, we develop a signaling model. We assume two players, a government and a rebel group, that are in an ongoing conflict. The rebel group does not know whether the government is reliable or not. An unreliable government will not abide by the terms of any peace agreement or truce, imposing costs on the rebel group if it accepts a peace agreement. In order for peacekeepers to function as signals of the government's type, there must be some differential cost to the two government types of allowing peacekeepers into the country. While both might prefer to avoid the interference of outsiders, the cost relative to benefits for an unreliable government is higher than the cost to a reliable government. Peacekeepers monitor behavior; focus international attention on a conflict; make bad behavior more costly in terms of international aid, diplomatic support, and legitimacy; and may provide a trip wire triggering a more robust military response against violation of a peace deal. For a government that intends to abide by the agreement, these actions by peacekeepers are not costly. But for a government that intends to restart the fight after suckering the rebels with a peace deal, peacekeepers will raise the cost of going back to war. Unreliable governments may also face more internal opposition to allowing peacekeepers in, as hardliners will anticipate these effects.

This section formalizes the argument and finds the equilibria of this signaling game. Nature begins by choosing whether the government (G) is reliable (probability r) or unreliable ($1 - r$). G observes this choice, but the rebel group (R) does not. G moves next. G has three choices: continue to fight; offer a peace agreement without peacekeepers; or offer a peace agreement with peacekeepers. There is a cost associated with offering peacekeepers, but this cost is differentiated by type. The cost/benefit ratio is higher for unreliable than for reliable Gs. R observes G's choice, and decides whether to accept G's agreement or to continue fighting. We normalize the payoffs of continued fighting to zero for both sides. We assume that there is some small cost (e) to G for offering an agreement that is rejected.

A reliable G gets payoff Z from having an agreement accepted, and R gets payoff S from this successful peace agreement. An unreliable G gets payoff Y from having an agreement accepted. Y may be different from Z, although in our empirical application we have been unable to identify proxies that effectively differentiate the two. G must also, however, pay some cost for allowing peacekeeping troops into the country. For an unreliable G, we can interpret this as the cost (b) of buying off nationalist interests or future reputational costs from having peacekeepers observe G's unreliability.[14] Even a reliable G bears some general sovereignty cost (a) from inviting peacekeepers in. However, for a reliable G, this cost is smaller relative to benefits than for an unreliable G. Thus, we assume that $Z - a > Y - b$. (Otherwise peacekeepers cannot possibly work as a signal.) R bears cost c from signing an agreement with an unreliable G. This cost could result from, for example, R beginning to disarm and thus being less able to fight G in the future. Figure 5.1 shows the game, and table 5.1 specifies the equilibrium outcomes.[15]

The bottom row of table 5.1 shows situations where the benefits of peace are low relative to the costs of peacekeepers for both types of governments. In this case, neither type of government is willing to bear the costs of peacekeepers. When the rebels have prior beliefs that the government is likely unreliable ($r < (c / (S + c))$), they will not accept any offers

---

[14] For a discussion of how the presence of peacekeepers affects the costs and benefits of reneging on the agreement, see Fortna 2008.

[15] We do not provide a formal proof of the equilibria in this chapter because of space constraints. As in most signaling models, two classes of equilibria arise, one in which the second player demands costly signals, and an accommodating one in which she does not. Because we are concerned with a set of cases involving deep animosity, we expect civil war belligerents, by definition deadly enemies, to play strategies that yield the demanding equilibrium rather than the accommodating one. We thus predict that the results from the demanding equilibria should hold, and we focus on them here.

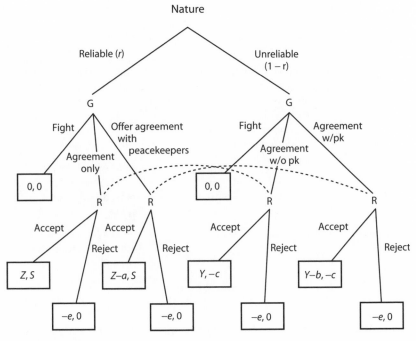

Figure 5.1 Nature

of peace, and so fighting will continue. But when the government is more likely reliable $(r > (c / (S + c)))$, rebels will be willing to take a chance and will accept the government's offer of a peace agreement without peacekeepers.

The next row, moving up, shows a situation where a reliable government is willing to bear the cost of peacekeepers, but an unreliable government is not. Here we get a separating equilibrium regardless of prior beliefs about the government's reliability, because the two types clearly distinguish themselves from one another. A reliable government will always offer peacekeepers, and the rebels will accept this offer. An unreliable government will not be willing to bear this cost; knowing this, rebels will reject all offers of agreements without peacekeepers.

The top row of table 5.1 illustrates the equilibria when the benefits of peace are high relative to the cost of peacekeepers for both types of governments. Here, if the chance that the government is reliable is high, all types will offer peacekeepers and rebels will accept this offer. In this case, an unreliable government has been able to bluff successfully. However, when prior beliefs that the government is reliable are low, rebels will not buy this bluffing strategy quite so easily. Here we get a complex semi-

TABLE 5.1
Equilibria

	$r < c / (S + c)$	$r > c / (S + c)$
$Z > a$ and $Y > b$	Semiseparating: reliable Gs offer peacekeepers. Unreliable Gs offer peacekeepers with probability $rS / (c - cr)$. R accepts offers with probability $(b + e) / (Y + e)$	Pooling: all types of G offer agreements with peacekeepers; all are accepted
$Z > a$ and $Y < b$	Separating: only reliable Gs offer agreements with peacekeepers; all offers are accepted	Separating: only reliable Gs offer agreements with peacekeepers; all offers are accepted
$Z < a$ and $Y < b$	No peace offers made	Pooling: all types of G offer agreements without peacekeepers; all offers are accepted

separating equilibrium. A reliable government will always offer peacekeepers. An unreliable government, knowing that bluffs will not always be successful, will not always be willing to offer peacekeepers. Thus, an unreliable government plays a mixed strategy, offering peacekeepers with some probability between 0 and 1, as specified in the table. The rebels will never accept an agreement without peacekeepers under these circumstances. On observing an offer of peacekeepers, the rebels will also play a mixed strategy, accepting the offer with some probability between 0 and 1 (as shown in the table).

Comparative Statics

This game thus has three possible outcomes: continued fighting, a cessation of hostilities with no peacekeeping troops, or a cessation of hostilities and the presence of peacekeepers, lending itself to empirical analysis via multinomial logit. The game gives rise to a large number of predictions, based on the parameters of the model and the outcome of interest. Here we will focus our attention on two sets of comparative statics: when we will observe peacekeepers relative to observing continued fighting, and when we will observe peacekeepers relative to a truce without peacekeepers. Tables 5.2 and 5.3 allow us to specify these comparative statics by showing the predicted outcomes. Table 5.2 focuses on the relative incidence of peacekeepers and continued fighting. Cells in which only agree-

TABLE 5.2
Peacekeeping Relative to Continued Fighting

	$r < c / (S + c)$	$r > c / (S + c)$
$Z > a$ and $Y > b$	Some peacekeeping and some fighting; higher proportion of peacekeeping	Peacekeeping only
$Z > a$ and $Y < b$	Some peacekeeping and some fighting; lower proportion of peacekeeping	Some peacekeeping and some fighting; lower proportion of peacekeeping
$Z < a$ and $Y < b$	Fighting only	XXX

ments with no peacekeepers are predicted are shown as empty (marked XXX), and the "agreements without peacekeepers" outcomes are neglected. Analogously, table 5.3 shows the relative incidence of peacekeepers and truces without peacekeepers; cells that predict only continued fighting are shown as empty (again, marked XXX), and the outcome of continued fighting is neglected.

These tables allow us to specify the following comparative statics.

Peacekeeping relative to continued fighting:

1. The incidence of peacekeeping will increase as Z and Y increase and as a and b decrease. That is, we will see more peacekeeping relative to continued fighting as the benefits of peace for the government increase, and as the costs of accepting peacekeepers decrease.

2. The incidence of peacekeeping will increase as r and S increase, and as c decreases. That is, we will see more peacekeeping relative to fighting when rebels believe the government is reliable, when the benefits of peace for the rebels are high, and when the costs of exploitation for the rebels are low.

Peacekeeping relative to agreements (or truces) without peacekeepers:

3. The incidence of peacekeeping will decline as r and S increase, and as c decreases. That is, we will see less peacekeeping relative to agreements without peacekeepers when the government is likely reliable, when the benefits of peace for the rebels are high, and when the costs of exploitation for the rebels are low.

4. The incidence of peacekeeping will increase as Z and Y increase and as a and b decrease. That is, we will see more peacekeeping relative to agreements without peacekeepers when the benefits of peace to the government are high and the costs of accepting peacekeepers low.

TABLE 5.3
Peacekeeping Relative to Agreement without Peacekeepers

	$r < c / (S + c)$	$r > c / (S + c)$
$Z > a$ and $Y > b$	Peacekeeping only	Peacekeeping only
$Z > a$ and $Y < b$	Peacekeeping only	Peacekeeping only
$Z < a$ and $Y < b$	XXX	Agreements only

Table 5.4 summarizes the predicted effects of the model's parameters.

This model shows how important it is to consider all three outcomes in order to get predictions that are not subject to selection effects. The incidence of peacekeeping relative to continued fighting, and relative to agreements without peacekeepers, is subject to different effects. In order to begin testing these propositions, we need to find proxies for the costs and benefits facing governments and rebels, and for rebels' beliefs. The next section turns to this problem and to specifying the observable implications on which we will focus.

Measuring the Variables

We draw on civil war data collected by Michael Doyle and Nicholas Sambanis.[16] We focus on the sixty-four cases in the period from 1989 to 1997. While peacekeeping as an institution was "invented" in the late 1940s, it was used primarily in interstate conflicts during the Cold War. The norm of noninterference in the internal affairs of states has since relaxed considerably, and peacekeeping has become a commonly accepted practice in civil wars only since the end of the Cold War.

For our purposes, the dependent variable is trichotomous: (1) wars in which fighting ends in victory for one side, or is ongoing ($N = 25$); (2) wars in which the belligerents reach an agreement to stop fighting but no peacekeepers are deployed ($N = 18$); and (3) wars in which an agreement is reached and peacekeepers are deployed ($N = 21$). Because we are interested in the demand for peacekeeping by the belligerents themselves, the measure of peacekeeping includes only consent-based peacekeeping, agreed to by the belligerents, not enforcement missions that do not require this consent.

[16] The data are adapted slightly from Doyle and Sambanis 2000. Data and data notes are available upon request from Fortna.

TABLE 5.4
Predicted Effects of Model's Parameters

Parameter	Peacekeeping relative to fighting	Peacekeeping relative to agreements without peacekeeping
Z, Y	+	+
S	+	−
a, b	−	−
c	−	+
r	+	−

In terms of the model presented above, the first category (1) represents decisions to continue fighting, or agreements (with or without peacekeepers) that are offered but rejected (and are therefore unobserved in the data). Agreements (in categories 2 and 3) include both cases of peace treaties and informal truces. The latter represent at least tacit agreement to stop fighting, and in some cases peacekeepers are deployed to oversee these truces.

Measuring rebels' beliefs, the costs and benefits of peace for various actors, and the costs of peacekeeping for the two types of government is more difficult. We do not have single straightforward proxies for each of these concepts. Instead we posit that a number of characteristics of the war and of the parties should affect the participants' beliefs and their assessment of costs and benefits.

The benefit of peace for both reliable and unreliable governments is a function of the costs of war, which we proxy with duration, on the theory that as the war drags on, the government's estimate of what it will cost to win outright rises. Duration might be thought of as a proxy for rebel costs as well. However, as the old maxim goes: for many rebel groups, not to lose is to win, while for governments not to win is to lose. Duration, we argue, is thus a better proxy of government costs than of rebel costs.[17]

---

[17] We also tried a measure of battle deaths as a proxy of both government and rebel costs, and therefore benefits of peace. Deaths had no significant effect on the likelihood of peacekeeping, a finding that is consistent with our predictions about agreements with and without peacekeepers. If deaths raise S along with Y and Z, this variable will have contradictory effects on the likelihood of peacekeeping. Omitting this variable does not affect any of the other results.

Z and Y should correlate positively with war duration.

The more mountainous the terrain, the easier it is for rebels to hide and the lower their costs of war. Rough terrain thus makes it harder for the government to find and defeat rebels, increasing the government's benefit from peace.

S should correlate negatively, while Z and Y may correlate positively with mountainousness.

A well-armed government that reneges on a peace agreement is more dangerous to rebel groups than one that is not well-armed.

c may therefore correlate positively with government army size.

R's assessment of G's reliability (r) may depend on the government's regime type. Relative to closed political systems, democracies are likely less able to be able to renege on a peace agreement once they have entered into it. Domestic audience costs and democratic political processes may bind democratic governments to their commitments more tightly than autocratic ones.

r should be higher for democracies.

There is a cost to both reliable and unreliable governments of letting peacekeepers in, because peacekeepers infringe on the state's sovereignty, and a country's prestige is at stake. Bangladesh, for example, was particularly unwilling to countenance peacekeepers in its civil war in the Chittagong Hill Tracts because Bangladesh prides itself on deploying peacekeepers elsewhere, helping other worse-off countries out of their civil war messes. Allowing peacekeepers in would entail admitting that it needed such help.[18] This cost might vary with the age of the country; those closer to independence might be more prickly about their newfound sovereignty and their prestige.

Both a and b should decrease with the number of years since the country gained independence.

The strength of a country's economy provides a proxy for how much a country will care about earning a negative reputation with the international community. Poorer countries who depend significantly on international development assistance will be much more sensitive to the negative effects of reneging on an agreement while peacekeepers are present

---

[18] Interviews by Fortna in Bangladesh, January 2002. The sovereignty costs of peacekeeping were also quite apparent in interviews with government officials in Mozambique, December 2002.

observing their behavior. Richer countries, meanwhile, will care much less about this cost to their reputation.

b should thus be lower the richer the country.

R's prior beliefs about G's reliability will be affected by their history of conflict:

r should be lower if these parties have fought before in the past.

Table 5.5 summarizes the relationship between observable measures in the data and the variables in the formal model. It also provides information on the measurement and data source for each variable.

Predictions

Because we have observable measures that tap into more than one variable in the model, predictions are a bit complicated. Some testable hypotheses can be derived, however. We start with predictions about agreements with peacekeepers relative to continued fighting.

Agreements with Peacekeepers, Relative to Continued Fighting

DURATION

Longer duration of conflict increases the government's benefit from peace (Z or Y, depending on G's type) and, following comparative statics point 1 (cs1) above, should increase the probability of peacekeeping agreements.

MOUNTAINOUS TERRAIN

Rough terrain has contradictory effects. To the extent that it increases the government's benefit from peace, it should increase the probability of peacekeeping agreements (cs1). But it also decreases the rebels' benefit from peace, decreasing the probability of peacekeeping relative to ongoing fighting (cs2).

GOVERNMENT ARMY SIZE

The larger the government's army, the more vulnerable rebels are to an unreliable government. Thus, we expect a negative relationship between army size and peacekeeping (cs2).

REGIME TYPE

Democracy increases the rebels' belief that that the government is reliable (r), which has a positive effect in the demanding equilibrium (cs2).

TABLE 5.5
Observable Measures

Observable measure	Relationship to model variables	Measurement and data sources[1]
Duration of war	Increases G's benefit of peace (Z & Y)	In months: (end year—beginning year $\times$ 12) for ongoing wars: (1999—beginning year $\times$ 12)
Mountains	Decreases R's benefit of peace (S)	Log (% mountainous + 1)^2
	Increases G's benefit (Z & Y)	
Government army size	Increases R's vulnerability (c)	Troops (thousands)
Democracy	Increases G's reliability (r)	Average Polity score over five years before the war[3]
Years sovereign	Decreases cost of peace-keeping for both types of G (a & b)	Year war began—year of independence[4]
Economic strength	Decreases cost of peace-keeping for unreliable G (b)	Real GDP per capita
Past war	Decreases r	Dummy for previous civil war between same parties (from Doyle and Sambanis 2000 "cluster" variable)

[1] Source is Doyle and Sambanis 2000 except as noted.
[2] Source is Fearon and Laitin 2003.
[3] Because regime type may be endogenous to the agreement—sometimes nondemocracies agree to democratic institutions or at least elections as part of the agreement—we use a measure of regime type taken before the war begins.
[4] Source is Correlates of War in addition to Doyle and Sambanis 2000.

YEARS SOVEREIGN

The longer a country has enjoyed sovereignty and the less prickly it is about the issue, the lower the cost of letting in peacekeepers, and the more likely they will be. We should see a positive relationship between the age of a country and peacekeeping (cs1).[19]

[19] Civil wars tend to occur in newer states, but as our universe of cases consists only of those experiencing civil war, any effect of a country's age on civil war onset should be selected out.

GDP/CAPITA

Similarly, the richer the country, the lower the cost of peacekeepers to unreliable governments (b). GDP per capita should thus have a positive effect on peacekeeping (cs1).

PAST WAR

If the parties' history involves previous rounds of fighting, the rebels are less likely to believe the government is reliable (r), which should decrease the probability of agreements with peacekeeping, relative to continued fighting (cs2).

Agreements with Peacekeepers, Relative to Agreements without Peacekeepers

The hypotheses for agreements with peacekeeping relative to agreements with no peacekeeping are more straightforward, because where measures tap into more than one variable in the model, the effects point in the same direction.

DURATION

By increasing the benefits of peace for the government (Z or Y, depending on its type), longer duration should make the government more willing to offer peacekeepers (cs4).

MOUNTAINS

Rough terrain increases the benefit of peace for the government, but decreases it for the rebel side. So both comparative static predictions (cs3 and 4) suggest that peacekeepers will be more likely in countries with mountainous terrain.

GOVERNMENT ARMY SIZE

The strength of the government's army should have a positive effect. It increases the vulnerability of rebels, and increases their demand for peacekeepers as the price of agreement (cs3).

REGIME TYPE

Democracy increases the rebels' beliefs that the government is reliable (r). This should decrease the probability of peacekeepers (cs3).

YEARS SOVEREIGN

If countries that have more recently won independence are indeed more sensitive to the infringement of peacekeepers on their sovereignty, then the cost of peacekeeping (a and b, depending on the government's type) is lower the older the state. This should increase the prevalence of peace-keeping among those wars that end with an agreement (cs4). We thus expect a positive relationship between years sovereign and peacekeeping.

GDP/CAPITA

Governments of richer countries, which care less about the reputational costs of peacekeepers if they renege on their agreements, will be more likely to accept peacekeepers. GDP per capita should increase the likelihood of peacekeeping (cs4).

PAST WAR

By decreasing the rebels' beliefs that the government is reliable (r), at least one previous round of conflict should increase their demand that the government incur the added cost of peacekeeping to prove its reliability (cs3). Peacekeeping should thus be more likely if this war is a repeat of earlier fighting.

Table 5.6 summarizes these predictions.

Empirical Testing

To test these predictions, we run a multinomial logit on the data set of civil wars. The dependent variable is the trichotomous outcome: continued fighting, agreement without peacekeeping, and agreement with peacekeeping. The results are shown in tables 5.7 and 5.8. The tables show the results of the same multinomial logit model. However, for ease of interpretation, we show the results both when continued fighting is the baseline (table 5.7) and when an agreement without peacekeepers is the baseline (table 5.8). For both, the results that interest us the most are shown first, for the use of peacekeepers relative to the omitted category.[20] Because some of the observations in this data set are not independent of each other (e.g., whether peacekeepers deploy to one conflict may be affected by whether peacekeepers have been involved in that country in the past), we calculate robust standard errors with observations clustered by country. In other words, the various civil wars in India are considered potentially related, whereas the civil war in Nicaragua is considered independent of the war in Peru.[21]

[20] The model also provides predictions about the use of agreements without peacekeepers relative to continued fighting. As these are of less interest, we do not discuss them here. However, their inclusion in the model is necessary to avoid selection bias, and the results are largely consistent with the signaling model's predictions.

[21] Note that the cluster variable used to calculate robust standard errors is slightly different from the cluster variable used to determine whether there was a previous war between

TABLE 5.6
Predicted Effects of Observable Measures

Measure	Peacekeeping relative to fighting	Peacekeeping relative to agreement without peacekeeping
Duration of war	+	+
Mountains	$\sim$[1]	+
Goverment army size	−	+
Democracy	+	−
Years sovereign	+	+
Economic strength	+	+
Past war	−	+

[1] This entry results from our observable measure being correlated with more than one model parameter. For example, mountainous terrain is positively correlated with Z and Y, but negatively correlated with S. The former leads us to predict a positive effect of peacekeeping relative to ongoing fighting, the latter a negative effect, leading to an ambiguous overall prediction.

Consider first table 5.7, where the first part shows the results for the incidence of peacekeeping relative to continued fighting. These results are quite strong and consistent with our model. Wars of longer duration are associated with more peacekeeping, indicating that higher potential peace benefits for the government lead to more peacekeeping, as predicted. More mountainous terrain, on the other hand, is associated with less peacekeeping. This result is consistent with the model if we assume that rough terrain is a better proxy for benefits to the rebels than benefits for the government. If rough terrain tends to decrease rebels' peace benefits by lowering the cost of ongoing fighting, we would predict the negative effect of mountains on peacekeeping that we find here.

The results show a strong negative effect of government army size on peacekeeping. This is consistent with the model, indicating that a larger government army makes rebels more vulnerable to government reneging, so reducing the incidence of agreements with peacekeeping (and agreements with no peacekeeping) relative to continued fighting. Similarly, democracy has a strong positive effect on peacekeeping, as the model

---

the same parties. In the Doyle and Sambanis data, the former is named *clust2* and the latter *cluster*. The former groups together all conflicts in a given country, whether or not they are related (so the Sikh conflict in India is in the same *clust2* cluster as the war in Kashmir). The latter only groups conflicts that involved the same parties (so the Sikh and Kashmir war do not share a cluster).

TABLE 5.7
Multinomial Logit Model, Incidence of Peacekeeping Relative to
Continued Fighting

	Coefficient	Robust std. error	Z
Peacekeeping			
Duration	0.0169**	0.0067	2.50
Mountains	−0.985**	0.446	−2.21
Government army size	−0.0113**	0.0031	−3.68
Democracy	0.282**	0.109	2.59
Years sovereign	−0.0406**	0.0196	2.07
Past war	−0.597	0.844	−0.71
GDP per capita	0.0013*	0.0006	1.93
Constant	1.640	1.289	1.27
Agreement without peacekeepers			
Duration	0.0110*	0.0063	1.74
Mountains	−1.430**	0.590	−2.42
Government army size	−0.0056**	0.0020	−2.83
Democracy	0.334**	0.113	2.95
Years sovereign	−0.0616**	0.0227	−2.72
Past war	−1.339	1.002	−1.34
GDP per capita	0.0013**	0.0006	2.06
Constant	2.813*	1.630	1.73

Number of observations   60
Pseudo R^2 0.391
* Significant at the .10 level.   ** Significant at the .05 level.

predicts, indicating that more reliable governments are associated with more peacekeeping (and less continued fighting). The sign on past wars is negative, as predicted, although not statistically significant. We find a positive effect of per capita GDP on peacekeeping, as expected, indicating that rich governments bear a relatively low sovereignty cost for allowing peacekeepers in.

One surprising result is the strong negative effect of years sovereign on the incidence of peacekeeping. We had hypothesized that newly sovereign governments would be more sensitive to the intrusive presence of peace-

TABLE 5.8
Multinomial Logit Model, Incidence of Peacekeeping Relative to Agreement without Peacekeepers

	Coefficient	Robust std. error	Z
Peacekeeping			
Duration	0.0059*	0.0035	1.68
Mountains	0.445	0.302	1.47
Government army size	−0.0057**	0.0026	−2.14
Democracy	−0.0517	0.0862	−0.60
Years sovereign	0.0210**	0.0098	2.14
Past war	0.742	0.830	0.89
GDP per capita	−0.00005	0.00014	−0.36
Constant	−1.174	0.932	−1.26
Continued fighting			
Duration	−0.0110*	0.0063	−1.74
Mountains	1.430**	0.590	2.42
Government army size	0.0056**	0.0020	2.83
Democracy	−0.334**	0.113	−2.95
Years sovereign	0.0616**	0.0227	2.72
Past war	1.339	1.002	1.34
GDP per capit	−0.0013**	0.0006	−2.06
Constant	−2.814*	1.630	−1.73

Number of observations   60
Pseudo R^2 0.391
* Significant at the .10 level.   ** Significant at the .05 level.

keepers, leading to a negative correlation between years sovereign and the parameters a and b. This led us to predict a positive correlation between years sovereign and peacekeeping, as states more confident in their sovereign status would be more willing to allow peacekeepers in. Instead, we find just the opposite. As we will see below, of those wars that end with an agreement, peacekeeping is more likely in older states. But as the negative and significant coefficients in both halves of table 5.7 indicate, the most likely outcome in older states, ceteris paribus, is continued fighting rather than agreement (with or without peacekeepers). It is possible that newly independent states are more susceptible to international pressure to negotiate an end to their civil wars, while older states can more easily resist this pressure.[22]

Overall, the results for peacekeeping relative to continued fighting provide strong support for the signaling model. With the exception of a state's age, all the results are in the predicted direction, and all but one of these effects are statistically significant.

Turn now to table 5.8, which shows the same multinomial logit model but makes agreements without peacekeepers the baseline category, so that we can directly see effects on the incidence of peacekeeping relative to these agreements. The results here are not as strong as for peacekeeping relative to continued fighting, but still suggestive. As expected, we find that war duration has a positive effect on peacekeeping. If governments see a high potential benefit of peace, they will be more willing to offer agreements with peacekeepers, leading to the result we find here. The sign of the coefficient for mountainous terrain is positive, as predicted, though it is not statistically significant. The effect of government army size runs counter to our predictions, however. A larger government army has a strong negative effect on peacekeeping.[23]

As noted above, we find a positive effect of years sovereign on peacekeeping. As predicted in our model, newer states appear to be more sensitive to infringements on their sovereignty, while older states are more likely to offer peacekeepers (given that an agreement is reached). The coefficient for past wars is positive, as the model predicts, but this effect is not significant. Neither democracy nor GDP/capita have effects that are statistically distinguishable from zero ($p > .9$).

Overall, we find that the model is less powerful at distinguishing between agreements with and without peacekeepers than between peacekeeping and continued fighting. The results in table 5.7 support our model strongly, while those in table 5.8 are more mixed.[24] Nonetheless, given that some of the proxies used here are crude, we believe the overall results suggest that there is a substantial signaling element to the demand for peacekeepers.

---

[22] On the rise and possible demise of a norm of negotiated settlement in civil wars, see Howard 2003.

[23] We treat this variable as a proxy for rebel vulnerability, but it may well also pick up the effect of the government's cost of war. If governments with larger armies have a lower cost of war and therefore a lower benefit of peace (Z and Y), this should decrease the demand for peacekeeping, yielding the result we see here.

[24] This, along with the fact that the results in table 5.7 show similar findings for both agreements with peacekeeping and those without, relative to continued fighting, may reflect the fact that the choice between agreement and fighting to the finish is more predictable than the choice of whether to invite peacekeepers if agreement is reached.

Conclusion

The small existing literature on where peacekeepers go focuses on supply—on when the international community chooses to deploy international personnel. Here we focus on the demand for this institution—when do belligerents agree to be peacekept.[25] We develop a signaling model in which governments choose whether or not to offer an agreement, and if so whether to offer to allow peacekeepers in. Rebels choose whether or not to accept this offer. The increased cost of peacekeeping to a government that intends to renege on the deal makes the offer of peacekeeping a credible signal of reliability. The model highlights the effects of the benefits of peace (or the cost of war), the cost of allowing peacekeepers to intrude, rebels' a priori level of trust in the government's reliability, and their vulnerability to exploitation.

While none of these variables can be observed outright, we propose at least crude proxies for testing the model's predictions. Most of these predictions are supported empirically. We find quite strong support for our expectations about agreements with peacekeeping relative to ongoing fighting. The findings about peacekeeping relative to agreements without peacekeeping are more mixed, but nonetheless generally support our expectations. As Keohane's work has long emphasized, focusing on strategic demands for institutions leads to powerful insights about their incidence.

[25] For analysis that combines the supply and demand side of where peacekeepers go, see Fortna 2008, chaps. 2 and 3.

CHAPTER 6

Women and International Institutions
THE EFFECTS OF THE WOMEN'S CONVENTION
ON FEMALE EDUCATION

Beth A. Simmons

Do INTERNATIONAL INSTITUTIONS have an important impact on the behavior of governments and other actors? This is a question that international relations research is now beginning to address. Decades have been spent understanding why governments join international institutions. Rational theorists underline the reduction of transaction costs, the routinization of reciprocity, and the expectation of future material benefits.[1] Sociological theories emphasize the less rational influence of world culture on the tendency for governments to join or adopt particular institutions,[2] while constructivist theorists in political science underscore the internalization of norms that joining international institutions represents.[3]

Skepticism of the power of international institutions to influence behavior abounds. Traditional realists believe international institutions typically do not alter the power or interests of governments.[4] Quite commonly these institutions are thought to reflect interests rather than shape them in any important way.[5] Theorists largely agree that international institutions—defined as rules that govern state behavior—are endogenous, but point out that this does not deny institutions an independent or an interactive effect on behavior.[6]

Neoliberal institutionalism has had an enormous impact on the way international relations scholars think about international institutions. The model of cooperation based on joint gains for contracting parties has stimulated theoretical and empirical work in a range of issue areas, from trade and monetary agreements to security and war-fighting regimes. But in one area, international rules have proliferated that are hard to understand from the standpoint of mutual contracting: human rights. These agreements are not about the joint games elaborated by Robert Keohane

[1] Keohane 1984.
[2] Ramirez and McEneaney 1997; Wotipka and Ramirez 2008.
[3] Risse and Sikkink 1999.
[4] Mearsheimer 1994–95.
[5] Downs, Rocke, and Barsoom 1996.
[6] Simmons and Martin 2002.

in his classic discussion of the demand for regimes. Human rights are not about transaction costs; indeed, they are not centrally about international transactions at all. They are not about joint gains: if a country's leaders want to improve its rights practices, they can do so without resorting to an international institution. And they are not enforced in the way first-generation neoliberal institutionalists envisioned: reciprocity, so central to regime enforcement for these theorists, is not generally available when it comes to rights practices. To my knowledge, no government has ever threatened to reciprocate for a rights violation by a treaty partner by violating its own people in retaliation.

Human rights regimes are based on a logic fundamentally different from the rational functionalism advanced by Robert Keohane now nearly three decades ago. The international human rights regime was pushed along largely by nonstate rather than state actors alone, and many of the smaller democracies rather than the major powers. These actors were motivated by ideas and values rather than mutual gains. They believed (or hoped) that international institutions could further social purposes by focusing attention and expectations that would have an effect on the legitimacy of human rights ideas, rather than simply mitigating the uncertainty inherent in cooperation under anarchy. The dynamics of the human rights regimes has been elucidated by theorists of ideas—an approach later embraced by Keohane in his study of the power of foreign policy ideas.[7]

While it does not reflect the original functionalist logic of neoliberal institutionalism, the international human rights regime is undeniably a set of institutions based on liberal ideas. One of the most important questions that the research paradigm that Robert Keohane did so much to advance asks about the effect that international institutions have on outcomes that affect the quality of human life. This chapter offers evidence of international institutional effects in one of the most difficult issue areas in which to demonstrate them: human rights. Without the benefit of mechanisms of reciprocity, governments that join human rights institutions find it increasingly costly to egregiously ignore these institutions' basic principles. I demonstrate this claim by examining the effect of the Convention on the Elimination of Discrimination against Women (CEDAW) on various measures of the educational gender gap around the world.

This chapter proceeds as follows. The first section discusses the global situation of women in recent decades. In much of the world, severe inequalities have traditionally existed and continue to exist between women and men. Differences in legal rights, family rights, nationality rights, and access to the means of self-betterment, employment, health care, and—

---

[7] Goldstein and Keohane 1993.

the focus of this chapter—education have plagued the prospects for women around the world. The CEDAW is the world's premier legal response to these inequalities. "Enforcement" of this agreement has been highly decentralized, through intergovernmental organizations designed to monitor governments' practices; international nongovernmental women's advocacy groups; and especially by domestic actors who demand that their government take their treaty commitment seriously. The second section discusses the data and methods I will use to demonstrate this point. The third section provides evidence that governments' international legal commitment improves women's and girls' access to education: it tends to improve their access to primary education, literacy training, and tertiary education. On the whole, the findings are remarkably robust: international legal commitments to address gender discrimination actually do improve, on the margins, the educational possibilities for the world's women. By focusing expectations and staking one's own reputation, official government commitments to improve women's access to education can have very real and very positive consequences.

The CEDAW: Women's Rights and International Law

By almost any measure, women's rights globally have largely been subordinated to those of men. Back in 1979, the year that the CEDAW was open for signature,[8] a report on the state of the world's women found that "Women and girls constitute one-half of the world's population, one-third of its labor force. They perform two-thirds of the world's work hours. They earn, by estimate, only one-tenth of the world's income. They own less than one-hundredth of the world's property. World-wide, women attend school half as often as men. Two out of every three illiterates are female."[9] By the turn of the millennium, women were still largely in dire straits compared to men. According to the World Health Organization,

[8] The CEDAW was the culmination of a series of multilateral negotiations on women's issues after World War II. In 1952 the General Assembly had adopted the Convention on the Political Rights of Women. Yet it would be years before states would again address women's issues in treaty form. Early in 1967, the United Nations' Commission on the Status of Women (CSW) began drafting a nonbinding Declaration on the Elimination of Discrimination against Women, which was adopted by the General Assembly in November of that year. The Economic and Social Council and CSW worked on strategies for implementation of the declaration over the next several years. One tack was to ask states voluntarily to submit reports on their implementation efforts, but in response they got very little cooperation. By the mid-1970s the CSW was working on a draft of a comprehensive and legally binding instrument, and by 1976 began to garner the comments of governments and specialized agencies. A series of working groups worked to finalize the agreement throughout 1979.

[9] Langley 1988, 45.

70 percent of the 1.2 billion people living in poverty are female. There are twice as many women as men among the world's 900 million illiterates. Economically, women continue to face a clear gender disadvantage: on average, women are paid 30–40 percent less than men for comparable work. In a number of ways, then, women face important disadvantages globally.[10]

In 1979, of governments of the world agreed to the Convention on the Elimination of All Forms of Discrimination against Women (CEDAW). The CEDAW was the first broad-based legal response to systematic gender inequality, and in its wake, interest in women's rights picked up over the course of the 1990s.[11] Still, resistance to explicit international legal machinery to support women's rights is fairly widespread. The Women's Convention came into force with a comparatively weak monitoring committee. The stature and powers of the committee were addressed in 1999 by the adoption by the UN Commission on the Status of Women of a no-reservations-allowed Optional Protocol giving individuals and groups of individuals a right to complain about their government's violation of the treaty provisions.[12] The Optional Protocol entered into force in December 2000.

The Women's Convention is widely viewed as "the starting point for delivery of justice for women."[13] It is quite an ambitious convention. Not only does it purport to provide women with equal political and civil rights; it was intended to eliminate *all forms* of discrimination against women. Article 1 is quite sweeping. It defines discrimination as "any distinction, exclusion or restriction made on the basis of sex which has the effect or purpose of impairing or nullifying the recognition, enjoyment or exercise by women, irrespective of their marital status, on a basis of equality of men and women, of human rights and fundamental freedoms in the political, economic, social, cultural, civil or any other field."[14] All measures that have the effect of discriminating against women are forbidden—even if governments did not intend to discriminate.[15] The treaty even obligates governments to "modify the social and cultural patterns of conduct of men and women, with a view to achieving the elimination of prejudices and customary and all other practices which are

---

[10] World Health Organization, Fact Sheet No. 251, June 2000, http://www.who.int/inf-fs/en/fact251.html (accessed July 8, 2003).

[11] Adopted and opened for signature, ratification, and accession by General Assembly Resolution 34/180 of December 18, 1979; entry into force September 3, 1981.

[12] CEDAW, Optional Protocol, Article 17. The Optional Protocol to the CEDAW can be accessed at http://www.bayefsky.com/treaties/cedaw_opt.php.

[13] Freeman and Fraser 1994, 124.

[14] CEDAW, Article 1.

[15] CEDAW Article 2.

based on the idea of the inferiority or the superiority of either of the sexes or on stereotyped roles for men and women."[16]

For all of the legal machinery that has been developed over the past two decades to address women's issues, we know very little about its effects on the actual realization of women's rights. No study to date has looked at the effects of the global legal centerpiece for guaranteeing women's rights, the CEDAW itself. A central difficulty is that the CEDAW contains broad obligations that are difficult to define precisely and even more difficult for governments to guarantee effectively. My strategy is to choose one of the most basic of rights—equal access to education—which is mentioned quite explicitly, and to test the proposition that governments that commit themselves to the CEDAW will make an effort to design policies to address educational equality. The evidence suggests that committing to the CEDAW has had some effect on spurring governments to take women's educational rights seriously.

Why look at education? Education is fundamental to a whole range of other rights that the CEDAW envisions women should equitably enjoy. Access to education influences the exercise of a broad range of social and political rights, and is one of the primary determinants of the gender gap more generally.[17] The level of education of a mother can have severe consequences for her own well-being and for that of her family. In twenty developing countries, under-five mortality was found to be significantly related to a lack of maternal education.[18] Education is one of the important factors found to influence contraceptive use,[19] which, as other studies show, contributes to a reduction in female and child mortality and morbidity.

The CEDAW addresses educational equality head-on. Article 10 requires that "States Parties shall take all appropriate measures to eliminate discrimination against women in order to ensure to them equal rights with men in the field of education." Governments are also required to provide a comparable quality of education for girls and boys in all types of schools, in rural as well as in urban areas, in preschool, general, technical, professional, and higher technical education, as well as in all types of vocational training.[20] Moreover, girls are to have a right to the same

---

[16] CEDAW, Article 5(a).

[17] Wils and Goujon 1998. Decades of recent research has confirmed that educating girls, especially at the primary through secondary school levels, has a large positive impact on women's earnings (relative to that of men). See, for example, Knowles, Lorgelly, and Owen 2002. For a review of the research on the greater return to female than to male education, see Psacharopoulos 1994. For household survey-based research that reaches similar conclusions in Taiwan see Spohr 2003 and in India see Duraisamy 2002.

[18] World Health Organization, Fact Sheet No. 251, June 2000.

[19] Sai 1993; Ainsworth, Beegle, and Nyamete 1996.

[20] CEDAW, Article 10(a).

curricula, the same examinations, teaching staff with qualifications of the same standard, and school premises and equipment of the same quality.[21] They are to have equal access to scholarships and educational grants.[22] Governments that become party to the CEDAW are required to address the literacy gap between men and women, and put programs in place to address the problem of female retention in schools.[23]

Why Comply?

Why should we expect an international treaty to affect women's educational status? Surely domestic developmental, social, and political factors are the primary determinants of a government's—indeed, a society's—commitment to educate the female population. Nonetheless, there are good reasons to believe that an international treaty commitment may, at the margins, make a positive contribution to a government's policy choice. Treaties raise audience costs. They use explicit language to express the serious intent of a government to live up to its substantive obligations. As such, they raise expectations and potentially reputational consequences related to flagrant noncompliance.

Treaty commitments may engage the interests of three kinds of audiences. First, since the obligations contained in treaties are intergovernmental, the state parties to a treaty have some interest in the extent to which other governments fulfill their obligations. Though arguably the most indifferent audience and hence a weak source of compliance pressure, there are good reasons to believe that at least some state parties value compliance by governments with which they have forged formal agreements. Theoretically, noncompliance with a specific legal obligation can create doubt about a government's broader commitment to the general principle that *pacta sunt servanda*: treaties are to be observed. As existential evidence of the value placed on compliance, governments have participated in the creation of institutions meant to monitor progress in meeting CEDAW obligations, and these institutions have been strengthened over time.

Treaties also engage the expectations of nongovernmental actors. Transnationally, nongovernmental organizations committed to human rights issues generally and women's rights issues in particular have grown and created a context of informal accountability. They have a clear interest in governmental compliance with CEDAW, and an incentive to independently monitor, publicize, and organize to improve the chances that a gov-

[21] CEDAW, Article 10(b).
[22] CEDAW, Article 10(d).
[23] CEDAW, Article 10(e and f).

ernment will live up to its commitments. Linkages to broader trans-national networks, foreign governments, and relevant international organizations improve the effectiveness of these groups in raising awareness and highlighting halfhearted government compliance, thus leveraging their influence locally and abroad.[24]

Most importantly, however, may be domestic audience costs. One of the primary effects of making a treaty commitment may be to raise or to change the expectations of one's own people. There are reasons to believe these changes may work in favor of treaty compliance. First, those who have a preference for implementing the substance of the obligation will now have a legal handle to press their claims. In some national contexts, treaties have direct consequences in national law, but even where they do not, claimants will be in a stronger moral position to press for treaty implementation. Moreover, treaty ratification should have the effect of increasing the size of the domestic coalition for compliance. To those who favor policies that improve women's rights can now be added those who prefer international treaty compliance in general. The possibility of a political alliance between those who are substantively affected and those with principled or strategic reasons to comply with a legal obligation has the potential for increasing local pressures on authorities to implement the treaty's main provisions.

Testing for Treaty Effects: Data and Methods of Analysis

One of the key provisions of the CEDAW is equal access to education for women. But does making a treaty commitment improve the chances their government will deliver? To begin to answer this question, it is important to develop indicators that can reasonably be interpreted as evidence of a government effort to meet treaty obligations by improving women's access to educational opportunities. Three key areas in which I look for treaty effects are the ratio of girls to boys in primary schools, the literacy gap between males and females, and the ratio of women to men in tertiary (post-high school) education. If the CEDAW has had an important impact on women's educational possibilities, we should see improvements in some or all three of these measures.

Ratio of Girls to Boys in Primary School

If governments have moved to implement the educational guarantees of the CEDAW, they should provide incentives for parents to send their girls

[24] Keck and Sikkink 1998.

to school. They can do this in a number of ways, two of the most effective being providing free, mandatory primary education and enforcing rules against child labor that interferes with education. With such efforts, parents have every incentive to allow their daughters to get a basic education.[25] We should therefore be able to observe change from year to year in the ratio of girls to boys attending elementary and secondary schools.[26] As this ratio rises, it is possible to infer a much greater government effort to provide a free and widely available opportunity for families to send their daughters to school. Obviously, this ratio alone does not capture all of the detailed requirements of the subparagraphs of Article 10,[27] but it is a good start for examining governments' commitment to the crucial first step: getting girls out of the house or the field or the factory and into the classroom. Figure 6.1 graphs the raw ratio over time. Clearly, on a global scale girls' educational opportunities have by this measure improved over the past two decades. Indeed, the data suggest that the upward trend began prior to the year in which the CEDAW was open for signature. The question we need to answer, however, is whether the public commitment to CEDAW has contributed anything to this upward trend.

The Gender Literacy Gap

Article 10(e) of the CEDAW specifically requires governments to make efforts to close the literacy gap between men and women. Parties are to ensure "The same opportunities for access to programmes of continuing education, including adult and functional literacy programmes, particularly those aimed at reducing, at the earliest possible time, any gap in education existing between men and women." This gap is calculated as the difference between the female and the male literacy rate prevailing in a given country (female literacy − male literacy).[28] A negative number indicates that women lag men in literacy. Figure 6.2 shows that there has been a significant improvement in the average literacy gap between 1970 and 2002, and again that this improvement began prior to the existence of the CEDAW treaty. Once again, I am interested in trying to assess the extent

[25] In some cultures, parents may resist, but with these policy changes we should be able to see widespread improvements in the gender ratio in elementary schools.

[26] World Bank, World Development Indicators.

[27] Admittedly, equal numbers in school need not mean equal education. A poignant example is given by Mai Yamani: "[In Saudi Arabia] the first school opened in 1903 was named Falah ('success'). This school was only for men. The first school of an equivalent nature opened in Jeddah only at the beginning of the 1960s, with the name Dar al-Hanan ('house of tenderness'). The objective of Dar al-Hanan was to produce better mothers and homemakers through Islamically guided instruction" (Yamani 2000, 141).

[28] World Bank, World Development Indicators.

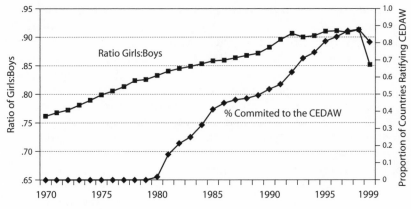

Figure 6.1   CEDAW and Girls' Education (Global Averages)

to which the treaty itself has influenced the rate of improvement in the literacy gap during this period.

Share of Women in Tertiary Education Enrollments

Finally, I consider whether making a CEDAW commitment has any effect on the possibilities for higher education for women. The treaty refers to equal opportunities for women in education *at all levels*, including professional and technical training. Are governments taking their treaty commitment seriously at the upper end of the educational spectrum? The

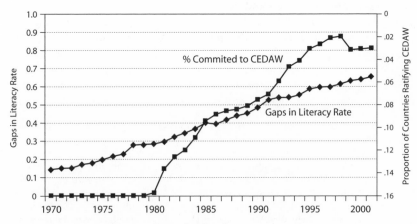

Figure 6.2   Gap in Literacy Rates by Gender, 1970–2002

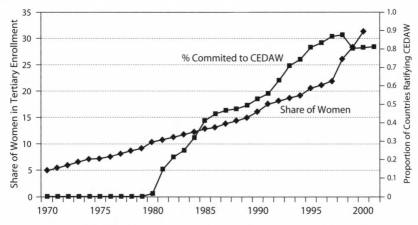

FIGURE 6.3   Women's Share in Tertiary Education Enrollment, 1970–2002

share of women in tertiary education[29] documents the extent of this effort. Figure 6.3 graphs yearly country averages for this measure. From a low of about 5 percent of all tertiary school students in 1970, countries on average had women in 30 percent of tertiary education slots in 2000.

Method of Analysis

The most obvious problem in assessing the effect of an explicit international legal commitment on these various indicators of women's educational progress is that of endogeneity: would governments have improved their performance with respect to the education of women, whether or not they had signed the CEDAW? Whether as a matter of modernization or socialization or world acculturation, women were "bound" to do better over time, so the argument might go, and the treaty commitment, one may reasonably argue, *reflects* rather than *shapes* governments' behavior in this regard.

Perhaps the most pervasive critique of researchers who attempt to isolate the effects of international agreements on state behavior is the charge of potential endogeneity: international institutions—treaties among them—do little to influence governments beyond what they would have done in their absence.[30] Institutionalists have developed a persuasive theoretical response based on game-theoretical analyses and principal-agent rela-

[29] School enrollment, tertiary, female (percent gross): United Nations Educational, Scientific, and Cultural Organization (UNESCO) Institute for Statistics; World Development Indicators.

[30] Mearsheimer 1994–95; Downs, Rocke, and Barsoom 1996.

tionships. Robert Keohane and Lisa Martin argue, for example, that principals develop international institutions to address their interests, but that they also only imperfectly control "agents" to whom enforcement and monitoring tasks have been delegated. Moreover, conditions change, and the structures that give rise to certain agreements need not persist. Therefore, while institutions may be endogenous, they may not simply be epiphenomenal of the interests or current practices of regime participants.[31]

The two-stage least-squares model employed here helps to control for the problem of treaty endogeneity. The selection equation models the influences on governments' decision to ratify the treaty in the first place. Treaty selection can be modeled as a function of exogenous influences on the propensity to ratify any treaty affecting women's status (e.g., the density of ratification in one's region, the nature of the domestic legal system, the predominance of Islam) as well as those factors that can be expected to influence compliance with the treaty's main provisions (e.g., performance on key dimensions of the treaty prior to ratification). My strategy is to use this selection equation as an instrument for the treaty commitment itself, and then ask what *additional effect* such a commitment has on the propensity to improve women's educational possibilities.[32]

The output equation, in addition to the instrumented treaty effect, contains a series of explanatory variables that control for obvious alternatives to the CEDAW hypothesis. These variables can be characterized as largely exogenous in the context of the educational policies under examination here. I control for obvious indicators of economic development, such as GDP per capita and in some specifications GDP growth and foreign aid as a proportion of GDP. I also control for key demographic factors, such as the relative youthfulness of the population (share of population under fourteen years of age) and the proportion of population living in urban areas. When we examine the ratio of girls to boys in primary schools and the literacy gap, it is reasonable to control for the social and economic structures that might affect this rate; I use the prevalence of child labor as a possible systematic explanation for gender bias in these cases. Since serious civil violence is another possible influence on gender ratios, I control for civil wars. Every output equation also attempts to address the socialization or acculturation possibility—the possibility that these rates are normatively driven *independently* of the legal norm of treaty compliance—by controlling for the average scores on the depen-

[31] Keohane and Martin 1999.

[32] Since the selection equation involves a time-series and a dichotomous dependent variable (treaty ratification), I control for the time dependence of observations by including a counting vector (a cumulative count of years without treaty ratification) and three cubic splines. See Beck, Katz, and Tucker 1998. In the output equation, time is handled through the use of a lagged dependent variable.

dent variable among the countries within the region. In every case, serial correlation is addressed by the use of a lagged dependent variable. Where it was found to be significant net of these other effects (only in the case of tertiary education), I also included a year trend to reduce the possibility that time alone could account for the upward drift in all three curves.

The models employed address the treaty endogeneity problem by developing instruments for CEDAW ratification. They control for developmental and demographic explanations, and reduce the possibility of extralegal socialization into the normative framework of women's rights by controlling for the practices of the surrounding region. Time trends are included where appropriate and serial autocorrelation addressed with the equivalent of lagged dependent variables.[33] In order to minimize the confusion of cause and effect, all explanatory variables—including the CEDAW commitment—are reported lagging their effects one, three, and five periods from the observed outcome. This specification recognizes that it may take time—bureaucratically, politically, logistically—for the influences discussed here to have effects on the outcomes in which we are interested. In short, the models used here do more than any empirical work to date to isolate the effect of the treaty per se by controlling for reasonable alternatives and explicitly endogenizing the treaty commitment itself.

Results

Has ratifying CEDAW had any measurable effects on women's and girls' access to education in those countries that are parties to the treaty? Tables 6.1–6.3 present some interesting evidence that, quite possibly, it has. There is some sensitivity to exact specification (which I will discuss below), but in general, these models produce credible results that the CEDAW has contributed positively to governments' propensity to take the educational opportunities afforded females much more seriously than they otherwise might have done.

Table 6.1 indicates the results for the ratio of girls to boys in primary education. The first point to make is that it is very difficult to find good explanations for changes in the encouraging upward trend depicted in figure 6.1. Unsurprisingly, the prior ratio has the strongest impact on the ratio one, three, and five years in the future. Only two or three of our control

[33] In the selection equation, the issue of how to handle time is complicated by the fact that treaty ratification is dichotomous. I therefore employ methods suggested by Beck, Katz, and Tucker by including a counting vector (counting the years from first observation without ratification) and a series of three cubic splines to handle the problem of time dependence among observations. See Beck, Katz, and Tucker 1998.

TABLE 6.1
Effects of the CEDAW on the Ratio of Girls to Boys in Primary School (two-stage
least squares; robust standard errors adjusted for clustering by country)

Explanatory variable	Lagged 1 year	Lagged 3 years	Lagged 5 years
CEDAW ratification	.226*	.668*	.549
	(.136)	(.386)	(.640)
Women's NGOs (#logged)	−.506***	−1.68***	−1.96***
	(.183)	(.571)	(.706)
Share of girls in primary school, t_o	.976***	.920***	.851***
	(.0043)	(.012)	(.022)
Average regional share of girls in primary school, t_o	.006	.024	.048*
	(.006)	(.018)	(.025)
Prevalence of child labor	−.003	−.019	−.047
	(.007)	(.020)	(.029)
GDP per capita (logged)	.115*	.266	.301
	(.061)	(.200)	(.307)
Overseas development assistance/GDP	−.0000	−.0000	−.000013
	(.0000)	(.0000)	(.000014)
GDP growth rate	.005	.031**	.043**
	(.008)	(.015)	(.021)
Civil war	.246	.540	.227
	(.170)	(.504)	(.759)
% population under 14 (logged)	.154	.027	.595
	(.231)	(.819)	(1.16)
% population urban (logged)	−.023	−.101	−.359
	(.152)	(.434)	(.641)
Constant	2.5***	8.92***	16.44***
	(.778)	(2.35)	(3.37)
Number of observations	2,693	2,418	2,154
Number of country clusters	141	137	130
R^2	.995	.971	.94

Instrumented: CEDAW ratification; women's INGOs.
Instruments: ratio of girls to boys in primary school prior to CEDAW ratification; average regional share of girls in primary school; prevalence of child labor; % population under 14 (logged); % population urban (logged); GDP per capita (logged); civil war; dummy for years including year of ratification, number of years without ratifying; % of region ratifying CEDAW and CRC; Islam; British legal culture; foreign development assistance/GDP; three cubic splines (based on years without ratifying CEDAW or CDC).
* = significant at .10; ** = significant at .05; *** = significant at .01

variables seem to bear any relationship to the improvement. One of these is GDP per capita (for the following year's ratio) and GDP growth rate (for the ratio three and five years hence). CEDAW ratification had a statistically significant impact on the ratio of girls to boys in primary school with a one- and a three-year lag, though there is little evidence this impact endures beyond three years. For the first year after ratification, the CEDAW can account for about a quarter of a percentage point increase in the ratio. By the third year, a CEDAW commitment accounts for an estimated two-thirds of a percentage point increase. Along with a country's wealth and growth rates, making a CEDAW commitment is one of the few factors that seem to have a systematic impact on the average national commitment to get girls into the classroom.[34] Surprisingly, the number of women's international nongovernmental organizations does not positively affect the ratio of girls to boys in primary school; if anything, the impact appears to be negative.

Ratification of the CEDAW seems also to have contributed on the margin to closing the literacy gap between women and men. Table 6.2 indicates that ratification is on average associated with a .06 improvement (closure) in the gender literacy gap. Since the average gap over the past three decades has been about 9.6 percentage points, and the average *improvement* in a year is about .29 percent, the estimated CEDAW effect is substantively significant as well.[35] Several factors stand out in explaining the rate of change of the literacy gap. The lagged dependent variable is negative in this case for an obvious reason: the larger the improvement in the previous period, the smaller we should expect that improvement to be in the next.[36] Strong regional improvement effects can also be discerned. Where child labor is most common, the gap in literacy between women and men worsens rather than improves. The ratio of young to old population also helps to close the gap, as newly educated girls increasingly outnumber the older generations, which were subject to even greater educational deficits. Development assistance does not help, but GDP growth does.

Finally, consider the effect of the CEDAW on a country's commitment to train women beyond high school. From admittedly very low levels of tertiary education participation, the CEDAW has had an important impact

---

[34] These results are robust to specifications using the first difference (improvements) as the dependent variable, as well as regional fixed effects. The results are disturbed somewhat by the inclusion of other kinds of fixed effects (country and year).

[35] These results are robust to the inclusion of year fixed effects, and they are enhanced greatly by the inclusion of regional fixed effects. CEDAW effects in this case are disturbed by the inclusion of country fixed effects, however.

[36] Improvements do not get larger and larger; they tend to degrade naturally over time. Similarly small improvements in the previous period leave more room for larger improvements in the next. This is reflective of a natural saturation in the rate of improvement over time.

TABLE 6.2

Effects of the CEDAW on the Literacy Gap between Men and Women (two-stage least squares; robust standard errors adjusted for clustering by country)

Explanatory variable	Lagged 1 year	Lagged 3 years	Lagged 5 years
CEDAW ratification	.062*	.066**	.066**
	(.035)	(.033)	(.032)
Improvement in the literacy gap, t_0	−.014***	−.018***	−.021***
	(.003)	(.003)	(.003)
Average regional improvement in literacy gap, t_0	.610***	.535***	.474***
	(.130)	(.122)	(.116)
Prevalence of child labor	−.009***	−.010***	−.011***
	(.003)	(.002)	(.003)
GDP per capita (logged)	−.010	−.0007	.010
	(.032)	(.032)	(.775)
Overseas development assistance/GDP	−.000003***	−.0000003**	−.0000002**
	(.0000001)	(.0000000)	(.00000009)
GDP growth rate	.003***	.003**	.0019
	(.0015)	(.001)	(.0015)
% population under 14 (logged)	.300***	.302***	.298***
	(.095)	(.098)	(.097)
% population urban (logged)	−.018	−.039	−.069
	(.073)	(.070)	(.069)
Constant	.731**	.742***	.771***
	(.282)	(.263)	(.248)
Number of observations	2,974	2,740	2,504
Number of country clusters	121	121	120
R^2	.35	.40	.46

Instrumented: CEDAW ratification.

Instruments: improvement in literacy gap prior to CEDAW ratification; average regional improvement in literacy gap; prevalence of child labor; GDP per capita (logged); foreign development assistance/GDP; GDP growth rate; % population under 14 (logged); % population urban (logged); dummy for years including year of ratification, number of years without ratifying; % of region ratifying CEDAW; Islam; British legal culture; three cubic splines (based on years without ratifying CEDAW).

TABLE 6.3
Effects of the CEDAW on the Ratio of Women to Men in Tertiary Education
(two-stage least squares; robust standard errors adjusted for clustering by
country)

Explanatory variable	Lagged 1 year	Lagged 3 years	Lagged 5 years
CEDAW ratification	.344***	1.10***	1.50***
	(.147)	(.400)	(.564)
Women's NGOs (#logged)	−.314***	−1.03***	−1.03**
	(.118)	(.375)	(.500)
Share of women in tertiary education, t_o	1.02***	1.03***	1.04***
	(.009)	(.029)	(.043)
% population under 14 (logged)	−1.21***	−4.25***	−6.80***
	(.336)	(1.103)	(1.56)
% population urban (logged)	.032	.195	.189
	(.106)	(.342)	(.494)
GDP per capita (logged)	.116	.388	.642*
	(.078)	(.243)	(.353)
Civil war	−.125	−.267	−.074
	(.098)	(.289)	.518
Year	.015**	.059**	.087**
	(.007)	(.024)	(.035)
Constant	−32.29**	−124.58***	−184.36***
	(14.45)	(47.00)	(69.07)
Number of observations	3,107	2,870	2,581
Number of country clusters	150	147	147
R^2	.99	.96	.93

Instrumented: CEDAW ratification; women's INGOs.

Instruments: Share of women in education prior to CEDAW ratification, % population under 14 (logged); % population urban (logged); GDP per capita (logged); civil war; year; dummy for years including year of ratification, number of years without ratifying; % of region ratifying CEDAW; average regional share of women in tertiary education; regional WINGO presence (logged); Islam; British legal culture; foreign development assistance/GDP; three cubic splines (based on years without ratifying CEDAW).

* = significant at .10; ** = significant at .05; *** = significant at .01

on the ratio of women to men in tertiary education. Ratification is associated with a .34 increase in the ratio, growing to a 1.50 increase within five years of ratification. This is the case when we control for the previous ratio, and include a time trend as well.[37] As in the model for primary school ratios, the endogenous effect of women's international NGOs is negative. The ratio is also apparently influenced by demographics—large youth populations make it less likely that women will enter a tertiary educational setting. Unsurprisingly, there is also a positive impact of GDP per capita: the wealthier the country, the more likely women are to participate in higher education.

It is important to keep in mind that these are very stringent models of CEDAW effects. Because they include the equivalent of a lagged dependent variable, these tests in effect capture *improvements* associated with CEDAW ratification. Because they include a time trend (where statistically significant),[38] they control for the simple linear progression of year-on-year improvement. Most importantly, because they endogenize the making of the treaty commitment itself, it is difficult to claim that these are improvements that "would have happened anyway." While these are tough tests, it is also worth pointing out that none of them suggests CEDAW is the only or even the most important effect on women's educational situation. Resources and demographics play an important role as well. Nonetheless, this is the first time it has been shown that, when their governments make an international legal commitment to work toward educational equality, the world's women have, on average, been made a bit better off than they would otherwise have been.

Conclusions

The study of international institutions is an important frontier in international relations and international law. A tremendous expenditure of political effort has gone into the codification of international affairs in the post–World War II period, and nowhere has this trend been more marked

[37] The CEDAW's effects on enrollment of women in tertiary education are also quite robust to various specifications: CEDAW's influence was strongly positive when the dependent variable was converted to first differences (more directly measuring improvements) and whether or not country or regional fixed effects were used. When year fixed effects were used, CEDAW effects remained large and positive, but were no longer statistically significant.

[38] A linear time trend proved significant and hence is only reported in the case of tertiary education. For primary school and literacy, the time trend was not at all statistically significant, and greatly increased the standard errors, including those for CEDAW. As a result, when the year time trend is included for those cases, CEDAW remains positive, but falls below traditional levels of statistical significance.

than in the recognition, promotion, and protection of human rights. From practically nothing before the Universal Declaration on Human Rights (1948), governments have constructed a dense web of treaties by which they have committed themselves to observe basic standards of rights protection. The CEDAW is an example of this general trend.

This chapter has demonstrated one empirical strategy for establishing a fairly nonintuitive outcome: treaties can have meaningful domestic effects, even in the absence of formal international machinery for their rigid enforcement. As Robert Keohane's neoliberal institutional research agenda should lead us to expect—though through mechanisms that are not likely to involve state-centric reciprocity but rather domestic political awareness and expectations—treaties raise expectations of performance, which governments are, of course, free to ignore, but which on occasion raise politically awkward questions about their sincerity and consistency. Of course, not every government will be concerned about these consequences of noncompliance, but where they are, the world's women will have a little better access to equal education as a result.

CHAPTER 7

Private Governance for the Public Good?

EXPLORING PRIVATE SECTOR PARTICIPATION
IN GLOBAL FINANCIAL REGULATION

Layna Mosley

IN 1971, ROBERT KEOHANE and Joseph Nye called for greater attention to the role of transnational actors. Scholars of international relations should, they argued, examine the effects of these actors on intergovernmental institutions (and on global governance more generally), as well as on the global distribution of wealth and power. As Helen Milner notes in chapter 1 in this volume, the ensuing decades have witnessed numerous analyses of the roles of nonstate actors, not only in economic realms, but also in human rights, the environment, and military operations. Many posit, following Keohane and his collaborators, that transnational actors represent a fundamental challenge to the state-centric, realist-oriented paradigm;[1] others maintain that powerful states retain control of the most important elements of global governance.[2] At the same time, the intensification of economic globalization and the accompanying advances in technology have rendered transnational actors—including multinational corporations, institutional investors, banks, and nongovernmental organizations—increasingly important to the politics of global governance.

The growth in importance of transnational actors, particularly those from the business sector, has been particularly dramatic in the area of global finance. The volume, velocity, and diversity of capital flows has increased markedly over the last two decades. At the same time, efforts to govern various aspects of global finance have expanded. One of the distinguishing features of contemporary financial governance is its reliance on public as well as private actors. In many instances, public (government) agents set rules, while a combination of public and private sector actors enforce the rules. Governance is now the province not only of

The author thanks Stanley Black, Phil Cerny, Eric Helleiner, Susan Minushkin, David Singer, Mariana Sousa, Ngaire Woods, participants in the Robert Keohane Festschrift Conference; the UCSD International Relations seminar; the 2005 LSE CARR Conference on Risk and Regulation; and the 2006 GARNET Conference on Global Financial and Monetary Governance, as well as two anonymous reviewers, for comments.

[1] E.g., Slaughter 2004.
[2] E.g., Drezner 2007.

"clubs" of powerful governments, but also of private sector actors, quasi-governmental agencies, and transgovernmental groups.

Despite the growth in private sector participation in global financial governance, recent scholarship in international political economy provides few systematic assessments of the sources of variation in international financial governance, and does little to investigate the consequences of this variation for equity and efficiency.[3] This chapter begins to address this shortcoming, moving from the general claim that private financial sector actors play an important role in governance to an exploration of the precise ways in which their participation affects outcomes. In this way the analysis reminds us that traditional intergovernmental institutions are only part of the story in global financial governance.

I begin with a discussion of contemporary global financial governance, with special attention to private actors. I hypothesize that, through a variety of mechanisms, private sector involvement could increase the effectiveness of global rules. I offer an initial assessment of this hypothesis, based on recent studies as well as on quantitative evidence. I suggest that the effects of private sector participation on financial system efficiency and stability may be more limited than optimists would hope. In closing, I note that private sector participation also has distributional consequences, as privately developed regimes tend to reflect financial sector interests.

Global Financial Governance

Mirroring a general trend in global economic governance, international and transnational efforts at financial regulation have increased dramatically in recent years.[4] Post–World War II financial governance focused on states as both participants in and subjects of regulation. The associated institutions were oriented toward nation-states as sovereign, central actors. Thus, the obligations created by intergovernmental institutions such as the IMF and the World Bank centered on "at the border issues," requiring governments to change the ways they treated external actors and flows (e.g., current account convertibility), but not to alter their domestic policies or institutions.[5] Following steady growth in the 1970s and 1980s,

---

[3] Recent exceptions include Mattli and Büthe (2003) on international product standards, Farrell's (2003) account of the EU-U.S. agreement on Internet data privacy, Sinclair's (2005) analysis of credit ratings agencies, and the contributions to Underhill and Zhang 2003.

[4] Armijo 2002; Drezner 2007; Eichengreen 1999; Goldstein et al. 2000. Drezner notes that "none of the financial standards now considered to be important by the IFIs existed prior to 1996" (2007, 19). Simmons (2001) points out, however, that governance efforts in international finance have been less comprehensive and less legalized than in international trade.

[5] Vogel 1996.

the pace and depth of global regulation increased dramatically in the 1990s. Some new regulatory systems were created, and other existing rules became more legalized. This expansion was both a cause and an effect of economic openness, partly in response to the growing international externalities generated by national actions.[6]

Many of these more recent governance efforts involve "behind the border" issues, requiring not only changes in governments' policies vis-à-vis external actors, but also revisions in national laws and policies, including taxation, banking regulation, and property rights protection.[7] These efforts generally aim to improve the functioning of global capital markets, by allocating investment efficiently, preventing volatility and crises, and reducing transaction costs. "Reregulation" has emerged at the international level,[8] and the subjects of public international law have shifted, from states to states plus firms and individuals. Contemporary efforts include providing higher quality information;[9] setting common accounting standards;[10] resolving economic crises via structural adjustment and orderly workouts for sovereign debt;[11] ensuring direct investors against threats of expropriation;[12] and encouraging prudential bank behavior.[13] These efficiency-enhancing measures also might promote a more equitable global distribution of capital, although this is by no means guaranteed.

For the study of international institutions, increased financial regulatory efforts raise two important issues: compliance with global rules and the accountability of rule makers. First, international rules achieve their aims only when the relevant actors—governments, banks, investment houses—comply. While compliance is always an issue in international relations,[14] it may be particularly problematic when the subjects of rules are firms and individuals; when commitments are not legally binding;[15] and when rules are highly technical. Creating rules that encourage compliance—attending to supervision, as well as regulation—is central. There are numerous mechanisms to promote compliance, as Ronald Mitchell's chapter in this volume details. In the financial realm, the participation of private actors may be one such mechanism.

Second, as contemporary efforts at global regulation have increased, so have concerns about accountability. At the limit, these concerns threaten

[6] Keohane 2002; Slaughter 2004; Drezner 2007.
[7] Kaul et al. 2003; Elkins, Guzman, and Simmons 2006.
[8] Kapstein 1992; Ronit and Schneider 2000; Vogel 1996.
[9] Mosley 2003b.
[10] Crouzet and Véron 2002.
[11] Conceição 2003; Eichengreen 1999.
[12] Simmons and Elkins 2004.
[13] Simmons 2001; Singer 2007.
[14] E.g., Downs, Rocke, and Barsoom 1996; Mitchell 1994; Simmons 2000.
[15] Slaughter 2004.

the sustainability of economic globalization. All international agreements have distributional consequences, both within and among states.[16] As neoliberal institutionalists recognize, but have not always emphasized, institutionalized cooperation may be used to achieve a variety of aims, only some of which enhance equity. Indeed, the neorealist concern with the distribution of gains from cooperation may be borne out by the character of global financial rules and rule-making. Many standards are set by regulatory clubs, in which a small group of powerful states—or the United States acting unilaterally—sets standards that ultimately evolve to govern most of the universe of states.[17] For instance, the 1988 Basel Accords on Capital Adequacy began as a U.S.-U.K. agreement that then expanded to cover other G-10 nations.[18] Later, the agreement's main directives were adopted by a variety of developing nations, often under pressure from the IMF, the World Bank, and private investors. The Basel Committee, though, remains oriented toward practices in major financial centers.[19]

As globalization has intensified, so have worries that global rules create winners and losers both across and within societies.[20] Some focus on the fact that the rules of dominant countries often become the rules for other nations in the region or across the world, even though these other nations might have very different preferences.[21] For instance, the success of efforts to reduce money laundering in the early part of this decade likely was driven as much by direct political pressures from the United States as by national governments' and private banks' desire to maintain a reputation for doing legitimate banking business.[22]

In other instances, the concern is that those who create the rules are not accountable directly to those affected by the rules. For instance, the governments and citizens of developing nations have little influence over most standards.[23] As Helen Milner notes in chapter 1, the design of international institutions may well be endogenous to the interests of powerful states—or, in this case, to the interests of powerful private sector actors within those states. For instance, the Financial Stability Forum (FSF), established in the late 1990s and the coordinating body for a dozen recent financial "codes and standards," consists of G-7 governments (three seats per country, for the finance ministry, central bank, and financial regulator), international financial institutions (sixteen seats for IMF, World Bank,

[16] Krasner 1991; Koremenos, Lipson, and Snidal 2001; Mattli and Büthe 2003; Rosenbluth and Schaap 2003.

[17] Conçeicao 2003; Drezner 2007; Helleiner 2002.

[18] Kapstein 1992; Simmons 2001.

[19] Oatley and Nabors 1998; Singer 2004.

[20] E.g., Grant and Keohane 2005; Keohane 2002.

[21] Eichengreen 2003; Keohane and Nye 2001, 2003; Simmons 2001.

[22] Helleiner 2002.

[23] Griffith-Jones and Ocampo 2003; Schneider 2005.

and Bank for International Settlements representatives), and single seats for Australia, Hong Kong, the Netherlands, and Singapore. While the FSF sets standards that aim to govern all nations, its composition reveals a club-oriented rule-making process that excludes developing nations.[24]

This latter concern about accountability is exacerbated by private sector participation in rule setting and rule enforcement. Private commercial actors—banks and investment houses, professional associations, and multinational corporations—often play a role in the implementation as well as the creation of international rules. Some regulatory regimes include private actors explicitly, delegating rule-making and enforcement authority to them, while others consult private actors informally. The overall result is a shift from governance via multilateral, intergovernmental cooperation to governance based on "transnational and transgovernmental cooperation."[25] While this shift may promote compliance, it also raises concerns about accountability. In the remainder of this chapter, I explore the implications of private involvement for the effectiveness of global rules. I suggest that if private sector involvement increases compliance with rules, the accountability trade-off may be one worth making. If not, however, concerns about accountability could undermine confidence in global financial regulation. Unfortunately, empirical evidence leans toward the latter.

The Role of the Private Sector

Neoliberal institutionalists have observed that global governance may take a variety of forms, ranging from international organizations with bricks-and-mortar headquarters, a professional staff, and a highly codified set of rules, to sets of informal but regular practices based on behavior and shared understandings. Contemporary efforts to govern global finance mirror much of this diversity. They include intergovernmental institutions (IMF, World Bank), transnational regulatory groups (International Organization of Securities Commissions), and private sector entities (credit ratings agencies, London Club). As Keohane and Nye's work anticipated,[26] a good deal of governance activity occurs outside traditional intergovernmental frameworks and institutions.[27] Rather than work through governments, private actors instead may work alongside governments in institutional design as well as in institutional implementation.[28]

[24] Vojta and Uzan 2003.
[25] Keohane and Nye 2001; Slaughter 2004.
[26] Keohane and Nye 1971a, 1977.
[27] Also see Keohane and Nye 2001; Kahler and Lake 2003.
[28] Farrell 2003; IMF 2003; Knill and Lehmkuhl 2002; Koremenos, Lipson, and Snidal 2001.

Types of Private Involvement

While a variety of nonstate actors may have interests in financial regulation, my analysis is confined to private (nongovernmental) commercial actors. Private commercial actors include financial institutions, corporations (national or multinational), industry and professional associations, and professional investors. I exclude noncommercial private actors, such as labor rights and development-oriented NGOs, from this analysis. Such groups could play a role in the governance of longer-term investment or the relief of public debt,[29] but their importance pales relative to commercial actors.

I categorize commercial private actors' involvement in financial governance into three broad types—as autonomous authorities (developing *and* enforcing rules); as joint sources of rules (developing rules in concert with governmental authorities); and as enforcers of standards (applying rules developed by other authorities). First, when private actors serve as autonomous authorities, they both regulate and supervise; states and IGOs delegate (or lose) part or all of their rule-making authority. Along these lines, Mattli's study of product standards depicts a movement, albeit a partial one, of authority from the "transnational public" to the "transnational private" sphere.[30]

Second, joint governance involves the participation of private agents alongside governmental authorities. They may take part in the establishment of rules. For instance, private actors (i.e. International Accounting Standards Board representatives) often sit alongside governments at the Financial Stability Forum, helping to develop key codes and standards. Third, private actors may act as supervisors: public authorities remain the creators of rules, but private actors bear primary or secondary enforcement responsibilities.[31] On the primary side, national auditors are responsible for implementing international auditing standards—self-enforcement. On the secondary side, private actors can provide additional incentives for governments or banks to follow global rules. For instance, the fiscal policy convergence associated with Economic and Monetary Union was enforced primarily by EU governments. But because private sector actors also were interested in who would qualify for EMU, and in how the euro would perform in world markets, they rewarded governments for compliance with EU rules.[32]

Table 7.1 classifies international financial rules along two dimensions, enforcement and establishment. For each dimension, rules are classified

---

[29] Haufler 2000.

[30] Mattli 2003. For similar accounts regarding other regulatory domains and issue areas, see Cutler 2003; Farrell 2003; Haufler 2000; and Stone Sweet 2004.

[31] Farrell 2003.

[32] Mosley 2004.

TABLE 7.1
The Public-Private Continuum in International Finance

	Enforcement		
Establishment	Public	Public-private	Private
Public	· Money launder-ing (**Financial Ac-tion Task Force**) · Debt relief and rescheduling (Paris Club, IMF, World Bank, G-7)	· Data dissemina-tion (IMF SDDS) · EU fiscal policy (EMU Conver-gence Criteria, Stability and Growth Pact, financial market pressures)	· **Bank supervision** (Basel II, agreed 2004)
Public-Private	· Financial Stability Forum's 12 key standards (**Fiscal transparency; monetary trans-parency; payment and settlement systems; insol-vency**)[1] · International Center for the Settlement of In-vestment Disputes arbitration	· **Bank supervision** (Basel Committee capital adequacy rules, 1988–2004)[2] · **Corporate gover-nance** (OECD) · **Securities regula-tion** (Interna-tional Organiza-tion of Securities Commissions) · **Insurance super-vision** (Interna-tional Association of Insurance Supervisors) · Structural adjust-ment programs (IMF) · Transparency: Global anticor-ruption move-ment[3]	· Antisweatshop movement (UN Global Compact, NGOs, corporate codes of conduct)

TABLE 7.1 (con't)
The Public-Private Continuum in International Finance

	Enforcement		
Establishment	*Public*	*Public-private*	*Private*
Private	· Financial reporting rules in the EU (using IASB rules)	· **Accounting rules** (International Accounting Standards Board) · **Auditing rules** (International Auditing and Assurance Standards Board) · International Chamber of Commerce[4]	· Sovereign Borrowing: Credit Ratings

[1] Not all of the FSF's twelve key standards fall into this cell. For instance, anti-money-laundering rules are primarily based in the public sector, accounting and securities regulations in the private sector.
[2] Note the contrast, below, between Basel I (1988) and II (2004).
[3] On the global anticorruption movement, see Sandholtz and Gray 2003.
[4] See Ronit and Schneider 2000.

as fully public, shared public and private, or fully private. The table includes the thirteen standards and codes used in the empirical assessment below (in bold), plus several others. The upper left cell contains cases in which national governments and intergovernmental institutions retain control of regulation *and* supervision. For instance, the Financial Action Task Force's anti-money-laundering rules were created by states, initially limited to G-7 countries. Although there are some private market pressures for financial centers to "know their lenders," the major impetus for compliance comes from powerful states.

In the lower right cell, private actors are autonomous authorities. For instance, while International Labor Organization conventions suggest norms that inform the antisweatshop movement, the majority of rule setting and enforcement happens privately, via multinational corporation codes of conduct and NGO monitoring and advocacy. Similarly, private credit ratings agencies (Moody's, Standard and Poor's, and Fitch-IBCA) develop guidelines regarding appropriate economic policies, and portfolio-market investors—who often rely on these ratings for asset allocation decisions—enforce these guidelines.[33]

Other areas of the table reflect mixed patterns, where private actors are involved in enforcement or establishment or both. For instance, international accounting standards are set by the IASB, operating independently of governments and funded by donations from accounting firms, stock exchanges, and underwriters. While IASB board members are drawn largely from the private sector, the IASB sometimes relies on public sector agents—such as the U.S. Securities and Exchange Commission, the IMF, and IOSCO—as additional enforcers.[34] A similar pattern exists for international auditing rules, established by the International Auditing and Assurance Standards Board (IAASB), and for insurance supervision, via the International Association of Insurance Supervisors.[35]

More generally, the FSF's key codes and standards are created by a private-public consortium, with some variation among the dozen standards (see table 7.1). Some standards were based on efforts (money laundering, data dissemination) that existed previously; in other cases, the FSF was the primary forum for developing rules, in the late 1990s. Five FSF standards reflect mixed establishment, but largely public enforcement: (1) insolvency; transparency in (2) fiscal and (3) monetary policymaking; payment systems of (4) central banks and (5) in the financial system.[36] In these cases, enforcement occurs largely through the IMF's and World Bank's regular surveillance and occasionally through inclusion in IMF standby arrangements.[37] Finally, the Basel Committee's revised rules ("Basel II," 2004) on bank capital adequacy included several rounds of consultation with private banks and investors (as did the 2004 revision of the OECD-based Principles of Corporate Governance). And Basel II relies on public (national banking regulators) as well as private market ("Pillar 3") enforcement.

Implications of Private Sector Participation

Private actors frequently, if not always, are involved *indirectly* in global governance. For instance, many firms lobby national governments re-

---

[33] Cantor and Packer 1996; King and Sinclair 2003; Mosley 2003a; Sinclair 2005.

[34] Quinn 2004.

[35] Recent corporate scandals and the passage of the Sarbanes-Oxley Act have increased public sector involvement in auditing standards.

[36] Payment and settlement systems are the "plumbing" that ensure the clearing of markets with respect to financial transactions.

[37] Schneider 2005; Sundararajan, Marston, and Basu 2001.

garding international trade treaties and policies.[38] Similarly, Jonathan Aronson's chapter in this volume reveals the influence of copyright holders in wealthy nations on the development of global intellectual property rules. And even the *direct* involvement of private actors in economic governance is not entirely new; older examples include the law merchants of early modern Europe, the pre–World War I London-based Corporation for Foreign Bondholders, and the interwar administration of the oil trade.[39]

What is somewhat new in much of contemporary global governance is not the involvement of private actors, but the often direct—without mediation by national governments or public agencies—nature of their participation. This has increased markedly during the last decade.[40] The contemporary role of private actors raises important questions, such as the relationship between the type of governance and the nature of regulatory outcomes (efficiency as well as equity). To return to the comparison with intellectual property rules, while copyright holders gain from TRIPs and related regulations, consumers, innovators, and developing nations may lose from such rules.

While some scholars have pointed out that intergovernmental organizations do not have a monopoly on governance,[41] they have done little to explore the effects of varying forms of governance on outcomes. For instance, Keohane and Nye briefly offer a matrix for contemporary global governance, suggesting three levels of authority (supranational, national, and subnational) and three genres of authorities (private, governmental, third sector).[42] But they do little beyond arguing for the importance of understanding "new agents in networks" and pointing out the rise of "trisectoral partnerships," involving intergovernmental institutions, private firms, and civil society groups. Moreover, while those in the policy community have examined the need to involve private sector actors in the resolution of crises,[43] they have paid less attention to their role in regulation more generally. The scant scholarship that explores the impact of private actors often employs a principal-agent framework, focusing on the interaction among legislatures, national regulators, and private interests;[44] or on the existence of multiple principals, some private and some public.[45]

[38] E.g., Grossman and Helpman 1994; Hiscox 2002; Milner 1988.

[39] Cutler 2003; Eichengreen 1999; Kahler 2004; Ronit and Schneider 2000; Stone Sweet 2004.

[40] Armijo 2002; Eichengreen 2003; Goldstein et al. 2000, Koremenos, Lipson, and Snidal 2001; Sandholtz and Gray 2003.

[41] E.g., Strange 1996; Porter 1999; Underhill 2000.

[42] Keohane and Nye 2001.

[43] E.g., Eichengreen 1999.

[44] Singer 2007.

[45] Büthe and Mattli 2005.

These approaches, however, stop short of exploring the impact of private sector participation on broader outcomes.

We also could investigate the *causes* of private sector participation. Some view private involvement as a deliberate choice by governments.[46] Private actors also could play a role in this process: it may be the threat of public sector regulation that spurs private agents to develop and implement regulatory frameworks. One might then assess the conditions under which governments retain ultimate control (but are influenced by the financial community), versus the circumstances under which governments delegate more fully to private actors.

Others treat private involvement as the (perhaps) unintended consequence of capital market openness and technological advances.[47] We could then imagine that more technical issues are likely to be characterized by greater direct private participation. Of course, even the most technical of rules has distributional consequences.[48] Still others argue that, when major nation-states are unable to agree among themselves, greater delegation to the private sector occurs.[49] Such delegation will be systematically more likely for some issues than for others: if states have the most difficulty agreeing to regulate the most distributionally contentious issues, they will leave the most challenging regulatory tasks to the private sector. This final possibility reminds us of the selection problem inherent in analyzing the effects of international institutions;[50] as both Helen Milner and Ronald Mitchell point out, institutions are endogenous to considerations of power, influence, and distribution. To some extent, studying the effects of institutions also requires analyzing their causes. As a starting point, however, the empirical examination below focuses on the consequences of direct private involvement. The causes of this involvement are left as a subject for future research.

The Impact of Private Sector Participation: Initial Evidence

One potential impact of private sector involvement concerns its effects on compliance. Private sector involvement in global governance could lead to more successful—in terms of rates of implementation—global rules. How might this happen? Here it is useful to distinguish again between private actors as enforcers of agreements against third parties (e.g. private markets pressuring national governments to comply), versus private ac-

---

[46] Drezner 2007; Farrell 2003; Pauly 2002.
[47] Helleiner 1994; Porter 1999; Strange 1996; Underhill 2000.
[48] Crouzet and Véron 2002; Cutler 2003; Mosley 2003b.
[49] Drezner 2007; Simmons 2001.
[50] E.g., Simmons and Hopkins 2005; von Stein 2005.

tors as self-regulators, implementing rules that govern their own behavior (e.g. accountants following IASB standards).

In terms of third-party enforcement, the causal argument is that market discipline is an effective means of supervision. If investors reward (via interest rates and capital flows) governments for compliance with global financial rules, governments will have greater incentives to follow the rules.[51] Market rewards also could reduce the slippage between announcing adherence to a standard versus implementing it in practice.[52] Market discipline, then, may increase regulatory bite.[53] Involvement in the establishment of rules also could play a role: if private actors participate in the development of standards, they will have better information about—and perhaps a more positive view of—those standards. If, on the other hand, they have little awareness of the standards, weak enforcement pressures can be expected.[54]

In terms of self-regulation, the argument is that private actors are more accepting of rules when these rules account for technical issues and expertise;[55] when rules are more consistent with their interests and beliefs; and, by implication, when they view these rules are more legitimate. In other words, if accounting standards closely match the views of professional accountants—as opposed to the views of labor unions or pension system stakeholders, for instance—then professional accountants are more likely to embrace the standards. Moreover, when individuals or governments have participated in the making of laws, they see such laws as more legitimate; greater legitimacy, in turn, leads to greater compliance.[56] Or, to take a slightly different tack, participants in rule-making are more able to commit credibly and, ultimately, more likely to actually comply.[57]

For an initial evaluation of these propositions—the "efficiency" hypothesis—I consider two types of evidence. First, studies of the linkage between government compliance with international standards and capital market outcomes allow us to assess the market discipline mechanism. These studies reveal a mixed pattern. On the positive side, Gelos and Wei find that international equity funds invest less in emerging markets with low macro-level policymaking and corporate transparency;[58] but data transparency has no impact on investment flows. Christofides and colleagues' study includes twenty-four emerging market nations;[59] for 1992

---

[51] E.g., Simmons and Elkins 2004.
[52] World Bank 2001.
[53] Germain 2001; Mosley 2003a; Hardie and Mosley 2008.
[54] IMF 2003; Mosley 2003b.
[55] Knill and Lehmkuhl 2002; Mattli 2003.
[56] Tyler 1990.
[57] Martin 2000.
[58] Gelos and Wei 2002.
[59] Christofides, Mulder, and Tiffin 2003.

to 2001, they find significant associations between accounting standards and insolvency procedures, on the one hand, and sovereign spreads, on the other. Similarly, Cady reports that—for seven nations, 1990 to 2002—subscription to the IMF's Special Data Dissemination Standard (SDDS) is associated with smaller sovereign spreads (lower risk premiums).[60]

Using a larger set (sixty-one developed or developing) of countries, Mosley reports that, after controlling for a variety of economic factors, countries that subscribe to the IMF's SDDS have lower interest rate spreads.[61] Glennerster and Shin assess the impact of various transparency-related reforms (the publication of IMF Article IV assessments; of IMF/ World Bank Reports on the Observance of Standards and Codes; and compliance with the SDDS) on sovereign spreads in twenty-three emerging market countries, during the period from 1999 to 2002.[62] Again, their analyses—which also account for potential endogeneity and selection bias—suggest that these transparency-enhancing events are associated with lower interest rate spreads, particularly for countries with a low initial level of transparency. Tong takes a slightly different approach, assessing the impact of SDDS fulfillment on equity investment analysts' forecasts of firm earnings.[63] Using data for thirty emerging market countries, covering 1990 to 2004, Tong finds that SDDS subscription increases the accuracy, and decreases the variance, of earnings forecasts.

Other studies provide a less sanguine view of the effectiveness of market discipline. Sundararajan and colleagues report that, for a cross-section of thirty-five developing nations in the late 1990s, adherence to the Basel I core principles has no impact on sovereign spreads.[64] Similarly, Schneider's analysis reveals no significant relationship between subscription to the SDDS and sovereign spreads.[65] One issue with these studies is that the number of countries sometimes is quite small (e.g. seven in Cady's, eleven

---

[60] Cady 2004.

[61] Mosley 2006. This result is based on annual data for the 1990–2000 period. A similar result obtains when sovereign spreads, rather than interest rate spreads generally, are used as the dependent variable. Using the former, however, reduces the sample to twenty countries. Moreover, this finding is robust to using a measure of compliance with—rather than subscription to—the SDDS.

[62] Glennerster and Shin 2008.

[63] Tong 2007.

[64] Sundararajan, Marston, and Basu 2001. Podpiera (2006), however, reports a statistically significant relationship between adherence to the Basel Accord's core principles and banking sector performance, measured in terms of nonperforming loans and net interest margin. Additionally, Demirigüç-Kunt, Detragiache, and Tressel (2006) find a positive relationship between a given country's compliance with Basel core principles and the soundness of that country's private banks.

[65] Schneider 2005. And Tong argues that, as SDDS participation grows, the number of analysts who forecast firms' earnings for that country declines. Public information may crowd out, rather than substitute for, private information.

in Schneider's). Another is that many studies use data from the early 1990s, but the movement toward standards did not begin until at least the mid-1990s. Their findings, however, also are supported by Mosley's assessment of the IMF's efforts to encourage the dissemination of national economic data; she reports that professional investors display little awareness of, and therefore little reaction to, adherence to the data standard (SDDS).[66]

Considering the bivariate relationships between country risk premiums and compliance with various standards suggests similarly mixed results.[67] There is a negative correlation ($-.35$ in 2005, and $-.47$ in 2006) between the overall level of compliance with the Financial Stability Forum's twelve codes and standards and a country's sovereign risk premium. For forty-eight developing and transition nations,[68] both 2005 and 2006 data suggest that greater compliance is rewarded with lower borrowing costs.[69] Negative correlations between sovereign spreads and compliance levels also exist, for emerging market nations, for every other key financial standard. While the correlations vary in magnitude ($-.03$ for auditing in 2006, compared with $-.39$ for securities regulation, $-.32$ for data dissemination, and $-.44$ for fiscal transparency), most range from $-.3$ to $-.4$, suggesting that market participants assign lower risk premiums to developing countries that meet international standards.

At the same time, however, when measures of overall compliance with key financial standards (from eStandards) or of compliance with the IMF's SDDS (based on IMF assessments of compliance) are included in multivariate models of stock market valuation or government bond market spreads, they often are not significantly associated with financial market performance.[70] While further development of quantitative measures of compliance (using a wider variety of standards) is necessary, these find-

---

[66] Mosley 2003b. Note, though, that Glennerster and Shin (2008) find pronounced sovereign debt market reactions to the IMF's release of country-specific macroeconomic information. At least indirectly, then, transparency-related standards and reforms appear to affect market participants' behavior.

[67] Compliance scores are from eStandards, as below. Country risk premiums are taken from Aswath Damodaran's data set, available at http://pages.stern.nyu.edu/~adamodar/New_Home_Page/datafile/ctryprem.html (accessed May 15, 2008).

[68] Countries included, based on data availability, are Argentina, Bolivia, Brazil, Bulgaria, Chile, China, Colombia, Croatia, Czech Republic, Dominican Republic, Egypt, Ecuador, Estonia, Guatemala, Honduras, Hong Kong, Hungary, India, Indonesia, Israel, Jordan, Kazakhstan, Latvia, Lebanon, Lithuania, Malaysia, Mexico, Morocco, Pakistan, Peru, Philippines, Poland, Romania, Russia, Saudi Arabia, Singapore, Slovakia, Slovenia, South Africa, Taiwan, Thailand, Tunisia, Turkey, United Arab Emirates, Ukraine, Uruguay, Venezuela, and Vietnam.

[69] For OECD nations ($N = 22$), the bivariate correlation between overall compliance and interest rate spreads is $-.02$ in 2005, but $-.48$ in 2006.

[70] Also see Mosley and Singer 2008.

ings call the "market discipline" mechanism into question. One possibility is that, while it is relatively cheap to sign onto international standards, actual compliance is more costly. Another possibility is adverse selection: perhaps governments—especially emerging market nations—that are more concerned with a reputation for creditworthiness[71] also are more likely to accede to (but not necessarily comply with) certain financial standards.

Second, we might consider the relationships between the degree of private sector involvement and the implementation of global standards. Do areas of global financial governance with greater private sector involvement demonstrate higher levels of compliance? Table 7.1 provides some sense of the variation in the degree of private actor involvement. I use compliance with standards as a proxy for their effectiveness. I rely on compliance measures developed by eStandards Forum,[72] a private-sector-based effort to monitor compliance and to provide cross-country summary data to market participants.

eStandards Forum provides assessments of compliance with twelve global standards,[73] listed in bold in table 7.1. These are available for between fifty-five and eighty-three developed and developing nations, depending on the standard. The data reported reflect scores in August 2006.[74] eStandards Forum assessments are on a five-point scale—"no compliance," "intent declared," "enacted," "compliance in progress," and "full compliance." I assign ordinal scores to these categories, ranging from 0 for no compliance to 4 for full compliance. Like any one-dimensional measure, these scores can overlook the complexity of regulatory efforts,[75] but they allow for useful macro-comparisons across countries and across standards.

Figure 7.1 reports the average levels of compliance with various standards for OECD countries, emerging market nations, and the entire sample. Higher scores represent greater compliance. Governance arrangements are classified as mostly public (on the left; money laundering, fiscal transparency, monetary transparency); mixed public-private (data dissemination, corporate governance, securities regulation, and insurance supervision); or mostly private (on the right; accounting and auditing).

---

[71] E.g., Tomz 2007.

[72] See IMF 2003, and www.estandardsforum.com. Compliance also could be assessed using reports (ROSCs) from the IMF–World Bank Financial Sector Assessment Program. See Petrie 2003; Schneider 2005.

[73] Until September 2005, eStandards Forum separated one of the twelve FSF key standards—payment systems—into general principles of payments and central bank payments. Compliance scores are now given for twelve standards.

[74] Data collected in August 2004 and August 2005 are similar; some 2006 averages are slightly—but not significantly—higher.

[75] E.g., Schneider 2003, 2005.

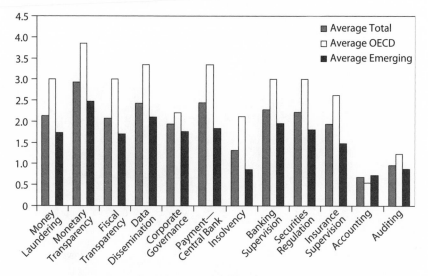

Figure 7.1   Compliance with International Standards

For this figure, the enforcement and establishment dimensions of table 7.1 are collapsed.[76]

As we would expect, given technical and political resources, compliance levels are highest among OECD countries. Variance tends to be greater among emerging market nations.[77] Compliance is highest for rules regarding monetary policymaking transparency, data dissemination, central bank payments systems, and banking supervision. The average compliance score for these measures ranges from 1.84 (payments in emerging markets) to 2.93 (monetary policy transparency in the entire sample). Monetary transparency and payments principles were publicly created rules, and one could argue that the pressure from powerful countries and from the IMF (especially for monetary policymaking) motivates compliance. Global banking regulations are based on a combination of public and private sector activity; the relatively high compliance with those rules provides modest support for the efficiency hypothesis. The next set of standards, in terms of compliance outcomes, includes securities regulation (overall compliance level of 2.22), money laundering (2.13), and fiscal transparency (2.08).

What do these outcomes tell us about the impact of private sector participation on regulatory performance? Figure 7.2 summarizes compliance

[76] A similar pattern emerges if we array rules according only to the nature of enforcement (as opposed to both establishment and enforcement).

[77] For banking supervision, however, OECD variance is markedly greater.

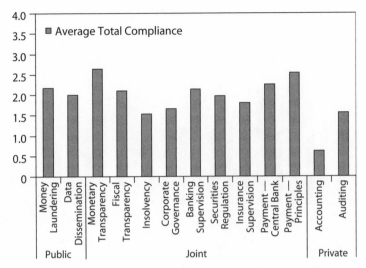

Figure 7.2 Compliance with Rule Establishment

according to the nature (public versus private) of rule establishment. It suggests, again, that the answer is mixed: fiscal transparency and data dissemination were established largely in the public sphere, while securities regulation and insurance supervision reflect a public-private balance. Despite these differences, their compliance levels are relatively similar, suggesting (not surprisingly) that other factors—perhaps IMF and World Bank pressure, as well as domestic technical capacity —are at play. Furthermore, among the standards with the lowest levels of compliance are corporate governance (1.94 overall compliance average), insolvency (1.53), auditing (0.96), and accounting (0.68). Two of these rules (insolvency and corporate governance) were established in a mixed public-private setting.

Auditing and accounting, on the other hand, were established almost entirely in the private sphere and rely mostly on private enforcement. Levels of compliance with auditing rules (1.22 in OECD nations, 0.87 in emerging markets) are below most of the publicly enforced rules, hinting at problems with private sector enforcement and rule establishment. Levels of compliance with accounting rules are particularly low, and—unlike every other standard—levels of compliance are lower in OECD (0.55) than in emerging market (0.72) nations, a pattern that was also reflected in 2004 and 2005 data.[78] Here, rule making is entirely based in the pri-

[78] The eStandards Forum's methodology for international accounting standards was updated in November 2004, to reflect revisions to IAS. Prior to this revision, the average level of compliance was 1.10 (still lowest among the thirteen standards).

vate sector, yet compliance is very low, at least by the judgments of the eStandards staff.

What, then, are we to conclude about the potential linkages between private sector participation and compliance? Global standards that are housed entirely in the private sphere do not have higher compliance. This may be the result of several factors. First, the four standards with the lowest average implementation—corporate governance, accounting, auditing, and insolvency—also are those that the World Bank is charged with overseeing, via the IMF/World Bank Reports on Standards and Codes (ROSCs). The IMF is responsible, using the voluntary ROSC assessments, for surveying the other standards; most ROSCs to date concern those eight codes,[79] although assessments of auditing and accounting, and of corporate governance, have become more common.[80] Perhaps, then, indirect market pressures—in which private actors respond to public reports on implementation—operate more strongly for IMF-monitored than for World Bank–monitored standards.[81] Second, the compliance data remind us that, when there are disagreements over the content of global standards, their effectiveness will suffer, regardless of the role of private actors. Recent tensions between U.S. and European governments and firms regarding accounting standards, for example, surely play a role in depressing compliance.[82]

Third, and more importantly, these patterns suggest that standards housed entirely in the private domain (with both private regulatory and supervisory roles) may lack teeth. Market-based enforcement assumes that investors are aware of the content of, and national compliance with, standards. If market participants are unaware of standards, or if they remain unconvinced of their utility, they are unlikely to base their asset allocation decisions on them. Alternatively, investors may find some standards difficult to evaluate with simple information shortcuts. If investors pay little attention to governments' compliance with global rules, governments' incentives to enact them will decline.[83] Moreover, if global capital markets are prone to booms and busts, as they were in the 1990s and continue to be today, they will be inconsistent enforcers of standards.[84]

And admittedly, the country and issue coverage of these data is skewed: there are no internationally recognized standards for hedge fund gover-

[79] Schneider 2003, 2005.

[80] Only a few assessments of insolvency have been performed. The World Bank continues to develop an assessment methodology in this area.

[81] This assumes that investors respond to the information contained in ROSCs, either on their own or via the effects of the reports on their information sources (such as credit ratings agencies). See Petrie's (2003) survey of ratings agencies, and Schneider 2005.

[82] E.g., Crouzet and Véron 2002; Glaum and Street 2003; Quinn 2004.

[83] Mosley 2003b; Petrie 2003.

[84] King and Sinclair 2003.

nance, nor are "offshore havens" such as the Cayman Islands included in the set of nations monitored by eStandards. Indeed, where offshore havens allow firms to escape the regulatory oversight of national governments, the only governance option may be the private sector. But absent a credible threat of public sector intervention and regulation—which may drive many private actors to cooperate on self-regulation in the first place—the prospects for any type of regulation of some financial sector activities seem bleak. More generally, this highlights the importance of selection in our analyses of institutional effectiveness: only a subset of international financial issues is subject to global governance; and, within that subset, the choice among private, private-public, and fully public regulation is not a random one.

Finally, the lack of a connection between private sector involvement and levels of implementation may highlight problems with self-regulation. Recent corporate accounting scandals and subsequent legislative changes in the United States and Europe remind us that private actors sometimes avoid, or defect from, self-regulatory commitments. The concentration of technical expertise in the hands of private actors could make it difficult for public sector agents to monitor independently the enforcement of international rules[85]– a classic principal-agent problem.[86] Therefore, while there is an argument to be made about the contribution of private actors to enforcement, there also are reasons to worry that this will not hold in all cases.

Conclusions and Future Directions

The preliminary evidence presented above suggests that market discipline may not be an effective means of enforcing global financial standards. This outcome may result, in part, from a lack of awareness of the content of global rules, in situations where private actors' role is more supervisory than regulatory (rendering them perhaps unaware of the specific content of new standards). In terms of policy, how might the international community address this issue? One possibility is to involve the private sector more heavily in establishing rules, as with recent revisions to banking and corporate governance standards. This strategy, though, would have dis-

[85] Underhill and Zhang 2003.

[86] Potoski and Prakash's (2005) study of U.S. firms, however, suggests that participation in a voluntary environmental standard (ISO 14001) renders firms' compliance more likely, even controlling for selection. For an analogous process to occur in finance, privately based standards would need to develop a positive "brand image" with market participants, IFIs, or national governments.

tributional effects: where private sector actors have greater involvement in the design of financial governance, those systems will reflect more closely the interests of organized finance.[87]

If this distributional prediction—private sector participation in the regulatory phase increases the effectiveness of supervision, but also alters the content of financial governance—is correct, it presents a conundrum for the international community. Given that private actors control a great deal of financial resources, and given that the success of rules could hinge on their responses to such rules, it is important to "bail in" these entities.[88] But private actors often will not act on the basis of public interest, and they are even less accountable to domestic publics than are indirectly democratic IGOs.[89] Another possibility, then, is to consider whether hybrid systems of governance (in which private actors play key roles, but are backstopped by public authorities) produce an appropriate balance between effectiveness and equity.

In terms of the domain of this chapter, further empirical assessments of the effectiveness hypothesis are necessary. Such studies should assess further the linkages between interest rate spreads and compliance (with a range of standards, rather than only data dissemination and banking regulations), using more countries and more recent years (as data become available). Event history analyses also could be useful, testing whether there are well-defined breaks in sovereign spreads that result from signing on to, or being judged in compliance with, a given standard. Additionally, to trace the causal mechanisms behind the effectiveness conjecture, we should systematically survey private investors regarding their views of various standards, and then assess whether investors' involvement (directly, or via business associations) in creating rules correlates with their awareness of and attitudes toward standards.

In broader terms, our understanding of the causes and consequences of new forms of global cooperation and governance remains limited. The challenge is much the same as Keohane and Nye identified: to move away from state- or intergovernmental-oriented paradigms, and to think systematically about the role of private actors.[90] Along these lines, we should continue to theorize about the causal mechanisms through which private sector participation interacts with other variables to produce regulatory outcomes in the realm of financial markets. Additionally, once we address the general phenomenon of private actors, we should assess differences in forms of private participation. It may be the case that some types of private

[87] E.g., Crouzet and Véron 2002; Simmons 2001; Slaughter 2004.
[88] E.g., Eichengreen 1999.
[89] Eatwell and Taylor 2002; Underhill and Zhang 2003; Vojta and Uzan 2003.
[90] Keohane and Nye 1977.

involvement (enforcement against other actors) promote compliance, while other types (self-regulation) detract from it.[91] Furthermore, research in this area should consider the linkages among various financial governance efforts. A country that responds to IMF pressures in the area of banking regulation may be more likely also to change its economic data dissemination practices. Perhaps, then, under such circumstances, the various substantive standards and rules in finance (many of which are listed in table 7.1) are not independent of one another. Rather, they might be treated as "regime complexes" or "networks of networks,"[92] each covering a set of problems and issues in the financial realm. Addressing such issues will allow scholarship on international governance to keep pace with evolving realities.

[91] Also see Cutler, Haufler, and Porter 1999.
[92] Raustiala and Victor 2004; Slaughter 2004.

CHAPTER 8

Power, Interdependence, and Domestic Politics in International Environmental Cooperation

Elizabeth R. DeSombre

ROBERT O. KEOHANE'S WORK HAS BEEN central to understanding international cooperation on environmental issues. The most obvious aspect of this contribution can be seen in the formulation of neoliberal institutionalist theory, which explains both the incentives for and process of cooperation. It indicates both why international environmental cooperation is a rational endeavor and how we might expect the types of cooperation to play out. Similarly, the concept of complex interdependence indicates the types of power dynamics that can underpin cooperation, suggesting that even in situations where everyone gains from cooperation, there will be some actors who have a greater ability than others to influence the shape and content of the cooperative arrangements that result.[1] Sometimes these actors are those that have traditionally been powerful, though it may be that they use different methods of persuasion on this issue area than others, in ways that can be understood via complex interdependence. And in other cases, neoliberal institutionalism helps to explain how traditionally powerless states come to play an important role in international environmental politics; resources other than military force or threats can be power resources in an environmentally interdependent world.

Because most environmental issues are themselves common pool resources and thus require cooperation from all relevant actors to mitigate a given problem, the powerful actors shaping cooperation may be those without large traditional power resources like military or economic might, but instead gain their influence simply through their ability to threaten credibly to stay outside the process of cooperation. This formulation allows us to understand the seemingly disproportionate level of influence developing countries have had in international environmental cooperation, and also predict the arenas in which their power will succeed or fail. Finally, opening up the institutionalist approach to further consideration of domestic politics can further help illuminate the specifics of this cooperative process, by suggesting what strategies states will pursue on

[1] Keohane and Nye 1977.

what issues (and what power resources they will bring to bear) when approaching international environmental cooperation.

Rational Environmental Cooperation

Most international environmental issues contain some aspect of prisoner's dilemma incentives: initial cooperation may be difficult despite benefits to those who participate, but the fact that cooperation brings collective benefits can, with the proper institutional structure, lead to successful international agreement. In most cases when facing a global environmental problem a state's first choice would be for the rest of the world to undertake the costly activities necessary to protect the environment, while it free rides on their efforts. In this situation the environmental problem would thereby be mostly mitigated (an outcome shared among all states in the system), without the state itself having to take action. The worst option, conversely, is to take unilateral action while the rest of the world does nothing; the state in question would thus bear all of the costs but gain no significant benefits, as the environmental problem would not be fundamentally ameliorated. In between are the two options most often encountered—the one most frequently predicted by economists, in which no states take substantial action in hopes of either successfully free riding or at least avoiding the sucker's payoff, and the cooperative outcome, in which all states obtain their second-best outcome by cooperatively restricting their behavior and thereby positively protecting the environmental amenity in question.

In fact, environmental issues fit a prisoner's dilemma model better than most issues of international cooperation. This issue structure is particularly relevant for environmental problems with characteristics of common pool resources—those that are not excludable (meaning that the resource can be accessed, either practically or legally, by all) but that are subtractable (meaning that they can be diminished by additional use).[2] Some argue that most environmental problems have these characteristics to a relevant degree.[3] In this structure the prisoner's dilemma is especially stark, because any major actor that remains apart from the cooperative system does not simply diminish the cooperation (as may be the case with fewer states in a free trade or development assistance agreement), but may be able to prevent it altogether. Consider, for instance, a fishery. Even if most of the relevant actors in the system agree to limit their fishing, the cooperation can be undermined by one actor that does not follow the lim-

---

[2] This is also sometimes called rival, or "joint of supply."
[3] Barkin and Shambaugh 1999; Keohane and Ostrom 1995.

its. Similar situations can be found in ocean or atmospheric pollution, where emissions by one sufficiently important state can weaken any reductions undertaken by all others, possibly even to the point where the reductions fail to accomplish significant environmental improvement. For common pool resources, the lack of involvement by one major state does not just decrease the quality of the cooperation, but may be able to undermine its effects completely. In a game-theoretic matrix, then, the differences between the payoffs for cooperation and defection are much larger for CPR issues than for public or club goods.

Many international environmental agreements take this incentive structure into consideration. In most recent environmental treaties there is not only the standard clause requiring a certain number of ratifications before the treaty enters into force, but also a mandate that those ratifiers account for a certain degree of the activity responsible for the environmental problem. For example, the Montreal Protocol on Substances that Deplete the Ozone Layer[4] only entered into force when at least eleven states, with emissions of ozone-depleting substances from 1986 collectively totaling two-thirds of global emissions of that year, ratified the agreement.[5] The Kyoto Protocol to the Framework Convention on Climate Change required ratification by fifty-five states that collectively account for 55 percent of greenhouse gas emissions of Annex I parties from 1990.[6] States know that moving ahead with cooperative agreements before a majority of those primarily responsible have signed on would be a foolish endeavor because of the CPR nature of these problems.

Similarly, unlike with many economic issues, staying outside of cooperative arrangements for environmental protection is not a neutral endeavor; it can itself be seen as a form of defection from cooperative arrangements, since on almost all global environmental issues all states contribute, or have the potential to contribute, to the problem. If a state does not enter into a trade agreement, it does not gain the advantages of the trade agreement, but the rest of the world can continue to cooperate and enjoy the benefits of free trade without it. But if a state chooses to remain apart from cooperative efforts to protect the environment, it may prevent others from succeeding in their quest to do so. This factor makes environmental issues in some ways more closely akin to security issues than to the economic issues with which they are more frequently compared, since states that choose to remain apart from security arrangements can

---

[4] Montreal Protocol on Substances that Deplete the Ozone Layer, 1987.

[5] Montreal Protocol on Substances that Deplete the Ozone Layer, 1987, Article 16.

[6] Kyoto Protocol to the United Nations Framework Convention on Climate Change, 1997, Article 25(1). Annex I parties are the developed states that have emissions reductions obligations under the agreement; 1990 is the base year from which emissions reductions are calculated.

have an impact on the overall functioning of the security system in a way that is less true of economic cooperation.

International institutions are especially good at addressing the incentive problems that can lead to collectively suboptimal choices in a prisoner's dilemma model, and we see that especially clearly in international environmental agreements. Environmental issues are particularly amenable to the Coasian incentives for international cooperation elaborated in *After Hegemony*.[7] International institutions are created precisely to address the lack of property rights (known more frequently in political science circles as legal liability)[8] inherent in many environmental issues, the creation and exchange of information is often the most central aspect of efforts to cooperate internationally on environmental issues, and the role of international institutions in decreasing transaction costs apparent in other issue areas (and discussed extensively by Michael Gilligan in this volume) is of importance in cooperation on environmental issues as well.

Coase's theorem predicts cooperation in a self-help system when actors recognize joint benefits from doing so; he nevertheless outlines a set of conditions required to make that cooperation possible.[9] Property rights are necessary because unless it is specified who has legal control over the resources about which actors negotiate, there is no ability to reach a cooperative arrangement about how to manage them. Property rights on the international level are of necessity imperfect. On the one hand, sovereignty itself is a strong property right, but it is precisely because sovereign authority cannot protect states from the impacts of environmental influxes across borders that international environmental cooperation is necessary. And because sovereignty is sufficiently strong, states are unwilling to cede too much influence to international organizations to make decisions for them.

In international relations, broadly, property rights are usually taken to be the kind of legal approaches represented by international regimes themselves;[10] these are the rules of the game and processes for cooperation set up by international institutions. But some aspects of property rights are more directly created in the way these regimes are negotiated. For instance, the United Nations Convention on the Law of the Sea specified the extent of ocean over which individual states could exercise sovereign control,[11] which then impacted the way international environmental agreements approached common governance of the ocean. In this case, a large number of fisheries treaties were renegotiated after the nego-

---

[7] Keohane 1984.

[8] Keohane, 1984, 88.

[9] Coase 1960.

[10] Keohane 1984, 89.

[11] United Nations Convention on the Law of the Sea (1982), Articles 55–75.

tiation of the law of the sea, to adapt their regulatory processes to the question of who actually had the legal right to regulate in which areas of the ocean.[12]

The broader context of property rights or legal liability can, in some cases, reflect what Haas, Keohane, and Levy termed the "contractual environment" that may be a necessary condition for addressing international environmental issues.[13] International institutions can improve the contractual environment, by providing an arena in which rule making can be easily done, and providing the kind of monitoring that allows for reciprocation in the case of free riding. In most cooperative exercises related to the prisoner's dilemma (and to an even greater extent in the CPR version most environmental issues represent) the biggest threat to cooperation comes when it is possible that others may free ride, since that fear alone can lead those who collectively benefit from cooperation to eschew participating in it.

The mechanisms of this sort contained in environmental agreements are generally weak: most data on compliance comes from self-reports from member states. This weakness relates to the endogeneity problem Ronald Mitchell identifies in his chapter in this volume: states that may consider not living up to their obligations under an agreement will be unlikely to agree to intrusive monitoring provisions. Nevertheless, the main advantage of reporting is to give states evidence that other states are living up to their obligations or reassurance that it is possible to know whether states are doing so or not. So even a minimal degree of reporting can begin to fulfill this function and make states more willing to enter into such agreements. Moreover, environmental agreements may have an implicit additional check on self-reporting, since information collected on the environmental conditions themselves can sometimes give a broader sense of whether or not states are giving accurate reports. For example, during the era when commercial whaling was allowed but the number and size of whales that could be caught were restricted by the International Whaling Commission, statistical analysis conducted by the organization suggested that the number of whales reported as caught within only a foot over the minimum size was statistically impossible;[14] it was thus possible to know that behavior reporting compliance was likely incorrect.

Focusing more directly on the legal liability aspect of property rights, the development of international environmental law has created a set of liability norms that impact the expectations states face as they negotiate international environmental agreements. Though honored sometimes in

[12] Peterson 1993.
[13] Keohane, Haas, and Levy 1993.
[14] Birnie 1985, 338.

the breach, these principles, such as the polluter pays principle or the precautionary principle, have been widely accepted as the starting point for international negotiations. There are certainly agreements in which straight power dynamics determine which states contribute the most to efforts to mitigate environmental problems,[15] though these power dynamics are themselves often environment-specific. But the well-known principle that states have "the sovereign right to exploit their own resources . . . and the responsibility to ensure that activities within their jurisdiction or control do not cause damage to the environment of other states"[16] serves as a basis for and is integrated into many recent international environmental agreements.[17]

But we can also think about property rights or legal liability on the domestic level as being a precursor to successful international cooperation. This is at least part of what Haas, Keohane, and Levy refer to as capacity, which includes the ability of states to credibly commit to being able to undertake the necessary domestic changes to live up to the international agreements they reach. If a state does not believe that the other states it is contracting with actually have the ability to follow through on their promises, it would be foolish to make an agreement with them, particularly in a CPR-laden prisoner's dilemma situation. Institutions themselves can help create this domestic capacity, including by creating a structure for economic assistance, an issue discussed further below.

Coase's second criterion is information. He notes that perfect information is the ideal; perfection is even less likely on the international level than in the domestic realm he describes, but certainly anything that moves closer to that goal makes cooperation in a self-help situation more feasible. The creation and exchange of information is often seen as one of the primary roles of international institutions for environmental protection. Uncertainty about the cause, extent, and implications of environmental problems is frequently given as a reason for lack of international cooperation. It can be difficult to undertake actions with certain short-term costs in the hopes they will produce (uncertain) benefits in the longer run. Doing so is even more difficult on the time scales at which many environmental problems operate, since the problems predicted would likely have their major impact long after the term in office of the decision makers in question has ended.

[15] As a power explanation would predict, sometimes these are ones in which those who bear the greatest effect of the pollution are the most responsible for contributing to the cleanup. See, for example, Bernauer 1996.

[16] Rio Declaration on Environment and Development, 1992, Principle 2.

[17] To name just a few examples: the Convention on the Prevention of Marine Pollution by Dumping of Wastes and Other Matter, 1972, preamble; Vienna Convention for the Protection of the Ozone Layer, 1985, preamble; Stockholm Convention on Persistent Organic Pollutants, 2001, Preamble.

Most international environmental agreements make information gathering their first priority in the process of addressing an environmental problem. It is now common for international environmental cooperation to begin with a "framework convention" that outlines agreement on the general concept at issue, but does not yet require specific abatement measures. Framework conventions almost always create provisions for research and information exchange. Some cynically regard such processes as consolation prizes when substantive cooperation is not yet possible, but frequently these agreements lay the groundwork for more and faster abatement than would otherwise have been possible. Sometimes the process of information gathering demonstrates to states that there are problems they have an interest in solving that previously they did not know about. For example, the required surveys of the health of forest resource conducted under the Convention on Long-Range Transboundary Air Pollution turned up damage to Germany's forests of which it was not aware; in the wake of this new knowledge it was transformed from a cooperation laggard to a leader.[18] This information at minimum modified its cardinal payoff values within a game-theoretic structure and may have actually changed its preference orderings as it began to care about addressing an issue it previously would not have wanted to expend much effort to mitigate. Similarly, the phaseout schedule for ozone-depleting substances under the Montreal Protocol has been substantially accelerated because of new information turned up by the scientific process coordinated and disseminated through the Vienna Convention process, indicating both that the ozone layer was more threatened than had previously been understood, and that options for addressing the problem were more realistic than previously imagined.[19]

Interestingly, however, complete information is not always directly advantageous to cooperation. Sometimes uncertainty creates an incentive to cooperate precisely because states are risk averse and want to protect themselves from possibly bad outcomes that might happen. In particular, sometimes not knowing how much a given state contributes to or suffers from a given problem may make a more cooperative outcome easier.[20] It has been suggested that the 1991 environmental protocol to the Antarctic Treaty, which contains a long-term ban on minerals mining on the continent, was made easier by the fact that states that claim territory in the region did not know whether they had vast mineral resources under their claimed land, since those who knew they had these resources might not have been willing to give up their access to them.[21] Savvy institutions

[18] Levy 1993, 92–93.
[19] Parson 2003.
[20] Na and Shin 1998.
[21] Susskind 1994, 66–67.

know how to use uncertainty to their advantage. For example, scientists affiliated with the United Nations Environment Programme (UNEP), overseeing negotiations to protect the Mediterranean Sea from pollution, allowed the popular understanding of the ocean as a purely nondirectional issue to persist, even though ocean currents are sufficiently slow and directional that some states experience more harm than others depending on where they are located in the current flow. They knew that providing clear information on who the winners or losers were from cooperation would decrease the willingness of some to cooperate, and thus chose to keep that information to themselves.[22]

The effort to decrease transaction costs, Coase's third criterion, is the most obvious impetus for multilateral cooperation generally, as discussed in Gilligan's chapter; again, this incentive is particularly strong in the area of the environment. The common-pool resource nature of environmental issues again contributes to the importance of this factor. One of the main arguments for multilateral cooperation rather than a large set of bilateral agreements across all relevant states is that the economies of scale represented by acting multilaterally can create an enormous savings in the costs of individual negotiations and procedures needed to maintain the agreements. Again, this difference is especially stark for CPR problems, because the costs of negotiation would likely increase as some number of actors are in cooperative agreements and others are outside; those outside would be able to demand greater concessions to join, and those inside would be increasingly likely to defect if it looked as though some major players would remain outside the system. Prisoner's dilemma scenarios are by definition contingent decisions, and a two-player game simplifies the extent of this contingency. Multilateral environmental cooperation dramatically reduces the transaction costs that come from states making contingent decisions under conditions where some nonparticipating states can undermine the effects of cooperation.

Similarly, the kind of economic aid that has become emblematic of international environmental agreements is also best distributed through international institutions, which avoids the specific bargaining over what will be provided, in return for what activities, each time a developing state asks for aid in return for action. This process has a dynamic similar to the one described above, in that states asking for aid would have the ability to strike a continually harder bargain over time as other states, sufficiently invested in the collaborative effort, could less afford to have defections by major developing states. Interestingly though, the large developing countries that first bargained for environmental aid might have

[22] Haas 1990.

been able to strike a better deal for themselves on the initial issues (such as ozone depletion) if they had asked for individual compensation rather than the creation of a general mechanism; similarly the developed countries might have been able to better target their aid to those whose participation was most needed if they had simply made side-payments to the major users of (for example) ozone-depleting substances among the developing countries.[23] It may have been for reasons of transaction costs that the developed countries did not push this option. Certainly for developing countries the principle that was created initially when the first global funding mechanisms to address environmental issues began has been easier to integrate into future agreements as a generalized obligation to provide aid for developing countries than would have been the case for particularized side-payments to influential states.

And, of course, international institutions for the environment can address the same kinds of transaction costs more generally ameliorated by international institutions, such as providing a place for policymakers from different states to interact regularly, with a set of rules about how those interactions will take place, that precludes having to discuss process any time a decision needs to be made. Most international environmental institutions, as is the case in most other international institutions, have specific decision rules that substantially lower transaction costs for future decisions. And since environmental agreements often require the changing of obligations, as new information about the condition of the environment and the impact of earlier rules becomes known, the creation of such a process is an enormous savings in transaction costs over beginning negotiation anew.

The specific refinement of these theories as they apply to efforts to create international environmental institutions and their financial mechanisms helps explain the issues on which cooperation transpires or fails to occur. The states in question need sufficient concern about the issue, capacity to undertake domestic and international efforts to address it, and a contractual environment in which commitments will likely be honored. While these may be necessary conditions for cooperation, they can often be created or augmented by existing institutions, or by a smaller subset of initially cooperating states. Environmental cooperation, because of its important reliance on information and resolution of uncertainty, the likelihood that it will involve repeated interactions and progressive tightening of rules, and the extent to which successful cooperation requires involving all or most states, relies particularly heavily on these factors.

[23] DeSombre and Kauffman 1996.

The Complex Interdependence of the Commons

Keohane's earlier work, less directly devoted to examining environmental issues, is nevertheless of particular importance in further elaboration of environmental cooperation. An essential but occasionally overlooked element in examining international environmental politics is the role of power. Because transboundary environmental issues appear to provide circumstances in which cooperation is better for all those involved than noncooperation, it is easy to overlook the extent to which threat and coercion may play a role in determining the existence and form of environmental cooperation. Access to resources, control over a market for particular goods, or even a lack of concern about an environmental issue can be a source of power for a state that wants to shape the structure of international cooperation to its benefit. That all states may be better off in the aggregate from environmental cooperation should not blind us to the fact that some may be better placed to gain more than others, and that the types of collective arrangements chosen to address these issues will impact how much a state gains.

Others have noted the role of power and coercion in providing the mechanism to create, or hold together, international cooperation with prisoner's dilemma incentives. These factors can also play a role at the point of creating cooperative outcomes in the first place. Though there are joint gains to be had from environmental cooperation, the impetus to push for it generally comes from one or a small number of states particularly concerned about a given issue. Such leadership can be expressed by organizing meetings, but it can also be expressed by using other means of persuasion to entice states toward cooperation. The United States, during the era when it was a leader in domestic and international environmental protection, often pushed other states to take collective action by using threats of economic sanctions.[24] In this case, the power was economic (and more specific than that since the sanctions in question involved access to particular markets) rather than military.

Several international environmental institutions, particularly those pertaining to fisheries, have also begun to use economic restrictions against nonparticipating states, led by initial unilateral action of this type by individual states such as the United States and Japan. A number of regional fishery management organizations now require that their members restrict trade in regulated species, only importing or transshipping fish caught by members of the agreements or by those vessels that can otherwise demonstrate that they are operating within its restrictions.[25]

[24] Charnovitz 1994.
[25] DeSombre 2005.

The CPR structure of international environmental problems (itself evidence of complex interdependence, as described by Keohane and Nye)[26] also gives particular opportunities to developing countries to use the kinds of power they gain from the fact that their participation is necessary for a successfully cooperative outcome to address environmental problems. It is here that Keohane and Nye's argument that "power resources specific to issue areas will be most relevant"[27] is clearest, since developing countries not only generally have little military power, but also have much less economic power than the major industrialized states that have traditionally been the instigators of international cooperation for the environment. The nonparticipation of developing countries in measures to protect the global atmosphere would ultimately create a sucker's payoff for developed country cooperation, in which costly mitigation efforts by developed states would be swamped by the increasing emissions from rapidly industrializing states. Because of this issue structure, developing states have been willing to make their participation in global environmental agreements conditional on measures providing them economic and technical aid. Their power is neither economic nor military: it is environmental. The power they (especially large developing states) have is the power to destroy an environmental resource. This power comes, in part, from the ability to demonstrate that they care less about the environmental problem than other states do.

The first serious instance of this "greenmail" was in the negotiation of the international agreements to protect the ozone layer. Developing states, led by China and India, did not ratify the 1987 Montreal Protocol initially, arguing that it would preclude development options that to them were of a higher priority than protection of the ozone layer. The result of their credible threat to stay outside of the agreement and develop using substances prohibited within it was the creation of the Montreal Protocol Multilateral Fund. Under this agreement developed states give money to meet the full "incremental costs" of developing countries in complying with the agreement; after its creation all the major developing countries joined the Montreal Protocol. All major global environmental agreements negotiated since then have contained such funding mechanisms.

A similar organization with a broader mandate created around the same time is the Global Environment Facility (GEF), a mechanism created to provide funding to developing countries to address four specifically global environmental problems: climate change, loss of biodiversity, ozone depletion, and issues of transboundary water resources.[28] It is no surprise that its focus is specifically on transboundary environmental issues (and

[26] Keohane and Nye 1977.
[27] Keohane and Nye 1977, 37.
[28] Fairman 1996.

particularly those of the global commons); despite the way that developing countries may prioritize environmental risks, the ones on which they have enough bargaining leverage to get compensation for their cooperative action are the ones that the developed world cares most about and cannot successfully address without the participation of the less developed countries. The GEF has been expanded since its origins to include persistent organic pollutants and land degradation,[29] the latter being the only issue that is not obviously transboundary. In addition it has been designated the funding mechanism for several specific international agreements.

Also notable is the structure of decision making under these mechanisms. In most international institutions providing economic assistance, voting is pegged to contributions, so that donors have the greatest degree of influence over how the funding is used, with recipients hardly able to influence prioritization of funding. From the beginning the negotiations to set up the Montreal Protocol Multilateral Fund focused on how its decisions would be made, with developing countries refusing to participate unless their concerns were assuaged. They first successfully prevented the entirety of the funding process from being simply overseen by the World Bank (though the Bank is still one of the implementing agencies for the process). Instead, they successfully lobbied for the creation of a new institution altogether, with an executive committee comprising seven donor and seven recipient countries with rotating terms. Projects are approved by "double majority" voting, in which any decision not taken by consensus requires a two-thirds majority, which must include a majority of states in both blocs.[30] Even in the Global Environment Facility decisions are made by consensus in a council with split representation: sixteen developing states, fourteen industrialized states, and two states with economies in transition.[31]

In addition, it has become the norm to exempt developing states from some of the initial burdens of international cooperation on the environment, as a way to persuade them to participate. The original version of the Montreal Protocol did this in 1987 by offering developing country parties a ten-year lag in the obligations they would have to meet, specifically in the hopes of enticing them into the agreement. The same is true to a greater extent in the Kyoto Protocol, where developing countries were given no initial emissions abatement obligations. Though this is given as one of the arguments against U.S. participation (following CPR

[29] GEF, "Types of Projects," http://www.gefweb.org/What_is_the_GEF/what_is_the_gef.html#Projects (accessed December 29, 2004).
[30] DeSombre and Kauffman 1996.
[31] GEF, "Council," http://www.gefweb.org/participants/Council/council.html (accessed December 29, 2004).

logic, an agreement that exempts these states from obligations is doomed to fail), the whole idea of the protocol process is to get to the stage where these states will eventually be given obligations, and getting them into the process by having them ratify the agreement helps work toward that eventuality.

Environmental issues are representative of a particularly physical type of interdependence that impacts the political arrangements used to mitigate international problems. Because of this characteristic, they provide different types of power resources to states that they use to influence the structure and process of international cooperation. States with traditional power resources may find that these are not necessary or even effective for enticing cooperation among others or removing the incentive to free ride, but that other ways in which states are globally linked may prove more conducive to changing their incentives to cooperate. Similarly, states—particularly developing states—without traditional power resources gain important influence in international environmental cooperation because the CPR structure of the problems mean their participation is necessary. If they are willing to refuse to participate unless compensated, their power to destroy the resource, which comes in large part because of the structure of the issue area, can be an important, and previously ignored, power resource.

Domestic Sources of International Environmental Cooperation

But even when international cooperation benefits all involved, how does it begin? What drives those states that choose to help organize or maintain cooperative agreements to do so? Perhaps this question can best be answered by looking inside of the state. Doing so can help explain under what conditions, and in what ways, states are willing to work to organize cooperation.

As we know, states are not unitary actors. For much neoliberal institutionalist theory that insight may be irrelevant, if we can understand the basic character and process of international environmental cooperation sufficiently without having to descend to the less parsimonious domestic level. But once we recognize the basic outlines of the way international cooperation works among states in the international system, the specifics of how it actually happens may be gleaned from looking at the domestic level. In some cases this information may allow us to predict the form and process of cooperation in a more nuanced way than a simple analysis of the gains to be had from a cooperative outcome might allow.

Looking further at the role of domestic politics may shed additional light on the way in which power is exercised in international environmental cooperation. That states in the aggregate may be better off with cooperation overlooks the fact that within a given state some actors prefer different outcomes. One of the implications of complex interdependence is that it brings to bear intragovernmental negotiations as well as intergovernmental ones, since the lack of clear hierarchy among issues means that different policies a government can pursue (including different linkage strategies) will have different domestic impacts.[32] This phenomenon is true of most issues of international cooperation. For instance, free trade may raise the overall economic wealth of a state, but put out of work those people who work for an industry in which international firms can better compete. It would not be surprising to find different domestic views of cooperation on free trade, depending on whether one is likely to lose a job from lower trade barriers or be made wealthy by the new export opportunities (or cheaper imports) it provides. Disaggregating the state and examining theories about the interaction between domestic politics and international relations under interdependence may explain the conditions under which states will be willing (or able) to pursue international cooperation or to use particular types of threats or other incentives to push for their preferred cooperative outcome on any issue. Examining this dynamic for environmental politics adds additional factors to straight economic considerations, however, because some actors advocate for the environment based not on self-interest per se but on a broader ethical or normative concern for ecosystems. As Keohane, Haas, and Levy note, "if there is one key variable accounting for policy change, it is the degree of domestic environmentalist pressure in major industrialized democracies, not the decision-making rules of the relevant international institution."[33]

Keohane and Milner examine the intersection between domestic politics and international relations (and particularly what they call internationalization, the increase of trade and investment flows across states), but their edited volume on the subject looks at it primarily for the impacts of the international on the domestic.[34] These impacts, however, also work the other way; it is trade linkages that allow a state to use its economic might to nudge others toward the form and content of international cooperation it might prefer. The United States or Japan can credibly threaten other states to exclude their fishery products from domestic markets if these states do not undertake the cooperative efforts either state is pushing internationally, precisely because the market for fish is international and the United States and Japan are the primary importers. It is the

[32] Keohane and Nye 1987.
[33] Keohane, Haas, and Levy 1993, 14.
[34] Keohane and Milner 1996.

dependence of other states on the U.S. or Japanese fishery markets (for example) that makes these threats sufficiently serious that target states change their preference orderings for cooperation.[35]

Why the United States, or any state, threatens in this particular form can only be understood by examining the domestic political structure. After all, considering the range of U.S. power resources, threatening imports of fishery products is a fairly small threat. Perhaps if this level of threat were sufficient to succeed in a goal, it would be a choice that would not need to open the state to further examination, because we could simply conclude that states threaten only the minimal action needed in order to get the cooperative ends they desire.

But sometimes this type of threat is not enough to accomplish the desired policy change. On one issue, for example, the United States threatened a number of states with refusing to accept their imports of shrimp if they did not agree to cooperative measures to protect sea turtles (which drown in shrimp fishing nets) that the United States was pursuing. Most states resisted but ultimately gave in, particularly after the import restrictions were enacted. French Guiana refused to go along with what the United States advocated. U.S. measures prohibiting the import of shrimp from states that did not accept these measures had no effect on French Guiana's behavior, because it did not export any shrimp to the U.S. market.

Why, then, did the United States threaten this type of measure when it had no chance of working against that particular state? Because the U.S. position internationally was determined by the intersecting concerns of its domestic actors: environmentalists concerned with sea turtle mortality and shrimp fishers concerned that they had to use costly turtle-protection measures when their international competitors did not. In the domestic political process that led the United States to make this threat, the point of commonality to appease both constituencies was to seek desired behavior change by refusing to import shrimp from states that did not adopt a policy to protect turtles. Environmentalists were happy because it was a measure that could (and, in fact, did) persuade other states to protect turtles. And the U.S. shrimping industry was happy because either other states would adopt the higher U.S. turtle protection standards and thus remove what they considered to be unfair competition, or the shrimp in question would not compete with that caught by U.S. shrimp fishers on the U.S. market. But since the measures to accomplish this were only politically possible as a way to simultaneously please both constituencies, a different (more effective, in the case of French Guiana) action would not have been issued.[36]

[35] DeSombre 2005.
[36] DeSombre 2000.

This example illustrates the broader underlying domestic political situation of a powerful state that can drive approaches to international cooperation. Not only does it suggest what kinds of approaches states might try to achieve or support cooperative outcomes, but it may suggest which issues states prioritize for cooperation. At minimum, we should look toward domestically regulated industries to push their states to work toward international cooperation. That means that understanding the domestic politics of regulation in a given state, particularly if it is an internationally influential state, will go a long way toward understanding what it will choose to push. Or, perhaps, resist: note that the United States, the most reluctant international player on climate change, had virtually no domestic process for addressing climate change at its time of greatest resistance to international regulation.[37]

Conclusion

Much of our current understanding of international environmental cooperation thus comes directly from Keohane's specification of the incentives generally for international cooperation. His work explains how the gains from cooperation on international environmental issues can provide the underlying incentive for doing so, and emphasizes the importance of cooperation in international relations more generally. He also points us to the necessary institutional mechanisms for overcoming the difficulties of cooperation in a self-help system. International environmental issues represent a strong form of a prisoner's dilemma, in which widespread cooperation is especially necessary for addressing the problems faced, and the difficulties of cooperation are particularly pronounced.

Moreover, the political dynamics within the cooperation on environmental issues can best be understood through a lens of complex interdependence. States value environmental concerns even though these issues have generally been considered low politics, and the power resources to which states have access for addressing them are different than the traditional power resources of military might or even economic wealth. The different types of power that allow states to have influence within this issue area can impact the shape or existence of international cooperative measures to address international environmental problems. Most interestingly, it accounts for the high degree of influence developing countries have had within recent global environmental agreements.

Finally, the next step in understanding this dynamic further is to allow for the influence that domestic politics has on whether states are willing

[37] DeSombre 2004.

to play coordinating roles internationally, on which environmental issues, and with what mechanisms of persuasion. Systemic theories of international cooperation can specify the broad outlines of issues on which cooperation would benefit its participants and even identify the power resources states might have available to them in working toward this cooperation. But it is when looking at the domestic politics of complex interdependence that the specific priorities of states in approaching environmental cooperation may be best understood.

While these factors may be of particular relevance to cooperation on international environmental issues, what they suggest more broadly is that environmental issues are not fundamentally different from most issues of cooperation under conditions of interdependence. Insight from international environmental cooperation and understanding what influences its creation and form contributes more broadly to understanding international institutions in a globalized world.

CHAPTER 9

The Dynamics of Trade Liberalization

Vinod K. Aggarwal

IN 1999, WORLD TRADE ORGANIZATION (WTO) participants in Seattle unsuccessfully attempted to launch a new trade round. Many commentators saw this as the swan song of the global approach to negotiations and began to call for alternative paths to liberalize trade. Suggestions for coping with the perceived complexity of the WTO included negotiating among a more restricted set of actors or limiting the set of issues discussed.[1] But the success of the November 2001 Doha meeting of the WTO in setting a timetable for negotiations seemed to once again restore faith in the global approach. Yet the seesaw continued. First came the dramatic collapse of the Cancún negotiations in September 2003, followed shortly thereafter by the success of the July 2004 WTO meeting in Geneva. Since then, WTO members have missed the January 2005 deadline for concluding the Doha Round as disagreements over trade concessions between developed and developing countries continue. Efforts to revive the Doha Round in 2007 have foundered, and President George W. Bush's expiration of Trade Promotion Authority (requiring up or down votes of trade bills in Congress without amendment) signals a very bleak prospect for any imminent conclusion of the multilateral round. In this environment, many countries look for other trade options, in particular the active pursuit of bilateral preferential trade agreements.

From the post–World War II era until the early 1990s, the General Agreement on Tariffs and Trade (GATT) was the primary vehicle to foster trade liberalization, with the most significant exception being the formation and evolution of a customs union in Europe. By contrast, trade protection has taken a variety of forms, with unilateral, bilateral, minilateral, and multilateral restrictions—both on a sector-specific and multiproduct basis. Robert Keohane's work has been particularly illuminating in developing an explanation for the persistence of trade liberalization in the face of these protectionist measures. Drawing on the seminal work of

I am especially grateful to Min Gyo Koo for his comments on this chapter. Edward Fogarty also provided valuable suggestions, and Vivek Narayanadas and Rene Schneeberger helped with background research. I am also indebted to the participants in the Robert Keohane Festschrift Conference.

[1] For an example of restricting countries, see Business Roundtable 2001; for an example of restricting issues, see Tyson 2000.

Ronald Coase and Oliver Williamson, Keohane applied a transaction costs approach to understand the persistence of the GATT regime in promoting openness in the face of declining U.S. hegemony.[2] Keohane's work, as highlighted by Helen Milner in the introduction to this volume, developed several themes, including the role and evolution of institutions in fostering cooperation, constraints on the provision of public goods, the role of reciprocity, the use of nonmilitary power in negotiations, and the importance of institutional design. This work has inspired research on the dynamics of trade liberalization and protectionism.[3]

My objective in this chapter is to build on the tradition of this trade cooperation and conflict-focused research program. In earlier work with Robert Keohane and David Yoffie,[4] we focused on the evolution of different forms of trade protectionism. Here, drawing on Keohane's work, the work of his other students, and that of other scholars who have studied trade issues, I focus on forms of trade liberalization.[5] To this end, the next section of this chapter begins by summarizing the general problem of understanding trade liberalization, the potential need and role of institutions, and the bargaining process leading to their creation. I then specify different forms of trade governance based on several criteria. The next major section presents an institutional bargaining game approach to analyze the evolution of trade accords. I show how such an approach can help us understand the building and modification of different types of international institutions in trade. The following section applies this institutional bargaining approach to examine the development of trade arrangements in northeast Asia by constructing scenarios that explore the interaction of different variables that lead to different modes of trade governance. The final major section concludes with an assessment of possible avenues to pursue a broader research program for understanding the dynamics of trade liberalization.

The Role of Institutions in Trade Liberalization

In thinking about trade liberalization, one can focus on several key questions. First, why is cooperation necessary in trade? Second, if cooperation is indeed necessary, how might institutions foster such cooperation? Third, from a bargaining perspective, how can institutions be created?

[2] Coase 1960; Williamson 1983; and Keohane 1984.

[3] Yarbrough and Yarbrough 1987; Mansfield and Milner 1999; Oye 1992; McKeown 1983 and 1991.

[4] Aggarwal, Keohane, and Yoffie 1987.

[5] Beth and Robert Yarbrough (1987), in particular, have been leaders in an effort to theorize about alternative modes of trade liberalization.

Fourth, what are the options with respect to the development of different types of trade governance mechanisms? Fifth, what underlying factors drive different forms of trade governance and how might they evolve? The first four of these questions are addressed in this section, while I consider the fifth in the next section.

The Need for Trade Cooperation

The conventional wisdom in international economics is that economic openness and integrated world markets ensure an optimal allocation of factors of production and maximize both aggregate world welfare and individual national welfare.[6] Yet, in practice, the benefits of globalization cannot always be realized by states pursuing independent policies; cooperative action is required. In particular, the changing distribution of costs and benefits from trade liberalization can result in strong political opposition both for and against further liberalization. For example, for commodity producers, price volatility and ultraspecialization can bring severe adjustment costs. Developing countries that emphasize manufactured exports face significant adjustment challenges as they compete with each other for market share, particularly in the face of the rise of the Chinese export juggernaut. And for their part, rich countries often face strong domestic lobbies in agriculture, textile, steel, and other sectors, creating pressure for trade restrictions.

Given these political constraints, countries may be either unwilling or unable to sustain processes of economic liberalization by themselves. While some countries continue to fully implement their market-opening commitments, others could slow or halt theirs. But their counterparts may find this unacceptable, and react by reneging on their own commitments. International cooperative action may therefore be required to avoid the unfortunate effects of this *temptation to free ride*. More formally, analysts have discussed the question of the *type of goods* involved in trade liberalization. Is free trade a public good from which all can benefit? Classical trade theory suggests that international trade liberalization should be seen as a public good that is easily provided because everyone's optimal strategy is to liberalize, independent of what others do. From this perspective, trade liberalization can be modeled nicely using a harmony game. By contrast, John Conybeare argues that free trade should be modeled as a prisoner's dilemma (PD) game, and not a public good.[7] Yet

---

[6] The first three subsections draw on Aggarwal and Dupont 2007.

[7] Conybeare 1984. Gowa 1989 provides a convincing response by showing that retaliatory efforts have public goods characteristics.

his analysis conflates the goods involved in a particular issue-area with the *game used to model it*. It may simply be that membership in the GATT, for example, is best modeled as an inclusive club good, and thus a different game may be more appropriate.[8]

If there are strong elements of a PD in the case of trade liberalization, how might the PD be resolved? One avenue that has been much discussed is the possibility of cooperation with iterated play.[9] Yet even under iteration, cooperation is not a foregone conclusion, for if actors overly discount the importance of future iterations owing to a dire economic or political situation at home for governments, they will be tempted to free ride.

Institutions and Cooperation in Trade

To address the problem of achieving trade liberalization, neoliberal institutionalists have examined the role that international institutions may play in facilitating cooperation in trade. First, institutions may help secure positive outcomes in bargaining processes. They can play the role of a third party and enforce a mutual agreement, making the parties more willing to settle on a bargaining outcome in the first place. Second, institutions may reduce distributive problems. They may eliminate some sharply asymmetric outcomes and may provide focal point solutions for both benefit and cost sharing. Third, institutions may be useful even if there is some powerful political entrepreneur, or hegemon, that provides public goods. Hegemons wish to coerce weaker actors to move away from free riding on the unilateral provision of goods and carry some of the burden. Institutions can facilitate the linkage of issues and decrease the temptation to free ride. Fourth, institutions can create a mechanism for exclusion, transforming public goods into club or private goods. For example, trade arrangements with fewer participants reduce the possibility of free riding (by definition) and ensure that gains from trade liberalization accrue only to the participants in the agreement.[10]

Institutional Creation

Although institutions can facilitate cooperation in several ways, how might institutions be formed in the first place? From the perspective of a power-based tradition, regimes affect the distribution of costs and benefits of state interaction. For analysts in this school,[11] institutions have

---

[8] See Aggarwal and Dupont 1999 for a formal analysis of goods, games, and institutions.
[9] See Axelrod and Keohane 1986; Cornes and Sandler 1996; Taylor 1987.
[10] Gowa 1989.
[11] Krasner 1991; Aggarwal 1985; and Knight 1992.

distributional consequences and can be used as devices to seek and maintain asymmetric gains. They can also help control other actors' behavior, both at home and abroad. The central theme in this literature has been the role of hegemonic powers in fostering the development of institutions through both positive and negative incentives.[12] Benevolent hegemons, for example, may provide public goods because their large size makes it worthwhile for them to take action on their own initiative to overcome collective action problems. But although this approach suggests that regimes may form when powerful states desire them, it does not tell us much about the nature of regimes, or actors' desire to pursue multilateral solutions as opposed to bilateral ones.

Building on these criticisms of the neorealist approach, neoliberal institutionalists have examined the specific incentives for states to create institutions—as opposed to simply engaging in ad hoc bargaining. As we have already discussed, institutions provide many useful functions in helping actors to coordinate their actions or achieve collaboration. This theoretical approach assumes that collaborative action is primarily demand driven—that is, actors create institutions because they are useful—but a mechanism for how to create them is not actually specified. An important theme of this work has been how existing institutions may constrain future institutional developments. One key constraint is the presence of existing institutions with broad mandates that influence the negotiation of more specific institutions, leading to the "nesting" of regimes within one another.[13]

A third approach to examining institutional innovation and change places emphasis on the role of expert consensus and the interplay between experts and politicians.[14] New knowledge and cognitive understandings may lead decision makers to calculate their interests differently, thereby directly affecting payoffs and play. From this perspective, institutions may fundamentally alter actors' preferences.

Classifying Modes of Trade Governance

What types of institutions are states likely to create to deal with the problem of trade cooperation? In examining regional, sectoral, and bilateral agreements, analysts often conflate different types of arrangements and use them synonymously. For example, the term *regional agreement* has been used to refer to accords as widely disparate as Asia Pacific Economic Cooperation (APEC), the North American Free Trade Agreement (NAFTA), bilateral free trade agreements both in and outside a region, and even

[12] Kindleberger 1973; Gilpin 1975; Krasner 1976; and Keohane 1984.
[13] Keohane and Nye 1977. See Aggarwal 1985 on nesting.
[14] Haas 1980.

sectoral agreements such as the Information Technology Agreement (ITA).[15] This conceptual ambiguity makes it difficult to develop causal arguments to account for the variety of trade arrangements.

To address this problem, I focus on several dimensions in classifying modes of trade governance: the number of participants; product coverage; geographical scope; market opening or closing; and institutionalization. I define the number of participants in terms of bilateral, minilateral, and multilateral participation in an agreement.[16] I use the term *bilateral* to refer to two countries and *minilateral* to more than two.[17] In terms of product coverage, the range is from narrow (a few products) to broad (multiproduct) in scope. Geographical scope differentiates arrangements that are concentrated geographically and those that bind states across great distances. A fourth dimension addresses whether these measures have been either market opening (liberalizing) or market closing (protectionist). Fifth and finally, one can also look at the degree of institutionalization or strength of agreements.[18] Based on these dimensions, table 9.1 presents a typology of trade agreements.

The table itself omits discussion of protectionist measures and degree of institutionalization for presentation purposes, although I do consider these elements in the scenarios of northeast Asian trade arrangements in a later section, "Trade Arrangements in Northeast Asia and Beyond."

Explaining Trade Governance Measures

Analysts have developed a wide variety of causal explanations for different trade liberalization measures. Given space constraints, I briefly consider some general arguments about specific forms, as well as efforts to account for variation and evolution across types of accords.

The first row in table 9.1 focuses on sectoral agreements (cells 1–6). These involved liberalization in a relatively small number of products, as

[15] See for example, Mansfield and Milner 1999, 592, who recognize the problematic nature of the term *regionalism* but use this term in their analysis.

[16] For theoretical completeness, I also consider unilateral approaches to liberalize trade.

[17] This usage differs from that of Yarbrough and Yarbrough 1992, which conflates third-party enforcement with these terms so that *bilateral* for them can also mean three countries, a highly counterintuitive use. Keohane 1990 refers to an agreement among three or more states as multilateralism. Richardson 1987 is consistent with my usage.

[18] Of these, the dimension of geographical scope is the most controversial. It is worth noting that this category is quite subjective, since simple distance is hardly the only relevant factor in defining a geographic region. Despite the interest that regionalism has attracted, the question of how to define a region remains highly contested. See the discussions by Mansfield and Milner 1999; Katzenstein 1997; and Aggarwal and Fogarty 2004, among others.

TABLE 9.1
Classifying Trade Arrangements

		Actor scope				
		Bilateral		Minilateral		
	Unilateral	Geographically concentrated	Geographically dispersed	Geographically concentrated	Geographically dispersed	Multilateral
Product scope	(1)	(2)	(3)	(4)	(5)	(6)
Few products	UK Corn Law removal (1846)	U.S.-Canada Auto Agreement (1965)	U.S.-Japan VIEs (1980s-1990s)	ECSC (1951)	EVSL (1997)	ITA (1997), BTA (1998), FSA (1999)
	(7)	(8)	(9)	(10)	(11)	(12)
Many products	APEC Individual Action Plans (IAPs)	Canada–U.S. FTA (1989) Australia–New Zealand CER (1983)	U.S.-Israel FTA (1985 U.S.-Jordan FTA (2001) Canada-Chile FTA (1997)	EC/EU (1958/1992) NAFTA (1993) Mercosur (1991)	APEC (1989) (trans regionalism) Lomé (hybrid inter-regionalism) EU-Mercosur (pure inter-regionalism)	GATT / WTO (1947/1995)

Source: Adapted from Aggarwal 2001.

in the classic example of British opening of its grain market with the removal of the Corn Laws in 1846.[19] Most analysis of British motivation for this unilateral action focuses on domestic politics, although others have emphasized Britain's international position as a hegemonic power.[20] Sectoral arrangements have also been pursued bilaterally, both on a geographically dispersed and transregional basis. These accords appear to be driven by politically strong but narrow interests pursuing greater economies of scale. The resulting arrangements tend to promote intraindustry trade, as with the U.S.-Canada auto accord.[21] Transnationally, voluntary import expansions (VIEs) have been used to pressure countries to open up their markets, which are directly tied to domestic pressure, often in the context of Super 301, a provision in U.S. law allowing for unilateral restrictions against countries that the United States believes are unfair traders.

In looking at sectoral accords, we might ask: Why don't we have more industry-driven specific agreements to capture private goods? Here the role of institutional constraints proves critical. The best example of this is Article 24 of the GATT, which calls for the coverage of "substantially all trade" when free trade areas or customs unions are developed. Indeed, when the Coal and Steel Community (ECSC) was created in 1951 (driven by both domestic interests and concern about international security), its members faced criticism for its creation. Although challenged as inconsistent with the GATT by Czechoslovakia, the ECSC members managed to obtain a GATT waiver of obligation, with the strong support of the United States, which was of course interested in encouraging West European states to work together to resist the Soviet Union.[22] Another example of an effort to promote sectoral accords also took place in the context of preexisting institutions. In 1997, APEC ministers agreed to Early Voluntary Sectoral Liberalization (EVSL) in nine sectors as a package for fast track liberalization. Article 24 was also important here, as this approach could run counter to the GATT. To address this potential conflict, one idea was to liberalize in areas where non-APEC countries would not compete and to promote voluntary liberalization without asking for extra-APEC reciprocity. In the end, however, this approach ran into difficulties, as several countries objected particularly to the liberalization of certain agricultural, forestry, and fishery products in the context of the East Asian financial crisis.

Finally, a new development in trade cooperation has been the effort to promote sector-specific multilateral liberalization, namely the ITA, the

---

[19] See Schonhardt-Bailey 1996.

[20] See McKeown 1983 and James and Lake 1989, among others.

[21] See Milner and Yoffie 1989.

[22] Curzon 1966, 266–68.

Basic Telecom Agreement, and the Financial Service Agreement (cell 6 in table 9.1). The emergence of these types of agreements is particularly important. Laura Tyson, for example, has argued that among multilateral trade options, this sectoral approach is a sound alternative to the multisector WTO approach.[23] Yet open sectoralism can be politically and economically hazardous, particularly if one considers the impact of one type of trade accord on another.[24] From a political perspective, sectoral market opening, driven by narrow domestic lobbies, is likely to *reduce* political support for multilateral, multisector negotiations. Because sectoral agenda setting involves a limited and easily polarized set of domestic interests, the margin for coalition building and political give-and-take is much slimmer. Moreover, from an economic perspective, such agreements may *reduce* economic efficiency. By liberalizing only specific, highly competitive sectors, open sectoral trade agreements can lead to incentives to invest in or discourage exit from the least efficient areas of the economy.

We turn next to broader multiproduct liberalization (cells 7–12). Unilateral liberalization was feasible for Britain thanks to its industrial strength, its limited investment in transaction-specific assets for trade, and its quasi-monopsony power in raw material and export markets—which contrasted with other countries' limited alternatives to importing British manufactured goods.[25] Contemporary examples of unilateral liberalization include measures taken by Australia, New Zealand, Hong Kong, and Singapore, driven often by globally minded state elites.

Bilateral arrangements involving both a regional and transregional scope have rapidly proliferated over the last few years. More often than not, such agreements draw upon not only geographic, historic, and cultural affinities but also complementarities in economic structure. Analysts argue that, in order to reduce the costs related to geographic distance and to maximize the benefits of economic size, neighboring countries will often form preferential trade agreements (PTAs) with one another, creating a natural trading bloc. Yet we have also seen examples of geographically dispersed bilateral agreements covering multiple products.[26] Some of these bilateral FTAs—for example, the U.S-Israel FTA and the U.S.-Jordan FTA—have been clearly motivated primarily by political-strategic rather than economic reasons.[27] Others, such as the FTAs between Japan

---

[23] Tyson 2000.

[24] For details of this argument see Aggarwal 2001 and Aggarwal and Ravenhill 2001.

[25] Yarbrough and Yarbrough 1992. McKeown 1983 makes a strong case that Britain did not exhibit hegemonic power in the move to liberalization in the nineteenth century but rather chose to liberalize on its own.

[26] For an insightful discussion comparing intra- versus cross-regional bilateral accords, see Solís and Katada 2007.

[27] Aggarwal and Urata 2006.

and Singapore and between South Korea and Chile are largely designed for the purpose of "training" or "capacity building" for countries with little prior experience in FTA formation.[28] And as with the recent U.S.–South Korea accord, these accords may reflect efforts to lock in key markets in the context of problematic global negotiations.

The emphasis of scholarly attention on regional accords is commensurate with the rise of such arrangements starting in the 1960s. Conventional explanations for the move toward minilateral regionalism have focused on both economic and political-strategic motivations. Some economic arguments include enlarging economies of scale without excessive global competition; increasing the attractiveness of an economy to foreign capital; and creating natural trading blocs according to geographic proximity.[29] Political-strategic economic reasons include signaling or strengthening one's bargaining position in relation to more powerful partners; responding to the erosion of U.S. support for multilateralism; locking in a domestic reform agenda; a domino effect; limiting free rider problems; reducing transaction costs between negotiating parties; and lowering the political salience of negotiations.[30]

It is worth noting that these explanations of "regionalism" actually fall into several cells of my typology, namely 2, 4, and 8—and, to some extent, cell 11 as well, indicating the conceptual ambiguity and underdifferentiation inherent in the existing literature on regionalism. Thus, it is useful to separately consider arrangements that span countries across continents (cell 11). The term *interregionalism* can itself be broken down into more specific types. I refer to an agreement as *pure interregional* if it formally links free trade areas or customs unions, as in the case of EU-Mercosur.[31] If a customs union negotiates with countries in different regions, but not with a customs union or free trade agreement, I refer to this as *hybrid interregionalism* (e.g., the Lomé Agreement). Finally, if an accord links countries across two regions where *neither* of the two negotiates has a grouping, then I refer to this as *transregionalism* (e.g., APEC). Aside from conventional political and economic motivations that drive regionalism, the EU's interregionalism also seems to be driven by its efforts to project its success in regional integration on an international basis.[32]

Finally, we have the case of global, multiproduct trading arrangements

[28] Koo 2006.

[29] On economies of scale, see Milner 1997; on foreign capital, see Lawrence 1996; and on natural trading blocs, see Frankel 1997.

[30] See respectively Milward 1992; Gilpin 1987 and Krasner 1976; Haggard 1997; Oye 1992 and Baldwin 1997; and Yarbrough and Yarbrough 1992, among others.

[31] Aggarwal and Fogarty 2004.

[32] Aggarwal and Fogarty 2004.

such as the GATT and its successor organization, the WTO. Both liberal economists and neoliberal institutionalists prefer this approach on the belief that it maximizes global efficiency and reduces transaction and information costs. Yet as we have seen, the WTO has increasingly encountered difficulties in hammering out new terms of trade liberalization. This, in turn, has fueled interest in preferential arrangements at the submultilateral level.

An Institutional Bargaining Game Approach
  to Analyze Trade Arrangements

The literature on different forms of trade arrangements has grown in recent years in step with the rise of such agreements. Yet most analysis does not adequately examine the choice of trade governance mechanisms in comparative perspective, although there are important exceptions.[33] The most innovative effort to look at explanations for the choice of trade accords builds on transaction cost and power-based arguments. Beth and Robert Yarbrough have argued that the *form* of trade accords is driven by the combination of transaction-specific investments and the possibility of hegemonically driven cooperation.[34] In brief, they argue that Britain's dominance combined with the lack of asset-specific investments in the nineteenth century to made unilateral multisectoral liberalization a viable option for the British. After World War II, although asset specificity increased, U.S. power enabled it to promote multilateral trade liberalization through the GATT. More recently, with relative U.S. decline, they argue that minilateralism (and bilateralism) is likely to rise as countries attempt to ensure that their asset-specific investments in trade are not impaired in view of the declining commitment to the WTO. Other analysts have considered whether regional accords serve as building blocks or stumbling blocks for multilateral liberalization.[35] And more recently, considerable debate has been generated about the implications of bilateral trade accords for the global trading system.[36]

Although these analytical approaches are insightful, they do not adequately account for the variety of trade accords. Almost all fail to distinguish between the implications of sectoral versus broader liberalization, and most have little to say about the difference between regionalism and interregionalism, be it on a bilateral or minilateral basis. In an effort to more adequately analyze and capture the implications of the rich variety

[33] Notably, Yarbrough and Yarbrough 1987; Oye 1992; and Katzenstein 1997.
[34] Yarbrough and Yarbrough 1987, 4.
[35] See, for example, Bhagwati 1991.
[36] See Aggarwal and Urata 2006 for a discussion.

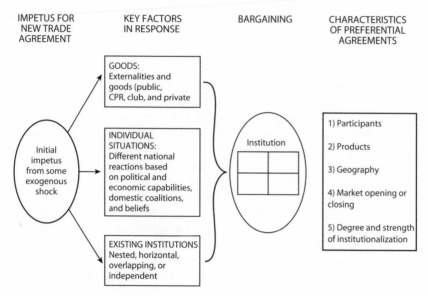

| IMPETUS FOR NEW TRADE AGREEMENT | KEY FACTORS IN RESPONSE | BARGAINING | CHARACTERISTICS OF PREFERENTIAL AGREEMENTS |

Figure 9.1   The Origins of Preferential Trade Agreements

of trade governance measures, I use an institutional bargaining game approach to examine such arrangements.[37] Although this approach does not provide a precise causal prediction of each type of accord, it provides a more systematic basis for examining both policy choices and connections among different types of arrangements and can be used to explore alternative scenarios.

As illustrated in figure 9.1, an institutional bargaining game approach begins by identifying an initial impetus for new trade accords, and then considers the goods involved, actors' individual situations, and the impact of existing institutions to construct a "bargaining game." The result of the strategic interaction leads to some type of preferential agreement with various characteristics. We examine each element in turn.

The process of a shift from an initial institutional equilibrium can come about with some external shock—for example, the end of the Cold War or simply a decline in U.S. hegemony. But contrary to realist accounts, the driving force for institutional change can also come from problems with existing institutions (as with the Doha Round of the WTO) or the Asian financial crisis of 1997–98. Countries respond to such external shocks in various ways based on the "goods" involved in the negotiations. As we have already seen, there is considerable debate over the types of goods

[37] See Aggarwal 1998. Owing to space constraints, my discussion of this approach is sharply abbreviated.

involved in trade negotiations (public goods, common pool resources, inclusive club goods, or private goods), but this step allows us to identify the basic underlying structure of the bargaining problem.

Next, we can consider factors that help us predict actors' payoffs. These include (1) an actor's international position, as defined by its overall power and its specific economic competitiveness in trade and security matters; (2) the makeup of its domestic coalitions, reflecting pressure groups that respond to underlying economic competitiveness based on such factors as trade complementarity and asset specificity; and (3) elite beliefs and ideologies. These factors vary by country and thus determine each country's preference ordering with respect to trade arrangements. Finally, preexisting institutions (if they exist) affect the play of a trade-bargaining game. Thus, in creating new arrangements or modifying existing ones, connections among existing and proposed institutions influence the outcomes.[38] An example of this is the concern about conforming to GATT Article 24's strictures on free trade areas and customs unions.

Finally, with respect to outcomes, if countries decide to create a new agreement or modify an existing one, they must decide on its characteristics. As shown in table 9.1, these features include the participants, products, geography, market opening or closing, and degree of institutionalization. One can also then consider additional rounds of play, which lead to further modification or creation of new institutions.[39]

Trade Arrangements in Northeast Asia and Beyond

Drawing on my work with Min Gyo Koo, I now turn to an institutional trade-bargaining game approach to explore organizational outcomes and implications in northeast Asia.[40] Ideally, we would simultaneously consider the variation in all the variables in our institutional bargaining game, namely the factors of goods, individual situations, and context of existing institutions to examine bargaining game payoffs and play. Given the many uncertainties involved, instead of formally trying to derive payoffs, I consider a narrower range of factors from these broad categories

[38] From a theoretical perspective, we can define four types of connections among institutions: (1) nested links, whereby narrow arrangements conform to broader accords; (2) horizontal connections, whereby arrangements reflect a division of labor without any hierarchy among institutions; (3) overlapping agreements, which may create tension among participants' obligations under each agreement; and (4) independent institutions, which govern distinct fields and thus have little or no interaction in functional terms.

[39] See Aggarwal 1998 for a discussion of this idea.

[40] This section draws on Aggarwal and Koo 2005.

to look at scenarios for trade outcomes in northeast Asia. To construct these scenarios, I assume a certain hierarchical order among the variables in our institutional bargaining game. I give pride of place to the status of extant broad-based, international institutions as a primary source of *initial impetus* for change. In particular, I assume that the status of the WTO and APEC may stimulate or impede the provision of trade liberalization as a public good.[41] Specifically, the weakness of each of these institutions should encourage the pursuit of a club good, whereas their strength will discourage such an attempt.

Given the nature (market opening) and geographic coverage (northeast Asia) of a prospective PTA, individual bargaining situations and institutional context determine the other elements of bargaining outcomes, namely the number of participants (1, 2, or 3), strength of institutions (for example, the degree to which the agreements are binding and the presence of dispute settlement procedures), and scope of products included. I focus on three variables in order of their presumed significance—the institutional strength of the WTO and APEC, alliances-type relationships (rapprochement, for example, in the China-Japan case), and economic complementary between countries. I draw the following causal relationships from my theoretical and empirical observations: the number of participants, strength, and scope of a prospective NEAFTA are a negative function of the strength of the WTO and APEC, and a positive function of alliances and economic complementarity (see figure 9.2).

Paths to a NEAFTA

How might we get to a NEAFTA from the current institutional mix in northeast Asia that consists of the participation of China, Japan, and South Korea in bilateral regionalism and transregionalism (general bilaterals), minilateral transregionalism (APEC and APT), and multilateral globalism (GATT/WTO)?

If both the WTO and APEC are *strong*, there is little raison d'être for a NEAFTA. Essentially, all the incentives for securing club goods (even through bilateral agreements) would be gone with the broad-based institutions operating and dominating the institutional space (outcome 1).

A combination of a *strong* WTO and a *weak* APEC creates some incentives for pursuing club goods, thereby permitting institutional room for

[41] Strictly speaking, the WTO and APEC are club goods to the extent that membership is required if a state is to benefit from trade liberalization that they materialize. With the former's global membership and the latter's spirit of "open regionalism," their provision of the broadest club goods virtually makes them global public goods.

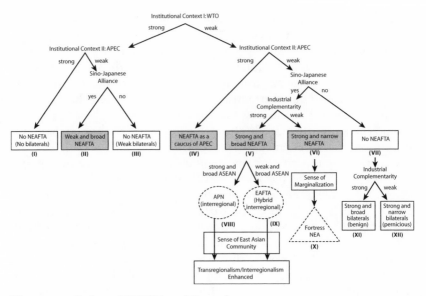

Figure 9.2   Paths to NEAFTA and Beyond

either trilateral or bilateral regionalism in northeast Asia. If there is significant security rapprochement between China and Japan (and thus possibly a trilateral arrangement including South Korea), a weak but broad NEAFTA might be a possibility (outcome 2). The logic here is that the strength of the WTO would dissuade a major focus on club goods. But the weakness of APEC would motivate politically secure northeast Asian countries to form a NEAFTA—immediately or by merging separate bilaterals—to maximize the benefit from the geographic proximity and size of their economies. By contrast, if there is no Sino-Japanese rapprochement, a NEAFTA would be highly unlikely because of strong concerns about relative gains between the two regional rivals. Yet this does not eliminate the possibility of some type of bilateral alliance or security agreement between Japan and South Korea and, potentially, between China and South Korea. Given the weakness of APEC, bilateral PTAs between these two dyads would remain a viable option, but their strength would likely to be weak in the presence of a *strong* WTO (outcome 3).

The combination of a *weak* WTO and a *strong* APEC is likely to result in a very weak NEAFTA. The WTO's weakness would motivate the three countries to pursue trilateral club goods, even without formal alliance arrangements among themselves, since a strong APEC would decrease relative gains concerns. In this case, however, a NEAFTA would be reduced to a caucus of the three countries *within* APEC—rather than a separate, strong negotiating body—since APEC operates as a principal locus of trade liberalization (outcome 4).[42]

Finally, if both the WTO and APEC are weak, considerable institutional space and a multiplicity of options are likely to emerge. If China and Japan achieve some type of security rapprochement, the formation of a *strong* NEAFTA is highly likely. In this case, the scope of a resulting NEAFTA is predicated on economic complementarity. If such complementarities exist among the three countries, they will broaden the scope of product coverage (outcome 5). If there are weak economic complementarities, we can expect a strong but narrow (or sectoral) NEAFTA (outcome 6). By contrast, if there is no alliance between China and Japan, a NEAFTA is not a possibility (outcome 7).

Beyond-NEAFTA Outcomes

Among the seven possible scenarios I have considered to this point, I further explore the likely paths from the three particular outcomes that are based on the combination of a weak WTO and a weak APEC.

To begin with, how would a *strong* and *broad* NEAFTA (outcome 5) evolve if we broaden our focus beyond northeast Asia? Within East Asia, if this type of NEAFTA is combined with a *strong* and *broad* ASEAN, the most likely outcome is an *interregional* arrangement—that is, a bilateral arrangement between two separate PTAs—possibly in the form of an ASEAN Plus NEAFTA (APN) (outcome 8). Alternatively, if a strong and broad NEAFTA links up with a broad but weak ASEAN, we can expect the advent of a *hybrid interregional* arrangement that creates an East Asian FTA (EAFTA)—currently manifesting itself in the reverse form of APT or East Asian Community (EAC) where ASEAN is united, but South Korea, Japan, and China are not. In this case, members would participate in their individual capacity as Southeast Asian states and South Korea, Japan, and China as members of NEAFTA (outcome 9).

Next, we can examine how an East Asian grouping—be it APN, APT, EAFTA, or EAC—might contribute to broader transregional or interregional arrangements such as APEC and ASEM. If an East Asian grouping is created that proves stable, the growing interconnectedness and the networked nature of interstate economic activities may produce an increasing awareness and sense of community among East Asian countries.[43] As either APN or EAFTA countries become more confident in their ability to

[42] According to this scenario, a NEAFTA as a caucus is likely to consolidate APEC as a *transregional* arrangement that combines its members as individual states rather than formal groupings.

[43] Terada 2003.

create their own transregional grouping, they might be more willing to extend their institutionalization efforts to the transregional level of APEC, thereby giving it new life. This could also lead to more an *inter-regional* rather than a transregional outcome, with the Australia New Zealand Closer Economic Relations (CER) Agreement, APN, and NAFTA operating within APEC as three distinct hubs. Similarly, the increasing sense of community within East Asia could facilitate the ASEM forum, leading to pure Asia-Europe interregionalism.

What about paths from outcome 6? In this case, we could end up with the formation of an exclusive, if not pernicious, "Fortress Asia" commensurate with the oft-voiced fears of a "Fortress Europe" and "Fortress America." The strategic relationship between northeast Asia and the rest of the world will be of key significance here. Most importantly, if the United States continues its focus on the Free Trade Area of Americas (FTAA) and the EU continues on an eastward and possibly southward expansion path, others may feel excluded. Under these circumstances, the decade-long perception between northeast and southeast Asians that Western regional arrangements are forming against them may well rekindle the Mahathir-promoted notion of an exclusive East Asian bloc (outcome 10).

Finally, in outcome 7, although I rule out some type of trilateral alliance, two separate dyads, Japan–South Korea on the one hand and China–South Korea on the other, are likely to have strong incentives to secure club goods through bilateral arrangements between themselves. In this case, the strength of bilateral arrangements would increase because of the weakness of both the WTO and APEC, and these bilaterals would operate as the dominant mode of trade liberalization in northeast Asia. If an individual dyad has strong economic complementarity, it might result in a *strong* and *broad* bilateral arrangement (outcome 11). This path can lead to *benign* bilateralism if it catalyzes a competitive dynamic to liberalize in other countries.[44] Conversely, if an individual dyad has weak economic complementarity, it might lead to a *strong* but *narrow* bilateral accord (outcome 12). In this case, it is plausible that the northeast Asian countries may be polarized between two camps—China versus Japan—on a sectoral basis, thereby undermining regional integration efforts. Ultimately, a pernicious web of competitive, sectoral bilaterals would likely damage other broad-based, multilateral trading accords.[45]

To conclude, the various scenarios derived from the institutional bargaining game model suggest the need to analyze the variety of institu-

[44] Bergsten 2001.
[45] Aggarwal and Ravenhill 2001; and Irwin 1993.

tional forms discussed in table 9.1. As I have argued, the more careful specification of arrangements helps us to move the discussion from a vague specification of contention between "regionalism" vs. "multilateralism" to a more nuanced analytical exploration based on the causal variables of goods, individual situations, and institutional context.

Conclusion

The puzzles of the necessity of cooperation in trade, of the creation and role of institutions in fostering cooperation, of the variety of institutional forms, and of their impact over time have stimulated a dynamic research program focusing on transaction costs, security externalities, reciprocity, and institutional design. As a consequence, our understanding of types of trade arrangements, their evolution, and likely impact on broader trading regimes has advanced considerably in the last two decades.

In this chapter, I have set out to build on these insights by more carefully specifying and examining the variety of liberalizing trade arrangements. A key step in this analytical effort to understand trade arrangements is to properly "differentiate" the dependent variable. To this end, I have sought to categorize the many forms of trade arrangements by the dimensions of number of actors, product scope of agreements, geography, degree of institutionalization, and orientation in terms of market opening or closing. This scheme allows us to more clearly specify and categorize not only trading accords but also to get a handle on the vast literature produced by political scientists and economists on trading arrangements.

I believe that this approach can help us assess how far we have come in our understanding of the diversity of trading accords and point to lacunae in our understanding of the dynamics of both trade liberalization and protection. In terms of research effort, many of the terms that I have used remain contested. For example, we have seen that the question of how to define "geography" has been debated. Similar issues can be raised about product scope: how many products define a sector? In the economics literature, much has been written about cross-elasticities of demand in defining "markets." To this point, the question of defining a sector adequately still remains. Similar questions arise with respect to defining levels of institutionalization and the extent to which an accord promotes or dissuades market opening.

With respect to causal arguments about types of agreements, much research has been done on specific accords. The most intriguing line of research, however, concerns the dynamics of trade arrangements. In this vein, Beth and Robert Yarbrough have attempted to specify a model to predict the origin of forms of trade liberalization.[46] Although this has been a fertile effort, the importance of looking at sectoral accords and differences among "regional agreements" suggests that much work remains to be done on the origin and evolution of trade arrangements. I have proposed an institutional bargaining game as a way to cut into this question, which focuses on types of goods, the source of national preferences, and institutional context, building on the insight of Robert Keohane and others. In particular, I have argued that the difference between club goods and private goods in trade is particularly salient. And in looking at countries' individual situations, I examined how international strategic and economic interests, government type, and beliefs about the value of pursuing trading arrangements beyond multilateralism are likely to impact the formulation and evolution of trading accords.

Although general theoretical arguments provide insights into the dynamics of the evolution of trading arrangements, careful empirical exploration of particular arrangements and how they are likely to change over time can advance our insights. In this chapter, I have sought to demonstrate the utility of an institutional bargaining game approach by exploring how trade arrangements are likely to evolve in northeast Asia. Specifically, I have examined how the strength or weakness of the WTO and APEC opens up or closes institutional space and showed how combinations of goods and individual's situations would result in a NEAFTA of varying strength. I have drawn on my classification of institutional variety to consider the alternatives of bilateral agreements as well as the possible development of a NEAFTA into East Asian regionalism, transregionalism, and interregionalism. In view of the dramatic rise of preferential trading arrangements in Asia and elsewhere, particularly after the end of the Cold War, I believe this line of inquiry is likely to be a progressive research program of value to both scholars and policymakers. Similar questions about the evolution in the Americas, Europe, the Middle East, and elsewhere would greatly enrich our understanding of the dynamics of the evolution of trade arrangements.

[46] Yarbrough and Yarbrough 1992.

Power and Interdependence
in a Globalized World

CHAPTER 10

International Intellectual Property Rights in a Networked World

Jonathan D. Aronson

> Interdependence among societies is not new. What is new is
> the virtual erasing of costs of communicating over distance as
> a result of the information revolution.[1]

GLOBALIZATION AND ITS GOVERNANCE evolve in fits and starts. The central themes of international relations are invented and reinvented, but the issues of power and the management of global relations remain constant. In parallel, research on fundamental concepts such as transnational relations, complex interdependence, regimes, institutions, transgovernmental relations, and globalization continues to grow more subtle and sophisticated. The use of intellectual property rights (IPR) to shape globalization and as a tool for governing it also is of growing importance.

This chapter situates the ongoing debate concerning intellectual property rights and international intellectual property (IIP) management in a framework related to global power and interdependence. Most writings on intellectual property concentrate on what is and is not legally permissible given changing technological parameters. By contrast, this chapter treats international intellectual property in terms of efforts by established firms to defend and extend their power and position and to protect their business models in the face of technological change and global interdependence.

As organizations increase in size, their innovative flare often wanes. Strong companies and countries seek to use intellectual property to maintain and reinforce their advantage. They try to reignite the innovative flair and also keep would-be competitors at bay.[2] Promising new technologies arise, so everyone still may benefit, but benefits are unequally distributed. Benefits may arrive more slowly and be smaller for those who need the most help. The economic gap between rich and poor companies

Some of the ideas in this chapter were initially presented at the conference Globalization, Civil Society and Philanthropy at the Rockefeller Archive Center, Sleepy Hollow, NY. I thank Manuel Castells, Peter Cowhey, the editors, and the anonymous reviewers for comments.

[1] Keohane and Nye 1998, 83.
[2] Christensen 1997; von Hippel 2005.

and countries widens and the poorest countries fall further behind.[3] The struggle is complex because the conflict pits gigantic corporate behemoths, often wedded to antiquated business models, against pesky, innovative startups that often can be crushed, purchased, or co-opted. These non-state actors are interdependent, but the power is asymmetrically distributed. The stakes are high—domination of the emerging global information economy. So the struggle to bend international rules, treaties, and institutions for self-interested purpose is intense.

The strong protection of intellectual property (IP), especially international intellectual property, may run counter to the interests of innovators and traditional and developing societies.[4] Strong IP protection crowds out and limits the distribution of what Keohane and Nye call "free information" that is created and distributed without financial compensation. Power and information are asymmetrically distributed. The proliferation of "commercial information" that is bought and paid for, by contrast, reinforces the power of strong states and commercial firms and may limit new ideas and innovators. Countries impose new nontariff barriers even as they lower or eliminate tariffs on imports. Similarly, as trade barriers are dismantled, global technology markets are being further regulated by ratcheting-up global IPR protection.[5]

In traditional societies elders passed down their wisdom to the next generation. It was their responsibility as ancestors to teach those that followed them what they needed to know. They were compensated with respect, not money. This mind-set is alien to international negotiators who argued that pushing the world toward strong intellectual property protection would ultimately lead to innovation in poorer countries. Under pressure from the industrial world, developing countries departed from their traditional position. They soon concluded that their positions were undermined by the new IP standards that they reluctantly accepted in 1994 in the Uruguay Round Trade-Related Aspects of Intellectual Property Rights (TRIPs) agreement.[6] After assessing the impact of TRIPs on their economies, developing countries began, individually and as a block, to focus their efforts on improving their bargaining position in the Doha Round trade talks and in the World Summit on the Information Society (WSIS) talks. The developed world grudgingly backtracked, at least with

[3] Collier 2007.

[4] Intellectual property covers patents, copyright, trademarks, trade secrets, and other more exotic protections. Patents industries (e.g., aerospace and biotechnology) rely on invention. Copyright industries (e.g., software and entertainment) are built on creative expression through literature, music, etc.

[5] Countries and companies try to improve their relative positions as tariff barriers fall. Countries often use nontariff barriers and antitrust policy; companies rely more on standards and IP protection.

[6] Maskus and Reichman 2004, 282.

respect to medicines, when it agreed to the 2001 Doha revision of the TRIPs agreement.[7]

Two developments accelerated the breakdown of the status quo. First, despite claims that "information wants to be free," the commercialization of the airwaves and the proliferation of ISPs offering Internet and Web access showed that users would pay for copyrighted and specialized information. Keepers of traditional knowledge were perplexed when outsiders, learning of ideas common in their societies, claimed this "newly discovered" intellectual property as their own.[8] Second, international firms are pushing to globalize their control over their IP. The creation of global broadcasting, communication, and information networks fostered interdependence but also deprived the elders of their knowledge advantage. "We are no longer linked to our past by an oral tradition which implies direct contact with others (storytellers, priests, wise men, or elders), but by books amassed in libraries, books from which we endeavor—with extreme difficulty—to form a picture of their authors."[9] Today, oral traditions are turned into scientific notes and books and newspapers are undercut by video images on YouTube.[10] Students worldwide still absorb traditional wisdom, but youth watch television and movies and learn what is new and what is cool more from their peers than their elders. They IM (Instant Message) their friends, update their lives on social networks like Facebook and MySpace, upload their photos and videos to Flickr and YouTube, stay on top of what is happening on deli.cio.us, do research on Wikipedia, and plan their next virtual World of Warcraft battles in Second Life.[11]

Why is this relevant to a volume that builds on the ideas of Robert Keohane? The short answer is that the control and handling of property rights (the ability to own and manage economic assets) is a fundamental building block needed to forge global governance regimes. IIP illustrates how nonstate actors and institutions wield influence. This chapter presumes that their self-interested IP initiatives, if left unchecked, could undermine efforts to manage cooperatively a globally interdependent ICT network infrastructure that fosters economic growth and technological innovation. Further, this is not merely a question of fine-tuning. There is growing evidence that we are at a new inflection point in the development

[7] Barma, Ratner, and Weber 2007, 28.
[8] McCalman 2002, 12–13.
[9] Lévi-Strauss 1968, 366.
[10] Google plans to create a vast online reading room by scanning and indexing all of the books in the Stanford and University of Michigan libraries and additional volumes from the libraries of Harvard, Oxford, and the New York Public Library (Markoff and Wyatt 2004).
[11] See Ito 2006. Diplomats are catching on. USC's Center for Public Diplomacy works with State Department officials in far-flung embassies on Second Life to discuss public diplomacy issues and initiatives.

of communications networks, infrastructure, and applications. This inflection point requires a strategic change in how the pieces of the ICT infrastructure fit together, and thus a shift in how innovative applications evolve. Shortly, current commercial and government structures will be inadequate to deal with future developments. Unless there is adaptation in the IPR realm and elsewhere, global economic prospects will diminish, perhaps markedly. The analytical tools pioneered by Robert Keohane to study complex interdependence may help fulfill the promise of this inflection point in global, converged ICT markets.[12]

The next section considers the prospects if industrial countries and global firms succeed in using IIP rules to enhance their power vis-à-vis other countries and competitors. Then, the impact of recent international negotiations and U.S. law concerning IP on the global power balance are considered. Finally, four scenarios for the future that relate to what occurs in the IIP arena are suggested. These scenarios lead to a set of recommendations on future approaches.

The Balance of Power Shifts

The major surprise of NAFTA and the Uruguay Round trade negotiations was the unexpected "progress" made on intellectual property. During the negotiations to create the TRIPs agreement, trade ministers trespassed on the turf patrolled by the guardians of the Paris Convention for the Protection of Industrial Property[13] and the Berne Convention for the Protection of Literary and Artistic Works,[14] which the United States did not sign until March 1989. The new, muscular WTO trumped an ossified World Intellectual Property Organization (WIPO). Signatories agreed that innovators should be fairly compensated for their ideas and that stronger, though not necessarily harmonized, IIP rights protection was needed. In short, the United States and other industrial countries shifted the negotiating focus to the WTO rather than use a weak international institution over which they exercised little leverage or create a new institution from scratch. Pressed to retain its relevance, WIPO met in 1996 to amend the Berne Treaty to take into account digital content and distribution.

Domestic and international IP protection, coupled with other regulations, traditionally maintained a delicate balance between the rights of in-

[12] As former Intel CEO Andy Grove noted, "an inflection point occurs where the old strategic picture dissolves and gives way to the new" (1996, 32). The evidence and arguments associated with this claimed inflection point are spelled out in Cowhey and Aronson 2009.
[13] Paris Convention for the Protection of Industrial Property 1883.
[14] Protection of Literary and Artistic Works 1886.

novators and the rights of users. Innovators pushed for greater protection; users sought affordable access.[15] Since the mid-1980s the balance has shifted in favor of IP owners and innovators as new domestic laws and international treaties have broadened and strengthened the scope of IP protection and extended its range into new information arenas. Organized industry lobbying interests brought more money to the table than diffuse users, so they usually prevailed. The net result was the expansion of the domain of intellectual property to cover "the intangible commons," what James Boyle has called "the Second Enclosure Movement." Some predict that this new extension of property rights will produce aggregate benefits to society on the scale associated with the first enclosure movement in Britain at the start of the industrial revolution. Or it could "slow down innovation, by putting multiple roadblock, multiple necessary licenses, in the way of subsequent innovation."[16]

IP protection and property rights extension has expanded. IP holders seem to assume "that the strength of intellectual property rights must vary inversely with the cost of copying."[17] However, if this presumption becomes law, this change could threaten the freedom, creativity, and dynamism of the Internet and perhaps the pace of technological innovation. The imposition of new IP standards could retard IT and wireless innovation, suppress creative risk-taking, and undermine development prospects. For example, what should constitute fair use of digital information available online? The United States, the largest market for exports of most developing countries, believes that countries that are unwilling to open their markets, discourage piracy, and improve protection of American IP rights should be subject to trade sanctions.

The distinction between real innovations that deserve IP protection and opportunistic patent and copyright protection also has blurred. Thus, biotech companies now patent DNA fragments and molecules from tropical forest plants and organisms that might yield new pharmaceuticals. Simultaneously, they prevent developing countries from seeking primary patents by exempting "plants and animals other than micro-organisms" from patent protection.[18] Process patents and "patent trolls" also are on the rise. Famously, Amazon.com claimed that the idea of one-click checkout was unique and patentable. Priceline.com made the same argument for its "name your own price" concept. The patent office concurred, granting broad, exclusive rights. Patent trolls buy up patents, often from a bankrupt firm, with no intention to use them themselves but only to

[15] Sell 1998, 107–40.
[16] Boyle 2003, 44.
[17] Boyle 2003, 42.
[18] TRIPs Article 27.3(b).

charge others for their use.[19] So when a newcomer spends heavily and comes up with a real breakthrough, the holders of patents and copyrights being displaced work to blunt the power of innovators. Others review their patent portfolios in order to charge a fee on any innovation that resembles one of their existing patents. Any new innovator that develops new processes or products that resemble existing patents or copyrights must anticipate that it will be subjected to expensive legal battles before it can proceed. Innovators respond in various ways, including embracing the concept of a cultural commons and the open source movement in software, to try to free themselves from the grapples of dominant players.[20] Even when a real breakthrough occurs, the innovator is likely to face sustained opposition to establishment of its right. For example, to establish its CDMA2000 3G wireless standard Qualcomm had to break down a long-established patent pooling system run by the European telephone oligopolists.

Globalization and interdependence involve greater access to resources and markets. But to what extent should countries be open for trade and competition and allow further interconnectedness of their economies? Who should decide—the countries themselves or international treaties signed by states but administered by international institutions? What will it mean if huge corporations use their clout and expertise to ensure that they gain advantage from global interconnectedness? As everyone competes, who should own and control information and ideas? What is it worth? How should creators and innovators be compensated?

NAFTA, WTO, and the Doha Round IP Negotiations

In short, since the 1980s international intellectual property protection has climbed the international economic agenda. Today, IP rules are tougher and more global, but not harmonized. The North American Free Trade Agreement (NAFTA), completed in 1993, provided for strong IPR protection in Canada, Mexico, and the United States and any future signatories. A year later signatories to the Uruguay Round TRIPs agreement, which was built on the Paris Convention, agreed to support somewhat

---

[19] Wikipedia defines *patent trolls* as entities that purchase a patent, often from a bankrupt firm, and then sue another company by claiming that one of its products infringes on the purchased patent. They enforce patents against purported infringers without ever intending to manufacture the patented product or supply the patented service themselves.

[20] Only a major player is likely to resist corporate behemoths. For instance, Microsoft was embraced in China only after it recognized that given weak enforcement of Chinese IP laws, it was, in Bill Gates's words, "easier for our software to compete with Linux when there's piracy than when there's not" (Kirkpatrick 2007, 83).

weaker baseline protection for copyright, patent, trademark, trade secret, and other forms of IPR. In retrospect, who won and who lost?

The TRIPs agreement included a laundry list of ground rules that signatories promised to use to provide IP protection. Countries promised to extend IP protection to cover new and innovative processes and products including computer programs, integrated circuits, plant varieties, and pharmaceuticals. They agreed to national treatment so the same IP protections applied for domestic and international, and for imported and locally produced goods and services. Poorer countries were allowed longer transition periods to come into conformance with the treaty. The least developed signatories could delay until 2016 before fully applying patent protection to pharmaceuticals. Implementation proved difficult to achieve because many developing countries had no existing IP institutions, few experienced experts, administrators, or lawyers, and no judges with the necessary expertise. And diverting scarce funds and manpower to create such expertise was not a high priority. Moreover, concerns quickly arose that restrictions on technology transfer via TRIPs might be hampering development prospects. Even strong supporters of free trade like Jagdish Bhagwati attacked TRIPs, complaining that it has "distorted and deformed an important multilateral institution [the WTO], turning it from its trade mission and rationale and transforming it into a royalty collection agency," especially for drug makers.[21]

NAFTA focused on these same issues but was stronger because only three countries were involved and because Mexico was highly motivated. Therefore, once ratified, the agreement was put into force without a lengthy transition period for signatories to come into compliance. Specifically, Article 17 of NAFTA increased IP protection on four fronts in the Americas: (1) it widened the range of what could be patented and established a long patent period; (2) copyright protection was extended to cover new technologies including software databases and sound recordings; (3) it narrowed the conditions under which compulsory licensing was allowed and beefed up contractual rights in copyrights; (4) the three signatories agreed to put the agreement into force quickly and to establish meaningful enforcement mechanisms to give it teeth.[22]

The initial declarations related to TRIPs at the Ministerial Conference in Doha, Qatar in late 2001 clarified existing obligations, particularly with respect to implementation, and set out a preliminary agenda. The Doha Declarations appear to aid developing countries by securing greater flexibility in using IP rights, especially as related to public health issues and domestically produced generic drugs. The ministers at Doha issued a

[21] Bhagwati 1991, 182.
[22] Callan 1998, 17–18.

separate declaration on public health and intellectual property. In light of the international AIDS crisis and other public health emergencies, ministers acted to mitigate the tension between improving public health and strengthening IP rights. For example, South Africa and others desperately wanted to reduce the cost of treating their HIV/AIDS populations with expensive AIDS drugs. The declaration recognized that to meet the demands of national public health emergencies governments like Brazil and India could suspend or alter certain IP rights obligations so that their firms could produce generics. Although the industrial countries and their pharmaceutical industries agreed to loosen their IP rights to deal with life-threatening epidemics, the United States and the EU insisted that profitable luxury and lifestyle drugs such as Viagra and weight-loss medicines were not granted more flexible IP treatment.

In addition to public health concerns, the Doha negotiations agreed to revisit several issues raised by TRIPs that are important to developing countries. New issues discussed in the Doha negotiations included the use of patents, trade secrets, and copyrights to protect traditional knowledge and folklore, the relationship of the Convention on Biological Diversity to the TRIPs agreement, and provisions to enhance the transfer of technology to developing countries. Other issues include efforts to protect plant and animal varieties and to refine the use of geographic location identification (such as the quality or reputation of products such as wine) to ensure that products originate from the place and manufacturer that is claimed.[23]

The United States long has been reluctant to join certain international agreements because it worried that doing so might restrict its sovereignty and freedom to act in its own interests. The U.S. refusal to sign on to agreements covering land mines, global warming, and the establishment of an international criminal court were in part driven by this concern. Similarly, the United States did not sign the Berne Agreement for more than a century to avoid having to repeal its own statute (17 U.S.C., section 601) that "required first publication in either the United States or Canada for a copyright to qualify for U.S. copyright protection under U.S. law."[24] U.S. publishers could get around the law, but even when the statute was allowed to expire in 1986, some U.S. copyright owners opposed ratification of the Berne Treaty because it contains a moral rights clause that allows an author "to object to any distortion, mutilation, or other modification . . . which would be prejudicial to his honor or reputation."[25] The television and movie industries that adapt creative works

[23] McCalman 2004.
[24] Bettig 1996, 221.
[25] Article 6bis.

alter screenplays, or "colorize" old movies, opposed this provision. Interests that were gathering to fight piracy and promote IIP protection and enforcement prevailed, and the United States signed the Berne Agreement. When the NAFTA and TRIPs agreements were negotiated, the United States made certain that they did not contain clauses related to moral rights.

The U.S. negotiators constantly reassured Mexico and other developing countries that the new IP agreements would help their economic prospects. Developing countries remain unconvinced. They distrust the United States and complain that it favors free trade when it is in its interest, but is protectionist when free trade undercuts American industries like steel, agriculture, software, or Hollywood.

An example of U.S. efforts to enhance its own industries came at the December 1996 WIPO conference in Geneva. The United States pushed for, but did not achieve the establishment of, new international IP norms for the information industry. According to Pamela Samuelson, the U.S. program consisted of six elements: It sought to (1) grant exclusive rights for copyright owners to control almost all temporary reproductions in the random access of computers; (2) treat digital transmissions of protected works as copies distributed to the public; (3) restrict the power of states to limit or make exceptions to the exclusive rights of copyright owners even for fair use and first sale privileges, (4) allow copyright owners to challenge the manufacture and sale of technologies or services that would make it possible to get around technological protections of copyrighted works; (5) protect the integrity of rights management information associated with protected works in digital form; and (6) create new legal protections for the contents of databases. Along with their European counterparts, American negotiators pursued "high protectionist norms" that "would enable their industries to flourish in the growing global market for information products and services."[26] In the aftermath of the Uruguay Round the United States continued to press to strengthen and harmonize IIP protection. In the absence of multilateral negotiations, it embarked on negotiations to establish model bilateral free trade agreements (e.g., with Jordan) and bilateral investment treaties (e.g., with Nicaragua) that contained TRIPs-plus provisions on IP. The idea was to ratchet up the level of IP protection by combining a process of "forum shifting," with coordinated bilateral and multilateral negotiations, and entrenchment of minimum acceptable standards of IP protection in international agreements."[27] Developing countries were promised that if they went along with the multilateral IP accords, the EU and the United States would relax some of the

[26] Samuelson 1997, 373.
[27] Drahos 2002.

standards in bilateral discussions. Although the EU was more flexible than the United States, this did not occur.

Increased Domestic IPR and Enforcement: the DMCA

Finding and maintaining the right balance between innovators and users recurs as a critical challenge facing policymakers. Paul Goldstein frames the public policy dilemma this way: "if society withholds property rights from creative work, the price that producers can charge for access to it will begin to approach zero; their revenues will diminish and, with them, their incentives to produce more. But if society confers property rights on creative works, prices will rise and the information produced will reach smaller, wealthier (or more profligate) audiences, even though it might be that the work could be disseminated to everyone else at no additional cost."[28]

During the Clinton years, the rights of property rights holders were strengthened and extended, especially with regard to digital content and distribution. Large commercial IP holders like the Intellectual Property Committee, the International Intellectual Property Alliance, and sector groups such as the Pharmaceutical Manufacturers Association, the Recording Industry Association of America, and the Motion Picture Association made lobbying for "hard law" and tough enforcement a priority. Their most stunning success came in 1998 when the Senate gave teeth to legislation implementing the WIPO treaty amendments. The Digital Millennium Copyright Act (DMCA) of 1998 tipped the delicate balance between the rights of innovators and the rights of users in favor of large firms that owned the copyrights.

TRIPs on the international level and the DMCA on the domestic level represented victories for large commercial interests that "institutionalized a conception of intellectual property rights based on protection and exclusion rather than competition and diffusion."[29] Critics doubted "that stronger IPRs stimulate local innovation, at least in the short to medium run" and predicted that small innovators in both rich and poor nations would suffer.[30] Those concerned more with equity and development also worried that consumers in developing countries would transfer more IP resources to rich firms than they received in return.

The Clinton administration supported the copyright industry, often fa-

[28] Goldstein 1994, 177.

[29] Sell 2002, 172. There were exceptions. The DMCA protected sites like YouTube from being sued for posting copyrighted material as long as the material was taken down after they were notified of infringement.

[30] Branstetter 2004, 369.

voring innovators over users. Its draft Intellectual Property White Paper proposed giving copyright owners control over all digital copyrighted works, their reproduction, and transmission. They favored eliminating fair-use rights whenever a product could be licensed and depriving the public of first-sale rights (including electronic forwarding). The Clinton administration proposed attaching copyright management information to digital copies of a work and to protect every digital copy of every work technologically. It argued for making online service providers into copyright police responsible for implementing pay-per-use rules and proposed that copyright rules should be taught to children in school.[31]

The white paper draft was toned down. Still, it helped inform the DMCA, which strengthened copyright protections. One key element of the DMCA was the "anticircumvention" provision that "restricts the cracking of code that protects copyrighted material" and "forbids the creation of code that cracks code that protects copyrighted material."[32] This provision made it illegal to circumvent antipiracy measures that are embedded within commercial software or to manufacture or distribute devices that can unscramble encryption codes.

The fundamental criticism leveled at the DMCA, and other laws designed to protect IPR, was that they "are so broadly drawn that all sorts of companies might use it to stifle competition."[33] Copyright protection grew out of print technologies. Built on English copyright foundations, American copyright law "created private rights to published works" while providing "for a legal public domain consisting of works on which copyrights had lapsed or to which it had never applied."[34]

The copyright industries are threatened by the changes transforming global online networks, especially interactions among digital youth. Social networking and mass collaboration change market dynamics and business and social prospects.[35] Faced with new technologies, publishers and authors' executors have tried to prevent works from going into the public domain.[36] This effort was designed to counteract Web and broadband communications technologies that allow the widespread, inexpensive distribution of perfect copies of digitized information. Digital books were slow to win widespread readership, but the popularity of Amazon's Kindle eBook reader may signal the beginning of acceptance. Still, the

[31] Samuelson 1996, 136.
[32] Lessig 2001, 187.
[33] Wildstrom 2003, 26.
[34] Starr 2004, 115.
[35] Rheingold 2003; Tapscott and Williams 2006.
[36] Google's attempts to digitize works published after 1923 have proceeded slowly. So far there is no provision to release "orphan" works into the public domain when nobody claims to own the copyright.

question remains: what is the appropriate manner for protecting digitally distributed intellectual property? One insightful critic asked, "Who will 'own' an interactive novel after it has been repeatedly interacted with?"[37] It becomes more difficult to effectively police and protect IPR that dynamically is reworked. The challenges for copyright holders of music and movies provide even more complex threats. In the face of significant drops in CD sales, the music industry is finally seeking new business models that are less dependent on rigid IPR enforcement. The movie and broadcast industries, taking note of the music industries' travails, have started to experiment with providing free downloads of shows and movies.

Copyright holders have attacked, with all the legal firepower at their disposal, efforts to use and modify IP in print and online. Notably, in 2001 the heirs of Margaret Mitchell tried to quash Alice Randall's *The Wind Done Gone*, a parody or sequel of *Gone with the Wind* from the perspective of the African slaves in the household, arguing that the story was theirs to control until 2031 (extended from 1992 by the new copyright law). The novel was published, but the tremendous expense of the legal battle may discourage writers and publishers from issuing future parodies and sequels.[38]

Music faces similar challenges. CD sales are falling sharply as teenagers everywhere continue to download free and also legal music. The more the music companies struggle to retain their old business model and prosecute offenders, the more negative the public's perception of them becomes. However, sales trends reveal new types of purchasing behavior. According to Nielsen SoundScan figures, CD sales in the first quarter of 2007 dropped 20 percent from the same period in 2006. Sales of digitized albums dropped by almost the same percentage, while sales of individual digitized songs jumped by nearly 20 percent during the same period.[39] Buyers never were loyal to the labels; now the buzz is turning from the performer to the song. Record company losses are real, but losses claimed to be due to software and IP violations are inflated. The copyright industry wrongly assumes that all those who illegally copy music, videos, or software would otherwise pay full retail price to obtain the pirated intel-

---

[37] Lanham 1993, 18.

[38] Lessig 2001, 198–99. Similarly, in 2004 Edgar Rice Burroughs's estate tried to curtail distribution of the novel *Tarzan Presley*, published in New Zealand, claiming that it infringed on IP rights by using the name Tarzan and aspects of the man-raised-by-apes character. The novel tells the story of Presley, "raised by gorillas in the wild jungles of New Zealand, scarred in battles with vicious giant wetas, seduced by a beautiful young scientist," who gets a record deal with Elvis Presley's producer and has thirty number 1 hits. Tom Cardy, "Legal Eagles target Tarzan," *Dominion Post*, December 2, 2004.

[39] Farrell 2007.

lectual property.[40] The only real choice for music barons is to reinvent their industry and dramatically alter their business practices and approaches. This process began with the introduction of Apple's iTune technology in April 2003 and its wildly successful iPod music player that blazed the way in providing a mechanism for distributing music over the Internet and still maintaining an IP revenue stream.

The problem is not that someone gets copyrighted materials cheaply, because otherwise they would not get it at all. It is routine for IP holders to charge less in poorer countries for their products and services than they do in major markets. Studios and broadcasters use variable pricing schemes to provide movies and television shows to developing countries for what they can get, not for what they think they should get. Their goal is to reduce incentives to piracy while maintaining profitability. Property rights owners can swallow low rates of return if doing so discourages outright piracy and makes them less vulnerable to less expensive alternatives (e.g., Linux). IP rights holders often are as concerned with creating the legal precedent of compensation for their innovations as they are in the absolute amount of compensation.

Piracy and parallel imports are much more disturbing to copyright holders. Piracy from music to movies, from BitTorrent to China, deprives legitimate copyright holders of revenue due to them. An even more serious problem comes when developing countries reexport cheap or pirated products to industrial countries, impacting sales to those who could otherwise afford to pay. Hong Kong after its return to China provides an example. IP holders want to be paid top prices in Hong Kong, but recognize they need to discount their prices to sell to the rest of China. Even after China's entry into the WTO, there remains a huge temptation to reexport legitimate and pirated products from China to Hong Kong and beyond. The problem is magnified because films usually are available on the Web before they open in theaters. The same is true for music and bestselling books. To partially counteract this phenomenon, starting with *The Matrix* movies, books, and CDs have been released simultaneously everywhere, despite time differences.[41]

By contrast, the patent-based pharmaceutical industry faces a different challenge than copyright sectors. It is far more expensive to develop, test, and gain approval for new drugs in industrial countries than to promote a rock band. Moreover, patents on drugs are shorter in duration and more difficult to extend than copyrights on creative works. This creates

---

[40] Schneier 2000, 25.

[41] Raymond Vernon's "product life-cycle" has less relevance in a globally networked world where new content is widely and simultaneously available. A remarkable account of the cross-platform marketing of the Matrix movies is found in Jenkins 2006.

incentives for pharmaceutical companies to concentrate on incremental improvements or on potential blockbusters that will sell for high prices to those who can afford them. There is little incentive to innovate on drugs for diseases that afflict the poor, so pharmaceutical company R&D does not concentrate on African and other tropical diseases because they do not believe that they will earn enough money to justify anticipated R&D expenditures needed to control these diseases. As a result, more R&D funds are spent by drug firms in industrial countries on diseases of pets than on diseases of the tropics.

Pharmaceutical firms are patenting the rainforest, but also seek full price for drugs everywhere. U.S. policy began to shift after the post-9/11 anthrax scare when Bayer, the sole producer of Cipro, the drug of choice for safeguarding against anthrax exposure, demanded full patent payment. The United States, citing the potential health emergency, pushed the German patent holder to accept lower royalties. The existence of the HIV/AIDS scourge reinforced this rethinking of U.S. policy. It was impossible to deny that cheaper HIV/AIDS drugs should be available in Africa and other poor, stricken countries. This persuaded the Bush administration, with pharmaceutical industry acquiescence, to agree to Doha Declaration changes in TRIPs to allow for price differentials. At the same time, the Bush administration staunchly opposed efforts to legalize the reimportation of approved drugs from Internet pharmacists located in Canada and elsewhere that would undercut pharmaceutical companies' patent payment receipts. Thus, the pharmaceutical industry is locked in a war with users to maximize its IP rights.

Intellectual Property and the Digital Divide

This chapter concludes with three cuts at international intellectual property issues: their impact on the digital divide, possible policy reforms, and their relevance within the international relations literature. A first consideration is whether the digital divide within and between countries is a temporary artifact of innovation, IP initiatives, and other policies, or is it more permanent? To grapple with this concern, four scenarios are considered (things fall apart; wealth and poverty; living well is the best revenge; and sustainable growth) that can be arrayed according to whether the digital divide is widening or narrowing and according to resource sustainability.

First, to paraphrase Chinua Achebe, things could fall apart if the digital divide widens, resources are squandered, and the environment is overwhelmed. Manuel Castells argues that "uneven development is the most dramatic expression of the digital divide," that the "social unevenness of the development process is linked to the networking logic and global

TABLE 10.1
Four Scenarios

	Nonsustainable resource use	Sustainable resource use
Widening digital divide	Things fall apart	Wealth and poverty
Narrowing digital divide	Living well is the best revenge	Sustainable growth

reach of the new economy," and that to be competitive within a networked world economy, countries, firms, and individuals need easy access to global flows of capital and information.[42] Further, the "transformation of liberty and privacy on the Internet is a direct result of its commercialization."[43] So it is probable that if legitimate legal capital flows and information flows are restricted by stringent IP protections, alternatives will be found. If many in poorer countries are shut out of the new economy, global criminal activities will arise to create illicit transnational networks instead.[44] Inevitably, such activities undermine the legitimacy and stability of governments and the civic culture and may lead to the destruction of the rule of law, the collapse of state authority, and even to violence and civil war.[45]

Second, the digital and economic divide could continue to widen while the economy remained relatively stable. This incremental, rich get richer, poor get poorer scenario might result in a segmented world with pockets of great wealth on islands of intense activity interspersed in seas of desperation. Information and IP catapult the techno-nomads, and a few entrepreneurs ride to significant wealth, but most people tread water or fall further behind into poverty and insecurity. Sustaining such a world depends on the ability of the United States to use its military, economic, and informational superiority to maintain the status quo.

Multinational firms are not the prime culprits responsible for poverty, corruption, and civil unrest. Most analysts agree that innovators should be compensated fairly for their breakthroughs so that they continue to invest in innovation. However, what constitutes fair use and fair payment varies across countries and sectors. Even IP hawks recognize that a

[42] Castells 2001, 265.
[43] Castells 2001, 170.
[44] Rose-Ackerman 1999.
[45] Cyberattacks aimed at crippling key networks increasingly erupt after politically provocative incidents. For instance, in 2007 Russian hackers bombarded Estonia's ICT infrastructure after a Soviet-era statue in Estonia was taken down (Vamosi 2007).

"country's level of development heavily influences the values placed on IP rights. Developing countries are leery of strong IP protection, which favors innovators over consumers, creative production over diffusion, and private interests over social goals."[46] This requires innovators and users to readjust their treatment of IP as circumstances change. The pendulum swung in the direction of strong and more harmonized IP protection during the 1990s, but it may now be starting to swing back toward balance.

Third, a more humane, but potentially disastrous scenario imagines that new technology and resource consumption will narrow the gap between rich and poor by pulling up the poor without sacrificing the advantages of the rich. In the words of Gerald Murphy, F. Scott Fitzgerald's friend, "Living well is the best revenge." The well-being of future generations may be sacrificed to prop up those now alive. Anyone with assets can live well for a time if he sells off his assets, if she drains her bank accounts. If those in industrial countries are entitled to the good life, why shouldn't the billions in China, India, and elsewhere seek parity? IT advance could help bridge the gap, but if billions more people consumed and polluted at the same level as those in rich countries, disaster would result. When resources are exhausted, individuals suffer, and civilizations may collapse.

If countries can burn through money and resources to maintain their lifestyles and improve the lot of others by relying on new breakthroughs, then Malthus was wrong. Technological breakthroughs may be magic pills that can improve everyone's situation while new ways to protect resources and the environment are devised. Some are confident that there is sufficient clean water and cheap energy to fuel growth and alleviate poverty and hunger. But if they are wrong, future generations will face problems we make worse today. This scenario was preferred by the Bush administration even though the gap between revenues and expenses was huge and growing. But can innovation close the gap while sustaining the planet?

Fourth, more optimistically, information and clean energy revolutions could be the instruments of sustainable growth and development that will lift the impoverished without decimating the planet. Communication and information technology needs could be inexpensive and widely available. None of the other alternatives leads to an equitable, sustainable future. To move this way, information needs to flow freely and IP needs to be a tool of innovation, not resistance. Instead IP holders usually threaten abusers with lawsuits and sanctions instead of enticing them to respect and protect IP through the use of positive rewards and incentives. The copyright industries increasingly threaten companies whose innovations make it possible to circumvent their IP and users of the offending mate-

[46] Callan 1998, 1.

rial. This is consistent with the first three scenarios, but not with the fourth. To grope in this direction, IP rights need to be exercised on behalf of information development everywhere.

Toward Rebalancing IIP

What is needed to restore the balance between innovators and users of IP, especially in developing countries? How might IP relations between industrial countries and firms and developing countries be improved? How might the IP balance between developed and developing countries be restored so that all sides benefit? Transparency, fairness, and generosity are required. Four steps would begin the process.

1. *Raise the bar for those claiming to establish intellectual property rights.* IP has become a tool to promote competitive advantage at the expense of would-be rivals instead of an incentive for innovators to innovate. Large firms use their financial heft and teams of lawyers to squash newcomers with new ideas. TRIPs in its present form may make achieving sustainable development more difficult for poor countries. Thus, IPR should be tied to the amount of money invested in research and development and not just to a fixed time frame. Efforts by copyright holders to extend the period of their copyrights should be curtailed and rolled back to help restore the balance between the IP protections afforded to innovators and the needs of users. In essence, strong property rights are only sustainable if they also lead to increased innovation and the extension of benefits to users.

2. *Promote local support for IPR in developing countries by assuring that their domestic innovators benefit.* Empirical studies suggest that strong IPR protection by developing countries increases both foreign direct investment and imports.[47] This finding has not convinced poorer countries to implement and enforce strong IP laws. Unless developing countries' innovators also benefit from IP protection, they have little incentive to crack down on piracy. Curbing corruption and illegal IP activities will be ineffective unless there are legal, profitable opportunities available. The dilemma that needs to be overcome resembles the situation with foreign food aid. It may feed the population during a time of drought and starvation, but if countries rely on foreign food charity long term, local farmers have little incentive to plant their crops or to improve their agricultural techniques.

3. *Provide foreign assistance to countries to implement their IP com-*

[47] Lesser 2001.

mitments and assist domestic entrepreneurs and firms develop opportunities tied to their national situation. Even countries that wish to create strong IP protection need help in creating laws and institutions. There is little appropriate expertise in most developing countries, and spending scarce human and capital resources on establishing a system of IP protection is likely to be a low priority. Therefore, outside help is needed and ought to be welcomed. As needed, foreign firms, governments, international institutions, and NGOs "should offer to advise countries that are drafting new legislation, help pay for local IPR improvements, and reward countries and firms that improve the IPR enforcement with favorable publicity indicating that strong IPR protection helped attract their investments."[48] In addition, networking between universities, firms, and experts in developed and developing countries to train experts, transfer technology, and create local partnerships is desirable.

4. *Developing countries need to keep it simple, honest, transparent, and consistent.* Greed and corruption discourage foreign investors and constrain the growth of legitimate business in developing countries. IP rules should be clearly articulated, transparent, and fairly and consistently enforced for both local and international copyright holders. In addition, installing a coherent, well-trained, and honest administrative and judicial system is important. For example, Botswana has grown rapidly since the 1980s in part because its mineral wealth was discovered after its administrative system was in place.

Intellectual Property and International Relations

Will the globalization of intellectual property rights widen or narrow the digital divide within and between countries? If rich countries and their largest firms maintain the upper hand versus poorer countries and smaller firms, how will that impact relations among these countries? If perceived inequities grow and developing countries cannot be competitive within a globalized, networked world economy, globalization could unwind into disarray. Information will not be free, but if new ideas and information are prohibitively expensive because of tough IP enforcement, those who seek these breakthroughs will take them by whatever means are available.

Similarly, if IP rights are strictly enforced, the digital divide persists, and growth and resource use slows substantially, the gap between rich and poor will grow. Large-scale piracy may discourage R&D and innovation, but profit maximization can be unsettling. The rights of IP holders need to be balanced against the benefits from affordable access to in-

[48] Aronson et al. 19983.

novations. The poorer the country, the less it can afford and the greater should be the price break for legitimate users. Otherwise, great wealth amid a sea of poverty will become unstable, requiring the United States to act to keep order. Fortunately, the spotlight recently shined on Africa and other desperately poor regions shows signs of leading to greater flexibility and balance on IP issues in international negotiations, despite the failure of the Doha Round to reach a successful conclusion in 2008.

Even if the gap between rich and poor narrows because developing countries' growth spurts using scarce resources, this is problematic. Without water, oil, and critical resources, decline continues and violence and conflict grow more likely. If access to affordable information resources continues to grow, the outlook would improve. Longer-term sustainability requires information and communication technology to be available globally. To make it available, international institutions, governments, and innovative firms need to readjust their treatment of IP so that the information revolution is global and the culture and practice of intellectual property evolve. Education, positive incentives, and the exercise of IP rights with compassion are at least as important as threats and legal enforcement. IP rights need to be exercised on behalf of information development and sustainability, not just profit. If this can be accomplished, it would be an important step toward building trust and cooperation in a complex, interdependent world.

CHAPTER 11

The Big Influence of Big Allies

TRANSGOVERNMENTAL RELATIONS

AS A TOOL OF STATECRAFT

Timothy J. McKeown

Keohane's Argument about Transgovernmentalism

Robert Keohane's treatment of transgovernmental relations between the United States and its allies[1] was an early challenge to the dominance of the unitary model of the state. Keohane argued for "the big influence of small allies"—they had far more influence on U.S. policy than one might expect. Some reasons for this are consistent with a unitary conception of the state—asymmetries of motivation and attention favoring the small country, the occasional American lack of appropriate instruments of influence, and the high value that the U.S. government placed on keeping friendly governments in power. What made his argument remarkable was his next step—to drop the unitary assumption and to argue that small states succeed when they enlist the support of subunits of the U.S. government and mobilize them to obtain concessions from U.S. leaders. They do this by exploiting their connections to these subunits and the subunits' dependence on outcomes that can only be supplied by foreigners. They also create or exploit transnational links to interest groups and the attentive public in the United States to enlist them as supporters.

In some respects the abandonment of the assumption of a unitary state has become accepted practice. Public choice models of executive-legislative relations imported into international relations theory and the burgeoning interest in a "democratic peace" have rendered the unitary model obsolescent if not obsolete. However, the structure of the state that they depict is generally limited to an executive confronting a legislature or voters. Such a simplification is necessary if one is confined to formal models with closed form solutions, but then the issues raised by Keohane cannot be pursued with fidelity to a richer empirical reality.

From the standpoint of public choice theories, the events recounted by Keohane are theoretically and empirically problematic. If a political scientist can see that small states are doing this, so too could a U.S. govern-

[1] Keohane 1971.

ment official. In work with Joseph Nye, Keohane noted, "Transgovernmental coalitions may be employed by sub-units of powerful states such as the United States as means by which to penetrate weaker governments."[2] Similarly, Huntington contended that

In the American empire, if it be that, the American presence was thus almost everywhere, American rule almost nowhere. American expansion has been characterized not by the *acquisition* of new territories but by their *penetration*. . . . The expansion of the American operational empire has . . . not been incompatible with the multiplication of national sovereignties in the Third World. Indeed, in some respects, [it] has facilitated the growth of American transnational operations. . . . Transnationalism is the American mode of expansion.[3]

Krasner also noted that government officials control the contact that foreign officials have with the home government, and they can exploit that to encourage or discourage transgovernmental contacts.[4]

If the success of transnational and transgovernmental contacts is related to their appearance of being unconnected to the influencing government's central decision-makers, then that government has a strong incentive to conceal any direction provided to ostensibly private or unauthorized interactions. Government officials who are colluding with foreign governments are also likely to have strong incentives to conceal their behavior. The public record might therefore understate the frequency of significant transgovernmental interaction, as well as high-level government knowledge and control of it. Some apparently transgovernmental or transnational interactions may, upon closer examination, turn out to be instances where one or both central governments play a controlling if concealed role.

What Exactly Are Transgovernmental Relations?

Modern governments are complex, multidivisional organizations, and interactions between them occur through many channels. Keohane and Nye noted the massive growth in the number of personnel and government agencies involved in U.S. foreign relations after 1945.[5] U.S. embassy staffs in important countries have for decades numbered in the hundreds (for example, by 1958 the U.S. Embassy in Saigon had 180 American employees [and an uncounted number of Vietnamese]).[6] These staffs often

[2] Keohane and Nye 1974, 47.
[3] Huntington 1973, 344.
[4] Krasner 1995.
[5] Keohane and Nye 1974.
[6] Montgomery 1962, 8.

include officials concerned with agriculture, labor, the environment, illegal drugs, atomic energy, public administration and public finance, and other program areas remote from traditional diplomatic concerns.

However, it is not just the sheer number of links or the reliance on officials from agencies outside of the foreign ministry that defines transgovernmentalism. Even if we conceive of government as a pure hierarchy, then the phenomena noted by Keohane could still emerge because control from the top is imperfect. In choice-theoretic parlance, transgovernmentalism occurs because governments confront an "agency problem"— efforts to control the behavior of subordinates are costly and sometimes fail. The existence of numerous low- or mid-level contacts between governments is a necessary but not sufficient condition for transgovernmentalism. When low-level contacts are encouraged by high-level officials and they maintain effective control over their subordinates, then the situation is simply one of delegation. While the politics of delegation is interesting in its own right,[7] it is not what Keohane addressed. In his cases transgovernmental contacts were interesting precisely because control from the top on at least one side was ineffective.

If control is imperfect, then an agency of one government might act as a coalition partner of an agency from another. This relationship is evoked by the Japanese term *gaiatsu*, connoting a situation where one Japanese ministry triumphs over another by enlisting foreign support for its own position.[8] Such a relationship was anticipated by Keohane and Nye, as well as by Keohane's 1983 argument about the demand for regimes, which contended that officials could build alliances with officials in other governments to strengthen their bargaining advantages within their home government.[9] Allison's account of bureaucratic politics as bargaining among independent organizational subunits presupposed a closed system, but as Risse-Kappen noted, transgovernmental phenomena imply a system that is open to intervention by external organizations.[10]

Subsequent Examinations of Transgovernmentalism in Alliances

Some have followed Keohane's 1971 argument by treating transgovernmental and transnational relations as weapons of the weak. Moon analyzed the transgovernmental and transnational channels whereby the Re-

---

[7] To the extent that delegation is studied at all, it is only in the context of legislative delegations of authority to the executive. Haftendorn 1999 shows that delegations within the executive are also rich in implications.

[8] Schoppa 1993.

[9] Keohane and Nye 1974; Keohane 1983.

[10] Allison 1971; Risse-Kappen 1995, 9.

public of Korea government influenced the U.S. government.[11] Kivimaki did likewise for Indonesia.[12] Others have treated transgovernmental influence as two-way.

Although Wendt and Friedheim analyze Soviet control of East Germany as a process in which "clients may become actively involved as a form of lobbyist influencing the domestic politics of patrons,"[13] their argument focuses on security assistance from the dominant partner being exchanged for influence over client policies, and the more general role of external assistance in changing the domestic politics of the recipient. They propose that aid could alter the membership of the winning coalition in the recipient by subsidizing that coalition's lack of responsiveness to its own society:

> Assistance enables constellations of societal interests to control power in subordinate states that otherwise would not or would at least be forced to make significant concessions to competitors. . . . [This] creates clients who have an "investment in subordination."[14]

Wendt and Friedheim did not provide empirical support for their contentions, but Sarotte's investigation of East German relations with the USSR sheds light on their case.[15] Although East Germany had Marxist-Leninist institutions, they did not prevent transgovernmental phenomena, because the Leninist norm and associated Communist Party rules against factions were violated.[16] In the late 1960s Erich Honecker and other high-level officials began to voice doubts about Party chairman Walter Ulbricht's détente-oriented policies toward West Germany. The Soviets used lateral relationships between East German and Soviet intelligence agencies to signal those opposed to Ulbricht's line that they wished East Germany to hold back from dealing with West Germany.[17] These transgovernmental contacts were especially important, because the East German agency provided the staff support for East German negotiators bargaining with the West German government, and the chief East

[11] Moon 1988.

[12] Kivimaki 1993.

[13] Wendt and Friedheim 1996, 250.

[14] Wendt and Friedheim 1996, 250.

[15] Sarotte 2001.

[16] Evangelista 1995 argued that it is difficult for transnational actors to obtain access to a Marxist-Leninist state, but that if they do manage to make contact at a high level, they could have a surprising amount of influence. This happens because top-level decision-makers in such system face a paucity of checks and balances or "veto players." However, if the official being reached is truly a top-level official, then this is a different situation from the one commonly envisioned in discussions of transgovernmental relations, where control from the top is subverted by outside influences.

[17] Evangelista 1995, 31.

German negotiator was an informant for the agency. The East Germans usually employed their intelligence agency, not their Foreign Ministry, for managing contacts with Western countries that did not extend diplomatic recognition.[18] Connections between the East German intelligence agency and its Soviet counterpart provided a channel through which the Soviet government could influence policies in East Germany while bypassing Ulbricht and the Foreign Ministry. Although Sarotte did not have access to Soviet intelligence archives, the importance of East Germany to the KGB (its station near Berlin was the largest outside the USSR) provides an indication that that Soviet agency had a great deal of business to conduct there.[19] The KGB recruited agents within Eastern European intelligence agencies to provide them with additional information and means of control.[20] Party secretary Brezhnev also communicated with Honecker directly, warning him that it would be dangerous to allow the disharmony within the politburo to become visible to the Bonn government, and hinting that the Soviet Union might intervene openly if developments strayed too far from Moscow's preferences.[21] If the Soviets had taken Leninist norms against factions seriously, the Soviets would have responded to the Honecker faction by alerting Ulbricht or scolding the Honecker supporters. Instead, the Soviet ambassador helped them to draft a letter to Brezhnev imploring him to encourage Ulbricht to resign.[22] All this suggests that transgovernmental relations were quite important, but not in the way that Wendt and Friedheim surmised. Neither the Honecker faction nor Ulbricht was particularly concerned about public opinion and did not respond to it, so the "subsidizing" unresponsive government" argument does not apply. However, Soviet troops on East German soil, ostensibly because of the formal alliance relationship between East Germany and the Soviet Union, did make highly credible any implicit or explicit threats by the Soviets to intervene openly in East German politics. That is not inconsistent with the Wendt-Friedheim thesis.

Crosby's examination of the North American Aerospace Defense Command (NORAD) also reveals two-way transgovernmentalism, but here too the historically crucial influence emanated from the dominant power. The United States exploited the institutional peculiarities of Canadian civil-military relations by using its contacts with the Canadian military to enlist them in implementing institutional arrangements that contravened Canadian government policies.[23] Canadian and U.S. air forces cooperated

---

[18] Evangelista 1995, 90.
[19] Andrew and Gordievsky 1990, 37.
[20] Shackley and Finney (2005, 26) discuss penetration of Polish intelligence by the KGB.
[21] Sarotte 2001, 281.
[22] Sarotte 2001, 105–6.
[23] Crosby 1998.

in constructing NORAD, bypassing the Canada-U.S. Permanent Joint Board on Defense to avoid involving Canadian government civilians in matters that both air forces knew would stimulate questions and objections from these officials. NORAD operates with a U.S. commander of Canadian forces in Canada, even in peacetime. It is a bilateral relationship in tension with NATO, and it raises the possibility of Canada's being entrapped in U.S. conflicts. It requires a declared non-nuclear-weapons state to accept nuclear weapons for defense purposes. These features significantly limit Canadian sovereignty, and they were in tension with declared Canadian government policy when NORAD was created. Particularly interesting from a theoretical standpoint is that this situation is one in which an international organization, rather than facilitating transgovernmental contacts, was the product of those contacts.

The NORAD proposal was presented to the Canadian government only after being approved by the U.S. and Canadian chiefs of staff and the U.S. government. While the Canadian government could have rejected the plan, the political costs of forcing the deliberations to begin anew would probably have been substantial. The U.S. government, by virtue of its capacity to manipulate transgovernmental relations with the Canadian armed forces, was able to control the framing of alternatives and hence the outcome.

Even more remarkably, the Canadian military made agreements with the U.S. military without informing senior civilian officials. It misrepresented NORAD to civilians as a NATO command, because this allowed treating it as merely an extension of an existing commitment.[24] General Charles Foulkes, the Canadian chief of staff, told his U.S. counterparts that he was forced to misrepresent the NORAD relationship to NATO to prevent interference by civilian ministers. Foulkes assured his government that the Canadian Air Defence commander retained "complete command and administration over Canadian troops and equipment," when this was manifestly untrue. The Canadian embassy in Washington informed the U.S. government that Canadian forces would only be actively assigned to NORAD in the event of an emergency. "Meanwhile, CINCNORAD, the Canadian Joint Staff in Washington the US Joint Chiefs of Staff and General Foulkes agreed in secret in August 1957 to delegate operational control of the Canadian Air Defence Command to the US Continental Air Defence Headquarters."[25] In an exchange of "confidential" letters the U.S. commander of NORAD, his Canadian deputy commander, General Foulkes, and the U.S. Joint Chiefs of Staff agreed that "Both countries will react automatically and in unison against any attack on the North

[24] Crosby 1998, 44.
[25] Crosby 1998, 43–44.

American continent." Foulkes said that he was "very doubtful" that the Canadian government would agree to this provision, but that it should be implemented nonetheless.

How could the U.S. government exploit this transgovernmental tie with such success? Crosby argues that

- Civilians control Canada's military primarily through its budget and procurement policies. The mechanisms for civilian review of specific military decisions are weak.
- The Canadian military's definition of national interest is shaped by professional standards that it receives from the U.S. military. The Canadian military is susceptible to them because it is from the U.S. military that it gains access to sophisticated military technology and a "seriousness of purpose" unavailable in Canada.
- In order to protect this access, and because cooperative defence programme planning for mutual security includes planning on the basis of collective, but largely US, monetary, industrial and technological resources, the security agenda of the Canadian military tends to reflect the security agenda of its alliance partner."[26]

The Theoretical Lessons

From the above cases, we can sketch the outlines of a theory of transgovernmental relations that develops the ideas present in embryonic form in Keohane's 1971 essay and his paper with Nye on transgovernmental relations.

1. Transgovernmental relations can be exploited by any government that cares to and has the capabilities and opportunity for success. Such tactics are not solely the tool of the small and the weak. Large, wealthy states can use the same tactics, but their success is not due to their size or wealth per se, but to their more robust hierarchical control arrangements. While such arrangements require the resources to invest in supervisory personnel and an effective communications system, resources are merely necessary but not sufficient for large powers to exploit transgovernmental contacts. Other governments are vulnerable to asymmetries in effective hierarchical control when they are not highly institutionalized and depend heavily on personal relations to manage the government. A lack of resources can exacerbate these problems, but even relatively poor governments can have highly effective hierarchical control (consider, for ex-

[26] Crosby 1998, 41.

ample, the success of hierarchical control in such low-income Marxist-Leninist governments as Albania's or North Korea's).

2. A key ingredient in successful exploitation of transgovernmental contacts is the control of reinforcement contingencies for a subunit of the foreign government by subunits of one's own. In the above studies the controlling government could effectively punish or reward foreign government subunits. Moreover, the rewards offered were ones that the top levels of the foreign government could not offer to their own subunits nearly as easily or inexpensively. Thus, resource dependency (where "resource" is defined to include political outcomes and not just material goods) is central to transgovernmentalism. This is consistent with the "resource contingency" analysis of power in organizations, and it is also suggested by Keohane and Nye.[27] Paul notes that the resource dependency of U.S. military aid recipients magnifies the effect of transgovernmental contacts; aid agencies also figure prominently in Huntington's and in Keohane and Nye's examples of transgovernmental relations.[28] In the U.S. case, this suggests that an analysis of aid flows or military sales and training agreements is a good starting point, especially when compared to the military budgets of the recipient governments.

3. The organizational structure of the influencing and the target governments is another critical theoretical ingredient—a point anticipated by Nye and Keohane's suggestion that governments' degree of central control ought to be a central concern in a theory of transgovernmental and transnational relations.[29] In the Canadian case, the relatively weak formal mechanisms for supervision of military subunits meant that top-level civilian officials were partially ignorant of the conduct of their own military and lacked the institutional control mechanisms that would have enabled them to intervene effectively if or when they learned of these activities. Correspondingly, the influencing government needs to have sufficient control of its own subunits so that they do not become beset by the same desire to please foreign government counterparts that one wishes to exploit in the target subunit.

4. The interests of central decision-makers and their respective governmental subunits need to be aligned in such a way that success is likely and desirable. If Canadian civilian officials had views on Canadian national security that were identical to those of the Canadian military, a transgovernmental strategy by Washington would have been superfluous. If Canadian military officers did not admire the U.S. military, or adhered to doctrines about continental defense that clashed with U.S. doctrines, then the

[27] Pfeffer and Salancik 1974; Keohane and Nye 1974, 49.
[28] Paul 1992; Huntington 1973, 348; Keohane and Nye 1974, 47.
[29] Nye and Keohane 1972, 380.

U.S. transgovernmental strategy would have worked much less well. If U.S. military officers did not have views on continental defense that coincided with those of their civilian leaders, overcoming their resistance to those leaders' views probably would have consumed the energy of the civilians and made the military reluctant and ineffective agents of a transgovernmental influence strategy. The transgovernmental "three-level game" need not end with successful transgovernmental manipulation.[30]

5. Beyond the choice-theoretic conception of interests as exogenous, a theory of transgovernmental relations might develop further Wendt and Friedheim's ideas on socialization of foreign subunit personnel by one's own subunits. Political scientists have long been aware of the importance of learning, and both the English school and the latter-day constructivists have argued for the importance of national governments being socialized into the international system.[31] This suggests that training programs, technical assistance, and aid for educational programs ought to come under scrutiny as possible instruments for socializing target audiences in foreign government subunits or populations.

6. Researching transgovernmental relations requires delving into territory that governments traditionally regard as extremely sensitive. Even where government documents have been declassified, they probably will be subject to significant redactions, as is the U.S. material on NORAD. This makes research on such relations especially challenging.

Against this rather pessimistic assessment, we can counterpose not only the achievements of the above studies, but also examples from archival research of other transgovernmental episodes. Relying on the archives is necessary if one lacks high-level informants and wishes to learn the precise nature of the control relationship between an agency ostensibly engaged in transgovernmental relations and its controlling authorities.

U.S. Military Assistance as a Transgovernmental Exploitation Tactic

> SEN. SPARKMAN: At a time when Indonesia was kicking up pretty badly—when we were getting a lot of criticism for continuing military aid—at that time we could not say what that military aid was for. Is it secret any more?
>
> SECRETARY MCNAMARA: I think in retrospect, that the aid was well justified.
>
> SEN. SPARKMAN: You think it paid dividends?

[30] Keohane and Nye 1974, 48.
[31] Breslauer and Tetlock 1991.

SECRETARY McNAMARA: I do, sir.

SEN. SPARKMAN: I believe that is all, Mr. Chairman.[32]

Almost every national government has uniformed military forces that are highly differentiated from civilian agencies. What was found in the NORAD case could occur wherever foreign governments interact with local militaries without close supervision by the local central government. The U.S. government invested in many such militaries, including the Indonesian army. Although the declassified record of U.S. assistance to Indonesia contains many redactions, we now understand "what that military aid was for."

U.S. aid objectives for Indonesia in the early 1960s were simple: maintain parity with bloc aid and strengthen the only significant organized opposition to the Communists—the army and the internal security forces.[33] A 1964 memorandum clarifies how aid was used to exploit transgovernmental ties.

> Our aid programs have been an essential tool . . . . Over the years, they have helped us keep open the communications between our two Governments and build up a limited but real leverage with the Sukarno regime, which we are using to prevent a dangerous drift away from the West. . . .
>
> Those forms of assistance which could help Indonesia maintain "confrontation" against Malaysia have been eliminated, and we do not intend to resume them so long as "confrontation" continues. . . .
>
> Our training programs give us a unique opportunity to shape the thinking of Indonesia's future civilian police and military leaders. . . . The program of assisting the national police has given us valuable influence in this key organization (the country's first line of defense against internal subversion) and has greatly enhanced its effectiveness.[34]

Even in the most difficult period in U.S.-Indonesian relations, nearly six hundred Indonesian civilians were training in the United States and third countries for "civil leadership," and seventy-five "carefully selected members of the Indonesian army" were training in the United States for "civic action service in management, civil administration, and technical fields."[35]

[32] Wolpin 1972, 8, citing U.S. Congress, Senate, Committee on Foreign Relations, Foreign Assistance, 1966, U.S. Senate, 89th Cong., 2nd sess., p. 693.

[33] Memo, Robert H. Johnson and George Weber to W. Rostow, February 22, 1961 re: Tentative FY62 Mutual Security Program, DDRS 1991: 3419.

[34] "Statement of Reasons for Continuation of Limited Assistance to Indonesia," attachment to memorandum, Rusk to President, June 22, 1964, NSAM 309, Box 5, NSAMs, National Security Files, Lyndon B. Johnson Library.

[35] Memo for the President, no author, July 21, 1964, re U.S. aid to Indonesia, White House Central Files Confidential Files, Box 46, FO 3–2 1963–64, LBJ Library.

The social psychological processes involved in such training and the reasons why it was likely to succeed were elucidated by Robert Price.[36] Although he did not completely reject functionalist accounts of military behavior in terms of generic features of formal organizations, or Huntington's attempt to explain the behavior of the military solely in terms of the political dynamics in the surrounding society,[37] Price emphasized how metropole militaries form reference groups for Third World officer corps, and how in Ghana many officers identified more closely with the British than with their own government. The removal of trainees from their normal social environment and their transport overseas to metropole military academies, their isolation with other trainees, and strong pressures from peers and highly esteemed superiors, are all consistent with what social psychologists had concluded about the circumstances under which socialization (or resocialization) is likely to be most effective.

Aid to Local Government as a Transgovernmental Relations Exploitation Tactic

Commentary on development written within the U.S. foreign policy bureaucracy in the 1950s and 1960s occasionally mentioned the need to strengthen the capacities of Third World governments. This sometimes involved aid to local governmental units, particularly in areas like northeast Thailand, which were subject to Communist-led insurgency during the Vietnam War. Although in the Thai case this was done "to make the Central Government effective in the remote provincial areas,"[38] and thus poses no challenge to a unitary view of the state, in other cases such aid had very different objectives.

An instance where aid to local government was intended not to buttress but to undermine the central government was Brazil during the Goulart regime of 1961–64. The U.S. government then was particularly concerned with rural Brazil, especially the Northeast.

In northeast Brazil the Ligas Camponeses of Francisco Juliao are mobilizing the peasants and urging them to assert their "rights."[39]

An integrated approach to rural poverty through extension services, cooperatives, land reform, self-help schools, roads, and so forth, can

[36] Price 1971.

[37] Huntington 1968.

[38] U.S. Department of State, Agency for International Development, *Country Assistance Strategy Statements,* April 1964, Far East, NLJ 93–91, LBJ Library.

[39] Memorandum from the President's Special Assistant (Arthur Schlesinger) to President Kennedy, March 10, 1961, Kennedy Library, Schlesinger Papers, White House Files, Latin America Report.

yield an enormous return not only in better living conditions but in the immeasurable elements of hope and self respect which are the strongest bulwarks against Castro-Communism. Yet for all of Northeast Brazil, probably the most poverty-stricken part of Latin America, the dollar needs are estimated at only $76 million over the next five years.[40]

The U.S. government believed Brazil to be balanced on a political knife-edge between the Left and the Right. It was prepared to channel U.S. aid directly to those groups most likely to be the strongest supporters of relatively orthodox economic development policies:

Success of the Alliance for Progress may . . . depend on the ability of the Alliance to build its own organized support of moderate groups by directing a substantial part of the available foreign funds to projects that specifically aim at strengthening major groups and institutions in the center at the same time that they contribute directly to socio-economic progress. Organized groups that may with particularly successful results be involved in the process of development are moderate labor unions and military organizations. The power of the revolutionary left among students may be reduced if AID can involve chosen educational institutions more fully in its program. The disbursing of aid through organizations somewhat independent of the government also minimizes US reliance on the current government as the only purveyor of evolutionary change.[41]

These suggestions led President Kennedy to call for substantial aid to Northeast Brazil and other sensitive regions timed to arrive before the 1962 Brazilian elections. For the Northeast, the United States agreed in February 1962 to a $33 million "immediate impact" loan-grant program, a $62 million "long-range development" program, and "a very substantial program for emergency food."[42] A formal agreement signed in April 1962 between representatives of the Brazilian central government and the U.S. government specified that funds for the Northeast would be administered by SUDENE, an organization created by the Brazilian government to foster the development of the Northeast.

By August, relations between the Agency for International Development

[40] Memorandum from the Under Secretary of State (Bowles) to Secretary of State Rusk, July 25, 1961, *Foreign Relations of the United States* (hereafter *FRUS*) 1961–63, American Republics, Brazil document no. 8.

[41] Research Memorandum From the Director of the Bureau of Intelligence and Research (Hughes) to the Assistant Secretary of State for Inter-American Affairs (Woodward), January 19, 1962, *FRUS* 1961–63, American Republics, Brazil, document no. 39.

[42] Memorandum from the Administrator of the Agency for International Development (Hamilton) to President Kennedy, February 9, 1962, *FRUS* 1961–63, American Republics, Brazil, document no. 220.

and SUDENE had broken down.[43] Although the agreement specified that "USAID may sign agreements for individual projects with SUDENE or other appropriate agencies or organizations in accord with applicable regulations," SUDENE claimed the authority to approve all negotiations between agencies within its jurisdiction. The Brazilians pointed to other language in the agreement that seemingly recognized SUDENE's claim that it alone was the proper organ of the Brazilian state to cooperate with AID.

> The government of the United States of Brazil is represented by SUDENE
> . . . in the co-ordination of programs in Northeast Brazil. . . . SUDENE
> is authorized to enter into project and other agreements, including loan
> agreements, to carry out specific projects. Activities under these proj-
> ects may be administered by SUDENE or by such other agency or or-
> ganization as may be mutually agreed.[44]

As its relations with Brazil's national government continued to deteriorate, the United States began to use its aid in the Northeast in more openly political ways, disbursing it in an attempt to defeat the leftist mayor of Recife's campaign to become governor.[45] United States Information Agency expenditures in Brazil increased drastically, and CIA funding of candidates in the 1962 election was so widespread that Weis characterizes it as "a prominent political party."[46] U.S. ambassador Lincoln Gordon even attempted to influence the promotion of general officers.[47] By December, the United States had suspended aid to the central government, but continued an "islands of sanity" policy of aiding state governments that were anti-Goulart. From then until the April 1964 coup, the United States committed approximately $100 million to ten such projects. About half of this money was earmarked for the Northeast, but not to SUDENE—it was given to friendly state governors.[48] Despite the language in the earlier U.S.-Brazilian aid agreement for the Northeast, and despite the Brazilian constitution's prohibition of agreements between Brazilian state and foreign governments, Goulart did not object for fear that the harmful domestic political consequences of blocking U.S. aid would be too great.[49]

The United States also developed a program aimed at Brazilian labor unions. Unions and the military were the two top priorities, because of

[43] Weis 2001, 338.
[44] Roett 1972, 82–83.
[45] Black 1977, 66–67.
[46] Weis 2001, 338.
[47] Weis 2001, 339.
[48] Black 1977, 65–66.
[49] Weis 2001, 339–40.

the central role they played in Brazilian politics.[50] What at first appears
to be a transnational contact between the AFL-CIO and its Brazilian
counterpart was in fact the product of a formal agreement between the
U.S. and Brazilian governments, requested not by the United States, but
by the Brazilians. In their April 1962 meeting Kennedy and Goulart decided that there should be more exchanges between U.S. and Brazilian
unions to counter Castro's influence in the labor movement.[51] In agreeing
to the Brazilian request, Kennedy said that "everyone is dissatisfied with
many of the AFL-CIO representatives in Latin America." Goulart agreed,
suggesting that they tried to intervene too openly in Latin American
union activities. This and other Alliance for Progress activities by the
United States had to be conducted so as not "to hurt national pride."

Faux Transnationalism: The Ford Foundation and U.S. Foreign Policy

Organizations that have an interest in appearing more detached from the
U.S. government than they really are will probably not disclose all of their
contacts with the government or how cooperative those relationships
have been. Thus, Ford Foundation official Peter Bell's discussion of the
foundation as a transnational actor notes that U.S. embassies are sometimes unhappy about its aid to "anti-American" groups, that agencies like
AID that contact the foundation want to tap its expertise in areas like education and population, and that foundation field staff are sometimes
wary of AID because of its lack of program continuity and its "use of aid
for political purposes."[52] This paints a picture of the foundation's relation
to the government as one in which a certain amount of contact is inevitable by virtue of the nature of the foundation's mission, but in which
some distance, detachment, and differences of opinion are all preserved.
Nor is Bell's viewpoint idiosyncratic or explained simply by a desire to
present the foundation in as favorable a light as possible. An author who
is far more critical of many foundation programs was unable to find
much evidence in its archives of links between the foundation and the
U.S. government, though he does find individuals who were involved in
both worlds and that sometimes the foundation funded projects that were
also funded and supported by the CIA.[53]

Neither author uncovered a relationship that both parties, but especially the foundation, sought to conceal. Far from keeping its distance

[50] Hughes to Woodward, January 19, 1962.
[51] Martin 1994, 295.
[52] Bell 1972, 125–26.
[53] Berman 1983, 86, 94, 113, 131–32, 143.

from government programs, the foundation in the 1950s and 1960s had a close, ongoing, and informal working relationship with government officials. Although it maintained its independence, the degree to which it coordinated its activities with the government was substantial. CIA officials repeatedly requested foundation funding for some agency projects, and asked for access to foundation officials or fellows abroad for intelligence-gathering purposes (the foundation granted access only to a list of those whose grants had expired).[54] During the Kennedy administration foundation trustee John McCloy periodically visited the National Security Council to learn of overseas projects the NSC wished the foundation to fund.[55] His visits spawned at least one "Dear Jack" letter from McGeorge Bundy that listed three projects for possible funding.[56] Declassified documents suggest that the foundation's collaborations with the government were known at middle and upper levels of these agencies, and they matter-of-factly took into account foundation programs when designing programs such as technical assistance.[57] Moreover, the involvement of the foundation was the perfect vehicle for activities that were best conducted outside the government, but with government direction. The following discussion within the NSC staff of the need for a new group to consider Africa policy illustrates this aspect of the foundation's activities:

[54] Bird 1992, 426–29; Berman 1983, 61.

[55] Bird 1992, 519.

[56] McGeorge Bundy to John McCloy, April 4, 1962, John F. Kennedy Library, National Security Files, Box 297, Ford Fdn 4/4/62–5/7/62. Other requests for Ford Foundation consideration of projects are in note to Amembassy Warsaw from Kaysen, n.d., Ford Fdn 4/4/62–5/7/63 and Marcus Raskin to Mac Bundy, 3/5/62, Ford Fdn 3/27/61–4/3/62.

[57] A 1968 interagency committee on youth spoke approvingly of a Ford Foundation grant to the OECD to study university reform, and suggested similar grants be "stimulated" by the government. Inter-Agency Youth Committee, July 1, 1968, DDRS 1991: 2705. A 1962 blind memorandum suggested that the Foundation be recruited to provide assistance to public authorities in Latin America to create the Latin equivalent of the TVA or the Port Authority of New York. Blind memo, March 1, 1962, John F. Kennedy Library, National Security Files, Box 297, Ford Fdn 3/27/61–4/3/62. A 1962 discussion suggested that embassies regularly take into account foundation programs when programming technical assistance. Summary Minutes of Meeting of the Interdepartmental Committee of Under Secretaries on Foreign Economic Policy, January 24, 1962, National Archives, Record Group 59, E Files: Lot 65 D 68, Interdepartmental Committee of Under Secretaries on Foreign Economic Policy. That same year an NSC staff member suggested involving the foundation in a program for Pacific Island Trust Territories controlled by the United States. Marcus Raskin to Mac Bundy, March 5, 1962, Ford Fdn 3/27/61–4/3/62, Box 297, National Security Files, John F. Kennedy Library. In 1951 staff from the Psychological Strategy Board discussed with the foundation creating a new public organization that would "help mold domestic public opinion on foreign policy." Memorandum for the Record by John Sherman, Psychological Strategy Board, December 6, 1951 re: Mr. Powell's Proposal for an Organization to Help Mold Domestic Public Opinion on Foreign Policy, DDRS 1986: 2384.

I want to arrange a small group under private auspices but with government participants' access to classified data to consider this problem [of increasing Soviet and Chinese involvement in Africa] over the next few months. I think I can get a little Ford money for the private scholars and can get some non-Africanists to work on it. . . . To do this successfully with a mixed Government, non-Government group I would need to do it (very unofficially of course) as a project with your blessing and sanction and as a White House rather than departmental project on the Government side, though of course with departmental participation.[58]

Sometimes foundation officials saw the foundation as an extension of AID. For instance, in discussing the impact of budget cuts on the AID program in 1968, former AID chief and then Ford Foundation official David Bell argued the case for picking up the most valuable AID programs that were cut from the budget and maintaining them with foundation support:

[I]t would seem sensible for us to be alert especially through the remainder of this year to salvage where we can valuable projects that may be dropped by AID for lack of funds, and to help identify and place usefully able people whom AID may be forced to let go. The carnage may be severe before the year is over, and even small efforts by us may have high marginal value.[59]

If we take as a measure of integration into the state the frequency of contact and the degree of cooperation, then the Ford Foundation in the 1950s and 1960s seems to have been remarkably well integrated into U.S. foreign policy decision-making. Arguably it was better integrated than most members of Congress.

Although it would be erroneous to claim that the foundation was controlled by the executive branch as if it were part of a hierarchy, the record of foundation-government relations from declassified documents is quite different from the one based on publicly available evidence. The more

[58] Memo for Mr. [McG] Bundy from Bill Bruebeck, May 16, 1964, Bruebeck memos, Box 1, Name File, National Security Files, LBJ Library.

[59] Kenya Meeting of Representatives, Agenda Paper, Session 7, Emerging Issues, "The Plight of Foreign Aid," circa June 1968, three-ring binder, Box 37, David E Bell Papers, John F. Kennedy Library. One former and one contemporary Ford Foundation official were involved in transition planning for the Kennedy inauguration. On Joseph Slater, see Ernest LeFever to Hubert Humphrey, November 10, 1960, HHH Legis, Box 150.B.15.8 (F), "Foreign policy, 1959–61," Hubert Humphrey Papers, Minnesota Historical Society, St. Paul. On George Gant, see Frank Coffin (interviewee), interview by Elizabeth Donahue, March 2–3, 1964, John F. Kennedy Library Oral History Program.

general problem that this case highlights is that the reliance on public information about the behavior of important individuals and organizations—a commonplace in political science case studies of international relations and foreign policymaking—can lead to erroneous conclusions when political decision-makers have an interest in concealing important aspects of their relationships from public view. Even when one attempts to probe more deeply, the interpretation of the declassified record is heavily influenced by what parts of that record are made available, and the rules governing the creation and dissemination of documents at the time that they were created.

Aside from an apparent lack of documentation of this relationship in the available Ford Foundation archives, earlier researchers were also handicapped by the very nature of the foundation's method for dealing with its government contacts: Only three members of the foundation's board of trustees were fully aware that some foundation projects were being promoted by the government. When these projects came before the board for approval, their connections to government policies and objectives were not revealed to the others.[60] Documentation of foundation-government contacts is easier to find in government files. Government documents that mention the Ford Foundation leave the impression that a working relationship with it was taken for granted and not particularly sensitive. (The fact that the contents of these documents were not even partially redacted lends credence to this conclusion).

Conclusions

"Complex interdependence" theories in the 1970s were rooted in the same developments that led to "sovereignty at bay" claims—the vast expansion of international transactions of all kinds, the concomitant increase in the complexity of the governmental task of overseeing those transactions, and the apparent lack of government control over them.[61] Another way in which scholarship of that era emphasized limitations on the capacity of the state to act rationally was the bureaucratic politics approach, which likewise argued that agency interests tended to frustrate the efforts of central decision-makers to make a hierarchically organized executive branch comply with its directives. Arguments about the importance of transnationalism and transgovernmentalism complemented these viewpoints—one stressing the problems of controlling private actions, the other emphasizing the limits of hierarchical control. Moreover, the appar-

[60] Bird 1992, 428.
[61] Vernon 1971.

ent importance of these phenomena as challenges to the state-centric conception of international relations was strengthened by how the state concealed the way in which it took advantage of these interactions when it served its purposes to do so. The failures to take control were far more visible than the successes.

Risse-Kappen's reassessment of transnationalism and transgovernmentalism perceptively noted that it is more useful to inquire how the world of governments interacts with the world of nongovernmental actors than to try to adjudicate whether a "society-dominated" or "state-centered" view of world politics is better.[62] Each government's capacity to control its own subunits and the international behavior of nongovernmental actors within its jurisdiction is an important capability, to be placed alongside more conventional capabilities such as military strength or economic resources.[63] The inability to prevent elements of one's own government from becoming coalition partners for foreign interests could be a significant liability, while the capacity to take advantage of weak control relationships in another national government is a possible source of advantage. It is more useful to view transgovernmental and transnational relations as complicating the exercise of state power rather than as invariably limiting it.

It is impossible to assess the consequences of transnationalism and transgovernmentalism for the capacity of national governments to maintain effective control over international interactions without knowledge of the internal processes of the governments. Particularly when control relationships are informal, as in the Ford Foundation case, or when state action involves actions of dubious legality, as in the case of the "islands of sanity" aid policy, it is not easy to assess the extent to which either the donor or the recipient government is aware of, consents to, or actively encourages the interactions in question. When governments choose to conceal their role behind the barrier of security restrictions, the odds that scholars can arrive at an accurate understanding of these interactions are poor.

Governments are reticent to reveal their role because both powerful and weak find it useful to uphold the legal doctrine of the formal equality of states—the former because it softens their apparent dominance, the latter because it similarly takes the edge off of their apparent weakness.[64] The "private" entities involved in such transactions may be even more reluctant to reveal that they do not have an arm's-length relationship to a government, especially when that government is unpopular, is suspected

[62] Risse-Kappen 1995, 5.
[63] Krasner 1995.
[64] Krasner 1999.

of attempting to manipulate or undermine another national government, or has falsely claimed that it has no control over "private" transactions of various types.

The observation that governments are involved in shaping transgovernmental and transnational interactions in ways that have not been publicly revealed also raises the possibility that the boundaries between public and private, or state and nonstate, are or are becoming fuzzy. Were the Ford Foundation programs mentioned above "private" or "public"? Was U.S. aid in Brazil after December 1962 consistent with Brazilian law? Was it an example of an unregulated transgovernmental transaction, or merely a rather loosely worded formal agreement between two sovereign national governments? These questions no longer have neat, simple answers.

Because many diplomatic historians work from an implicitly realist perspective, and because official compendia of declassified material such as *Foreign Relations of the United States* are also seemingly compiled with a realist worldview, it requires primary sources to determine whether and how governmental control of transnational and transgovernmental relations is an important aspect of diplomacy. Given the political sensitivity of many of the relationships that exist, we cannot expect an easy path of discovery, but even our limited accomplishments thus far are enough to suggest that a reconsideration of how transgovernmental and transnational phenomena affect and are affected by the actions of national government is in order.

CHAPTER 12

On Taking Religious Worldviews Seriously

J. Ann Tickner

> We need to take alternative worldviews—including religious worldviews—more seriously.
>
> Robert Keohane[1]

> The twenty-first century is dawning . . . as a century of religion.
>
> Samuel Huntington[2]

> The study of other people's religious beliefs is now no longer merely desirable, but necessary for our very survival.
>
> Karen Armstrong[3]

WRITTEN IN THE IMMEDIATE AFTERMATH of the attacks of September 11, 2001, the final chapter of Robert Keohane's *Power and Governance in a Partially Globalized World* challenges scholars of international relations (IR) to reflect on whether their theories of world politics are adequate for explaining such acts of what he calls "informal violence."[4] Claiming that we face a moral imperative to understand world politics better, he suggests that 9/11 could best be understood through synthesizing insights from institutionalism, classical realism, and constructivism.[5] Given the increasing urgency to make sense of world politics in light of this catastrophic event, Keohane claims that no perspective has a monopoly on wisdom. He chastises the discipline for the parochialism of its paradigmatic disputes and urges IR scholars to pay more attention to synthesis

---

I would like to thank my late husband Hayward R. Alker for his helpful suggestions on this chapter. I shall miss his careful consideration and support of all my scholarship.

[1] Keohane 2002, 283.

[2] Huntington 2004, 15.

[3] Armstrong 2004, 304.

[4] Keohane distinguishes informal violence, which he defines as violence by nonstate actors with the capacity to inflict great harm with small material capabilities, from formal violence, which is state-controlled. He prefers this term to *terrorism* because, since the latter has such negative connotations, it is difficult to define in an analytically neutral and consistent way (Keohane 2002, 272, 274).

[5] Keohane 2002, 283.

and less to differentiating their views from those of others.[6] Keohane's inclusion of this concluding self-reflective chapter on the globalization of informal violence in a selection of his writings over 1990s, is intended to illustrate the values and also the limitations of his institutionalist approach for understanding such events.[7] He claims that understanding the tragic events of 9/11 also demands taking other worldviews, including religious worldviews, seriously.

Keohane advocates synthesis of theoretical insights. However, I believe that the most appropriate synthesis may be even more challenging than he suggests. As Keohane claims, incorporating religious motivations into mainstream IR theory, which he describes as relentlessly secular, is difficult. Theories built upon the epistemological and ontological foundations of secular rationalism are not particularly useful for understanding religious motivations or worldviews of those who express a deep hostility to modernity and secular thinking. Indeed, the social sciences, which have emerged out of Western Enlightenment thought, are themselves part of the secular rationalist thinking that adherents to conservative religious worldviews attack.

Taking up Keohane's challenge, I first examine the worldviews of some of those who commit violence in the name of religion. Focusing more widely than on the events of 9/11, I examine some worldviews of both Christian and Islamic groups that support religious violence. Similarities are striking. The rhetoric of both Christian and Islamic extremist groups demonstrates a sense of rootlessness and loss of identity; all exhibit deep hostility to secular rationalism, modernity, and globalization. While they depend on modern technologies to spread their message and plan their strategies, all are deeply suspicious of liberal international institutions and the "new world order."[8] I then examine the broader economic and cultural contexts from which contemporary religious violence is emerging. Albeit in an extreme and perverted form, perpetrators of violence and their supporters emerge out of a more prevalent search for identity and cultural values, an attempt to answer the question "Who are we?"—a search that Samuel Huntington has termed the most distinctive feature of the contemporary world.[9]

In the next part of the chapter, I take up Keohane's challenge to synthesize insights from institutionalism, realism, and constructivism in order to help understand informal violence and the religious worldviews that are

---

[6] The need for synthetic thinking is supported by Audrey Cronin (2002, 57), who suggests that political science has ignored terrorism because it does not fit neatly into the realist or liberal paradigms.

[7] Keohane 2002, 2.

[8] Juergensmeyer 2000, 222.

[9] Huntington 2004.

driving it. I first discuss the contributions of Keohane's institutionalist approach. I then suggest that synthesizing secular social science perspectives, such as neoliberal institutionalism, and antisecular, antimodern religious worldviews may not be possible within these three approaches. I draw on the writings of Hans Morgenthau to demonstrate classical realism's discomfort with secular rationalism for understanding human motivation. I use constructivist Vendulka Kubálková's work to demonstrate that linguistic constructivism can provide a more useful tool for understanding religious beliefs and quests for meaning and identity that are so important to adherents of the conservative religions that I discuss. I suggest that religious worldviews may be better understood using hermeneutic, reflexive, and dialogical methodologies traditionally associated with religious studies and some forms of linguistic constructivism. These methodologies cannot be fully assimilated within instrumental rationalist conceptions of social science.

In the concluding section, I draw on feminist secular and religious scholarship that provides us with some ways of getting beyond the difficulties of theoretical synthesis. First I discuss Western feminist writings that offer new possibilities for transcending the religious/secular knowledge divide. I then discuss some Islamic scholarship, critical of conservative religious thought yet sensitive to reactions against Western modernity, that could help us recognize different forms of modernity not so closely linked with Western secularism.

Violence in the Name of God

Although the overall incidence of terrorism did not increase in the late twentieth century, there was an increase in religious violence.[10] Individuals who support or commit religious violence see themselves as "saints" or "martyrs" striving for a more perfect and more simplified world.[11] They deplore moral ambiguity and uncertainty and see the world in Manichaean terms where no compromise is possible. They use militaristic language, frequently from religious texts, to describe a world in a perpetual state of war—a battle between good and evil. If evil means are necessary to achieve good ends, they will be used.[12] Worldviews are surprisingly similar—whether they are Christian or Islamic. All decry secularism,

---

[10] By one measure, the number of terrorist attacks in the 1990s averaged 382 per year, whereas in the 1980s, the number averaged 543. However, the number of people killed in each attack increased in the 1990s, as did the number of terrorist organizations classified as "religious" (Cronin 2002, 42–43).

[11] My illustrations rely on interviews conducted by Juergensmeyer 2000 and Stern 2003.

[12] Juergensmeyer 2000, 149.

materialism, and modernity, which create confusion and fear amid a general lack of authority and which are manifest through tolerance of "inappropriate" sexual behavior and lack of racial hierarchy.[13] Material wealth, engendered by capitalism, leads to moral decadence. Yet motives are material as well as spiritual and emotional: heavenly rewards are promised to perpetrators of religious violence, but so are material incentives.

Extremist religious groups decry international institutions, the building blocks of a liberal world order. They express strong hostility to a world order based on secular morality and on global institutions such as the United Nations.[14] Kerry Noble, one of the former leaders of an American Christian cult Covenant, the Sword, and the Arm of the Lord (CSA), based in rural Arkansas, states that the strength of international institutions promoting world government, including the United Nations and international banks, are indications that the Antichrist, whose forces also include the IMF, the Council on Foreign Relations, and the "One-Worlders," is already here.[15] A study of American right-wing rural Christian militias reveals a similar fear of a "new world order" and an "invasion" of the United States by the United Nations.[16] Leaders of the Pakistani jihad group Lashkar e Taiba (Army of the Pure), a member of the International Islamic Front, bin Laden's umbrella organization, assert that the West enslaves Muslim countries through debts to the IMF, the World Bank, foreign aid, and loans.[17] Contrary to CSA's fears of a UN invasion, Army of the Pure claims that the United Nations is a spy for the United States, and international institutions are synonymous with American imperialism.

Many of the violent, religiously motivated individuals whom Jessica Stern interviewed indicate a sense of wounded masculinity. Indeed, gender and race are central for understanding the worldviews of perpetrators and supporters of religious violence. Almost all who commit violence in the name of religion are men.[18] Many express ambivalence toward women, homophobia, and fears of being marked "feminine." Followers of right-wing militia movements in the United States are mainly lower-middle-class white men, and it is through militias that these individuals believe that American manhood can be restored. Militias believe they are engaged in

[13] Scott Thomas (2005, 10–11) sees the global resurgence of religion, which he claims is a far more wide-ranging phenomenon than extremism or fundamentalism, as part of a larger crisis of modernity in the West.

[14] Walter Russell Mead 2006 asserts that it is no coincidence that the *Left Behind* novels show the Antichrist rising to power as the secretary-general of the UN.

[15] Stern 2003, 11–17.

[16] Kimmel and Ferber 2000.

[17] Stern 2003, 119.

[18] Some women have played a prominent role in violent groups; however, groups in which women play a prominent role tend to be motivated by secular political ideologies or ethnic separatism. See Juergensmeyer 2000, 196.

an armed struggle against a state that is controlled by feminists, environmentalists, blacks, and Jews.[19] Christian identity groups see the state as emasculating and blame feminists and their nonwhite coconspirators for their humiliation.[20] Many members of radical religious movements see themselves as soldiers, and many are military veterans.

While the leaders of extreme religious movements are often middle-aged and affluent, their followers tend to be young urban males experiencing economic hardships, unemployment, and social marginalization. While leaders of these movements see their role as purifying the world, operatives are often influenced by pragmatic incentives such as money, which is frequently provided to "martyrs'" families.[21] In Pakistan many male children are educated at religious schools or madrassas because they receive free books, housing, and board. Often poor families and those in refugee camps cannot afford the cost of the textbooks and transportation frequently required at public school.[22] Racial hierarchies are also prevalent in extremist religious movements. Recruits for Islamic extremism are coming increasingly from Africa, where anti-Americanism is on the rise. But Al Qaeda is highly tiered, and Africans are, for the most part, not admitted to the upper ranks; they do, however, provide willing foot soldiers for religious violence.[23]

Ian Buruma and Avishai Margalit claim that the issue of women lies at the heart of Islamic "Occidentalism," which they define as a dehumanizing picture of the West painted by its enemies.[24] Most conservative Muslims are not political Islamists but advocates of enforcing public morality that is largely about regulating female behavior.[25] Jessica Stern claims that the religious violence we face today is not only a response to political and economic grievances, often attributed to neoliberal economic globalization, but also to what she terms, using the language of Sartre, a "God-shaped hole" where values like tolerance and equal rights for women are irritating to those who feel left behind by modernity.[26] All extremist religious movements display a deep hostility to modern rationalism, secular thinking, materialism, and economic globalization. They draw selectively on religious texts, often militant or violent, to exhort their followers to "return" to what they define as a "traditional" way of life. They consider themselves to be unconstrained by secular values or

[19] Kimmel and Ferber 2000, 595.
[20] Stern 2003, 286.
[21] Stern 2003, 4–5.
[22] Stern 2003, 293.
[23] Stern 2003, 237–48.
[24] Buruma and Margalit 2004, 7.
[25] Buruma and Margalit 2004, 128.
[26] Stern 2003, 282.

laws and display a complete sense of alienation from the existing social system.[27] While those who are willing to kill in the name of religion are a small minority, they represent, albeit in an extreme and perverted form, feelings of threat, alienation, and loss of identity that are far more widespread and symptomatic of larger trends.

Some Broader Implications of the Religious War of Ideas

Mark Juergensmeyer suggests that the moral leadership of the secular state has become increasingly challenged after the end of the Cold War, a struggle, also portrayed in Manichaean terms, that provided contesting models of moral politics—communism and democracy.[28] Today, communism and democracy have been replaced by the single model of the global market, a model that, according to Juergensmeyer, is devoid of political ideals and lacks clear standards for moral behavior. The political conservatism of the 1980s and the shift in the global economy to the neoliberal consensus began what has continued to be a widening income inequality throughout the world. This has reinforced a public sense of insecurity that results in disaffection with political leaders and the growth of right-wing religious movements that feed on the public's perception of the immorality of government.

While disillusionment with the secular state is characteristic of conservative religious groups, their relations with actual states are complex. Many groups, both Christian and Muslim, are using the state to increase their political influence. This is eroding the boundary between religion and politics even in secular societies, a phenomenon that has caught international relations scholars and policy analysts by surprise. Modernization theory, popular in both the academy and the policy world in the 1950s and 1960s, assumed that, as newly independent countries began to follow the path to development previously taken by the West, they would become increasingly secular.[29] Today when, in many parts of the world, Western values and economic modernization are regarded as culturally alien and a threat to indigenous values, these predictions seem strangely out of place. In the Muslim world there is a positive correlation between supporters of the Islamic faith and educational and occupational prestige that challenges the assumption that religious beliefs erode with modernization.

Occidentalism epitomizes the resentment against Western modernity's belief in the superiority of secular reason and science as the only way to understand natural phenomena. While modernization theory, which is based on secular rationalist knowledge, has ceased to be of central con-

[27] Cronin 2002, 41.
[28] Juergensmeyer 2000, 225–26.
[29] See, for example, Lerner 1958.

cern to Western development theory, it has come under increased scrutiny outside the West where scholars are searching for definitions of modernity that are more compatible with religion and local cultural values. While Westerners promote the globalizing of Western values as a way to build a democratic international society of states outside the West, the legacy of colonialism and the association of modernity with secularism and the West play an important role in religion's resurgence.

Fears about loss of identity in the face of secular modernization exist within the West also. They are intensifying cultural clashes that reinforce exclusionary international (often racialized) boundaries. In the face of what he has famously called a "clash of civilizations," Samuel Huntington has suggested that the attacks of 9/11 have mobilized America's identity as a Christian nation. Huntington claims that the religious component of their identity has taken on new meaning for Americans. According to Huntington, this identity is Anglo-Protestant—an identity he clearly favors over a more multiracial, inclusionary one, but one that is unlikely to foster tolerance and cooperation.[30] Huntington's "clash" is mirrored by "jihadists" whose vision of the world is similar. Sayyid Qutb articulated this clash as early as the 1960s, when he claimed that the world was divided into two camps—those who are followers of Islam and those who are not.[31]

I have suggested that the reemergence of conservative religious movements has challenged the predictions of modernization theory and the universal acceptance of a liberal world order based on certain Western values and Western-led international institutions. Their growing influence on the state and politics, even in secular societies, has confounded political analysis that looks to rationalist, materialist explanations for political behavior. To understand these new phenomena requires the IR discipline to pursue some new avenues, as Keohane suggests.

Incorporating Religion into Theories of International Relations: Problems of Synthesis

Keohane suggests a synthetic role for institutionalism, classical realism, and constructivism in helping understand the events of post-9/11 world politics. Institutionalism can help us understand new patterns of asymmetric interdependence manifest in terrorist activities. He also suggests that the attacks pose a fruitful test for institutionalist theory in terms of their potential for increasing or decreasing multilateralism. He claims that classical realism could help us understand the human desire to hate,

[30] Huntington 2004, 340.
[31] Esposito and Voll 2003, 240.

and constructivism the role of ideas, the importance of which, he claims, he has come to a greater appreciation of over the decade of the 1990s.[32] I shall now examine some insights that these three approaches might provide to help understand some of the issues discussed earlier. My discussion of realism and constructivism will demonstrate the difficulties of theoretical synthesis of social scientific knowledge and knowledge that can help us understand religious worldviews. I will begin with Keohane's reflections on the adequacy and limitations of neoliberal institutionalism as defined in this volume.

Keohane's Neoliberal Institutionalism

Keohane claims that our theories provide important components of an adequate post-9/11 conceptualization of world politics, but that we need to alter some of our assumptions in order to rearrange these components into a viable theoretical framework.[33] The 9/11 attacks did not focus on world political economy, nor were international institutions directly involved.[34] Acts of informal violence require that institutionalism's association of nonstate actors with forms of nonmilitary power must be rethought. These acts, which have the capacity to achieve high levels of damage on a global scale, have called into question IR theory's assumption that the state is both the primary perpetrator of large-scale international violence and the primary protector against it. Large-scale informal violence has strengthened global networks through which the means of violence flow, while potentially weakening economic and social exchange, which liberals see as the foundation of cooperation and interdependence. Ironically perhaps, the scope and magnitude of informal violence has increased through the decline in the cost and increase in speed of communications and transportation in a globalizing world. The power of ideas, in this case religious ideas, in a networked global society allows nonstate actors with relatively little military capability to mobilize supporters and execute acts of informal violence with large-scale consequences.

Keohane claims that, while it has focused on nonmilitary power, institutionalism has always been clear that military power dominates economic power.[35] An institutionalist understanding of power as asymmetric interdependence, often used to explain economic issues, can also be useful for explaining acts of informal violence. In the case of the attacks of 9/11, informal violence has increased the vulnerability of the United States through an asymmetry of information. The United States is a rela-

[32] Keohane 2002, 272.
[33] Keohane 2002, 293.
[34] Keohane 2002, 18.
[35] Keohane 2002, 276.

tively open society, whereas the identity and location of terrorist networks is hard to track down. Religious violence has also increased U.S. vulnerability through an asymmetry of beliefs, whereby those motivated by religious violence see rewards in the afterlife rather than in material gains so vital to the payoff structures of instrumental rationality. Given the hugely unequal material capabilities between the United States and Al Qaeda, this suggests that greater emphasis on conceptualizing power in terms of ideas and beliefs is needed.

Writing in the wake of the 9/11 attacks, Keohane also reflects on the prospects for global institutions. While democratically elected leaders are likely to be motivated by national self-interest rather than by global interests, they do benefit politically from implementing policies that are compatible with international norms and that are endorsed by the United Nations. However, the subsequent invasion of Iraq seemed to confirm Keohane's worst-case scenario, that the United States would become more unilateral after 9/11. Since Keohane's chapter was written, the United States has faced a sharp decline in its moral standing in the world as well as a declining level of domestic support for the war, both of which suggest a possible return to a more multilateral foreign policy to fight global terrorism. However, framing U.S. foreign policy in terms of civilizational clashes and identity issues, about which Huntington is so pessimistic, does not bode well for multilateralism. Additionally, the growing importance of nonstate actors with the capacity to commit large-scale violence, as well as the number of states that regard international institutions as illegitimate tools of Western domination, are challenges to the legitimacy of a modern world order based on Western secular liberal norms.

Daniel Philpott sees the origins of the secularism of international relations theories, such as neoliberal institutionalism, in what he calls the "Westphalian synthesis." The Treaty of Westphalia of 1648, often termed a landmark in the origins of the modern state system,[36] signaled the defeat of religion, not as a force in politics, but as a scheme for organizing international authority. Westphalia established the right of sovereign authorities to govern religion in their territory as they pleased, thus establishing state sovereignty and the norm of nonintervention.[37] Set in motion by the Protestant Reformation and the subsequent development of religious freedom, the separation of church and state resulted in the gradual secularization of the interstate political realm.

The ontological assumptions of the Westphalian synthesis, together with the commitment to international relations as a social science, so central to the evolution of the international relations' discipline, particularly in the

---

[36] This claim has been the subject of an ongoing dispute. For counterarguments see Krasner 1993 and Teschke 2003.

[37] Philpott 2002, 73–74.

United States, have reinforced IR's neglect of religion and, more importantly, its inability to incorporate religion into its theories. The radical revival of Islam has challenged the Westphalian synthesis and its associated modern social scientific commitments. The ultimate goal of radical revivalists is the Islamization of the international political order—replacing the secular state system and Western-led international institutions with an Islamic system under God's rule. Nonstate actors claim religious authority and kinship with people outside their state, but they also look to state institutions to promote Islam.[38] Support for Islamic movements is statist and transnational at the same time.[39] The questioning of the fundamental principles around which the Westphalian state system is organized presents a profound challenge to IR theory. Secular rationalism is ill equipped to understand the mixed motivations, from the transcendental to the materialist, that characterize not only radical Islam, but also the other conservative religious movements that I have described. Therefore, it may be necessary to look beyond conventional social science to other theoretical traditions to help understand these worldviews and to design policies and institutions to deal with them. To this end, I now turn to realist Hans Morgenthau's *Scientific Man vs. Power Politics* to help us understand deeper problems associated with the reaction against secular modernity and rationalism that I have described.

Morgenthau's Classical Realism

Writing in the aftermath of World War II and deeply affected by European fascism, Hans Morgenthau evokes themes that are strikingly similar to some of those discussed earlier in this chapter. In *Scientific Man vs. Power Politics*, Morgenthau points to disillusionment with modernity and its association with secular rationalism, a disillusionment that, as I have indicated, is central to contemporary fundamentalist thinking in a variety of religions. Morgenthau disputes the liberal claim that, in a liberal society, reason, revealing itself in the "laws" of economics, would reign and of necessity bring about harmony, the welfare of all, and world peace.[40] Liberals believe that this benign society would come about through "reason" that has its own inner force, not dependent on human

[38] Philpott 2002, 89.

[39] The Christian Right in the United States tends to look to state institutions to promote Christianity and to see religion and the state as coincidental. Its support for the Iraq War and an imperial foreign policy (God and country) are indications of this. This is quite consistent with the Westphalian principle of *cuius regio, eius religio* and further complicates the Westphalian synthesis.

[40] Morgenthau 1946, 25.

intervention.[41] In a severe indictment of liberalism and rationalism, Morgenthau is strikingly pessimistic about the ability of scientific reasoning to solve social problems. Suggesting that "man's" nature has three dimensions, the biological, the rational, and the spiritual, he concludes that the rationalistic or instrumentalist conception of "man," portrayed by liberal social science, has completely disregarded the emotional and spiritual aspects of life.[42] Disavowing positivism's belief that the social world is subject to laws similar to those in the natural world, Morgenthau claims that science may have allowed "man" to master nature but it has not answered the reason for "man's" existence, a search so prevalent in today's religious resurgence.[43] While *Scientific Man vs. Power Politics* is a severe indictment of an attempt to construct a "scientific" theory of world politics, a "scientific" model is, nevertheless, the one to which Morgenthau aspired in all his writings. His rigid separation of rationality and emotion is itself a product of modern secular reasoning. Rationality has the potential to overcome what he sees as dangerous emotions. I shall return to this later in the chapter.

Kubálková's Linguistic Constructivism

Scientific Man vs. Power Politics is grounded in the interpretive or hermeneutic tradition, an intellectual approach closer to theology and to contemporary IR postpositivist approaches than to realism's subsequent devolution to a more "scientific" neorealism. The hermeneutic tradition is also an important foundation for much of contemporary IR constructivism, an approach that Keohane suggests can also help us understand post-9/11 global politics. In an essay whose goal is to develop what she calls an international political theology, Vendulka Kubálková claims that it is not possible to study religion adequately in a positivist framework. Arguing for a rule-oriented constructivist approach, she asserts that there

---

[41] Interestingly, in the introduction to *Power and Governance in a Partially Globalized World*, Keohane expresses his own reservations about being labeled a liberal for some of the same reasons. He claims that his institutionalist theory does have its roots in liberalism but that it has nothing to do with the liberal view that commerce necessarily leads to peace, that people are basically good, or that progress in human history is inevitable (Keohane 2002, 3).

[42] Morgenthau 1946, 122.

[43] Morgenthau 1946, 125. I use the term *man* rather than *human*, which is more prevalent in contemporary usage, because Morgenthau uses man both in the text and in the title of his book. While I understand that this was the convention in the 1940s, I believe that its usage has deeper implications. The association of men and masculinity with reason and women and femininity with emotion is deeply rooted in Cartesian thought. Historically it has had important implications for assigning men and women to different (unequal) roles and competencies.

is a profound difference between positivist and religious understandings of the world. Indeed, positivists' reliance on logic and the positive evidence of the senses demonstrates a search for nonreligious foundations for secure knowledge. She advocates a shift to an insider's perspective on knowledge-building.[44] Such a perspective, characteristic of hermeneutic and postpositivist thought more generally, has religious antecedents in late-eighteenth-century romanticism, which was a revolt against modern rationalism.[45] Kubálková states that, up until two hundred years ago, religions provided the dominant mode of thought, and many schools of thought, such as phenomenology and hermeneutics, have their roots in religious theorizing. The stress on identity, the inside/outside distinction, phenomenology, and hermeneutics, all characteristic of postpositivist thought, has always been central to religious thought and practice. Thus, postpositivist approaches to knowledge cumulation are likely to be better at understanding religious worldviews than positivist ones.

Religious and secular thought start from different ontologies—all religions share a distinction between ordinary and transcendental reality. Religious thinkers see human experience as only one dimension of a multidimensional reality that is ordered by design but is not adequately knowable by sensory perception alone. Creating gods is a necessary feature of the human search for identity and transcendence. A believer must follow the dictates of conscience that are beyond the realm of "rational choice."[46] While constructivism has also been secular, Kubálková claims that approaching human action through linguistic constructivism—as a world created through human action and the meaning that humans give to their actions—is the methodological path by which we can incorporate religion into international relations. Linguistic constructivism is useful for understanding the religious worldviews I have described and for understanding contemporary events, for the way we construct our world is crucial to how we act upon it.[47]

Kubálková and Morgenthau both claim that fundamental questions about human existence cannot be answered in modern secular "scientific" terms. Both are searching for a way to understand human motivations, which, as they suggest, are not adequately explainable in instru-

[44] For a detailed examination of the contrast between insider and outsider perspectives on knowledge-building and how they are used in IR theory, see Hollis and Smith 1990.

[45] Kubálková 2003, 85–89.

[46] Kubálková 2003, 86–90.

[47] Comparison of U.S. responses to the attack on the World Trade Center in 1993, when five people were killed and approximately one thousand injured, and 9/11, when more than three thousand were killed, illustrates my argument. Whereas the 1993 attack was considered a crime, 9/11 was declared an act of war. These very different reactions were the result of the comparative levels of destruction rather than the acts themselves, which were motivated by similar goals. See May 2003, 39.

mental rationalist terms. Both helpfully suggest ways in which we need to rethink contemporary knowledge production in order to better understand religious worldviews. Their realist and constructivist analyses have taken us further into questioning the adequacy of the epistemological foundations of Western modern secular knowledge as well as the problems of theoretical synthesis for understanding religious worldviews. And Kubálková's linguistic constructivism provides theoretical openings for understanding these worldviews. I shall conclude with contributions of some recent secular and religious feminist writings that offer new insights into transcending the divide between secular and religious thinking. Feminists outside the West are also contributing to new thinking about different paths to modernity that are less Western-centered and allow for the inclusion of alternative religious and cultural traditions.

Some Feminist Rethinkings of Modern Knowledge and Modernity

Beyond Gendered Theology

Conservative religions in all the Abrahamic traditions are deeply patriarchal. Reactions from both Western and non-Western critics of modernity are frequently expressed as calls for the (re)activation of restrictive policies on women, often justified in the name of religion. Feminist theologians have offered important critiques of patriarchal religious beliefs and practices and suggested reconstructions and revisions of theology that are less patriarchal and can provide the bases for more benign, more inclusive, and less conflictual religious worldviews. Muslim feminists have claimed that, while Islam is being used as an instrument of oppression against Muslim women, this is because it is being interpreted by men to suit their purposes. Raffat Hassan asserts that there are no Koranic statements that justify the rigid restrictions that have been imposed on women in the name of Islam.[48] When Muslim women fight for their rights, they are frequently accused of betraying their religion and culture and of becoming Western. Indeed, for Islamic feminists, modernity itself is problematic because it is equated with being Western. Rather than reject Islam altogether, Islamic feminists are attempting to reconstruct an alternative reading of Islam that is less patriarchal and does not endorse the disempowerment of women.

Christian feminist theology has also engaged in both critical analysis of conventional texts and in a constructive rereading of texts, both of which involve an awareness of the ambivalence that religious texts have created for women. Feminist theologians, following a practice in feminist method-

[48] Hassan 1999, 260.

ology more generally, question the assumption that there can be a gender-neutral "universal" person who reads a text from an "objective" point of view. A feminist reader of the Scripture assumes a reflexive attitude—that the gender, race, and socioeconomic status of the reader must be taken into consideration when assessing a claim or meaning of a text.

Feminist theologians in the Christian tradition have drawn inspiration from, but gone beyond, liberation theology, a radical Christian tradition that emerged in the black U.S. and Latin American Catholic churches in the 1970s and 1980s. Liberation theology believes that marginalized and oppressed peoples must participate in constructing their own religious thinking out of their lives and experiences.[49] Rather than invoking the authority of texts selected by religious hierarchies, liberation theology involves a form of knowledge-building whereby ordinary people come to understand religion through engagement in a hermeneutic, dialogic process. Constructing religious worldviews is reflective, ongoing, and emergent. It is consistent with a sense of empathy and compassion—to *feel with*, which Karen Armstrong suggests is as pivotal in all Abrahamic religious traditions as are the belligerent elements emphasized by fundamentalists.[50] Such nonpatriarchal religious interpretations are more inclusive. A nongendered dialogic reading of religious texts, which suggests that God can be both male and female, is a way to less conflictual religious self-understandings and worldviews.

Beyond Gendered Knowledge

Secular feminists have similar problems with the gendering of secular knowledge. Women have had an ambiguous and complicated relationship with secular rationalism and "objective" reasoning that have been foundations for modern knowledge, including social scientific knowledge. For this reason secular feminists have constructed useful critiques of the historical development of secular rationalist thinking of which conservative religions are so critical and about which Morgenthau was so pessimistic. A feminist reexamination of the early modern Westphalian era, so central to the establishment of the modern secular Western state system, reveals that it was not a good time for women. During the early stages of state formation and the beginnings of capitalism in Europe, women experienced a contraction of social and personal options.[51] Origins of an emerging, more highly gendered division of labor can be seen in seventeenth-century Europe, when definitions of male and female were

[49] Watson 2003, 1.
[50] Armstrong 2004, 295.
[51] Kelly-Gadol 1977, 139.

becoming polarized in ways that were suited to the growing division of labor between work and home required by early capitalism. The notion "housewife" began to place women's unremunerated work in the private domestic space, as opposed to the public world of economic and political activities and waged labor inhabited by men. Evolving notions of citizenship were based on male, property-owning heads of households: since the status of men defined that of their wives and children, gender discrimination became a constitutive feature of the modern state where activities in the male-dominated public sphere were accorded more importance than those in the private sphere inhabited largely by women.[52] The separation of the public and private spheres contributed to the knowledge base and boundaries within which contemporary Western political and economic thought has been constructed.[53]

Women have rarely been the subjects or producers of knowledge, secular or religious. Modern knowledge, with its claims to universality and objectivity, has generally been constructed by men from knowledge of men's lives in the public sphere. Men's historical roles as political and economic actors have provided the intellectual framework for Western knowledge about politics and economics. The separation of the public and private spheres, reinforced by the scientific revolution of the seventeenth century, has resulted in the legitimation of what are perceived as the "rational" activities (such as politics and economics) in the former while devaluing the "natural' activities (such as household management, child-rearing, and caregiving) of the latter.[54] Feminists argue that broadening the base from which knowledge is constructed to include the experiences of women can actually enhance objectivity.[55]

Modern knowledge depends on the Cartesian separation of the intellect (valued in public sphere behavior) and the emotions (more acceptable in the private sphere).[56] These are hierarchically ordered and gendered; the mind is associated with men and emotions with women, and, as Morgenthau claims, it is the task of (masculine) reason to tame dangerous (female) emotions.[57] Feminists believe that emotion and intellect are mutually constitutive and sustaining, and that emotions can be a positive as well as a negative force. Armstrong claims that, since the scientific revolution of the seventeenth century, even Western theology has been characterized by inappropriate reliance on reason. This has reinforced the

[52] Toulmin 1990, 133.

[53] Pateman 1998, chap. 1.

[54] Peterson 1992, 202.

[55] Harding 1991, 123.

[56] Recent work in neuroscience has overthrown the scientific evidence for this claim. See Damasio 2005.

[57] See note 43.

tendency to impose dogmatic religious beliefs that are causing many of today's problems.[58]

For feminists, rationality is contextual and emergent out of social relations in which the individual is embedded. Contextualized rationality whereby the producer of knowledge reflects on her or his role in the production of knowledge is a more robust ideational foundation from which to build less conflictual worldviews. Like feminist theologians, many secular feminists also advocate a dialogic contextual model of knowledge-building whereby knowledge emerges through conversations with texts and subjects.[59] Brooke Ackerly builds on, but goes beyond, democratic political theory in designing a deliberative democratic model of social criticism that she defines as an ongoing process to bring about incremental uncoerced models of social change.[60] Working with rural women and social activists in Bangladesh, Ackerly constructs a framework that combines scholarship with action. She argues that effecting social change in social, political, and economic institutions must come, not just from theorists, but also from the experiences of those whose lives are impacted by injustices that they seek to remedy. Analogous to processes used by liberation theologists, she recounts meetings among rural women and social activists who use stories, analogies, and emotions in noninstitutionalized settings to construct better understandings of their situations in order to change them. Building knowledge through an interactive dialogic process that includes multiple voices, rather than constructing knowledge aimed at discovering some objective universal truth, could provide a useful foundation for the construction of less conflictual worldviews. Although not specifically religious, such an approach could also contribute to bridging religious and secular divides.

Beyond Traditional/Modern Divides

As Chris Brown suggests, there are a number of different ways of being modern; the modernity associated with the liberal, largely post-Christian, humanist West is not a universal model.[61] Feminists outside the West are contributing to a reconceptualization of modernity that could allow for the incorporation of local religious and cultural traditions. Islamic feminists have made important contributions to a growing literature on "multiple modernities" that offers a critique of the adequacy of Western modernization theory. This literature attempts to get beyond the tradi-

[58] Armstrong 2004, 294.

[59] For a discussion of dialogic feminist methodologies for international relations see Tickner 2005.

[60] Ackerly 2000, 14.

[61] Brown 2002, 299.

tional/modern divide and the exclusive association of modernity with the spread of Western secular norms, institutions, and economic arrangements that are a source of such hostility to conservative religious groups both inside and outside the West.[62] The conceptualization of non-Western modernities is a theoretical effort to create new ways of reading and seeing aspects of social life that have been judged and dismissed as regressive and backward.[63]

Turkish feminist Nilufer Gole criticizes modernization theory for its portrayal of non-Western countries as being temporally behind the West in development. In the second half of the twentieth century, modernization and Westernization were believed to be synonymous. Gole claims that she sees evidence of a decoupling of these two concepts. She points to concomitant processes of the globalization of capitalism and the indigenization of modernity. She hypothesizes alternative forms of "hybrid" modernity—the blending of global capitalism with the recognition of different sets of values and cultures. Whereas in the West the public sphere was historically formed as a bourgeois sphere excluding women, in Muslim contexts of modernity, women are the markers of public space. She points to the example of Kemalist Turkey, where the public visibility of women implied a radical change in the definition of the public and private spheres and was a central feature of Turkish modernity.[64] Gole's analysis suggests that modernization can take different forms in different contexts. She is attempting to build alternative visions of modernity that would make possible mutual respect for, and understanding of, different worldviews.

Conclusion

Keohane challenges IR theorists to take other worldviews, including religious worldviews, more seriously if we are to understand the roots of what he calls "informal violence." His introductory chapter to *Power and Governance in a Partially Globalized World* concludes with the suggestion that, since 9/11, we face a moral imperative to understand world politics better. Better understanding should enable people to design better policies and institutions.[65] Responding to this challenge, I have attempted to offer some insights to help us better understand the worldviews of those who commit violence in the name of religion. I believe that these views are an extreme version of more general frustrations with secular modernity

[62] Eisenstadt and Schluchter 2001.
[63] Gole 2000, 41–45.
[64] Gole 2000, 51.
[65] Keohane 2002, 18.

and liberal capitalism and the policies, institutions, and knowledge supporting them, which date back to the Westphalian era, when a system of secular states began to replace religiously based polities. I have suggested that Keohane's synthesis of institutionalism, realism, and constructivism may not be adequate for understanding religious worldviews. Neoliberal institutionalism *is* helpful for understanding new forms of asymmetric power between powerful states and global networks engaged in informal violence that favor the latter. It also helps us understand some of the challenges that these nonstate actors pose for both states and multilateral institutions. However, an adequate understanding of the religious worldviews that such actors hold requires building knowledge that is itself critically reflective of secular rationalism—a form of knowledge that is limited in its ability to explain religious motivations and practices. Following Keohane's suggestion that contestation between different IR approaches can play a positive role in social science scholarship, I have outlined some ways in which insights from classical realism and linguistic constructivism are useful for such an endeavor. Going beyond these IR theoretical traditions, I have discussed feminist writings that offer insights into a radical rewriting of religion and more synthetic forms of knowledge-building. In part, humans create their world through the meaning they give to their actions. Less patriarchal religious interpretations can help us get beyond the constitutive gendered hierarchies of the conservative religious worldviews that are generating conflict and violence. Less gendered, more reflexive understandings of modern knowledge-building can help us transcend religious/secular divides and the exclusive association of modernity with a secular Western model. Dialogic, reflexive forms of knowledge can produce greater understanding of the "other's" religious beliefs, an understanding that, as Karen Armstrong's epigraph at the beginning of this chapter suggests, may no longer be merely desirable but necessary for our very survival.

Afterword

CHAPTER 13

Robert Keohane: Political Theorist

Andrew Moravcsik

THIS VOLUME CLOSES with a backward look. The fifteen years from 1970 to 1985 witnessed the emergence of the new subdiscipline of international relations now widely known as "international political economy" (IPE). No one contributed more to this process than Robert Keohane.[1] Working in part with Joseph Nye, he laid the theoretical foundation for IPE in three books—*Transnational Relations and World Politics, Power and Interdependence*, and *After Hegemony*—and many related essays.[2] Among his numerous contributions to international relations, these are the most essential.

This chapter has two aims. The first is to summarize the basic contribution of this work to general international relations theory. In it, Keohane introduced three fundamental causal premises about international politics, which have served as core elements of the discipline of international political economy ever since. These premises highlight the important impact on state behavior of, respectively, shifts in state preferences induced by globalization, shifts in interstate power induced by asymmetries in interdependence, and shifts in the distribution of information induced by international institutions. Taken together, these three factors offer a coherent explanation of patterns of international cooperation in world politics.

The second aim of the chapter is to place these theoretical innovations in historical perspective. Keohane's background and intellectual style, combined with a distinct set of historical circumstances both in the outside world and in academia, explain the emergence of these particular theoretical contributions at this juncture in the history of international relations. Critical is that Keohane's temperament and training have always been closer to those of a political philosopher than a political scientist. Drawing on additional biographical material, the chapter traces how Keohane deployed the skills of a "political theorist" at a moment when international economic issues were becoming more important in American and global politics, and realist international relations theory was fac-

---

[1] The chapters in this volume were initially delivered at a conference held in honor of Robert Keohane at Princeton University.

[2] Keohane and Nye 1972, 1977; Keohane 1984.

ing theoretical challenge. This circumstance created a unique moment for major intellectual breakthroughs—a historical "window of opportunity" that has now closed.

Keohane's Fundamental Theoretical Contributions

Robert Keohane's scholarship between 1970 and 1985 opened a new substantive area for inquiry. The work focused on new issues (international political economy, not international security), new actors (transnational actors, not states), new forms of interaction (transnational and transgovernmental relations, rather than interstate relations), new outcomes (international cooperation rather than international conflict), and new structures (international institutions, not "pure" anarchy). It advanced provocative hypotheses, most notably the claim that institutionalized cooperation persisted after the decline of postwar American hegemony. These aspects have been much discussed—and are treated in detail elsewhere in this volume.[3] Keohane's most fundamental contributions lie, however, at the level of basic international relations theory.

Three basic causal premises about international politics emerged from Keohane's epochal theoretical work in this period. One way to think about them is to posit a simple model of rationalist international cooperation divided into three stages: (a) the formation of state preferences; (b) interstate bargaining and strategic interaction; and (c) institutionalization of the bargain. If we assume states are rational, we can expect that they will first determine preferences across "states of the world," then bargain with one another to realize those goals as best they can, and finally seek to preserve the result by institutionalizing the bargain.[4] Keohane's three major works in this period can be viewed, respectively, as addressing the fundamental theoretical causes of state behavior at each of these three stages in turn. *Transnational Relations and World Politics* introduces state preferences, driven by globalization, as a variable shaping state behavior. *Power and Interdependence* introduces a new conception of interstate bargaining power, derived from asymmetrical interdependence, as a variable influencing state behavior. And *After Hegemony* introduces international regimes, driven in turn by the distribution of information, as a way to explain the preservation of bargains. Taken together, they provide a coherent synthetic account of state cooperation in world politics. Despite the addition of many other theories, these three claims remain to

---

[3] Gourevitch 1999; Griffiths 1999, 185–90; Milner, chap. 1 in this volume.

[4] Lake and Powell 2000; Fearon 1998; Moravcsik 1998, chap. 1. The final stage then feeds back, of course, into future rounds of preferences, bargaining, and institutionalization.

this day the most important theoretical pillars of modern international political economy. Beneath the surface of new actors, issues, processes, and outcomes, these remain the most fundamental theoretical contributions of Keohane's career. Let us explore each in turn.

State Preferences and Societal Interdependence

On the surface, the purpose of *Transnational Relations and World Politics* is to explore the importance for world politics of interaction among private actors, as distinct from states and international organizations. Keohane and Nye term such activities *transnational relations* and categorize them according to the nature of the items being moved across borders by the private parties: information, goods, money, or people.[5] The existence of transnational relations increases "societal interdependence" and makes countries more "sensitive" to one another. They make policy processes more "pluralistic," "complex," and "fragmented." They introduce new actors, issues, and processes. Keohane and Nye would later call the ideal type of this world *complex interdependence* and contrast it to the realist ideal type of pure interstate relations dominated by zero-sum security conflict.

Most of the examples Keohane and Nye cite—among them international trade and monetary policy, farm policy, international trade union federations, interstate airline regulation, global inequality, newspaper sales offices, and, above all, multinational firms—are economic in nature, though transnational nongovernmental groups (both revolutionary or reformist), religious groups, and mass communication comprise an interesting residual of cases.[6] In later writing, Keohane would speak also of social and ecological globalization, with global warming being a good example of the latter, as well as some politico-military forms.[7] The focus on transnational private activity opened a new substantive field of inquiry in the discipline of international relations. In the conclusion to *Transnational Relations*, Keohane and Nye propose a research agenda based on comparisons of the impact of transnational interaction across issue

[5] Keohane and Nye 1971a, 332, from which other citations in this paragraph come.

[6] Keohane and Nye 1971a, 333–36. Without the inspiration and active encouragement of economist Raymond Vernon, who was studying multinational corporations at the same research institute where Nye was active, Keohane later recollected, "I am not sure we would have gone down the transnational relations route." Cohen 2008, 29.

[7] Keohane 2004. The sense that economics is the dominant source of examples is also supported by intense collaborative work Keohane and Nye did with C. Fred Bergsten in the mid-1970s, which brought together economists and political scientists, as well as their engagement with the ideas of Ernst Haas, Richard Cooper, Charles Kindleberger, and other economists. Much of Keohane and Nye's work in this period also responds to liberal and radical political economy on multinational corporations, dependency, and inequality.

areas, an agenda that would be carried out by international political economists over the next two scholarly generations.

Yet we should not let a superficial focus on new actors ("transnational relations") and new issues ("international political economy") obscure the deeper implication of the *Transnational Relations and World Politics* for general international relations theory. The more fundamental implication of the existence of transnational relations is the following: *State prefer-ences about the management of world politics are a potentially positive-sum variable, rather than a zero-sum constant, as realists had claimed.*[8]

On the model of trade and other forms of economic cooperation, it seems reasonable to assume that domestic interest groups have considerable invest-ment in the transnational social relations in which they are engaged—a cir-cumstance Keohane and Nye would later call *societal interdependence*. Keo-hane and Nye argued that governments will not—and, empirically, do not—always override the interests of transnational actors, even when pursuing security interests and in wartime. Not only can transnational relations shift basic state preferences (that is, underlying interests), but they can impose new external constraints and opportunities for state behavior, and alter the nature of relative interstate power, with traditional statecraft and mil-itary might playing lesser roles.[9] Transnational societal relations must thus be understood as part of the basic structure of the international system in which states are embedded—over which they have some, but limited, con-trol. It follows that states can be assumed to gain some mutual benefit by facilitating and managing the activities in common—though of course this does not rule out interstate conflict over control of such activities.

This is a potentially revolutionary conclusion for international rela-tions theory, not least because it displaces the centrality of zero-sum power analysis favored by realists like Morgenthau and Waltz. Realists have long maintained that the precise preferences, interests, beliefs, and domestic politics of states are epiphenomenal, because they can be as-sumed to be conflictual (zero-sum). If preferences are fixed, then relative material power is all that shapes state behavior in the end; this establishes realism's core insight: "the autonomy of the political."[10] Keohane and Nye insisted, by contrast, that international politics (in the realist sense) is *not*

[8] Keohane recalls that the role of varying preferences and bargaining in politics was a les-son learned from Thomas Schelling's *Strategy of Conflict*, of which he says, "It is probably difficult to overestimate the impact of this book on my generation of graduate students, par-ticularly his discussions of mixed motive games, focal points, and bargaining" (personal communication, February 2008).

[9] Keohane and Nye 1971b, 721.

[10] Hans J. Morgenthau, *Politics among Nations: The Struggle for Power and Peace* 3rd edition (New York: Alfred Knopf, 1960), 13, 16.

autonomous; it is critically influenced by its transnational social context. Hence, as they argue, the hierarchy among issue areas breaks down, with military issues no longer dominant. It follows that if transnational relations vary greatly, then preferences can vary correspondingly—and one cannot simply take them by assumption. The ultimate significance of this line of argument—though Keohane and Nye themselves do not push it all the way to this conclusion—is that any empirical analysis of interstate power and strategic interaction cannot be conducted in isolation; it requires a *prior* understanding of state preferences derived from detailed empirical analysis of issue-specific societal interdependence. Realist theories of state behavior cannot stand on their own, and claims for the autonomy and parsimony of such theories are simply invalid.[11]

Economic examples are prominent in Keohane and Nye's development of this point. They point to financial markets and communications, with which foreign ministries are not competent to deal. They highlight tensions that arise between competing policy options, for example between the interests of U.S. multinational firms and the national interest in promoting economic development and stabilizing the international economy.[12] Similarly, they cite Cooper's claim that in economic policy, governments faced a range of strategic choices, including defensive protectionism, assertion of national jurisdiction, and policy coordination through international institutions—implying that conflict and cooperation are choices rather than foregone conclusions in the mixed-motive environment.[13] Such "complex" tensions may arise even in areas of "high" foreign policy. Keohane and Nye point to a declining separation between "high" and "low" politics, and offer a suggestive reanalysis of Norman Angell's famous pre–World War I prediction that great power war was obsolete, arguing that a century later interdependence and expectations may now have increased to a level where his claim is becoming more accurate.[14] Overall, they conclude, there is good reason to believe that the level and nature of transnational relations, and resulting levels of "societal interdependence," will influence foreign policy decisions.

A final implication of variation in patterns of societal interdependence and state preferences is the increasing importance of domestic politics.

[11] Here I extend the implications of Keohane and Nye's writing one step beyond what they wrote at the time. See, however, Keohane and Nye 1975. For subsequent analyses that develop the methodological implications, see Baldwin 1979; Frieden 1979; Moravcsik 1997. On Keohane's own ambivalence about domestic politics and variation in state preferences, see notes 16 and 17 below.

[12] Keohane and Nye 1971b, 741–42.

[13] Keohane and Nye 1971b, 744.

[14] Keohane and Nye 1971b, 724.

Individuals and groups within societies are likely to have differential links to global society, and therefore might be expected to have different interests in how it should be managed—in contrast to what some expect to be more homogeneous preferences for a public good like "security."[15] (Indeed, transnational and domestic forces can never be clearly separated in analyses of interdependence; interdependence, by its very nature, involves the interaction between domestic and foreign societal actors.) Keohane and Nye underscore this point by attributing the rising "politicization" of international economics to a conjunction of "secular trends" toward increased government responsibility for economic welfare and economic internationalization, which makes governments "more sensitive to external disturbances that may affect developments within their own societies."[16] Bureaucratic politics is fragmenting, they argue, citing the fact that by the early 1960s, forty-four U.S. federal bureaucracies were already represented in the London embassy.[17] Keohane and Nye provide examples of how private groups work through domestic politics, form transnational alliances, and invoke international organizations, in order to oppose or circumvent the will of their home governments.

Transnational Relations is more typology than theory. Keohane and Nye undermine the realist ideal type by outlining the complexity of potential causal connections, and set forth a research agenda for studying them, but offer no rigorous explanation of the effects of transnational relations. Forty years later, however, one is still struck not just by the enduring importance of the substantive and theoretical innovations outlined above, but by the many concrete phenomena highlighted in the volume, many of which have become the object of intensive research over the next generation of scholarship: transnational alliances, "two-level games," the "democratic deficit," the backlash against globalization, transgovernmental networks, the boomerang effect of transnational advocacy groups, and multilevel governance, to name a few. Most fruitful has been the vast literature on the ways in which interdependence and domestic politics impact state preferences across international economic policy. Yet Keohane and Nye themselves did not continue in this vein and explore this implication of their theory in detail—a task many of their students willingly took up.[18] What interested them about networks was not their substantive impact on preferences, but their impact on international political processes—to which we now turn.

[15] Keohane and Nye 1975, 397–98.
[16] Bergsten, Keohane, and Nye 1975, 5–7.
[17] Keohane and Nye 1971b, 724.
[18] A large number of his students, including many in this volume, did turn to the domestic politics of interdependence. Keohane did return to this issue in an edited volume with one of them (Keohane and Milner 1996).

Power and Asymmetrical Interdependence

In *Power and Interdependence*, Keohane and Nye begin by summarizing the world of *Transnational Relations* as the ideal type of "complex interdependence," characterized by high societal interdependence, intense transgovernmental interaction, and complex domestic politics. Military force is an inappropriate tool in most such cases, primarily because of its high collateral costs. There is thus little reason to assume a "hierarchy of issues" in world politics, with security at the top; instead we should view world politics as a complex and changing set of issue-specific interactions. Keohane and Nye contrast this ideal type of "complex interdependence" to a realist ideal type in which security issues dominate the agenda and military force is effective.[19]

Power and Interdependence seeks to develop positive theories to explain state behavior under such conditions. If power is not exercised by those with a dominant control over coercive power resources, such as military force—as realists claim—where does it come from? Without a conception of power, the notion of complex interdependence seems naive or utopian.[20] Keohane and Nye's answer comes in the form of the concept of *asymmetrical interdependence.*[21] The central theoretical claim of the book, and Keohane's second major contribution to IR theory, is this: *Interstate power stems not from the possession of coercive power resources, but from asymmetries in issue-specific interdependence.*

Asymmetrical interdependence functions as follows. The more resources one country possesses (or the less it needs), the stronger it is; conversely, the less a country has of it (or the more it needs), the weaker it is. Bargaining relationships, Keohane recalls arguing, "might be symmetrical, as in the case of Germany and France; it might be asymmetrical, as in the case of the United States and Guatemala."[22] This is a subset of a general and widely employed set of bargaining models in which players with more intense or immediate preferences are disadvantaged vis-à-vis those with less intense preference or more patience, and will be compelled to sacrifice relatively more in order to get what they want. In the context of international

---

[19] Keohane and Nye 1977, chap. 2. Keohane's attitude toward domestic politics and variation in state preferences remains ambiguous throughout his career. He backtracks in *After Hegemony*, dropping the assumption of varying preferences and "fragmented" domestic politics, and returning to a state-centric view favoring "systemic" explanations with fixed positive-sum preferences.

[20] Keohane 2004, 5.

[21] This is Keohane and Nye's own retrospective understanding as well. "In *Power and Interdependence*, Nye and I had already sought to integrate Realism and Liberalism by using a conception of interdependence which focused on bargaining." (Keohane and Nye 1987, 733).

[22] Keohane 2004, 5.

relations, asymmetrical interdependence offers what is potentially an extremely parsimonious model of bargaining, since it derives bargaining power from the same basic source as state preferences.[23]

Keohane and Nye pose a second theoretical question in *Power and Interdependence*, to which they provide only an inductive analysis: What explains international order? Here Keohane and Nye conduct simple empirical probes. In their most important empirical chapter, they assess four explanations for variation over the twentieth century in international rules in money and oceans policy. A first ("economic process") explanation stresses simple technocratic adaptation to technological or economic change. A second ("overall power" or realist) explanation posits that the most powerful country militarily (the "hegemon") makes the rules, with power shifting to match changes in its power. A third ("issue structure") explanation predicts that the most powerful country within an issue area, understood in "asymmetrical interdependence" terms, sets the rules. A fourth ("international organization") explanation posits that rules encoded in international institutions—or *international regimes*, as they came to be called—remain in place even in the face of pressures for change.[24] Keohane and Nye interpret the evidence over time to support the view that a world of "complex interdependence," which they associate with the third ("issue structure") and fourth ("international organization") explanations, is supplanting a more traditional state-centric explanation, which they associate with the first and second explanations.[25]

Their discussion of international regimes and organizations hints at the importance of "agenda-setting" and institutionalization. Yet this finding is more suggestive than conclusive, leading to a further puzzle: If international organizations are becoming more important in shaping state behavior, why is this so? This leads us on to *After Hegemony*.

International Regimes and Information

International institutions have played a secondary role in the works discussed up to this point.[26] In *Transnational Relations*, the focus is on "trans-

---

[23] Keohane recalls that this insight came from Schelling's work and from Albert Hirschman's *National Power and the Structure of Foreign Trade*, which was the subject of much discussion at Harvard when Keohane spent a year of leave there in 1972.

[24] For a definition and discussion of international regimes, see Krasner 1983b.

[25] The economic process explanation is not inconsistent with "complex interdependence." Keohane and Nye treat convergent economic interests as necessary but insufficient for cooperation.

[26] To be sure, both Keohane and Nye had worked on international organizations. Keohane's dissertation concerned influence within the UN General Assembly. Keohane describes the field in the 1960s as "an old-fashioned descriptive, atheoretical enterprise" (personal communication, February 2008). Nye worked on European integration, focusing on the convergence of economic and social preferences (Keohane and Nye 1975, 379).

national" or "transgovernmental coalitions," with international institutions simply providing one among a number of convenient sites or logistical instruments to assist in forming them.[27] *Power and Interdependence* goes a bit further, treating institutions as instruments to link issues and set agendas. Yet neither work succeeds in offering a micro-foundationally grounded explanation of how and why institutions alter the behavior of states. They leave any claims open to the traditional realist criticism that they rest ultimately on little more than a conviction that statesmen comply out of ethical or idealistic belief—a view derided as "moralistic," "legalistic," or "utopian." A convincing rationalist account of why states should construct and comply with the norms and principles of international law and organization remained absent. Yet international institutions, if we are to believe *Power and Interdependence*, seem to have increased in importance and influence since the mid- twentieth century. This is the central puzzle Keohane addresses in *After Hegemony*.

In contrast to the ever broadening inductive mode of *Transnational Relations* and *Power and Interdependence*, *After Hegemony* remains tightly focused on developing a rigorous theoretical answer to this question, even if it means setting aside other factors that might be relevant in explaining international cooperation. The effects of "economic process" and "transnational relations" on state interests, for example, analyzed in *Transnational Relations* and *Power and Interdependence*, are assumed rather than analyzed; the analysis begins by taking "the existence of mutual interests as given," and moves on immediately to "examine the conditions under which they will lead to cooperation."[28] *After Hegemony*'s tight focus is, from Keohane's perspective, a cardinal intellectual virtue, because it formulates the problem of cooperation in a more tractable form. By bracketing underlying interests, Keohane distinguished "cooperation" from "harmony." Harmony is a situation where preferences converge automatically, such that each actor's policies independently facilitate the achievement of the goals of others. Cooperation, by contrast, is a situation in which motives are mixed and uncertainty over behavior will prevent optimal outcomes unless active steps are taken. Shared interests are necessary, but insufficient, to explain cooperation. For Keohane, this was a decisive moment. "I gave this talk about cooperation," he recalls, "and Fred [Bergsten] said right away, 'What's the difference between cooperation and harmony?' And I realized that that was the key to the puzzle."[29]

[27] Keohane and Nye 1975, 399–401.

[28] Keohane 1984, 6.

[29] "That is, I wasn't going to argue that there was harmony. There's not harmony; there's conflict in international politics. It's decentralized realm, it's anarchy in a certain sense. So cooperation has to be something different, and it comes out of conflict. It's mutual adjustment to conflict. Once you see cooperation that way—not as harmony, which made it so seem

He later explained: "Harmony is apolitical. No communication is necessary, and no influence need be exercised. Cooperation, by contrast, is highly political: somehow, patterns of behavior must be altered. . . . [Under] a variety of conditions strategies that involve threats and punishments as well as promises and rewards are more effective in attaining cooperative outcomes than those that rely entirely on persuasion and the force of good example."[30]

Empirically and methodologically, the strict separation of harmony and cooperation might be viewed as a somewhat dangerous assumption, for without exploring baseline shifts in the economic costs and benefits that affect state interests, it is difficult to know for sure how to what extent the changes in cooperation one observes might actually explained by economic factors and domestic politics.[31] Theoretically, however, bracketing the origins of state preferences proved an extremely fruitful strategy, for by doing so, Keohane could focus his full attention on developing a rigorous rationalist account of international institutions.

Keohane developed this theoretical advance in a dialectical relationship with two basic strands of scholarship. The first was Waltzian neorealism. He was impressed by the parsimony and power of Waltz's work—more so, he recalls, than most of his colleagues at the time—and sought to emulate it.[32] In this respect *After Hegemony* is a theoretically conservative book: Keohane quite deliberately eschews the construction of polar opposite ideal types found in *Transnational Relations* and *Power and Interdependence* and, as we have seen, sets aside previous claims about the fragmentation of domestic politics and preferences. Instead he affirmed as many tenets of Waltzian realism as possible: states as actors, (bounded) rationality and self-interested state behavior, fixed preferences, the role of hegemonic power. Whereas Waltz assumed that uncertainty about future intentions would rule out cooperation, however, Keohane treats information as a variable and institutions as a means to manipulate it, thereby facilitating cooperation.[33] He recalls:

---

odd, how would you ever get cooperation to fit in international politics if it's harmony? Once you see that it's actually a form of discord which generates cooperation, mutual adjustment instead of conflict, then you can get a handle on it, because it becomes very similar to the problem of conflict. It's the obverse side of conflict" (Keohane 2004, 3).

[30] Keohane 1984, 53.

[31] Indeed, Keohane's own empirical analysis in *After Hegemony* repeatedly suggests the importance of domestic and economic factors. Keohane 1984, chap. 9, especially 207, 208–9, 211, 212–13, 215.

[32] Personal communication, February 2008.

[33] There has been a subsequent debate on this issue. Joseph Grieco and others argue that realists in fact assume "relative-gains seeking." However, the link between realism and relative-gains seeking has been criticized for its lack of conceptual clarity, while some realists deny that realism actually assumes conflictual preferences. For a review, see Baldwin 1993.

[Waltzian neorealism] was clearly a powerful intellectual construction [but] it was missing any attention to information—to the variation in how much information people have, and how much uncertainty there is. . . . and therefore the role of institutions was omitted. Once I realized that institutions serve principally to reduce uncertainty and provide information and credibility, then it was clear how the institutions fit into the missing part of Waltz's theory. A rebel against orthodoxy is always greatly in the debt of the people who can express what is the dominant view with utter clarity and logic.[34]

At the level of general international relations theory, therefore, the fundamental theoretical innovation in *After Hegemony* is to treat information as a basic element of the international system. This is Keohane's third major theoretical contribution to IR theory: *Variation in the nature and distribution of information is a systemic variable in world politics that helps explain the ability of states to overcome collective action problems.* By theorizing the precise role played by the quantity, quality, and distribution of information in world politics, we can understand state behavior better than with models that attend only to preferences, power, and strategic ideas. International institutions are one source of high-quality information otherwise unavailable to states, so the functional use of international institutions by self-interested, rational states is one implication of this basic theoretical insight—he one in which Keohane was most interested.[35]

To work out the precise link between information and institutions, Keohane turned to a second source of theoretical inspiration: the transaction costs economics of Ronald Coase, Oliver Williamson, George Akerlof, and other industrial organization economists.[36] The basic premise of this body of thought is that information is functionally useful, but costly to decentralized actors—in this case, to states—and its absence can induce "market failures" in otherwise competitive markets. In order to

---

[34] Keohane 2004, 2.

[35] Other potential sources of information about the intentions and actions of other states include diplomacy, the pattern of strategic interaction itself, direct observation of domestic politics, and independent social and cultural interactions, which have generated their own literatures. E.g., Oye 1986.

[36] Keohane recalls, "The most important piece of work was by an economist at Berkeley named George Akerlof, who later, much later, won the Nobel Prize for this article, called *The Market for Lemons.* Akerlof showed how in an economic market, the used-car market, there could be market failure. . . . [International] institutions were like the used-car dealer . . . because they made it possible for these otherwise separate and distrustful entities-the buyer and the seller, or the two countries-to make a deal which they would both benefit from, even though they were, in some sense, in a partially adversarial situation" (Keohane 2004, 2). Among the colleagues Keohane credits with pointing him toward this literature are Charles Kindleberger, Tim McKeown, James Rosse, and Laura Tyson. See Keohane 1982 for the seminal ideas and citations.

cooperate, governments must ascertain which parties are most interested, what agreements are possible, how best to structure those agreements, what behavior to expect of one another, who is complying with the agreements, and how they are to be collectively enforced—activities that, if constantly negotiated from scratch, impose potentially high (transaction) costs and risks. In world politics, "world government does not exist, making property rights and rules of legal liability fragile; information is extremely costly and often held unequally by different actors; transaction costs, including costs of organization and side-payments, are often very high."[37]

Insofar as international institutions generate high-quality information and reduce uncertainty about the intentions and actions of other states in regard to these things, they can reduce the costs and risks of cooperation. In Keohane's words, international regimes "contribute to cooperation not by implementing rules that states must follow, but by changing the context in which states make decisions based on self-interests."[38] Institutions can further cooperation by establishing forums for decision-making, linking issues together, providing incentives for states to exchange concessions, sharing information, specifying property and voting rights, assigning liability, creating dispute resolution mechanisms. They increase interactions (or iterations) among states, permitting states to observe one another and assess one another's willingness of the other to comply with cooperative agreements, coordinating coordinated and reciprocal "tit-for-tat" behavior. "Viewing international regimes as information-providing and transaction cost-reducing entities rather than as quasi-governmental rule-makers helps us to understand [their] persistence."[39] Keohane generally refers to this approach as *functional regime theory*, *neoliberal institutionalism*, or, later, *institutionalism*.[40]

One attractive implication of this approach is that it explains why modern international institutions are *neither* idealistic organizations appealing to utopian ideals *nor* authoritative monopolists of coercive force, superstates with an army and a police force on the model of the nation-state. Instead they are highly decentralized institutions, often informal or semiformal, to which nations belong voluntarily. The essence of such "international regimes" is that they set norms, principles, and procedures for interstate interaction. In this way Keohane sought to construct a maximally parsimonious argument why rationalist, self-interested states would construct and comply with international institutions—one that could com-

[37] Keohane 1984, 87.
[38] Keohane 1984, 13.
[39] Keohane 1984, 100–101.
[40] Keohane 1989.

bat the traditional realist objection that international law and institutions are utopian and idealistic. He concludes:

> International regimes are valuable to governments not because they enforce binding rules on others (they do not), but because they render it possible for governments to enter into mutually beneficial agreements with one another. They *empower* governments rather than shackling them.[41]

So far we have seen what international regimes do and why states create them, but not why they have an independent causal impact. Governments could, after all, simply constantly negotiate and renegotiate institutions at will to suit their immediate interests, always tracking underlying interests and power. To explain their autonomous impact, Keohane adds one more critical assumption, namely that regimes themselves are particularly expensive to establish and reform—much more so than individual agreements. This is so ostensibly because they link together a much thicker and more complex stream of preexisting agreements. If regimes were costless to build, there would be little point in constructing them. In this case, agreements would also be costless. Under these circumstances, governments could wait until specific problems arose, then make agreements to deal with them; they would have no need to construct international regimes to facilitate agreements. It is precisely the costliness of agreements, and more so regimes themselves, that make them important. The high price of regime-building helps existing regimes to persist.[42]

It is worthwhile, therefore, for governments (and domestic social groups) to economize to a certain extent in negotiation and adjustment by sticking with established patterns. Keohane's most famous set of empirical predictions follows: International institutions tend to impart a status quo bias. Governments would rather muddle through, building on and complying with the rules of a somewhat inconvenient regime, than seek to renegotiate the entire arrangement. Regimes persist, even if the interests

[41] Keohane 1984, 13.

[42] Keohane 1984, 102–3, more generally, 100–103, where he notes: "In world politics, international regimes help to facilitate the making of agreements by reducing barriers created by high transaction costs and uncertainty. But these very difficulties make it hard to create themselves in the first place. The importance of transaction costs and uncertainty means that regimes are easier to maintain than they are to create. Complementary interests are necessary but not sufficient conditions for their emergence. The construction of international regimes may require active efforts by a hegemonic state, as the IMF and GATT did after World War II; or regime creation in the absence of hegemony may be spurred on by the pressures of a sudden and severe crisis, such as that which led to the IEA. Even with complementary interests, it is difficult to overcome problems of transaction costs and uncertainty. Once an international regime has been established, however, it begins to benefit from the relatively high and symmetrical level of information that it generates, and from the ways in which it makes regime-supporting bargains easier to consummate."

that give rise to them shift. And within this institutionalized realm, the power to influence outcomes is wielded by those who control the agendas of international institutions.

To test this set of claims, Keohane turns to case studies of postwar Western trade, money, and oil politics. He seeks to isolate the importance of institutions, using declining U.S. hegemonic power (e.g., the decline of the United States from a half to a quarter of world GNP in the postwar generation) as a baseline. His central empirical claim is that the creation of postwar economic regimes in all three areas required the exercise of U.S. hegemonic power, exercised primarily in the form of asymmetrical policy adjustment and investment in the system by the United States, but that the decline of U.S. power did not lead to disorder and conflict, as realism would predict. Instead, cooperation persisted beyond expectations, even as hegemonic power declined—and this, he argues, is due to the stabilizing power of international regimes. Keohane observes, for example, continued multilateral trade liberalization, even in the face of slower growth, protectionist pressures, and bilateralism. In money and oil, where the collapse of the Bretton Woods fixed rate system and the replacement of the Seven Sisters with OPEC might be viewed as marking massive regime change, Keohane nonetheless points to considerable elements of institutional continuity.[43]

Keohane employs hegemonic stability theory as a baseline against which to test the institutionalist claims—a move often treated, even by Keohane himself, as a test of realism against institutionalism. In fact, however, most of his empirical arguments about hegemonic construction of postwar international institutions are not realist but based on "asymmetrical interdependence" arguments, whereby the hegemon assumes the brunt of adjustment or directly subsidizes the adjustment of less willing or able partners.[44] Overall military might and zero-sum security conflict play rel-

---

[43] There is surely some tendency on Keohane's part to code the cup as half-full of money and oil, certainly, even if the argument about trade is more convincing. With regard to oil, he seeks to offset the rise of OPEC with an entire chapter to the prospects for intra-Western cooperation in the International Energy Agency, though ultimately conceding that the case might be the most favorable for hegemonic stability theory. In money, he stresses continued, if weakened, cooperation at the IMF, monitoring and lending to deficit countries, at the same time as the dollar standard and fixed exchange-rate system collapsed. Be that as it may, our primary concern here is the theoretical contribution of the book, which remains that of providing a plausible account of the functional role of international institutions.

[44] In a zero-sum bargaining situation, asymmetrical interdependence means that the possession of issue-specific resources accords a country bargaining leverage. In the cooperative international environment, Keohane argues, the logic is reversed: The more issue-specific resources a country has, the less costly it is on the margin for it to contribute to provision of the public or collective good. At the limit, the U.S. hegemon can provide the public good itself, as in the case of financial assistance, a reserve currency, and order in the Middle East.

atively little role—though Keohane does acknowledge some impact.[45] Yet the primary role of hegemony in *After Hegemony* is not to advance a general theoretical claim—Keohane does not, in fact, claim that regime construction *generally* requires a hegemon—but to demonstrate that the transaction costs of regime creation are higher than the costs of regime maintenance, thereby bolstering the core institutionalist claim about the decisive role of information.[46]

With these three claims, Keohane (and Nye) had brought together new causal understandings of state preferences, interstate bargaining, and institutionalization, which would serve as a common foundation for the new discipline of international political economy over the next generation. Taken together, they established a comprehensive rationalist account of how states cooperate. After 1985, Keohane himself moved on. He has remained among the most prolific and influential scholars in the field. His work on ideas and international relations, interdependence, feminist theory, European integration, the environment, alliances, international law, anti-Americanism, qualitative methods, and democratic accountability displayed remarkable variety and energy, and considerable conceptual innovation has made important contributions to our understanding of world politics. But it would not have the same revolutionary impact on international relations theory.

The Emergence of International Political Economy in Historical Perspective

Three factors converged at this particular point in time to account for the emergence of the new field of IPE, and for the singular foundational importance of Keohane's specific theoretical insights: developments in world politics, developments within international relations theory, and Robert Keohane's particular characteristics among the founding generation of IPE theorists.

It is appropriate for us to begin—as Keohane himself would in analyzing

[45] It might reasonably be objected by realists that the ultimate motivation was one of security conflict with the USSR, as Joanne Gowa and others have recently argued, without which the United States would not have found the domestic political will to pursue an enlightened policy of regime construction. Liberals might respond that the sources of this Cold War security conflict itself had more to do with specific state preferences (respective domestic regime type, patterns of interdependence, and national ideologies of East and West) than with the distribution of power per se.

[46] The construction of international regimes may require active efforts by a hegemonic state, as with the IMF and GATT after World War II, but it may also occur in the absence of hegemony, as in the case of the EU, or spurred on by the pressures of a sudden and severe crisis, such as that which led to creation of the International Energy Agency.

258 · Chapter 13

a social phenomenon—with the deeper historical determinants of the theoretical breakthroughs. The 1960s and 1970s witnessed a critical juncture in modern political economy. Economic interdependence, the use of economic instruments of power, and the management of international regimes—what we would today term "globalization"—became salient public issues in Western, and particularly American, foreign policy.[47] Problems of inflation, the declining dollar, and trade competitiveness were increasingly salient on public agendas, and with the collapse of Bretton Woods, the global economy entered an era of increasingly unfettered international capital mobility, with everything that entailed. An important aspect was the increasing sense of vulnerability of the United States as its economic hegemony declined, beginning with John F. Kennedy's famous inaugural observation that the balance of payments, alongside the nuclear balance, was the incoming American president's chief foreign policy concern. Policy think tanks were springing up to study the phenomenon. G-7 cooperation was launched in this period as a transgovernmental means to manage these issues. This was the period of intense discussion about GATT, the IMF, OPEC, as well as various radical alternatives, such as the Group of 77 and the New International Economic Order.[48] This period also saw increasing public and scholarly attention to the activities of multinational corporations, the dependency of neoimperialism, revisionist theories of the Cold War, and economic influences on U.S. foreign policy—all of which linked political economy issues to the burning issue of intervention in Vietnam and other developing countries. Keohane and Nye were also influenced, as we have seen, by the writings of a number of economists, such as C. Fred Bergstein, Richard Cooper, Charles Kindleberger, Raymond Vernon, Albert Hirschman—and, later, by transaction costs economics.

Though, unlike Nye, he eschewed a life of policy activism, Keohane was engaged with these outside trends. Looking back, he speaks of his inherited sense of moral commitment:

[47] Keohane said his purpose was "to contravene the notion that world politics is only about security affairs, and that political economy is not an important part of it. When we started this work in 1970, people were ignoring multinational enterprises. They were looking only at the state system. They considered economic relations among the advanced countries to be low politics, not very interesting. What was interesting was the U.S.-Soviet conflict, nuclear weapons, international crises. Our view was that that was also interesting, but the increasingly important phenomenon of political economy-of the use of politics to shape the economy, of the use of economic wealth to shape politics-was not being studied" (Keohane 2004, 2).

[48] To be sure, Keohane did not address directly the issue of North-South relations, preferring to work on regimes among developed Western countries, but the theoretical advances were applied to these issues by others, including some participants in this volume.

I've always been a student of international politics because I cared about the outcomes, not just for curiosity. I thought (maybe with hubris) that one could make some difference in how people behave in the world if they think differently about it. . . . if they redesign their policies or institutions there could be more mutually beneficial collaboration without giving up one's own interests, [and] the world would be a better place.[49]

The new concept of power developed in *Politics and Interdependence* was a response to the collapse of Bretton Woods and the first oil shock in 1971–73, which demonstrated as clearly as any issues in modern times the power of "asymmetrical interdependence." Keohane's mentor and Nye's colleague Stanley Hoffmann penned an influential essay explaining why the United States was unable to deploy military force to offset Saudi Arabia's exercise of economic influence.[50] *After Hegemony* responded directly to the post–Bretton Woods concern about the stability of the international economic order in the face of rising interdependence. In Keohane's first issue as editor of *International Organization*, "right after the oil crisis," he wrote:

There was a crisis . . . of interdependence . . . growth had slowed down or stopped in the West. There was a general sense that we had to restructure the system after Bretton Woods collapsed, and so it was a moment when it was clear that people needed to think politically about the world economy, because it wasn't automatically taking care of itself.[51]

Keohane's work also came at a critical juncture in international relations theory, a moment when the hold on the field of realists like Morgenthau, Waltz, and Kissinger was eroding—which served to focus Keohane's thought. Keohane and Nye's challenge to realism was part of a broader trend. Kenneth Waltz's neorealist reformulation in the book *Theory of International Politics* was a powerful and appealing synthesis, but it attracted many critics. In part this was a function of its exclusive focus on military matters, and its difficulty in explaining the new economic trends we have just described. But there were also purely theoretical concerns. We have seen that in each book, Keohane (and Nye) were reacting against a realist ideal type—without which the theoretical revolution underlying the emergence of IPE would have lost much of its force.

The parsimony of neorealist theory left much out that was of potential interest. For Keohane, who ran a joint Bay Area international relations seminar with Waltz during the late 1970s, the parsimony of neorealism

[49] Keohane 2004, 3.
[50] Hoffmann 1975, 4–5.
[51] Keohane 2004, 3.

was a both a model and spur that led him to highlight what was missing—as we have seen above. He was not alone. Almost every major theoretical innovation of the past quarter-century in international relations has been a reaction to neorealism. Even Waltz's students, most of whom continued to call themselves "realists," tended to dilute neorealist assumptions by adding exogenous changes in state preferences—giving rise to so-called "neoclassical" realism.[52] Theories of the democratic peace, the focus on ideas, and the study on nonrational decision-making and theories of domestic politics also gained ground in this period.

At an even more fundamental level, the reconceptualization of power that underlay Keohane and Nye's approach to international political economy, in which coercive military force is replaced by asymmetrical interdependence and institutional agenda control, was part of a revolution across the discipline of political science. It was an application of Robert Dahl's pluralist politics model to the international system, with implications perhaps more far-reaching in international politics than even in U.S. politics.[53]

Keohane was thus in the right place at the right time—politically and academically—to make these breakthroughs. Yet there is also something in his own distinctive cast of mind that contributed to his success. In this regard, one might be tempted to focus on intellectual curiosity and tenacity, breath of interests, intensity and focused energy, an ability to collaborate with a wide range of interdisciplinary scholars, older and younger, a willingness to mentor students who disagree with him, and an utter fearlessness about directing the field in directions that he cannot, for methodological reasons, follow. Those who have worked with him have benefited from—and have been spurred on by—these characteristics. Yet here I shall focus on the intellectual style of his scholarship—a style that is reflected in the general theory that emerged—and its relationship to these external challenges.

Keohane was a member of the transitional or "founding" generation of the subdiscipline of modern international political economy. He played a role akin to that of Dahl in American politics, or Samuel Huntington and Gabriel Almond in comparative politics. As such he was a bridge between styles of thought: He was trained by scholars who were historians or political theorists—and at a university, Harvard, that prided itself on resisting modernizing trends. Yet he himself trained professional students of IPE. Keohane was suspended between these two generations—belonging to neither and yet, in a sense, to both. This generational position tells us much about his unique conceptual abilities.

Like those who taught him, Keohane brought to his scholarship the

[52] E.g., Walt 1987. For a critique see Legro and Moravcsik 1999.
[53] Keohane and Nye 1975, 395–96.

training and temperament of a political philosopher, as well as those of a political scientist. "I was always interested in political theory," he observes. "I'm a theorist by nature, and I love political theory more than anything else."[54] Those who had the greatest formative influence on him, his mentors Hoffmann and Judith Shklar, were political theorists, temperamentally unsuited to modern political science. Hoffmann has questioned—in public if not in print—the discipline's obsession with the intricacies of regime theory. Keohane recalls that when he told Shklar that he was working on *After Hegemony*, she responded that it would be "a small book with large type and large margins" because "there's nothing to say about international cooperation."[55] Keohane himself initially yearned to follow in their footsteps. But for the presidency of John F. Kennedy, anti-Communism, and his mother's social democratic admonitions to improve the world, as he tells it, he would have become a political philosopher.[56]

Keohane has always characterized himself as a political theorist, and traces of his fundamental commitment to political philosophy remain in his work. Keohane is above all a conceptual thinker. If other early IPE scholars brought other skills—one thinks of Robert Gilpin's historical sweep, John Ruggie's sociologically informed treatment of ideational factors, Joseph Nye's practical policy engagement, Peter Katzenstein's knowledge of comparative European institutions, Ernst Haas's complex analysis of endogeneity, Stephen Krasner's blunt analysis of power—Keohane's work stands out for its conceptual clarity. Throughout his career, he has focused tenaciously on "big questions" of international relations, more than detailed empirical and methodological issues. He possesses a special ability to distill fundamental conceptual dichotomies and core principles underlying disciplinary debates. In stylizing the positions of his opponents, often more crisply than they had themselves, he succeeded in redefining the contours of the discipline—as we see not just in volumes analyzed above, but in the debates recounted in the edited volumes entitled *Neorealism and Its Critics* and *Neo-Liberalism and Its Critics*.[57] Often these positions are based on close exegesis of theoretical texts, as in his readings of Hans Morgenthau, Kenneth Waltz, Ernst Haas, and the transaction costs economists. Though his work is informed by a remarkably broad empirical understanding of international relations, Keohane ultimately privileged conceptual clarity over empirical complexity.[58] This is evident,

---

[54] Keohane 2004, 1.

[55] Keohane 2004, 3.

[56] Keohane 2004, 1.

[57] Keohane 1986a; Baldwin 1993.

[58] Keohane has preferred edited volumes or article- or chapter-length empirical inquiries. A book-length study of American foreign policy over two hundred years remains unfinished.

for example, in his ambivalent attitude toward the role of "domestic politics" in world politics: His early work with Nye highlighted the fragmentation and complexity of politics among interdependent nations. Yet in *After Hegemony* he sets them aside, preferring to side with Waltz in preference for so-called systemic arguments about power and information—a decision that was, in the end, more aesthetic than empirically grounded.[59] All these habits of mind can be seen, at least in part, as marks of Keohane's affinity to normative political theory.

Another indicator of Keohane's ambivalent position in modern scholarship, poised between political theory and political science, is his attitude toward methodology. He advises students to study methods and might thus be considered—on the basis of his influential methodological writings with Gary King and Sidney Verba—a methodological modernist.[60] Yet he stresses also—at greater length and, one senses, with more passion—that students "should also have the context, because nothing is more dangerous than addressing a problem in a hard science way without an understanding of the context of the concepts that are involved. It's bound to be misleading and even dangerous."[61] One senses that Keohane, for all his encouragement and respect for the application of modern scientific methods in political science, remains ambivalent about the result.[62]

Keohane's distinctive "transitional" style of scholarship stands out in sharp contrast to the work of the generation that followed him—that of his students. The younger generation is, and has had to be, far more specialized. They have been *professional* international political economists from the start, practitioners of normal science, within a subdiscipline that has been subjected to a relentless process of specialization. It has sheered off almost entirely from international security, and has developed its own internal theoretical, methodological, and substantive subcategories that proceed increasingly in separate tracks.

Much of this has been for the good. Contemporary scholarship is conceptually more self-aware, with theories now spanning nearly the full spectrum of possible political and social processes. In many areas—such as the study of "endogenous tariff theory" or game-theoretical models of collective action problems—debates are many academic iterations deep, resulting in an extremely high level of methodological and theoretical specialization. Many are trained in statistics, mathematics, economics, or history, and engage in interdisciplinary work. Formal and quantitative

---

[59] Keohane's justification for this position is, in the end, essentially aesthetic (Keohane 1984, 25–26, 35, 69; Keohane 1986b).

[60] King, Keohane, and Verba 1994.

[61] Keohane 2004, 6.

[62] It is striking that some his most important theoretical advances were made in collaboration with Nye, who remains even more distanced from these developments.

methods have been refined—and we are now in the process, thanks in part to Keohane's coauthored efforts, of improving qualitative methods.[63] Many illogical, imprecise, and invalid claims have been rooted out.

But, like any process of Weberian rationalization, academic specialization comes at a cost to the individual. Each scholar is condemned to say more about less. The fundamental paradigmatic issues to which Keohane devoted his scholarly career have receded into the background. Each scholar lays a brick on the edifice of IR theory, but each is less concerned or less aware about the shape of the wall itself. Political scientists today tend to be more analytic and less synthetic, understanding parts of the whole, but not the system itself. It has become unfashionable in IPE circles to conduct debates about "isms" and "grand theory"— though such debates do occasionally have a tendency to sneak in by other names.[64] The logic of specialization places each individual in a Weberian "iron cage."

Keohane himself, by contrast, was fortunate to emerge as a scholar at an earlier moment in the development of the global political economy and in the discipline of international relations—a moment to which his particular training and temperament as a "political theorist" proved remarkably well suited. From 1970 to 1985, these three factors converged to create a foundational body of international relations theory. Yet there would never again come a historical moment when the tectonic shifts in public policy and international relations theory would dovetail so perfectly with one scholar's instincts as a political theorist. The vocational skills of a "political theorist" no longer fit the state of a subdiscipline that has become too crowded, specialized, and high-tech to make full use of them. No scholar writing on IPE today—whether so inclined or not, and whether possessed of the requisite talent or not—can realistically hope to emulate the style of scholarship and superordinate stature Keohane achieved. Yet without his epochal theoretical breakthroughs, none could be what they are today. It is this that has earned him a unique spot in the history of international relations theory.

[63] King, Keohane, and Verba 1994.

[64] Despite their dismissal of paradigmatic debates, recent works tend to replicate similar categories, distinguishing "international" and "domestic" levels of analysis, "political" and "economic" causes, or dividing the field into theories focusing on "preferences," "power," "institutions." See, for example, Lake and Frieden 1999; Lake and Powell 2000.

Bibliography

Abbot, Kenneth W., and Duncan Snidal. 1998. Why States Act through Formal International Organizations. *Journal of Conflict Resolution* 47(1): 3–32.

———. 2000. Hard and Soft Law in International Governance. *International Organization* 54:421–56.

Abdelal, Rawi. 2007. *Capital Rules: The Construction of Global Finance*. Cambridge: Harvard University Press.

Ackerly, Brooke A. 2000. *Political Theory and Feminist Social Criticism*. New York: Cambridge University Press.

Admati, Anat R., and Motty Perry. 1987. Strategic Delay in Bargaining. *Review of Economic Studies* 54(3): 345–64.

Aggarwal, Vinod K. 1995. *Liberal Protectionism: The International Politics of Organized Textile Trade*. Berkeley and Los Angeles: University of California Press.

———. 1996. *Debt Games: Strategic Interaction in International Debt Rescheduling*. New York: Cambridge University Press.

———, ed. 1998. *Institutional Designs for a Complex World: Bargaining, Linkages, and Nesting*. Ithaca, N.Y.: Cornell University Press.

———. 2001. Economics: International Trade. In *Managing a Globalizing World: Lessons Learned*, ed. P. J. Simmons and C. Oudraat, 234–80. Washington, D.C.: Carnegie Endowment for International Peace.

Aggarwal, Vinod K., and Cedric Dupont. 1999. Goods, Games, and Institutions. *International Political Science Review* 20(4): 393–409.

———. 2007. Collaboration and Coordination in the Global Political Economy. In *Global Political Economy*, ed. John Ravenhill, 28–49. Oxford: Oxford University Press.

Aggarwal, Vinod K., and Edward A. Fogarty, eds. 2004. *EU Trade Strategies: Between Globalism and Regionalism*. London: Palgrave.

Aggarwal, Vinod K., Robert Keohane, and David Yoffie. 1987. The Dynamics of Negotiated Protectionism. *American Political Science Review* 81:345–66.

Aggarwal, Vinod K., and Min Gyo Koo. 2005. Beyond Network Power: The Dynamics of Formal Economic Integration in Northeast Asia. *Pacific Review* 18(2): 189–216.

Aggarwal, Vinod K., and John Ravenhill. 2001. Undermining the WTO: The Case against "Open Sectoralism." *Asia-Pacific Issues* 50:1–6.

Aggarwal, Vinod K., and Shujiro Urata, eds. 2006. *Bilateral Trade Arrangements in the Asia-Pacific: Origins, Evolution, and Implications*. New York: Routledge.

Ainsworth, Martha, Kathleen Beegle, and Andrew Nyamete. 1996. The Impact of Women's Schooling on Fertility and Contraceptive Use: A study of Fourteen Sub-Saharan African Countries. *World Bank Economic Review* 10(1): 85–122.

Alesina, Alberto, and Allen Drazen. 1991. Why Are Stabilizations Delayed? *American Economic Review* 81:1170–88.

Allison, Graham T. 1971. *Essence of Decision: Explaining the Cuban Missile Crisis.* Boston: Little, Brown.

Andersson, Andreas. 2000. Democracies and UN Peacekeeping Operations, 1990–1996. *International Peacekeeping* 7(2): 1–22.

Andrew, Christopher, and Oleg Gordievsky. 1990. *KGB: The Inside Story of Its Foreign Operations from Lenin to Gorbachev.* New York: HarperCollins.

Andrews, David M. 2006. *International Monetary Power.* Ithaca, N.Y.: Cornell University Press.

Angell, Norman. 1912. *The Great Illusion: A Study of the Relation of Military Power to National Advantage.* Toronto: McClelland and Goodchild.

Armijo, Leslie Elliot, ed. 2002. *Debating the Global Financial Architecture: What's Democracy Got to Do with It?* Albany: State University of New York Press.

Armour, Henry O., and David J. Teece. 1980. Vertical Integration and Technological Innovation. *Review of Economics and Statistics* 62(3): 470–74.

Armstrong, Karen. 2004. *The Spiral Staircase: My Climb out of Darkness.* New York: Alfred A. Knopf.

Aronson, Jonathan, Michael Brownrigg, Karen B. Crockett, Keith E. Maskus, and Richard H. Steinberg. 1998. *Protecting International Intellectual Property.* A Report for the Pacific Council on International Policy. Los Angeles: PCIP.

Arrow, Kenneth. 1964. The Role of Securities in Optimal Allocation of Risk Bearing. *Review of Economic Studies* 31(2): 91–96.

Axelrod, Robert. 1984. *The Evolution of Cooperation.* New York: HarperCollins.

Axelrod, Robert, and Robert Keohane. 1986. Achieving Cooperation under Anarchy: Strategies and Institutions. *World Politics* 38:226–54.

Baldwin, David A. 1978. Power and Social Exchange. *American Political Science Review* 72:1229–42.

———. 1979. Power Analysis and World Politics: New Trends versus Old Tendencies. *World Politics* 31:161–94.

———. 1989. *Paradoxes of Power.* New York: Basil Blackwell.

———, ed. 1993. *Neorealism and Neoliberalism: The Contemporary Debate.* New York: Columbia University Press.

Baldwin, Richard E. 1997. The Causes of Regionalism. *World Economy* 20(7): 865–88.

Banks, Jeffrey, and Barry Weingast. 1992. The Political Control of Bureaucracies under Asymmetric Information. *American Journal of Political Science* 36: 509–24.

Barkin, J. Samuel, and George E. Shambaugh, eds. 1999. *Anarchy and the Environment.* Albany: State University of New York Press.

Barma, Naazneen, Ely Ratner, and Steven Weber. 2007. A World without the West. *National Interest* 90 (July–August): 23–30.

Barnett, Michael N., and Martha Finnemore. 2004. *Rules for the World: International Organizations in Global Politics.* Ithaca, N.Y.: Cornell University Press.

Barro, Robert J., and David B. Gordon. 1983. Rules, Discretion and Reputation in a Model of Monetary Policy. *Journal of Monetary Economics* 12:101–20.

Barton, John H., Judith L. Goldstein, Timothy E. Josling, and Richard H. Stein-berg. 2006. *The Evolution of the Trade Regime: Politics, Law, and Economics of the GATT and the WTO*. Princeton: Princeton University Press.

Beardsley, Kyle. 2004. UN Involvement in International Crises: Selection, Endo-geneity, and Authority. Paper presented at Annual Meeting of the International Studies Association, Montreal.

Beck, Nathaniel, Jonathan N. Katz, and Richard Tucker. 1998. Taking Time Se-riously: Time-Series-Cross-Section Analysis with a Binary Dependent Variable. *American Journal of Political Science* 42:1260–88.

Bell, Peter D. 1972. The Ford Foundation as a Transnational Actor. In *Trans-national Relations and World Politics*, ed. Robert Keohane and Joseph S. Nye Jr., 115–28. Cambridge: Harvard University Press.

Bergsten, C. Fred. 2001. Fifty Years of Trade Policy: The Policy Lessons. *World Economy* 24(1): 1–13.

Bergsten, C. Fred, Robert O. Keohane, and Joseph S. Nye Jr. 1975. International Economics and International Politics: A Framework for Analysis. *International Organization* 29:3–36.

Berman, Edward H. 1983. *The Influence of the Carnegie, Ford, and Rockefeller Foundations on American Foreign Policy: The Ideology of Philanthropy*. Al-bany: State University of New York Press.

Bernauer, Thomas. 1996. Protecting the Rhine River against Chloride Pollution. In *Institutions for Environmental Aid: Pitfalls and Promise*, ed. Robert O. Keo-hane and Marc A. Levy, 201–32. Cambridge: MIT Press.

Bernauer, Thomas, and Peter Moser. 1996. Reducing Pollution of the Rhine River: The Influence of International Cooperation. *Journal of Environment and Development* 5(4): 391–417.

Bettig, Ronald. 1996. Copyrighting Culture: The Political Economy of Intellec-tual Property. Boulder, Colo.: Westview Press.

Bhagwati, Jagdish. 1991. *The World Trading System at Risk*. Princeton: Prince-ton University Press.

———. 2004. *In Defense of Globalization*. New York: Oxford University Press.

Bird, Kai. 1992. *The Chairman: John J. McCloy, The Making of the American Es-tablishment*. New York: Simon and Schuster.

Birnie, Patricia. 1985. *International Regulation of Whaling*. New York: Oceana Publications.

Black, Jan K. 1977. *United States Penetration of Brazil*. Philadelphia: University of Pennsylvania Press.

Bodansky, Daniel. 2001. International Law and the Design of a Global Climate Change Regime. In *International Relations and Global Climate Change*, ed. Urs Luterbacher and Detlef F. Sprinz, 201–19. Cambridge: MIT Press.

Boyle, James. 2003. The Second Enclosure Movement and the Construction of the Public Domain. *Law and Contemporary Problems* 66(3): 33–74.

Branstetter, Lee G. 2004. Do Stronger Patents Induce More Local Innovation? *In-ternational Economic Law* 7(2): 359–70.

Breitmeier, Helmut, Oran R. Young, and Michael Zürn. 2006. *Analyzing Inter-national Environmental Regimes: From Case Study to Database*. Cambridge: MIT Press.

Breslauer, George W., and Philip E. Tetlock, eds. 1991. *Learning in U.S. and Soviet Foreign Policy*. Boulder, Colo.: Westview Press.

Brown, Chris. 2002. Narratives of Religions, Civilization and Modernity. In *Worlds in Collision: Terror and the Future of Global Order*, ed. Ken Booth and Tim Dunne, 293–302. New York: Palgrave-Macmillan.

Brown Weiss, Edith, and Harold K. Jacobson, eds. 1998. *Engaging Countries: Strengthening Compliance with International Environmental Accords*. Cambridge: MIT Press.

Burley, Anne-Marie, and Walter Mattli. 1993. Europe before the Court: A Political Theory of Legal Integration. *International Organization* 47:41–76.

Buruma, Ian, and Avishai Margalit. 2004. *Occidentalism: The West in the Eyes of Its Enemies*. New York: Penguin.

Business Roundtable. 2001. The Case for U.S. Trade Leadership: The United States Is Falling Behind. February. Available from http://www.businessroundtable.org/publications/publication.aspx?qs=2496BF807822B0F19D2 (accessed May 22, 2008).

Büthe, Tim, and Walter Mattli. 2005. Accountability in Accounting? The Politics of Private Rule-Making in the Public Interest. *Governance* 18(3): 399–429.

Cady, John. 2004. Does SDDS Subscription Reduce Borrowing Costs for Emerging Market Economies? Working Paper 04/58. Washington, D.C.: International Monetary Fund.

Callan, Bénédicte. 1998. *Pirates on the High Seas: The United States and Global Intellectual Property Rights*. New York: Council on Foreign Relations.

Calvert, Randall, Matthew McCubbins, and Barry Weingast. 1989. A Theory of Political Control and Agency Discretion. *American Journal of Political Science* 33:588–611.

Cantor, Richard, and Frank Packer. 1996. Determinants and Impact of Sovereign Credit Rating. *Federal Reserve Bank of New York Economic Policy Review* 2:37–53.

Cardy, Tom. 2004. Legal Eagles Target Tarzan. *Dominion Post*, December 2.

Carter, Timothy. 2007. United Nations Intervention Decisions: A Strategic Examination. Unpublished manuscript, Wayne State University.

Castells, Manuel. 2001. *The Internet Galaxy*. New York: Oxford University Press.

Charnovitz, Steve. 1994. Encouraging Environmental Cooperation through the Pelly Amendment. *Journal of Environment and Development* 3(1): 2–38.

Chayes, Abram, and Antonia Handler Chayes. 1995. *The New Sovereignty: Compliance with International Regulatory Agreements*. Cambridge: Harvard University Press.

Christensen, Clayton M. 1997. *The Innovator's Dilemma: When New Technologies Cause Great Firms to Fail*. Cambridge: Harvard Business School Press.

Christofides, Charis, Christian Mulder, and Andrew Tiffin. 2003. The Link between Adherence to International Standards of Good Practice, Foreign Exchange Spreads, and Ratings. Working Paper 03/74. Washington, D.C.: International Monetary Fund.

Clark, Ann Marie. 2001. *Diplomacy of Conscience: Amnesty International and Changing Human Rights Norms*. Princeton: Princeton University Press.

Coase, Ronald H. 1937. The Nature of the Firm. *Economica* 4(16): 386–405.
———. 1960. The Problem of Social Cost. *Journal of Law and Economics* 3(1): 1–44.
Cohen, Benjamin. 1998. *The Geography of Money*. Ithaca, N.Y.: Cornell University Press.
Collier, Paul. 2007. *The Bottom Billion: Why the Poorest Countries Are Failing and What Can Be Done about It*. New York: Oxford University Press.
Conceição, Pedro. 2003. Assessing the Provision Status of Global Public Goods. In *Providing Global Public Goods: Managing Globalization*, ed. Inge Kaul, Pedro Conceição, Katell Le Goulven, and Ronald U. Mendoza, 152–79. Oxford: Oxford University Press.
Connolly, Barbara, and Martin List. 1996. Nuclear Safety in Eastern Europe and the Former Soviet Union. In *Institutions for Environmental Aid: Pitfalls and Promise*, ed. Robert O. Keohane and Marc A. Levy, 233–79. Cambridge: MIT Press.
Conybeare, John A. C. 1980. International Organization and the Theory of Property Rights. *International Organization* 34:307–34.
———. 1984. Public Goods, Prisoners' Dilemmas and the International Political Economy. *International Studies Quarterly* 28:5–22.
Cornes, Richard, and Todd Sandler. 1996. *The Theory of Externalities, Public Goods, and Club Goods*. New York: Cambridge University Press.
Coulon, Jocelyn. 1998. *Soldiers of Diplomacy: The United Nations, Peacekeeping, and the New World Order*. Toronto: University of Toronto Press.
Cowhey, Peter F., and Jonathan Aronson. 2009. *The Inflection Point: Global Governance in the Internet Age*.
Cronin, Audrey Kurth. 2002. Behind the Curve: Globalization and International Terrorism. *International Security* 27(3): 30–58.
Crosby, Ann D. 1998. A Middle-Power Military in Alliance: Canada and NORAD. *Journal of Peace Research* 34(1): 37–52.
Crouzet, Philippe, and Nicolas Véron. 2002. Accounting for Globalization: The Accounting Standards Battle. Available at http://www.nicolasveron.info/ETR_3bis.pdf (accessed May 22, 2008).
Curzon, Gerard. 1966. *Multilateral Commercial Diplomacy*. New York: Praeger.
Cutler, Claire A. 2003. *Private Power and Global Authority: Transnational Merchant Law in the Global Political Economy*. Cambridge: Cambridge University Press.
Cutler, Claire A., Virginia Haufler, and Tony Porter, eds. 1999. *Private Authority in International Affairs*. Albany: State University of New York Press.
Damasio, Antonio R. 2005. *Descartes' Error: Emotion, Reason, and the Human Brain*. London: Penguin.
Darst, Robert G. 2001. *Smokestack Diplomacy: Cooperation and Conflict in East-West Environmental Politics*. Cambridge: MIT Press.
Davis, Christina L. 2003. *Food Fights over Free Trade: How International Institutions Promote Agricultural Trade Liberalization*. Princeton: Princeton University Press.
Debreu, Gerard. 1959. *Theory of Value*. New York: Wiley.

De Jonge Oudraat, Chantal. 1996. The United Nations and Internal Conflict. In *The International Dimensions of Internal Conflict*, ed. M. E. Brown, 489–535. Cambridge: MIT Press.

Demirigüç-Kunt, Ash, Erica Detragiache, and Thierry Tressel. 2006. Banking on the Principles: Compliance with Basel Core Principles and Bank Soundness. Working Paper 06/42. Washington, D.C.: International Monetary Fund.

Den Elzen, M.G.J., and A.P.G. de Moor. 2001. *The Bonn Agreement and Marrakesh Accords: An Updated Analysis*. RIVM Report 728001017. National Institute of Public Health and the Environment, Bilthoven, The Netherlands.

DeSombre, Elizabeth R. 2000. *Domestic Sources of International Environmental Policy: Industry, Environmentalists, and U.S. Power*. Cambridge: MIT Press.

———. 2004. Understanding United States Unilateralism: Domestic Sources of U.S. International Environmental Policy. In *The Global Environment*, ed. Regina Axelrod, David Downie and Norman Vig, 181–99. Washington, D.C.: CQ Press.

———. 2005. Fishing under Flags of Convenience: Using Market Power to Increase Participation in International Regulation. *Global Environmental Politics* 5(4): 73–94.

DeSombre, Elizabeth R., and Joanne Kauffman. 1996. The Montreal Protocol Multilateral Fund: Partial Success Story. In *Institutions for Environmental Aid*, ed. Robert O. Keohane and Marc A. Levy, 89–126. Cambridge: MIT Press.

Deutsch, Karl W., Sidney A. Burrell, Robert A. Kann, Maurice Lee Jr., Martin Lichterman, Raymond E. Lindgren, Francis L. Lowenheim, and Richard W. Van Wagen. 1957. *Political Community and the North Atlantic Area: International Organization in the Light of Historical Experience*. Princeton: Princeton University Press.

Diehl, Paul F. 1993. *International Peacekeeping*. Baltimore: Johns Hopkins University Press.

Dixit, Avinash K. 1996. *The Making of Economic Policy: A Transaction-Cost Politics Perspective*. Cambridge: MIT Press.

Downs, George W., David M. Rocke, and Peter N. Barsoom. 1996. Is the Good News about Compliance Good News about Cooperation? *International Organization* 50:379–406.

———. 1998. Managing the Evolution of Multilateralism. *International Organization* 52:397–419.

Doyle, Michael W., and Nicholas Sambanis. 2000. International Peacebuilding: A Theoretical and Quantitative Analysis. *American Political Science Review* 94:779–801.

———. 2006. *Making War and Building Peace: United Nations Peace Operations*. Princeton: Princeton University Press.

Drahos, Peter, with John Braithwaite. 2002. *Information Feudalism: Who Owns the Knowledge Economy?* New York: New Press.

Drezner, Daniel. 2007. *All Politics Is Global: Explaining International Regulatory Regimes*. Princeton: Princeton University Press.

Duraisamy, P. 2002. Changes in Returns to Education in INDIA, 1983–94: By Gender, Age-Cohort and Location. *Economics of Education Review* 21(6): 609–22.

Durch, William J., ed. 1993. *The Evolution of UN Peacekeeping.* New York: St. Martin's Press.

———. 1996. *UN Peacekeeping, American Policy, and the Uncivil Wars of the 1990s.* New York: St. Martin's Press.

Eatwell, John, and Lance Taylor, eds. 2002. *International Capital Markets: Systems in Transition.* Oxford: Oxford University Press.

Eichengreen, Barry. 1999. *Toward a New International Financial Architecture.* Washington, D.C.: Institute for International Economics.

———. 2003. Governing Global Financial Markets: International Responses to the Hedge Fund Problem. In *Governance in a Global Economy: Political Authority in Transition,* ed. Miles Kahler and David A. Lake, 168–98. Princeton: Princeton University Press.

Eisenstadt, Shmuel N., and Wolfgang Schluchter. 2001. Paths to Early Modernities—a Comparative View. In *Public Spheres and Collective Identities,* ed. S. Eisenstadt, W. Schluchter, and B. Wittrock, 1–18. Piscataway, N.J.: Transaction.

Elkins, Zachary, Andrew T. Guzman, and Beth A. Simmons. 2006. Competing for Capital: The Diffusion of Bilateral Investment Treaties, 1960–2000. *International Organization* 60:811–46.

Esposito, John L., and John O. Voll. 2003. Islam and the West: Muslim Voices of Dialogue. In *Religion in International Relations: The Return from Exile,* ed. Fabio Petito and Pavlos Hatzopoulos, 237–69. New York: Palgrave Macmillan.

Evangelista, Matthew. 1995. Transnational Relations, Domestic Structures, and Security Policy in the USSR and Russia. In *Bringing Transnational Relations Back In: Non-state Actors, Domestic Structures, and International Institutions,* ed. Thomas Risse-Kappen, 146–88. Cambridge: Cambridge University Press.

Fairman, David. 1996. The Global Environment Facility: Haunted by the Shadow of the Future. In *Institutions for Environmental Aid,* ed. Robert O. Keohane and Marc A. Levy, 55–87. Cambridge: MIT Press.

Fang, Songying. 2005. International Institutions and Bargaining. Ph.D. diss., University of Rochester.

Farrell, Henry. 2003. Constructing the International Foundations of E-Commerce: The EU-US Safe Harbor Arrangement. *International Organization* 57:277–306.

Farrell, Nick. 2007. US CD music sales fall. *The Inquirer,* March 22. http://www.theinquirer.net/?article=38413 (accessed May 22, 2008).

Fearon, James D. 1998. Bargaining, Enforcement, and International Cooperation. *International Organization* 52:269–305.

Fearon, James D., and David D. Laitin. 2003. Ethnicity, Insurgency, and Civil War. *American Political Science Review* 97:75–90.

Findlay, Trevor. 2002. *The Use of Force in UN Peace Operations.* Oxford: SIPRI and Oxford University Press.

Finnemore, Martha. 1996. *National Interest in International Society.* Ithaca, N.Y.: Cornell University Press.

Finnemore, Martha, and Kathryn Sikkink. 1998. International Norm Dynamics and Political Change. *International Organization* 52:887–917.

Florini, Ann. 1996. The Evolution of International Norms. *International Studies Quarterly* 40:363–89.

Fortna, Virginia Page. 2004a. Does Peacekeeping Keep Peace? International Intervention and the Duration of Peace after Civil War. *International Studies Quarterly* 48:269–92.

———. 2004b. Interstate Peacekeeping: Causal Mechanisms and Empirical Effects. *World Politics* 56:481–519.

———. 2008. *Does Peacekeeping Work? Shaping Belligerents' Choices after Civil War*. Princeton: Princeton University Press.

Fortna, Virginia Page, and Lise Morjé Howard. 2008. Pitfalls and Prospects in the Peacekeeping Literature. *Annual Review of Political Science* 11:283–301.

Frankel, Jeff A. 1997. *Regional Trading Blocs in the World Economic System*. Washington, D.C.: Institute for International Economics.

Freeman, Marsha A., and Arvonne S. Fraser. 1994. Women's Human Rights: Making the Theory a Reality. In *Human Rights: An Agenda for the Next Century*, ed. L. Henkin and J. L. Hargrove, 103–31. Washington, D.C.: American Society of International Law.

Frieden, Jeffrey. 2000. Actors and Preferences in International Relations. In *Strategic Choice and International Relations*, ed. David A. Lake and Robert Powell, 39–76. Princeton: Princeton University Press.

Garrett, Geoffrey. 1992. International Cooperation and Institutional Choice: The European Community's Internal Market. *International Organization* 46:533–60.

Garrett, Geoffrey, and George Tsebelis. 2001. The Institutional Determinants of Intergovernmentalism and Supranationalism in the EU. *International Organization* 55:357–90.

Gelos, R. Gaston, and Shang-Jin Wei. 2002. Transparency and International Investor Behavior. Working Paper 9260. Cambridge, Mass.: National Bureau of Economic Research.

Germain, Randall. 2001. Global Financial Governance and the Problem of Inclusion. *Global Governance* 7(4): 411–26.

Gilligan, Michael J. 2004. Is There a Broader-Deeper Tradeoff? *International Organization* 58:459–84.

Gilligan, Michael J., and Ernest J. Sergenti. 2007. Does Peacekeeping Keep Peace? Using Matching to Improve Causal Inference. Unpublished manuscript, New York University and Harvard University.

Gilligan, Michael, and Stephen John Stedman. 2003. Where Do the Peacekeepers Go? *International Studies Review* 5(4): 37–54.

Gilpin, Robert. 1975. *U.S. Power and the Multinational Corporation*. New York: Basic Books.

———. 1981. *War and Change in World Politics*. New York: Cambridge University Press.

———. 1987. *The Political Economy of International Relations*. Princeton: Princeton University Press.

Glaum, Martin, and Donna L. Street. 2003. Compliance with the Disclosure Requirements of Germany's New Market: IAS versus US GAAP. *Journal of International Financial Management and Accounting* 14(1): 64–100.

Glennerster, Rachel, and Yongseok Shin. 2008. Does Transparency Pay? *IMF Staff Papers* 55(1): 183–209.

Globerman, Steven. 1980. Markets Hierarchies and Innovation. *Journal of Economic Issues* 14(4): 977–98.

Goldstein, Judith. 2001. *Legalization and World Politics*. Cambridge: MIT Press.

Goldstein, Judith, Miles Kahler, Robert O. Keohane, and Anne-Marie Slaughter. 2000. Introduction: Legalization and World Politics. *International Organization* 54:385–400.

Goldstein, Judith, and Robert O. Keohane. 1993. *Ideas and Foreign Policy: Beliefs, Institutions, and Political Change*. Ithaca, N.Y.: Cornell University Press.

Goldstein, Paul. 1994. *Copyright's Highway: The Law and Lore of Copyrighting from Gutenberg to the Celestial Jukebox*. New York: Hill & Wang.

Gole, Nilufer. 2000. Global Expectations, Local Experiences: Non-Western Modernities. In *Through a Glass Darkly: Blurred Images of Cultural Tradition and Modernity over Distance and Time*, ed. Wil Arts, 40–55. Boston: Brill.

Gourevitch, Peter. 1999. Robert O. Keohane: The Study of International Relations. *PS: Political Science and Politics* 32(3): 623–28.

Gowa, Joanne. 1989. Rational Hegemons, Excludable Goods, and Small Groups: An Epitaph for Hegemonic Stability Theory. *World Politics* 41:307–24.

Grant, Ruth W., and Robert O. Keohane. 2005. Accountability and Abuses of Power in World Politics. *American Political Science Review* 99:29–44.

Grieco, Joseph M. 1988. Anarchy and the Limits of Cooperation: A Realist Critique of the Newest Liberal Institutionalism. *International Organization* 42: 485–507.

Griffith-Jones, Stephany, and José Antonio Ocampo. 2003. What Progress on International Financial Reform? Why So Limited? Paper prepared for the Expert Group on Development Issues, Government of Sweden.

Griffiths, Martin. 1999. Robert Keohane In *Fifty Great Thinkers in International Relations*, 185–90. London: Routledge.

Grossman, Gene M., and Elhanan Helpman. 1994. Protection for Sale. *American Economic Review* 84:833–50.

Grove, Andy. 1996. *Only the Paranoid Survive*. New York: Doubleday.

Gruber, Lloyd. 2000. *Ruling the World: Power Politics and the Rise of Supranational Institutions*. Princeton: Princeton University Press.

Haas, Ernst. 1980. Why Collaborate? Issue-Linkage and International Regimes. *World Politics* 32:357–405.

Haas, Peter M. 1990. *Saving the Mediterranean*. New York: Columbia University Press.

Haas, Peter M., Robert O. Keohane, and Marc A. Levy, eds. 1993. *Institutions for the Earth: Sources of Effective International Environmental Protection*. Cambridge: MIT Press.

Haftendorn, Helga. 1999. The "Quad": Dynamics of Institutional Change. In *Imperfect Unions: Security Institutions over Time and Space*, ed. Helga Haftendorn, Robert O. Keohane, and Celeste A. Wallender, 162–94. New York: Oxford University Press.

Haggard, Stephan. 1997. Regionalism in Asia and the Americas. In *The Political*

Economy of Regionalism, ed. Edward Mansfield and Helen Milner, 20–49. New York: Columbia University Press.

Haggard, Stephan, and Robert R. Kaufman. 1995. *The Political Economy of Democratic Transitions*. Princeton: Princeton University Press.

Hardie, Iain, and Layna Mosley. 2008. Turkey's Convergence Tale: Market Pressures, Membership Conditionality and EU Accession. Unpublished manuscript, University of Edinburgh.

Harding, Sandra. 1991. *Whose Science? Whose Knowledge? Thinking from Women's Lives*. Ithaca, N.Y.: Cornell University Press.

Hasenclever, Andreas, Peter Mayer, and Volker Rittberger. 1997. *Theories of International Regimes*. Cambridge: Cambridge University Press.

Hassan, Raffat. 1999. Feminism in Islam. In *Feminism and World Religion*, ed. Arvind Sharma and Katherine K. Young, 248–78. Albany: State University of New York Press.

Haufler, Virginia. 2000. *A Public Role for the Private Sector: Industry Self-Regulation in a Global Economy*. New York: Carnegie Endowment for International Peace.

Hawkins, Darren, David A. Lake, Daniel Nielson, and Michael Tierney. 2006. *Delegation and Agency in International Organizations*. New York: Cambridge University Press.

Helleiner, Eric. 1994. *States and the Reemergence of Global Finance: From Bretton Woods to the 1990s*. Ithaca, N.Y.: Cornell University Press.

———. 2002. The Politics of Global Financial Regulation: Lessons from the Fight against Money Laundering. In *International Capital Markets: Systems in Transition*, ed. John Eatwell and Lance Taylor, 177–204. Oxford: Oxford University Press.

Helm, Carsten, and Detlef Sprinz. 2000. Measuring the Effectiveness of International Environmental Regimes. *Journal of Conflict Resolution* 44(5): 630–52.

Hirschman, Albert O. 1980. *National Power and the Structure of Foreign Trade*. Expanded ed. Berkeley and Los Angeles: University of California Press.

Hiscox, Michael. 2002. *International Trade and Political Conflict: Commerce, Coalitions, and Factor Mobility*. Princeton: Princeton University Press.

Hoffmann, Stanley. 1975. Oil and Force. *Commentary* 59 (April): 3–6.

Hollis, Martin, and Steve Smith. 1990. *Explaining and Understanding International Relations*. Oxford: Oxford University Press.

Hovi, Jon, Detlef F. Sprinz, and Arild Underdal. 2003a. The Oslo-Potsdam Solution to Measuring Regime Effectiveness: Critique, Response, and the Road Ahead. *Global Environmental Politics* 3(3): 74–96.

———. 2003b. Regime Effectiveness and the Oslo-Potsdam Solution: A Rejoinder to Oran Young. *Global Environmental Politics* 3(3): 105–7.

Howard, Lise Morjé. 2003. The Rise and Decline of the Norm of Negotiated Settlement. Paper presented to the Georgetown Junior Faculty Workshop on Intervention, October 23–24, Washington, D.C.

Huntington, Samuel P. 1957. *The Soldier and the State: Changing Politics of Civil-Military Relations*. Cambridge: Harvard University Press.

———. 1968. *Political Order in Changing Societies*. New Haven: Yale University Press.

Huntington, Samuel P. 1973. Transnational Organizations in World Politics. *World Politics* 25:333–68.

———. 2004. *Who Are We? The Challenges to America's National Identity.* New York: Simon and Schuster.

Ikenberry, G. John. 2001. *After Victory: Institutions, Strategic Restraint, and the Rebuilding of Order after Major Wars.* Princeton: Princeton University Press.

Independent Evaluation Office (IEO). 2003. *The IMF and Recent Capital Account Crises: Indonesia, Korea, Brazil.* Washington, D.C.: Independent Evaluation Office, International Monetary Fund.

———. 2004. *The IMF and Argentina, 1991–2001.* Washington, D.C.: Independent Evaluation Office, International Monetary Fund.

International Monetary Fund (IMF). 2003. International Standards: Background Paper on Strengthening Surveillance, Domestic Institutions, and International Markets. Washington, D.C.: International Monetary Fund, Policy Development and Review Department.

Irwin, Douglas A. 1993. Multilateral and Bilateral Trade Policies in the World Trading System: An Historical Perspective. In *New Dimension in Regional Integration,* ed. Jaime Melo and Arvind Panagariya, 90–119. Cambridge: Cambridge University Press.

Ito, Joi. 2006. WoW presentation at 23C3. December 30, http://video.google.com/videoplay?docid=5160442894955175707&q=Joichi+Ito&total=62& start=0&num=10&so=0&type=search&plindex=0 (accessed May 23, 2008).

Jakobsen, Peter Viggo. 1996. National Interest, Humanitarianism or CNN: What Triggers UN Peace Enforcement after the Cold War? *Journal of Peace Research* 33(2): 205–15.

James, Alan. 1990. *Peacekeeping in International Politics.* New York: St. Martin's Press.

James, Scott, and David Lake. 1989. The Second Face of Hegemony: Britain's Repeal of the Corn Laws and the American Walker Tariff of 1846. *International Organization* 43:1–29.

Jenkins, Henry. 2006. *Convergence Culture: Where Old and New Media Collide.* New York: New York University Press.

Joskow, Paul L. 1985. Vertical Integration and Long-term Contracts: The Case of Coal Burning Electric Generating Plants. *Journal of Law, Economics and Organization* 1(1): 33–80.

Juergensmeyer, Mark. 2000. *Terror in the Mind of God: The Global Rise of Religious Violence.* Berkeley and Los Angeles: University of California Press.

Kahler, Miles. 2004. Global Governance Redefined. Paper presented at the seminar on Globalization, Equity and Democratic Governance, Duke University, October 24.

Kahler, Miles, and David A. Lake, eds. 2003. *Governance in a Global Economy: Political Authority in Transition.* Princeton: Princeton University Press.

Kapstein, Ethan Barnaby. 1992. Between Power and Purpose: Central Bankers and the Politics of Regulatory Convergence. *International Organization* 46:265–87.

Katzenstein, Peter J. 1997. Introduction: Asian Regionalism in Contemporary Perspective. In *Network Power: Japan and Asia,* ed. Peter J. Katzenstein and Takashi Shiraishi. Ithaca, N.Y.: Cornell University Press.

Kaul, Inge, Pedro Conceição, Katell Le Goulven, and Ronald U. Mendoza, eds. 2003. *Providing Global Public Goods: Managing Globalization.* Oxford: Oxford University Press.

Keck, Margaret E., and Kathryn Sikkink. 1998. *Activists beyond Borders: Advocacy Networks in International Politics.* Ithaca, N.Y.: Cornell University Press.

Kelly-Gadol, Joan. 1977. Did Women Have a Renaissance? In *Becoming Visible: Women in European History,* ed. Renate Bridenthal and Claudia Koonz, 137–64. Boston: Houghton Mifflin.

Keohane, Robert O. 1971. Big Influence of Small Allies. *Foreign Policy* 2:161–82.

———. 1980. The Theory of Hegemonic Stability and Changes in International Economic Regimes, 1967–1977. In *Change in the International System,* ed. O. R. Holsti, R. Siverson and A. George, 131–62. Boulder, Colo.: Westview Press.

———. 1982. The Demand for Regimes. *International Organization* 36:325–55.

———. 1983. The Demand for International Regimes. In *International Regimes,* ed. S. D. Krasner, 141–71. Ithaca, N.Y.: Cornell University Press.

———. 1984. *After Hegemony: Cooperation and Discord in the World Political Economy.* Princeton: Princeton University Press.

———, ed. 1986a. *Neorealism and Its Critics.* New York: Columbia University Press.

———. 1986b. Theory of World Politics: Structural Realism and Beyond. In *Neorealism and Its Critics,* ed. Robert Keohane, 158–203. New York: Columbia University Press.

———. 1989a. Neoliberal Institutionalism: A Perspective on World Politics. In *International Institutions and State Power: Essays in International Relations Theory.* Boulder, Colo.: Westview Press.

———. 1989b. *International Institutions and State Power: Essays in International Relations Theory.* Boulder Colo.: Westview.

———. 1990. Multilateralism: An Agenda for Research. *International Journal* 45(4): 731–64.

———. 2002. *Power and Governance in a Partially Globalized World.* New York: Routledge.

———. 2004. Theory and International Institutions Interview. Interview by Harry Kreisler, Institute for International Studies, University of California, Berkeley, March 9. http://globetrotter.berkeley.edu/people4/Keohane/keohane-cono.html (accessed May 23, 2008).

Keohane, Robert O., Peter M. Haas, and Marc A. Levy. 1993. The Effectiveness of International Environmental Institutions. In *Institutions for the Earth,* ed. Peter M. Haas, Robert O. Keohane, and Marc A. Levy, 3–26. Cambridge: MIT Press.

Keohane, Robert O., and Marc A. Levy, eds. 1996. *Institutions for Environmental Aid: Pitfalls and Promise.* Cambridge: MIT Press.

Keohane, Robert, and Lisa Martin. 1995. The Promise of Institutionalist Theory. *International Security* 20:39–51.

———. 1999. *Institutional Theory, Endogeneity, and Delegation.* Cambridge: Weatherhead Center for International Affairs, Harvard University.

———. 2003. Institutional Theory as a Research Program. In *Progress in International Relations Theory: Appraising the Field,* ed. C. Elman and M. Elman, 71–107. Cambridge: MIT Press.

Keohane, Robert O., and Helen V. Milner, eds. 1996. *Internationalization and Domestic Politics*. Cambridge: Cambridge University Press.

Keohane, Robert O., and Joseph S. Nye Jr. 1971a. Transnational Relations and World Politics: An Introduction. *International Organization* 25:329–49.

———. 1971b. Transnational Relations and World Politics: Conclusion. *International Organization* 25:721–48.

———, eds. 1972. *Transnational Relations and World Politics*. Cambridge: Harvard University Press.

———. 1974. Transgovernmental Relations and International Organizations. *World Politics* 27:39–62.

———. 1975. International Interdependence and Integration. In *Handbook of Political Science*, ed. F. Greenstein and N. Polsby, 363–414. Andover, Mass.: Addison-Wesley.

———. 1977. *Power and Interdependence: World Politics in Transition*. Boston: Little, Brown.

———. 1987. Power and Interdependence Revisited. *International Organization* 41:725–53.

———. 1998. Power and Interdependence in the Information Age. *Foreign Affairs* 77(5): 81–94.

———. 1999. *Power and Interdependence*. 2nd ed. Boston: Scott, Foresman.

———. 2001. *Power and Interdependence*. 3rd ed. New York: Longman.

———. 2003. Redefining Accountability for Global Governance. In *Governance in a Global Economy: Political Authority in Transition*, ed. Miles Kahler and David A. Lake, 386–411 Princeton: Princeton University Press.

Keohane, Robert O., Joseph S. Nye, and Stanley Hoffmann, eds. 1993. *After the Cold War: International Institutions and State Strategies in Europe, 1989–1991*. Cambridge: Harvard University Press.

Keohane, Robert O., and Elinor Ostrom, eds. 1995. Local Commons and Global Interdependence: Heterogeneity and Cooperation in Two Domains. London: Sage.

Kimmel, Michael, and Abby L. Ferber. 2000. "White Men Are This Nation": Right-Wing Militias and the Restoration of Rural American Masculinity. *Rural Sociology* 65(4): 582–604.

Kindleberger, Charles P. 1973. *The World in Depression, 1929–1939*. Berkeley and Los Angeles: University of California Press.

King, Gary, Robert O. Keohane, and Sidney Verba. 1994. *Designing Social Inquiry: Scientific Inference in Qualitative Research*. Princeton: Princeton University Press.

King, Michael R., and Timothy J. Sinclair. 2003. Private Actors and Public Policy: A Requiem for the New Basel Capital Accord. *International Political Science Review* 24(3): 345–62.

Kirkpatrick, David. 2007. How Microsoft Conquered China. *Fortune*, July 23, 78–84.

Kirschner, Jonathan. 1995. *Currency and Coercion*. Princeton: Princeton University Press.

Kivimaki, Tivo. 1993. Strength of Weakness: American-Indonesian Hegemonic Bargaining. *Journal of Peace Research* 30:391–408.

Klotz, Audie. 1995. *Norms in International Relations: The Struggle against Apartheid*. Ithaca N.Y.: Cornell University Press.

Knight, Jack. 1992. *Institutions and Social Conflict*. Cambridge: Cambridge University Press.

Knill, Christoph, and Dirk Lehmkuhl. 2002. Private Actors and the State: Internationalization and Changing Patterns of Governance. *Governance: An International Journal of Policy, Administration and Institutions* 15(1): 41–63.

Knowles, S., P. K. Lorgelly, and P. D. Owen. 2002. Are Educational Gender Gaps a Brake on Economic Development? Some Cross-Country Empirical Evidence. *Oxford Economic Papers*, n.s. 54(1): 118–49.

Koo, Min Gyo. 2005. From Multilateralism to Bilateralism? A Shift in South Korea's Trade Strategy. In *Bilateral Trade Arrangements in the Asia-Pacific: Origins, Evolution, and Implications*, ed. Vinod K. Aggarwal and Shujiro Urata, 140–59. New York: Routledge.

Koremenos, Barbara. 2001. Loosening the Ties That Bind: A Learning Model of Agreement Flexibility. *International Organization* 55:289–325.

———. 2005. Contracting around International Uncertainty. *American Political Science Review* 99:549–65.

Koremenos, Barbara, Charles Lipson, and Duncan Snidal. 2001. The Rational Design of International Institutions: Explaining the Form of International Institutions. *International Organization* 55:761–99.

———. 2004. *The Rational Design of International Institutions*. New York: Cambridge University Press.

Krasner, Stephen D. 1976. State Power and the Structure of International Trade. *World Politics* 28:317–47.

———, ed. 1983a. *International Regimes*. Ithaca, N.Y.: Cornell University Press.

———. 1983b. Structural Causes and Regime Consequences: Regimes as Intervening Variables. In *International Regimes*, ed. Stephen D. Krasner, 1–22. Ithaca, NY: Cornell University Press.

———. 1985. *Structural Conflict: The Third World against Global Liberalism*. Berkeley: University of California Press.

———. 1991. Global Communications and National Power: Life on the Pareto Frontier. *World Politics* 43:336–66.

———. 1993. Westphalia and All That. In *Ideas and Foreign Policy: Beliefs, Institutions and Political Change,* ed. Judith Goldstein and Robert O. Keohane, 235–64. Ithaca, N.Y.: Cornell University Press.

———. 1995. Power Politics, Institutions, and Transnational Relations. In *Bringing Transnational Relations Back In: Non-state Actors, Domestic Structures, and International Institutions*, ed. Thomas Risse-Kappen, 257–79. Cambridge: Cambridge University Press.

———. 1999. *Sovereignty: Organized Hypocrisy*. Princeton: Princeton University Press.

Krasno, Jean, Bradd C. Hayes, and Donald C. F. Daniel, eds. 2003. *Leveraging for Success in United Nations Peace Operations*. Westport: Praeger.

Kratochwil, Friedrich, and John Gerard Ruggie. 1986. International Organization: A State of the Art on an Art of the State. *International Organization* 40: 753–75.

Kubálková, Vendulka. 2003. Toward an International Political Theology. In *Religion in International Relations: The Return from Exile*, ed. Fabio Petito and Pavlos Hatzopoulos, 79–105. New York: Palgrave Macmillan.

Kydland, Finn E., and Edward C. Prescott. 1977. Rules Rather Than Discretion: The Inconsistency of Optimal Plans. *Journal of Political Economy* 85(3): 437–91.

Lake, David A. 1983. International Economic Structures and American Foreign Economic Policy, 1887–1934. *World Politics* 36:517–43.

———. 1996. Anarchy, Hierarchy and the Variety of International Relations. *International Organization* 50:1–33.

Lake, David A., and Jeffry Frieden. 1999. *International Political Economy: Perspectives on Global Power and Wealth*. Boston: Bedford/St. Martin's.

Lake, David A., and Robert Powell, eds. 2000. *Strategic Choice and International Relations*. Princeton: Princeton University Press.

Lanham, Richard. 1993. *The Electronic Word: Democracy, Technology, and the Arts*. Chicago: University of Chicago Press.

Langley, Winston. 1988. *Human Rights, Women, and Third World Development*. Boston: William Monroe Trotter Institute.

Lawrence, Robert Z. 1996. *Regionalism, Multilateralism, and Deeper Integration*. Washington, D.C.: Brookings Institution.

Legro, Jeffrey W. 1997. Which Norms Matter? Revisiting the "Failure" of Internationalism. *International Organization* 51:31–63.

Legro, Jeffrey W., and Andrew Moravcsik. 1999. Is Anybody Still a Realist? *International Security* 24(2): 5–55.

Lerner, Daniel. 1958. *The Passing of Traditional Society: Modernizing the Middle East*. Glencoe, Ill.: Free Press.

Lesser, W. 2001. The Effects of TRIPs-Mandated Intellectual Property Rights on Economic Activities in Developing Countries. Prepared for WIPO. Available at http://www.wipo.org/about-ip/en/index.html?wipo_content_frame=/about-ip/en/studies /index.html.

Lessig, Lawrence. 2001. The Future of Ideas: The Fate of the Commons in a Connected World. New York: Random House.

Lévi-Strauss, Claude. 1968. *Structural Anthropology*. Trans. Claire Jacobson and Brooke Grundfest Schoepf. Vol. 1. London: Penguin.

Levy, Marc. 1993. European Acid Rain: The Power of Tote-Board Diplomacy. In *Institutions for the Earth: Sources of Effective International Environmental Protection*, ed. Peter Haas, Robert O. Keohane and Marc Levy, 75–132. Cambridge: MIT Press.

Lipson, Charles. 1991. Why Are Some International Agreements Informal? *International Organization* 45:495–538.

Mansfield, Edward, and Helen V. Milner. 1999. The New Wave of Regionalism. *International Organization* 53:589–627.

Mansfield, Edward, Helen V. Milner, and B. Peter Rosendorff. 2002. Why Democracies Cooperate More: Electoral Control and International Trade Agreements. *International Organization* 56:477–514.

March, James, and Johan Olsen. 1998. The Institutional Dynamics of International Political Orders. *International Organization* 52:943–70.

Markoff, John, and Edward Wyatt. 2004. Google Is Adding Major Libraries to Its Database. *New York Times,* December 14.

Martin, Edwin M. 1994. *Kennedy and Latin America.* Lanham, Md.: University Press of America.

Martin, Lisa. 1992. *Coercive Cooperation.* Princeton: Princeton University Press.

———. 2000. *Democratic Commitments: Legislatures and International Cooperation.* Princeton: Princeton University Press.

———. 2005. The President and International Agreements: Treaties as Signaling Devices. *Presidential Studies Quarterly* 35(3): 440–65.

———. 2006. Distribution, Information, and Delegation to International Organizations: The Case of IMF Conditionality. In *Delegation and Agency in International Organizations,* ed. Darren G. Hawkins et al., 140–64.

Mas-Colell, Andreu, Michael D. Whinston and Jeffrey R. Green. 1995. *Microeconomic Theory.* New York: Oxford University Press.

Maskus, Keith, and Jerome Reichman. 2004. The Globalization of Private Knowledge Goods and the Privatization of Global Public Goods. *Journal of International Economic Law* 7(2): 279–320.

Masten, Scott E., James W. Meehan, and Edward A. Snyder. 1991. The Costs of Organization. *Journal of Law, Economics and Organization* 7(1): 1–25.

Mattli, Walter. 2003. Public and Private Governance in Setting International Standards. In *Governance in a Global Economy: Political Authority in Transition,* ed. Miles Kahler and David A. Lake, 199–225. Princeton: Princeton University Press.

Mattli, Walter, and Tim Büthe. 2003. Setting International Standards: Technological Rationality or Primacy of Power? *World Politics* 56:1–42.

May, Elaine Tyler. 2003. Echoes of the Cold War: The Aftermath of September 11 at Home. In *September 11 in History: A Watershed Moment?* ed. Mary L. Dudziak, 35–54. Durham, N.C.: Duke University Press.

McCalman, Phillip. 2002. The Doha Agenda and Intellectual Property Rights. Available at http://www.adb.org/Economics/pdf/doha/McCalman.pdf (accessed May 23, 2008).

———. 2004. Foreign Direct Investment and Intellectual Property Rights: Evidence from Hollywood's Global Distribution of Movies and Videos. *Journal of International Economics* 62(1): 107–23.

McCubbins, Mathew D., and Thomas Schwartz. 1984. Congressional Oversight Overlooked: Police Patrols versus Fire Alarms. *American Journal of Political Science* 28:165–79.

McGillivray, Fiona, and Alastair Smith. 2000. Trust and Cooperation through Agent-Specific Punishments. *International Organization* 54:809–25.

McKeown, Timothy. 1983. Hegemonic Stability Theory and 19th Century Tariff Levels in Europe. *International Organization* 37:73–91.

———. 1991. A Liberal Trading Order? The Long-Run Pattern of Imports to the Advanced Capitalist States. *International Studies Quarterly* 35:151–72.

McLean, Elena V., and Randall W. Stone. 2005. Two-Level Bargaining and the Kyoto Protocol. Presented at the 101st Annual Meeting of the American Political Science Association, Washington, D.C., September 1–4.

Mead, Walter Russell. 2006. God's Country? *Foreign Affairs* 85(5): 24–43.

Mearsheimer, John J. 1994–95. The False Promise of International Institutions. *International Security* 19(3): 5–49.

———. 2001. *The Tragedy of Great Power Politics*. New York: W. W. Norton.

Meunier, Sophie. 2005. *Trading Voices: The European Union in International Commercial Negotiations*. Princeton: Princeton University Press.

Miles, Edward L., Arild Underdal, Steinar Andresen, Jørgen Wettestad, Jon Birger Skjærseth, and Elaine M. Carlin, eds. 2002. *Environmental Regime Effectiveness: Confronting Theory with Evidence*. Cambridge: MIT Press.

Milgrom, Paul, and John Roberts. 1990. Bargaining Costs, Influence Costs, and the Organization of Economic Activity. In *Perspectives on Positive Political Economy*, ed. James E. Alt and Kenneth A. Shepsle, 57–89. New York: Cambridge University Press.

———. 1992. *Economics, Organization, and Management*. Englewood Cliffs, N.J.: Prentice Hall.

Milner, Helen V. 1988. *Resisting Protectionism: Global Industries and the Politics of International Trade*. Princeton: Princeton University Press.

———. 1997. *Interests, Institutions, and Information: Domestic Politics and International Relations*. Princeton: Princeton University Press.

Milner, Helen V., and David Yoffie. 1989. Between Free Trade and Protectionism: Strategic Trade Policy and a Theory of Corporate Trade Demands. *International Organization* 43:239–72.

Milward, Alan S. 1992. *The European Rescue of the Nation-State*. London: Routledge.

Mitchell, Ronald B. 1994. Regime Design Matters: International Oil Pollution and Treaty Compliance. *International Organization* 48:425–58.

———. 2002. A Quantitative Approach to Evaluating International Environmental Regimes. *Global Environmental Politics* 2(4): 58–83.

Mitchell, Ronald B., and Patricia Keilbach. 2001. Reciprocity, Coercion, or Exchange: Symmetry, Asymmetry and Power in Institutional Design. *International Organization* 55:891–917.

Moe, Terry. 1990. The Politics of Structural Choice: Toward a Theory of Public Bureaucracy. In *Organization Theory: From Chester Barnard to the Present and Beyond*, ed. Oliver E. Williamson, 116–53. New York: Oxford University Press.

Montgomery, John. 1962. *The Politics of Foreign Aid*. New York: Praeger, Council on Foreign Relations.

Moon, Chung-in. 1988. Complex Interdependence and Transnational Lobbying: South Korea in the United States. *International Studies Quarterly* 32:67–89.

Moravcsik, Andrew. 1997. Taking Preferences Seriously: A Liberal Theory of International Politics. *International Organization* 51:513–53.

———. 1998. *The Choice for Europe: Social Purpose and State Power from Messina to Maastricht*. Ithaca, N.Y.: Cornell University Press.

———. 1999. A New Statecraft? Supranational Entrepreneurs and International Cooperation. *International Organization* 53:267–306.

Morgenthau, Hans J. 1946. *Scientific Man vs. Power Politics*. Chicago: University of Chicago Press.

Morse, Edward L. 1976. *Modernization and the Transformation of International Relations*. New York: Free Press.

Mosley, Layna. 2003a. *Global Capital and National Governments*. Cambridge: Cambridge University Press.

———. 2003b. Are Global Standards the Answer? National Governments, International Finance, and the IMF's Data Regime. *Review of International Political Economy* 10(2): 332–63.

———. 2004. Government-Financial Market Relations after EMU. *European Union Politics* 5(2): 181–209.

———. 2006. Constraints, Opportunities and Information: Financial Market-Government Relations around the World. In *Globalization and Egalitarian Redistribution*, ed. Pranab Bardhan, Samuel Bowles and Michael Wallerstein, 87–112. Princeton: Princeton University Press.

Mosley, Layna, and David Andrew Singer. 2008. Taking Seriously: Equity Market Performance, Government Policy, and Financial Globalization. *International Studies Quarterly*, forthcoming.

Mullenbach, Mark J. 2005. Deciding to Keep Peace: An Analysis of International Influences on the Establishment of Third-Party Peacekeeping Missions. *International Studies Quarterly* 49:529–55.

Na, Seong-lin, and Hyun Song Shin. 1998. International Environmental Agreements under Uncertainty. *Oxford Economic Papers* 50(2): 173–85.

Neack, Laura. 1995. UN Peace-keeping: In the Interest of Community or Self. *Journal of Peace Research* 32(2): 181–96.

North, Douglass C. 1990. *Institutions, Institutional Change, and Economic Performance*. New York: Cambridge University Press.

Nye, Joseph S., and Robert O. Keohane. 1972. Transnational Relations and World Politics: A Conclusion. In *Transnational Relations and World Politics*, ed. Robert O. Keohane and Joseph S. Nye, 371–98. Cambridge: Harvard University Press.

———. 1993. The United States and International Institutions in Europe after the Cold War. In *After the Cold War: International Institutions and State Strategies in Europe, 1989–1991*, ed. Robert O. Keohane, Joseph S. Nye and Stanley Hoffmann, 104–26. Cambridge: Harvard University Press.

Oatley, Thomas, and Robert Nabors. 1998. Redistributive Cooperation: Market Failure, Wealth Transfers, and the Basle Accord. *International Organization* 52:35–54.

Onuf, Nicholas. 1989. *World of Our Making: Rules and Rule in Social Theory and International Relations*. Columbia: University of South Carolina Press.

Oye, Kenneth A., ed. 1986. *Cooperation under Anarchy*. Princeton: Princeton University Press.

———. 1992. *Economic Discrimination and Political Exchange: World Political Economy in the 1930s and 1980s*. Princeton: Princeton University Press.

Pahre, Robert. 1998. *Leading Questions: How Hegemony Affects the International Political Economy*. Ann Arbor: University of Michigan Press.

Parson, Edward A. 2003. *Protecting the Ozone Layer*. Oxford: Oxford University Press.

Pateman, Carole. 1988. *The Sexual Contract*. Stanford: Stanford University Press.

Paul, T. V. 1992. Influence through Arms Transfers: Lessons from the US-Pakistani Relationship. *Asian Survey* 32(12): 1078–92.

Pauly, Louis W. 2002. Global Finance, Political Authority, and the Problem of Legitimation. In *The Emergence of Private Authority in Global Governance*, ed. Rodney Bruce Hall and Thomas J. Biersteker, 76–90. Cambridge: Cambridge University Press.

Peterson, M. J. 1993. International Fisheries Management. In *Institutions for the Earth*, ed. Peter M. Haas, Robert O. Keohane, and Marc A. Levy, 249–305. Cambridge: MIT Press.

Peterson, V. Spike. 1992. Transgressing Boundaries: Theories of Knowledge, Gender and International Relations. *Millennium* 21(2): 183–206.

Petrie, Murray. 2003. Promoting Fiscal Transparency: The Complementary Roles of the IMF, Financial Markets, and Civil Society. Working Paper 03/199. Washington, D.C.: International Monetary Fund.

Pfeffer, Jeffrey, and Gerald R. Salancik. 1974. Bases and Use of Power in Organizational Decision Making—the Case of a University. *Administrative Science Quarterly* 19(3): 453–73.

Philpott, Daniel. 2002. The Challenge of September 11 to Secularism in International Relations. *World Politics* 55:66–95.

Pisano, Gary. 1990. Using Equity Participation to Support Exchange: Evidence from the Biotechnology Industry. *Journal of Law, Economics and Organization* 5(1): 109–26.

Podpiera, Richard. 2006. Does Compliance with Basel Core Principles Bring Any Measurable Benefits? *IMF Staff Papers* 53(2): 306–25.

Porter, Tony. 1999. Hegemony and the Private Governance of International Industries. In *Private Authority in International Affairs*, ed. Claire A. Cutler, Virginia Haufler, and Tony Porter, 257–82. Albany: State University of New York Press.

Potoski, Matthew, and Aseem Prakash. 2005. Green Clubs and Voluntary Governance: ISO 14001 and Firms' Regulatory Compliance. *American Journal of Political Science* 49:235–48.

Price, Richard. 1998. Reversing the Gun Sights: Transnational Civil Society Targets Land Mines. *International Organization* 52:613–43.

Price, Robert M. 1971. A Theoretical Approach to Military Rule in New States: Reference Group Theory and the Ghanaian Case. *World Politics* 23:399–430.

Psacharopoulos, George. 1994. Returns to Investment in Education—a Global Update. *World Development* 22(9): 1325–43.

Putnam, Robert D. 1988. Diplomacy and Domestic Politics. *International Organization* 42:427–61.

Quinn, Lawrence Richter. 2004. What's the State of International Standards? *Strategic Finance* 85(10): 5–39.

Raiffa, Howard. 1982. *The Art and Science of Negotiation*. Cambridge: Harvard University Press.

Ramirez, Francisco O., and Elizabeth H. McEneaney. 1997. From Women's Suffrage to Reproduction Rights? Cross-National Comparisons. *International Journal of Comparative Sociology* 66:6–24.

Raustiala, Kal, and David Victor. 2004. The Regime Complex for Plant Genetic Resources. *International Organization* 58:277–309.

Reinhardt, Eric. 2001 Adjudication without Enforcement in GATT Disputes. *Journal of Conflict Resolution* 45:174–95.

Rheingold, Howard. 2003. *Smart Mobs: The Next Social Revolution.* Cambridge, Mass.: Perseus.

Richardson, J. David. 1987. Comment. In *U.S. Trade Policies in a Changing World Economy*, ed. Robert M. Stern, 287–90. Cambridge: MIT Press.

Risse, Thomas. 2000. "Let's Argue": Communicative Action in World Politics. *International Organization* 54:1–39.

Risse, Thomas, and Kathryn Sikkink. 1999. The Socialization of International Human Rights Norms into Domestic Practice: Introduction. In *The Power of Human Rights: International Norms and Domestic Change*, ed. Thomas Risse, Stephen C. Ropp, and Kathryn Sikkink, 1–38. Cambridge: Cambridge University Press.

Risse-Kappen, Thomas, ed. 1995. *Bringing Transnational Relations Back In: Non-state Actors, Domestic Structures, and International Institutions.* Cambridge: Cambridge University Press.

Roett, Riordan. 1972. *The Politics of Foreign Aid in the Brazilian Northeast.* Nashville: Vanderbilt University Press.

Ronit, Karsten, and Volker Schneider. 2000. *Private Organizations in Global Politics.* London: Routledge.

Rose-Ackerman, Susan. 1999. *Corruption and Government: Causes, Consequences and Reform.* New York: Cambridge University Press.

Rosenbluth, Frances, and Ross Schaap. 2003. The Domestic Politics of Banking Regulation. *International Organization* 57:307–36.

Rosendorff, B. Peter, and Helen V. Milner. 2001. The Optimal Design of International Trade Institutions: Uncertainty and Escape. *International Organization* 55:829–58.

Rudolph, Christopher. 2001. Constituting an Atrocities Regime: The Politics of War Crimes Tribunals. *International Organization* 53:655–91.

Sai, F. T. 1993. Political and Economic Factors Influencing Contraceptive Uptake. *British Medical Bulletin* 49(1): 200–209.

Samuelson, Pamela. 1996. The Copyright Grab. *Wired*, January, 135–38, 188–91.

———. 1997. The U.S. Digital Agenda at WIPO. *Virginia Journal of International Law* 37(2): 369–439.

Sandholtz, Wayne, and Mark Gray. 2003. International Integration and National Corruption. *International Organization* 57:761–800.

Sandholtz, Wayne, and John Zysman. 1989. 1992: Recasting the European Bargain. *World Politics* 42:95–128.

Sarotte, M. E. 2001. *Dealing with the Devil: East Germany, Détente, and Ostpolitik, 1969–1973.* Chapel Hill: University of North Carolina Press.

Schneider, Benu, ed. 2003. *The Road to International Financial Stability: Are Key Financial Standards the Answer?* London: Palgrave Macmillan and Overseas Development Institute.

———. 2005. Do Global Standards and Codes Prevent Financial Crises? Some Proposals on Modifying the Standards-Based Approach. Discussion Paper No. 177. Geneva: UNCTAD.

Schneider, Gerald, and Lars-Erik Cederman. 1994. The Change of Tide in Political Cooperation: A Limited Information Model of European Integration. *International Organization* 48:633–62.

Schneier, Bruce. 2000. *Secrets and Lies: Digital Security in a Networked World.* New York: John Wiley & Sons.

Schonhardt-Bailey, Cheryl, ed. 1996. *Free Trade: The Repeal of the Corn Laws.* Briston: Thoemmes Press.

Schoppa, Leonard J. 1993. Two-Level Games and Bargaining outcomes: Why Gaiatsu Succeeds in Japan in Some Cases but Not Others. *International Organization* 47:353–86.

Sell, Susan. 1998. *Power and Ideas: North-South Politics of Intellectual Property and Antitrust.* Albany: State University of New York Press.

———. 2002. Intellectual Property Rights. In *Governing Globalization: Power, Authority and Global Governance,* ed. David Held and Anthony Grew, 171–88. London: Polity Press.

Shackley, Ted, with Richard A. Finney. 2005. *Spymaster: My Life in the C.I.A.* Dulles, Va.: Potomac Books.

Shambaugh, George E. 1999. *States, Firms, and Power: Successful Sanctions in United States Foreign Policy.* SUNY Series in Global Politics. Albany: State University of New York Press.

Shelanski, Howard A., and Peter G. Klein. 1995. Empirical Research in Transaction Cost Economics: A Review and Assessment. *Journal of Law, Economics and Organization* 11(3): 335–61.

Simmons, Beth A. 1998. Compliance with International Agreements. *Annual Review of Political Science* 1:75–93.

———. 2000. International Law and State Behavior: Commitment and Compliance in International Monetary Affairs. *American Political Science Review* 94:819–35.

———. 2001. The International Politics of Harmonization: The Case of Capital Market Regulation. *International Organization* 55:589–620.

Simmons, Beth A., and Zachary Elkins. 2004. The Globalization of Liberalization: Policy Diffusion in the International Economy. *American Political Science Review* 98:171–89.

Simmons, Beth A., and Daniel J. Hopkins. 2005. The Constraining Power of International Treaties. *American Political Science Review* 99:623–31.

Simmons, Beth A., and Lisa Martin. 2002. International Organizations and Institutions. In *Handbook of International Relations,* ed. Walter Carlsnaes, Thomas Risse, and Beth A. Simmons, 192–211. London: Sage.

Simon, Herbert. 1991. Organizations and Markets. *Journal of Economic Perspectives* 5(1): 25–44.

Sinclair, Timothy J. 2005. *The New Masters of Capital: American Bond Rating Agencies and the Politics of Creditworthiness.* Ithaca, N.Y.: Cornell University Press.

Singer, David. 2004. Capital Rules: The Domestic Politics of International Regulatory Harmonization. *International Organization* 58:531–65.

———. 2007. *Regulating Capital: Setting Standards for the International Financial System.* Ithaca, N.Y.: Cornell University Press.

Slantchev, Branislav L. 2003. The Principle of Convergence in Wartime Negotiations. *American Political Science Review* 97:621–32.

———. 2004. How Initiators End Their Wars: The Duration of Warfare and the Terms of Peace. *American Journal of Political Science* 48:813–29.

Slaughter, Anne-Marie. 2004. *A New World Order*. Princeton: Princeton University Press.

Slunaker, Ryan. 2005. Managing International Common Pool Resources: An Analysis of the International Regime History of the Northern Pacific Fur Seal Commons. B.S. thesis, University of Oregon.

Snidal, Duncan. 1985a. Coordination versus the Prisoners' Dilemma: Implications for International Cooperation and Regimes. *American Political Science Review* 79:923–42.

———. 1985b. The Limits of Hegemonic Stability Theory. *International Organization* 39:579–614.

———. 1991. Relative Gains and the Pattern of International Cooperation. *American Political Science Review* 85(3): 701–26.

———. 1996. Political Economy and International Institutions. *International Review of Law and Economics* 16(1): 121–37.

Solís, Mireya, and Saori Katada. 2007. Understanding East Asian Cross-Regionalism: An Analytical Framework. *Pacific Affairs* 80(2): 229–57.

Spohr, C. A. 2003. Formal Schooling and Workforce Participation in a Rapidly Developing Economy: Evidence from "Compulsory" Junior High School in Taiwan. *Journal of Development Economics* 70(2): 291–327.

Sprinz, Detlef, and Tapani Vaahtoranta. 1994. The Interest-Based Explanation of International Environmental Policy. *International Organization* 48:77–105.

Starr, Paul. 2004. *The Creation of the Media: Political Origins of Modern Communications*. New York: Basic.

Stedman, Stephen John, Donald Rothchild, and Elizabeth M. Cousens, eds. 2002. *Ending Civil Wars: The Implementation of Peace Agreements*. Boulder, Colo.: Lynne Rienner.

Stein, Arthur A. 1982. Coordination and Collaboration Regimes in an Anarchic World. *International Organization* 36:299–324.

———. 1983. Coordination and Collaboration: Regimes in an Anarchic World. In *International Regimes*, ed. Stephen D. Krasner, 115–40. Ithaca, N.Y.: Cornell University Press.

Steinwand, Martin C., and Randall W. Stone. 2008. The International Monetary Fund: A Review of the Recent Evidence. *Review of International Organizations* 3(2): 123–49.

Stern, Jessica. 2003. *Terror in the Name of God: Why Religious Militants Kill*. New York: Harper Collins.

Stone, Randall W. 2002. *Lending Credibility: The International Monetary Fund and the Post-Communist Transition*. Princeton: Princeton University Press.

———. 2004. The Political Economy of IMF Lending in Africa. *American Political Science Review* 98:577–91.

———. 2008. The Scope of IMF Conditionality: How Autonomous Is the Fund? *International Organization*, forthcoming (Fall).

Stone, Randall W., Branislav L. Slantchev, and Tamar R. London. 2008. Choosing How to Cooperate: A Repeated Public-Goods Model of International Relations. *International Studies Quarterly* 52:335–62.

Stone Sweet, Alec. 2004. Islands of Transnational Governance. In *Restructuring Territoriality: Europe and the United States Compared*, ed. Christopher K. Ansell and Giuseppe Di Palma, 122–44. Cambridge: Cambridge University Press.

Strange, Susan. 1983. Cave! Hic Dragones: A Critique of Regime Analysis. In *International Regimes*, ed. Stephen D. Krasner, 337–54. Ithaca, N.Y.: Cornell University Press.

———. 1988. *States and Markets*. London: Pinter.

———. 1996. *The Retreat of the State: the Diffusion of Power in the World Economy*. Cambridge: Cambridge University Press.

Sundararajan, V., David Marston, and Ritu Basu. 2001. Financial System Standards and Financial Stability: The Case of the Basel Core Principles. Working Paper 01/62. Washington, D.C.: International Monetary Fund.

Susskind, Lawrence E. 1994. *Environmental Diplomacy*. New York: Oxford University Press.

Tapscott, Don, and Anthony D. Williams. 2006. *Wikinomics: How Mass Collaboration Changes Everything*. New York: Portfolio.

Taylor, Michael. 1987. *The Possibility of Cooperation*. Cambridge: Cambridge University Press.

Terada, Takashi. 2003. Constructing an "East Asian" Concept and Growing Regional Identity: From EAEC to ASEAN+3. *Pacific Review* 16(2): 251–77.

Teschke, Benno. 2003. *The Myth of 1648: Class, Geopolitics, and the Making of Modern International Relations*. London: Verso.

Thomas, Scott M. 2005. *The Global Resurgence of Religion and the Transformation of International Relations*. London: Verso.

Thucydides. 1982. *The Peloponnesian War*. Trans. Richard Crawley, revised by T. E. Wick. New York: Modern Library.

Tickner, J. Ann. 2005. What Is Your Research Program? Some Feminist Answers to IR's Methodological Questions. *International Studies Quarterly* 49:1–21.

Tomz, Michael. 2007. *Reputation and International Cooperation: Sovereign Debt across Three Centuries*. Princeton: Princeton University Press.

Tong, Hui. 2007. Disclosure Standards and Market Efficiency: Evidence from Analysts' Forecasts. *Journal of International Economics* 72(1): 222–41.

Toulmin, Stephen. 1990. *Cosmopolis: The Hidden Agenda of Modernity*. Chicago: University of Chicago Press.

Trachtman, Joel P. 1996. The Theory of the Firm and the Theory of the International Economic Organization: Toward Comparative Institutional Analysis. *Northwestern Journal of International Law and Business*. 17(2–3): 470–555.

Tsebelis, George. 1994. The Power of the European Parliament as a Conditional Agenda-Setter. *American Political Science Review* 88:128–42.

Tsebelis, George, and Geoffrey Garrett. 2001. "The Institutional Foundations of Intergovernmentalism and Supranationalism in the European Union." *International Organization* 55(2): 357–90.

Tyler, Tom. 1990. *Why People Obey the Law.* New Haven: Yale University Press.

Tyson, Laura. 2000. What Really Sabotaged the Seattle Trade Talks. *Business Week,* February 7.

Underhill, Geoffrey R. D. 2000. The Contribution of International Relations Theory to Organized Business. In *Organized Business and the New Global Order,* ed. Justin Greenwood and Henry Jacek, 20–38. New York: St. Martin's.

Underhill, Geoffrey R. D., and Xiaoke Zhang, eds. 2003. *International Financial Governance under Stress: Global Structures versus National Imperatives.* Cambridge: Cambridge University Press.

Vamosi, Robert. 2007. Cyberattack in Estonia—What It Really Means. c/net News.com, May 29. http://news.com.com/Cyberattack+in+Estonia—what+it+really+means/2008-7349_3-6186751.html (accessed May 23, 2008).

Vaubel, Roland. 1986. A Public Choice Approach to International Organization. *Public Choice* 51:39–57.

Vernon, Raymond. 1971. *Sovereignty at Bay: The Multinational Spread of U.S. Enterprises.* New York: Basic.

Voeten, Erik. 2001. Outside Options and the Logic of Security Council Action. *American Political Science Review* 95:845–58.

Vogel, Steven K. 1996. *Freer Markets, More Rules: Regulatory Reform in Advanced Industrial Countries.* Ithaca, N.Y.: Cornell University Press.

Vojta, George, and Marc Uzan. 2003. The Private Sector, International Standards, and the Architecture of Global Finance. In 2003. *International Financial Governance under Stress: Global Structures versus National Imperatives,* ed. Geoffrey R. D. Underhill and Xiaoke Zhang, 283–301. Cambridge: Cambridge University Press.

Von Hippel, Eric. 2005. *Democratizing Innovation.* Cambridge: MIT Press.

von Stein, Jana. 2005. Do Treaties Constrain or Screen? Selection Bias and Ttreaty Compliance. *American Political Science Review* 99:611–22.

Vreeland, James Raymond. 2003. *The IMF and Economic Development.* Cambridge: Cambridge University Press.

Walt, Stephen. 1987. *The Origins of Alliances.* Ithaca, N.Y.: Cornell University Press.

Waltz, Kenneth N. 1979. *Theory of International Politics.* Reading, Mass.: Addison-Wesley.

Watson, Natalie K. 2003. *Feminist Theology.* Grand Rapids, Mich.: Wm Eerdmans.

Weber, Katja. 1997. Hierarchy amidst Anarchy: A Transaction Cost Approach to International Security Cooperation. *International Studies Quarterly* 41:321–40.

Weis, W. Michael. 2001. The Twilight of Pan-Americanism: The Alliance for Progress, Neo-colonialism, and Non-alignment in Brazil, 1961–64. *International History Review* 23(2): 322–44.

Wendt, Alexander, and Daniel Friedheim. 1996. Hierarchy under Anarchy: Informal Empire and the East German State. In *State Sovereignty as Social Construct,* ed. Thomas Biersteker and Cynthia Weber, 240–77. Cambridge: Cambridge University Press.

Werner, Suzanne, and Amy Yuen. 2005. Making and Keeping Peace. *International Organization* 59:261–92.

Wildstrom, Stephen. 2003. The Best-Laid Plans of Copyright Law. *Business Week*, February 24, 26.

Williamson, Oliver E. 1983. *Markets and Hierarchies: Analysis and Antitrust Implications*. New York: Free Press.

———. 1985. *The Economic Institutions of Capitalism: Firms, Markets, Relational Contracting*. New York: Free Press.

———. 1989. Transaction Cost Economics. In *Handbook of Industrial Organization*, vol. 1, ed. Richard Schmalensee and Robert Willig, 135–82. Amsterdam: North-Holland.

Wils, Annababette, and Anne Goujon. 1998. Diffusion of Education in Six World Regions, 1960–90. *Population and Development Review* 24(2): 357–68.

Wolpin, Miles D. 1972. *Military Aid and Counterrevolution in the Third World*. Lexington, Mass.: D. C. Heath.

World Bank. 2001. *Finance for Growth: Policy Choices in a Volatile World*. Oxford: Oxford University Press and the World Bank.

Wotipka, Christine Min, and Francisco O. Ramirez. 2008. World Society and Human Rights: An Events History Analysis of the Convention on the Elimination of All Forms of Discrimination Against Women. In *The Global Diffusion of Markets and Democracy*, ed. Beth Simmons, Frank Dobbin, and Geoffrey Garrett, 303–43. Cambridge: Cambridge University Press.

Yamani, Mai. 2000. Muslim Women and Human Rights in Saudi Arabia: Aspirations of a New Generation. In *The Rule of Law in the Middle East and the Islamic World: Human Rights and the Judicial Process*, ed. E. Cotran and M. Yamani, 137–43. London: I. B. Tauris.

Yarbrough, Beth V., and Robert M. Yarbrough. 1987. Cooperation in the Liberalization of International Trade: After Hegemony, What? *International Organization* 41:1–26.

———. 1992. *Cooperation and Governance in International Trade*. Princeton: Princeton University Press.

Young, Oran R., ed. 1999. *The Effectiveness of International Environmental Regimes: Causal Connections and Behavioral Mechanisms*. Cambridge: MIT Press.

———. 2003. Determining Regime Effectiveness: A Commentary on the Oslo-Potsdam Solution. *Global Environmental Politics* 3(3): 97–104.

Zacarias, Agostinho. 1996. *The United Nations and International Peacekeeping*. London: Tauris Academic Studies.

Zeng, Ka. 2004. *Trade Threats, Trade Wars: Bargaining, Retaliation, and American Coercive Diplomacy*. Ann Arbor: University of Michigan Press.

Index

movie and broadcast industries, and intellectual property rights, 196–97
Mullenbach, Mark J., 90, 90n13
multifinality, 80
multilateralism, use of term, 169n17
multiple principals, and agency problems, 35–37
music industry, and intellectual property rights, 196–97
mutual contracting, 108–9

negotiations, in transaction costs approach, 63, 65
neoliberal institutionalism, 3–5, 26, 147, 181, 254; impact of, 108–9; and incorporation of religious worldviews, 230–32; methodological issues, 21–25, 80–83, 87, 181; paradigm of, 5–21. *See also* Keohane, Robert O.; neorealism
neorealism, 3–5, 252–53, 259–60
networks of networks, 146
Nielsen SoundScan, 196
9/11 attacks. *See* terrorist attacks of September 11, 2001
Noble, Kerry, 226
no-institution counterfactuals: and incentive structures, 77; and normative structure of problems, 80
nongovernmental organizations (NGOs), 113–14, 121
noninterference in internal affairs. *See* peacekeeping
nonstate actors, in neoliberal institutionalist paradigm, 5–12
NORAD (North American Aerospace Defense Command), 208
normative structure of problems, 79–80
North, Douglass C., 53
North American Free Trade Agreement (NAFTA), 54, 190–91; Article 17, 191
North Atlantic Treaty, 54
Northeast Asia, trade agreements in, 176–81
Nye, Joseph S., Jr., 3, 16, 32, 126, 135, 157, 245–50, 261, 262n61

Occidentalism, 227–29
open source movement, 190
organizational cultures, pathological, 35n17
output equation, in two-stage least-squares analysis, 118–19

pacta sunt servanda, 113–14
Pahre, Robert, 33
Paris Convention for the Protection of Industrial Property, 188
patent protection, 189–90, 197–98
patent trolls, 189–90, 190n19
Paul, T. V., 211
peacekeeping, 10–11, 23, 71; in civil wars, 87–107; consent based, 90; demand side, 88, 90, 90n13; signaling model of, 88–89, 91–94
pharmaceutical industry, and intellectual property rights, 197–98
Pharmaceutical Manufacturers Association, 194
Philpott, Daniel, 231
piracy, of intellectual property, 196–97
Podpiera, Richard, 138n64
postagreement behavior, and incentive structures, 77
Potoski, Matthew, 144n86
power: in environmental politics, 156–58; and interdependence, 230–32, 249–50; in neoliberal institutionalist paradigm, 12–15
power resources, 12–14; and environmental issues, 159; and institutional design, 42, 48–49; in international transactions, 59; and transnational relations, 14–15
Prakash, Aseem, 144n86
preferential trade agreements (PTA), 172
preinstitutional interests, use of term, 71–72
Price, Robert, 214
Priceline.com, 189
price mechanism, 52–54
primary education, ratio of girls to boys in, 114–15, 119–21
principal-agent problem, 35–37, 117–18, 135, 144
prisoner's dilemma, 78; and environmental issues, 13, 16, 148–51, 154, 162; and international cooperation, 54; trade liberalization as, 166–67
private commercial actors, defined, 131
private sector, role in financial governance, 130–44
private sector actors: and global financial regulation, 11, 21, 126–46; and international intellectual property rights,

societal interdependence, 245–48
sociological theory, 108
South Korea. *See* Northeast Asia
Soviet Union, and East Germany, 207–8
state preferences, 245–48
status quo bias, and international institutions, 255–56
Stedman, Stephen John, 89–90, 90n13
Stern, Jessica, 226–27
Stone, Randall W., 6, 8–9, 37
Sundararajan, V., 138
supermajority voting rules, 47
Super 301 (provision in U.S. law), 171
sustainable growth, 200–201
systemic theory, 4–5, 163

tariff wars, 78
technology transfer, 191
terrorism, 26–27, 223n4. *See also* informal violence
terrorist attacks of September 11, 2001, 18, 223–24, 229–32, 234n47
testing, for treaty effects, 114–19
Thailand, 214
Thomas, Scott, 226n13
Tickner, J. Ann, 17–18, 24
time consistency problem, 38–40
Tong, Hui, 138, 138n65
Trachtman, Joel P., 59
trade agreements, sectoral, 169–72
trade cooperation, need for, 166–67
trade governance, modes of, 168–74
trade liberalization, 164–82; multiproduct, 172–74; as public good, 166–67; sectoral agreements, 169–72
trade linkages, and environmental politics, 160–61
trade policy, and transaction costs approach, 57
Trade Promotion Authority, 164
trade protection, 164–65
trade relations, 14, 17, 42, 46–47
transaction, defined, 58–60, 64
transaction costs: defined, 52–53; effort to decrease, 154–55; measurement of, 61, 64
transaction costs approach, 22, 41–43, 50–65, 165; defining and measuring variables, 58–62; and international cooperation, 9–10; selection bias in, 62–65; testing, 56–58; and trade relations, 17

transaction costs economics (TCE), 51, 258; and decentralized cooperation theory, 51–56
transactions, future, in transaction costs approach, 63
transgovernmentalism, 15, 206–10
transgovernmental relations, 204–22; defined, 205–6; exploitation tactics, 212–17; research issues in, 212, 220–22; theory of, 210–12
transnational actors, role of, 126–27
transnational relations, 14–15, 24, 245–48
transregionalism, use of term, 173
treaty commitments, 113–14
treaty effects, 114–19, 125
treaty endogeneity, 118–19
Treaty of Westphalia (1648), 231
Tressel, Thierry, 138n64
TRIPs (Trade-Related Aspects of Intellectual Property Rights) agreement, 186, 188, 190–91
trisectoral partnerships, 135
Tucker, Richard, 119n33
two-stage modeling, 23, 82, 118
Tyson, Laura, 172, 253n35

uncertainty, 153–54
unilateralism, U.S., 34
unitary state, assumption of, 204
United Nations, 31; Commission on the Status of Women (CSW, 1952), 110n8, 111; Convention on the Law of the Sea, 150–51; Environment Programme (UNEP), 154. *See also* peacekeeping
United States: declining power, 33–34, 33n5, 256; foreign aid, 212–17; foreign policy, 217–20; and intellectual property rights, 189, 192–98; military preeminence, 33n5; and threat of economic sanctions, 156, 160–61; and transgovernmental relations, 208–10
United States–Canada auto accord, 171
upstream/downstream problems, 75
users, and intellectual property rights, 189–90

variables: in signaling model, 96–99; in transaction costs approach, 58–62
Vaubel, Roland, 34
Verba, Sidney, 262
Vernon, Raymond, 197n41, 245n6, 258